Annual Franchise and Distribution Law Developments 2024

Eleanor Vaida Gerhards

Joseph S. Goode

AMERICAN BAR ASSOCIATION

Forum on Franchising

Cover Design by ABA Design.

Printed in the United States of America

28 27 26 25 24   5 4 3 2 1

TABLE OF CONTENTS

ABOUT THE AUTHORS

ELEANOR VAIDA GERHARDS

Eleanor Vaida Gerhards is a partner at the national law firm of Fox Rothschild LLP where she concentrates her practice on commercial transactions and regulatory compliance matters. As Co-Chair of the firm's Franchising and Distribution Practice Group, she routinely serves as outside general corporate and franchise counsel to startups, and emerging and established regional, national, and international franchise clients. Elle focuses on guiding the structuring of franchise programs, drafting of franchise documents, franchise acquisitions, administration and negotiation of supply chain agreements and relationships, foreign brand entry into the U.S. market, and master franchising and multi-unit licensing and area-development arrangements. She also works regularly with "accidental" franchisors on the conversion of licensing, subscription, or distribution models to franchise systems.

Elle has been recognized by Chambers USA as a leading national franchise attorney, named a "Legal Eagle" by Franchise Times for the last nine years, a "Rising Star" by Superlawyers, a Pennsylvania "Lawyer on the Fast Track" by the Legal Intelligencer as well as recognized by Who's Who Legal Franchising and named among Philadelphia's Business Journal's 40 under 40. Elle is an active member of the ABA Forum on Franchising. She's written multiple articles for the ABA Franchise Law Journal and ABA Forum's Franchise Lawyer newsletter as well as authored chapters in the ABA book Exemptions and Exclusions under Federal and State Franchise Registration and Disclosure Laws and the ABA Franchise

Deskbook Selected State Laws, Commentary and Annotations, Third Edition. She is a past member of the ABA Forum on Franchising Women's Caucus and ABA Forum on Franchising Program Committee. Elle previously presented at the ABA Forum on Franchising Annual Meetings in San Diego, California in 2022, Nashville, Tennessee in 2018 and Miami, Florida in 2016. The International Franchise Association has designated Eleanor as a Certified Franchise Executive and she serves as Co-Chair of the IFA Philadelphia Women's Franchise Network. She is a former member of the IFA Legal Symposium Task Force and multiple past presenter at the IFA Legal Symposium, including participating on the panel for the 2023 Judicial Update.

In her free time, you will find Elle hiking, golfing, playing board games, puzzling, cheering on her Philadelphia sports teams, and clowning around with her husband, Jeff, two children Samuel (Age 11) and Abigail (Age 9), the family Bernedoodle Harper, and bunny Cannoli, in their suburban Philadelphia hometown of Blue Bell, Pennsylvania. Elle is also an avid reader, gardener, and competitive bocce player.

JOSEPH S. GOODE

Joseph S. Goode is the Managing Partner of Laffey, Leitner & Goode LLC, a litigation boutique based in Milwaukee, Wisconsin. He is a trial lawyer who focuses his practice on complex business disputes with heightened emphasis in franchise and dealership law, intellectual property, probate, and real estate litigation, shareholder and fiduciary disputes, and non-competition and trade secret litigation. He has significant jury, bench trial, and arbitration experience in various jurisdictions around the United States. Joe is a graduate of the University of Wisconsin-Madison (B.A., History, 1989) and Syracuse University College of Law (J.D., cum laude, 1994). He also has a master's degree in public administration from the Maxwell School of Citizenship and Public Affairs at Syracuse University (M.P.A., 1994).

Each year since 2007, Joe has been named a Wisconsin Super Lawyer, starting first in 2006 as a "Rising Star." In 2017, 2022, and 2024, the organization named Joe a "Top 50" lawyer in the State of Wisconsin. In 2017 and 2022, Super Lawyers further designated Joe one of the "Top 25" lawyers in Milwaukee. Since 2011, he has been included annually in The Best Lawyers in America for his work in Commercial Litigation, Franchise Law, Appellate Practice, First Amendment Litigation, Real Estate Litigation, and Intellectual Property Litigation. In 2015, 2017, 2018, and 2021, Best Lawyers named Joe "Franchise Lawyer of the Year" for the City of Milwaukee. Franchise Times has listed Joe as one of its "Legal Eagles" every year since 2017.

Joe is a member of the Milwaukee Bar Association, the State Bar of Wisconsin, the Seventh Circuit Bar Association, and the American Bar Association. He is actively involved in the ABA Forum on Franchising where he has co-authored articles for the *Franchise Law Journal* and the *Franchise Lawyer*. Joe also co-authored the Litigation Chapter of the 2023 Forum publication *Representing*

Franchisees. Joe is a regular presenter at Forum workshops and currently serves on the Publications Committee. In 2025, Joe will join the Forum's Governing Committee. At various times since 2011, Joe has also presented at the International Franchise Association's Legal Symposium in Washington D.C. He is an American Bar Association Fellow as of 2023.

Joe has a strong sense of purpose and giving back. He is the President of the Board of Directors of Milwaukee's Historic Third Ward Association, the Past President of the Dane County Humane Society Board of Directors where he served for 15 years, and a member of the Board of Directors of Washington D.C.'s Animal Wellness Action. Three times (2017, 2019, and 2022), San Francisco's Animal Legal Defense Fund has awarded Joe and his firm with its prestigious "Advancement in Animal Law Pro Bono Achievement" Award for their tireless work pursuing animal welfare in the courts of the United States. In 2021, the Wisconsin State Bar placed Joe in its Pro Bono Honor Society for his work during the 2020 presidential election cycle.

When Joe is not working on client matters, he is struggling with his golf game, traveling, and hanging out with his far better half, his wife Dina. Joe and Dina share their historic home in Milwaukee with their dog Harlow and cats Audrey and Valentino.

FOREWORD

The book *Annual Franchise and Distribution Law Developments 2024* remains one of the strongest pieces of scholarship of our Forum on Franchising. It is a daunting task to take on, but each year, two valuable and committed members of the Forum do just that. This year, our colleagues Eleanor Vaida Gerhards and Joseph S. Goode took on this immense job. Among busy lives and legal practices, they took on the task of culling through and summarizing all the relevant legal developments in franchise case law this year—we are so grateful. And while this book represents and remains a pinnacle of our legal scholarship, this year I also want to point out that it also represents another one of the Forum's great traits—*friendship and comradery*.

Our authors wrote in their own acknowledgements about their joy in working together as a team on this large project, as well as the support of their families, friends, clients, and firms. When I took on the Annual Developments book myself in 2018, my co-author, Elliot Ginsburg, and I discussed how we are "friends-for-life" after completing that task; and we still are. The same was true when I co-chaired the Annual Meeting in 2020 with Gary Batenhorst—and we remain friends-for-life. I hope the same is true for Elle and Joe. One of the greatest gifts of participating in the Forum is the friendship that comes with that participation. We work side-by-side with colleagues, getting to know them, their hearts, and their intellects, and we find a connection that is not necessarily found in all professional places. Friendship and comradery are values of the Forum and they are gifts that our members receive when they participate in the Forum in any number of ways—writing, speaking, attending, planning, networking, and all other kinds of Forum activities. My hope for our readers is that they too continue to participate in the Forum and gain the friendships that our authors and so many others in the Forum have developed and treasure.

On behalf of the Governing Committee of the Forum, the 47th Annual Forum Co-Chairs Earsa Jackson and Erin Johnsen, and the entire membership of the Forum, I formally and specifically share our gratitude to the authors of *Annual Franchise and Distribution Law Developments 2024*, Eleanor Vaida Gerhards of Fox Rothschild in Philadelphia and Blue Bell, Pennsylvania and Joseph S. Goode of Laffey, Leitner & Goode, LLC Milwaukee, Wisconsin. They worked together and with many people at their firms to get this book to our readers to elevate the study of franchise law. It is a great effort to make this happen and to do it while conducting their busy law practices and the myriad of other responsibilities that they have as in-demand leaders is nothing short of remarkable. Thank you, Elle and Joe!

This year's book continues to showcase the high level of legal thinking and analysis that brings members back to the Annual Meeting each year. Cases of public interest, like *United States of America v. Burgerim Group USA, Inc.*, are covered, as well as many cases about the fundamental building blocks of franchise law, such as statutory interpretation. Our authors will showcase their work at the Annual Meeting in Phoenix and our readers will want to make sure to block their calendars to see their signature plenary presentation.

Many thanks go to Dan Oates, who edited the *Annual Franchise and Distribution Law Developments 2024* book. Dan is a member of our Governing Committee, the current Publications Officer, and the co-chair for next year's 48th Annual Forum, and he also authored his own book—*Annual Franchise and Distribution Law Developments 2022*—along with Susan Tegt, who has been nominated this year to be an incoming member of the Governing Committee. Dan is quite familiar with the work that goes into writing this book, and is a great editor, due in part to his prior work as the Editor-in-Chief of the Forum's Franchise Law Journal. I also share our thanks to the Forum's International Division, led wonderfully this past year by Nicola Broadhurst, and the authors in this division and in our Forum who contributed sections for specific country developments in franchising. The Forum also thanks the ABA publications staff and team for their aid in the publishing process.

I hope you settle in, read, and enjoy *Annual Franchise and Distribution Law Developments 2024*. As you peruse its chapters, remember that people and friends are behind this book and please be inspired to remain or become involved in our Forum and all it has to offer our members. Thank you again to Elle and Joe for their commitment and hard work on this essential book.

Elizabeth M. Weldon
Chair, Forum on Franchising

ACKNOWLEDGMENTS

"It won't take that much time if you stay on top of it," they said. "You two will really like working together," they said. "It will be a good experience," they said. Save the actual commitment of time to prepare this book, all this turned out to be true when the Forum on Franchising asked us last fall to prepare *Annual Franchise and Distribution Law Developments* for the 2024 Forum in Phoenix, Arizona. As the authors of this publication, we really have enjoyed working together and it has been a great experience. Teamwork actually is a thing and our collective efforts in preparing this book have absolutely paid off. The only real sacrifice came at the expense of our golf games, which suffered miserably due to the pressing needs of our day jobs and those attendant to this book. But as an initial acknowledgement, the two of us want to acknowledge each other who have actually had a great deal of fun working together and preparing this book for publication for those reading it.

But enough about us.

First and foremost, the authors wish to thank this year's Annual Meeting co-chairs, Earsa R. Jackson, Clark Hill PLC, and Erin Conway Johnsen, Garner, Ginsburg & Johnsen, P.A, for entrusting us with the honor of authoring Annual Developments and allowing us to present the book at the plenary session this year. We appreciate the confidence and faith you placed in us and the opportunity to present at the Annual Forum's signature event.

We also thank last year's Annual Development speakers and authors, Charles Marion, Blank Rome LLP, and Annie Caiola, Caiola & Rose, who graciously lent their expertise and experience, especially in the early months of this endeavor, to steer us down the right path to organize our plan of attack. We also thank our Program Director, Daniel J. Oates, Miller Nash LLP, for taking on the monumental task of reading and editing summaries of over 400 franchise and distribution law cases and keeping the authors in line.

We are also appreciative to Nicola Broadhurst, Stevens & Bolton LLP, and the Forum's International Division which provided the summaries of developments from around the world that appear in Chapter 9. Thanks to Eugenia Kolivos, Michael Joffe and Anika Di Pietro (Corrs Chambers Westgarth, Australia), Kristof Zadora and Dylan Verhulst (Monard Law, Belgium), Noah Leszcz (Cassels Brock & Blackwell), Dominic Hui (Ribeiro Hui, China), Kentaro Tanaka and Taro Matsumoto (Japan), Stewart Germann, CFE (Stewart Germann Law Office, New Zealand), Sławomir Uss and Krzysztof Misarko (Sołtysiński Kawecki & Szlęzak, Poland), Thivanka Hettiarachchi and Kasuni Ranaweera (Sri Lanka), Jane Wang, Charles Chen and Shelley Hsu (Taiwan), and Nicola Broadhurst and Alasdair McDowell (Stevens & Bolton LLP, United Kingdom).

The authors are both very grateful to Annalise Ehlenbach, Joe's tenacious and uber-competent legal assistant at Laffey, Leitner & Goode LLC, and Stacey Ritterson, dedicated Client Service Specialist to Elle at Fox, who each went above and beyond every single day for nearly a year tracking, logging, and assigning the cases and formatting our trusted developments master tracker to keep the authors and writers on task and organized. It was often Annalise and Stacey who found glitches in the authors' system and brought concerns and problems to the authors' attention. It was also Annalise and Stacey who offered the most practical and needed suggestions on how to resolve issues when they arose.

The entire team of Fox Rothschild's Knowledge Management Department particularly Nina del Valle (Legal Research Lead), P. McLane Daniel (Senior Research Manager), Gina Diez (Legal

Research Manager) and Genevieve Schmidt (Senior Research Analyst) were instrumental in creating a seamless process to extract and distribute the cases and regulatory updates to us for review. The tireless attorney resource team lead by Helen Sayen and Lindsay Stoner who donated their expertise at the bitter end to assist with the formatting and preparation of this book's table of contents, table of authorities and index.

Elle would like to personally thank Craig Tractenberg, Co-Chair of Fox's Franchise Practice, for assisting Elle with summarizing many of the most substantive and impactful cases as well as: Eric Michaels for lending his LLM background for summarizing the tax cases; Fox Rothschild Summer Associate, Madison Faizon, rising 3L at the University of Richmond School of Law from our Philadelphia office for assisting with all of the international chapter editing; and Fox Rothschild Summer Associate, Sakina Bhatti, rising 3L at Pennsylvania State University, Penn State Law from our Kansas City office for organizing, marshaling, summarizing, assembling, and analyzing the dozens of hotel brand sex trafficking cases.

Finally, Elle would like to thank her "hub" Jeff who always picked up the slack at home when her nights and weekends were spent on this book. As a special thank you by Elle to her immensely supportive and loving family, she allowed her children, Sam and Abbie, to ghost write her personal acknowledgments which are transcribed here verbatim: *I would also like to thank my family especially my son Sam and my daughter Abigail. They have been so unbelievably patient and cooperative throughout this process. My son Sam is just so special to me and is loved by me with all my heart. He is just one of my favorite people to hang out with, he is creative and funny and overall just a really great son to have. My daughter Abigail is also really fun and nice and she loves to golf with her family. She is also great to hang out with and trustworthy and brave. Abigail is so beautiful and I am so lucky to have her as a daughter.*

ACKNOWLEDGMENTS

For his part, Joe would like to personally thank his Milwaukee colleagues Maura K. Logue, Mark M. Leitner, John W. Halpin, Katherine W. Schill, Sarah Thomas Pagels, and Benjamin W. Kuhlmann who diligently assisted him in reading cases for the reporting year and helped in drafting sections of this book. Their insights and hard work elevated the final work product to what we now present to you. Joe would also like to thank Mackenzie Retzlaff, a 3L at Marquette University Law School, for her early work assisting Joe on case squibs and assessing case write ups for elevation into this book. "It takes a village" comes to mind and being surrounded in that village by capable and kind colleagues reminds Joe of why he got into this business in the first place. Finally, Joe would like to thank his wife Dina, whose patience and personal sacrifice to allow him to work on this project amidst a flurry of too many other professional obligations, cannot be adequately described in words, but is absolutely reflected in the work product in this book.

INTRODUCTION

In the day and age of digital everything, what's the value of a good old-fashioned, printed book? Modern day thinking might say, there is none. After all, in this world of ours everything we do is computer generated and accessible online. The proliferation of artificial intelligence is only growing this phenomenon. While the digitization of the world is beyond our realm as authors of this year's *Annual Franchise and Distribution Law Developments*, the question persists: why keep doing a printed book year after year as part of the ABA Forum on Franchising?

When lawyers sit down with a new client, be it for a piece of litigation or a transactional need, we are trained to gather a full understanding of the facts to advise the client on the legal implications of those facts. For the last 47 years, the Forum on Franchising has been the voice of franchise practitioners and the communal place where those impacted by franchising worldwide get together to learn, voice positions, and share insights and knowledge in the practice of franchise law. While we could presumably stop doing this book and leave you all to fend for yourselves on recent developments in the law affecting your franchise and distribution clients, that largely diminishes the value of the Forum as an association of similarly situated practitioners and this exercise, which for years has been one of the heralded outputs of our annual meeting.

The law moves incrementally. Some will say not fast enough and others will express shock at its speed. But move it will. The idea here is to place two individuals in a position to help our members do the work that is otherwise improbable for them to accomplish on their own. Because franchising is a regulated industry, and because the very definition of "franchise" at times comes into dispute, the law intervenes to help sort out what this all means to that client, to the lawyers practicing in this area, and to the greater good affected by developments in franchise law.

This book is a deliberate digest of reported decisions in franchise and distribution law for the period August 1, 2023 through July 31, 2024. It reflects the work of not just the two named authors but numerous individuals identified in the Acknowledgements who helped make it happen. But making it happen and "making it happen" are two different things. We report below on more than 400 cases in this book and that itself reflects editorial decisions by the two of us on which of the myriad other cases we read would make the final cut for the book. Every day for nearly the last year, we have obtained a report from Westlaw telling us what cases were decided in state and federal courts that might be worthy of reporting. Most often those reports had 30-plus cases listed on them which required us to assess their initial worth before diving deeper into their actual value for this publication. What you see below is the outcome of that work.

What we personally find most valuable about this publication is the level of consistency in reporting style year in and year out. In answer to the question of, what is the "the value of a good old-fashioned, printed book," consider picking a topic from the Table of Contents (let's use "Binding Non-Signatories" to Arbitration from Chapter 8, Section VI(B)). Now, for all the years this book has sat on your shelf at work, review that section of the book. You now have before you years of decisional law that will guide your work in answer to the client's questions about whether a non-signatory can be bound to an arbitration clause. It's pretty brilliant, in our view.

While the Acknowledgments demonstrate that we had lots of help pulling this book together, we take full ownership of the content. Countless editing by us, Daniel J. Oates, and the folks at the ABA assuredly helped to make this a better product. But they are not to blame for any errors you see. Any mistakes you find lay at our feet.

With thanks.

Eleanor Vaida Gerhards
Joseph S. Goode
August 27, 2024

CHAPTER 1

The Elements of a Franchise Relationship

I. Introduction

Whether a franchise relationship exists is often the initial question asked by a defendant when a plaintiff asserts rights under state and federal franchise laws. The Federal Trade Commission ("FTC") has its Franchise Rule ("Rule 436") and various states have their own version of that rule. Many state relationship laws similarly define what is and what is not a protected "franchise" or "dealership." Most of these laws contemplate courts looking at essentially three elements: (1) whether the party invoking franchise protection has the right to use or associate with the trademarks and intellectual property of the defendant; (2) whether the plaintiff paid franchise fees (directly or indirectly) in exchange for the trade rights associated with the relationship at issue; and (3) whether the putative franchisee was substantially involved in a "marketing plan" imposed by the defendant or whether the relationship alleged meets the law's definition of a "community of interest" between the parties. Within each of these elements are further definitional tussles that have for years led to creative and at times expansive rulings over what is (or is not) a franchise.

In this reporting year (2023-2024), there was a limited number of reported cases focused on the essential elements of the franchise relationship. All three cases reported below dealt blows to would-be franchisees seeking protection under various state franchise laws based on findings that the alleged franchisee had not paid a franchise fee as required to assert protection under the laws in Minnesota, Massachusetts, Florida, and California. Most interesting of these is *Cambria Co. v. M&M Creative Laminants, Inc.*, where the Minnesota Court of Appeals determined, as a matter of first impression in Minnesota, that post-purchase services of a countertop installation company for quartz countertops it had acquired from a manufacturer were not indirect franchise fees under the Minnesota Franchise Act such that the installer could not claim franchise protection under the statute.

II. Essential Elements of a Franchise

Cambria Co. v. M&M Creative Laminants, Inc., 995 N.W.2d 426, 431, 2023 WL 5340399 (Minn. Ct. App. 2023). Cambria Company LLC ("Cambria") is a Minnesota manufacturer and fabricator of quartz countertops. M&M Creative Laminants, Inc. ("M&M") is a Pennsylvania contractor that installed countertops into homes and other buildings. Between 2008 and 2017, Cambria and M&M entered into a series of "business-partner agreements" ("BPAs"). These BPAs (1) allowed M&M to order countertops on credit in exchange for payment within a certain period; (2) included terms and conditions limiting Cambria's liability; and (3) required M&M to use specific business equipment and attend training at Cambria's facility in Minnesota. M&M purchased countertops from Cambria on credit for 8 years, but routinely failed to timely pay its invoices when due.

In May 2017, Cambria notified M&M that it was terminating the BPAs for M&M's failure to timely pay its invoices. M&M responded that it would not pay any amounts outstanding until the parties agreed on how to terminate the relationship. Cambria responded by filing suit against M&M for its failure to pay the outstanding invoices. M&M counterclaimed against Cambria, alleging that the termination violated Section 3 the Minnesota Franchise Act ("MFA"), which requires good cause for termination and 90 days' notice of termination. M&M also alleged breach of contract, unjust enrichment, tortious interference with contract, and unfair competition claims.

The parties filed cross-motions for summary judgment on the MFA claim, and Cambria also challenged the breach of contract, tortious interference, unfair competition and unjust enrichment claims brought by M&M. The district court granted Cambria summary judgment on the MFA claim and certain of M&M's other claims, leaving certain claims for trial. At trial, the jury awarded Cambria over $275,000 in damages for breach of contract. Following a separate bench trial, the court awarded Cambria its attorneys' fees and costs.

The Minnesota Court of Appeals affirmed the trial court's decision in all respects. First, it found that M&M did not qualify as a franchise under the MFA and provided guidance to practitioners clarifying the statutory definition of what constituted a franchise fee. Specifically, the court noted that to qualify for protection under the MFA, the purported franchisee must show through an express or implied contract that (1) it has been granted the right to offer or distribute goods or services using the franchisor's name, marks or commercial symbols; (2) the franchisor and franchisee have a "community of interest" in the marketing of goods or services at wholesale, retail, or otherwise; and (3) the franchisee paid a franchise fee (either directly or indirectly). While the Court of Appeals noted that the MFA defines a "franchise fee" as "any fee or charge" that is required to be paid to the franchisor, including "any payment for goods or services," it held that "the purchase of goods or an agreement to purchase goods at a bona fide wholesale price" is not a franchise fee.

In its summary judgment ruling, the trial court expressly rejected M&M's argument that a fabrication service (such as adding a sink hole or polishing or edging countertops) constituted a franchise fee under the statute and relied on the Uniform Commercial Code ("UCC") in reaching this decision. On review, the Court of Appeals noted that there was no express precedent on the issue of whether paying for incidental fabrication services converts a bona fide wholesale price agreement to an indirect franchise fee under the MFA, which in its eyes made the trial court's reliance on the UCC reasonable. Under the UCC, when faced with a hybrid contract for both goods and services, the court is to classify the parties' contract using the predominant purpose test and determine whether the "dominant characteristic" is for goods for services. In affirming the trial court's decision, the Court of Appeals found that the dominant characteristic of the BPA was for the sale of countertops, not fabrication services. Finding that M&M's payment of a "bona fide wholesale price" was not a franchise fee under the statute, the Court of Appeals determined that if it were to recognize payments for post purchase services as franchise fees, it would significantly diminish the unambiguous language in the MFA that disclaims payments at a "bona fide wholesale price" as franchise fees.

Cognex Corp. v. Air Hydro Power, LLC, No. CV 22-10051-NMG, 2023 WL 5833112 (D. Mass. Sept. 8, 2023). Cognex Corporation ("Cognex"), a manufacturer of barcode readers gave notice to one of its distributors, Air Hydro Power, LLC ("Air Hydro"), that it did not intend to renew its distribution agreement. After Air Hydro filed suit against Cognex in Florida state court, Cognex filed a breach of contract claim seeking damages against Air Hydro Power, LLC for its alleged breach of the parties' forum-selection clause and violations of the covenant of good faith and fair dealing. In response, Air Hydro filed counterclaims, alleging violations of various state franchise acts, breach of the covenant of good faith and fair dealing, tortious interference, promissory estoppel, and unjust enrichment.

The United States District Court for the District of Massachusetts granted Cognex's motion to dismiss each of Air Hydro's counterclaims. The court barred Air Hydro's claim under the Florida Franchise Act applying the choice-of-law provision in the distribution agreement designating Massachusetts law. The court rejected Air-Hydro's argument that because Massachusetts lacks a franchisee-protection statute, applying the choice-of-law provision would be contrary to Florida's policy decision to protect franchisees. The court concluded that the Florida Franchise Act (unlike other Florida consumer protection statutes) does not specifically include an anti-waiver provision. Therefore, no Florida policy interest is damaged by applying the Massachusetts choice of law provision in the distribution agreement. As a result, Air Hydro was not entitled to assert claims under the Florida Franchise Act.

The court also dismissed the distributor's claims that Cognex violated the Florida Deceptive and Unfair Trade Practices Act Claim, the Indiana Franchise Act, and the Indiana Deceptive Franchise Practices Act because the business relationship between the parties did not meet the definition of franchise under the FTC Rule or any state franchise act as it was lacking the "fee element." The court cited the FTC Franchise Rule, which defines a required payment as "all consideration that the franchisee must pay to the franchisor or an affiliate, either by contract or by practical necessity, as a condition of obtaining or commencing operation of the franchise."

Neither the purchase of demonstration equipment or recommended software constitute a "required payment" under the FTC Rule because neither purchase was a required condition of commencing operation or a practical necessity of operating the business. Although the agreement stated that Air Hydro would purchase and maintain products for demonstration as recommended by Cognex, the purchases were not required. Rather, if Air Hydro did not make the product purchases, Cognex would eliminate certain discounts. The court concluded the recommended purchases were an incentive program that provided potential discounts, not a fee. Similarly, Air Hydro was not required to purchase a software license. Although the software license facilitated resales, it was not so critical to operations to be considered a practical necessity. Finally, the costs incurred by Air Hydro to build demonstration facilities were deemed sunk costs to further its own business goals and not a required payment to Cognex.

The court also dismissed Air Hydro's claim that Cognex breached the covenant of good faith and fair dealing when it did not compensate Air Hydro for unsold demonstration equipment because there was no expectation under the distribution agreement that Air Hydro would receive reimbursement. Similarly, Air Hydro's claim for tortious interference with a business relationship was dismissed. The court found that the distribution agreement expressly permitted Cognex to transfer sales leads within a territory, and therefore, Air Hydro could not establish the conduct was improper, an essential element to state a claim. The court also decided that any reliance by Air Hydro on Cognex's alleged oral promise to renew the agreement was unreasonable given the explicit terms of the written agreement, and dismissed the promissory estoppel claim in its decision.

Quick Dispense, Inc. v. Vitality Foodservice, Inc., No. 823CV02322FWSADS, 2024 WL 655996 (C.D. Cal. Feb. 2, 2024). Plaintiff Quick Dispense, Inc. ("Quick Dispense") and Defendant Validity Foodservice, Inc. ("Validity") entered into a distributorship agreement, a sales agent agreement, and an independent contract services agreement (collectively, "the Agreement"). Pursuant to the Agreement, Validity would distribute Nestlé branded goods to Quick Dispense to sell in an exclusive territory. On May 1, 2023, Validity informed Quick Dispense that it would not be renewing the Agreement. Six months later, Quick Dispense filed suit for: (1) violations of California Franchise Investment Law; (2) breach of contract; (3) breach of implied contract; (4) wrongful termination/non-renewal in violation of California Franchise Relations Act ("CFRA"); (5) declaratory relief; (6) unfair business practices in violation of California Business and Profession Code Section 17200 ("UCL"); and (7) intentional interference with prospective economic advantage. Shortly after, Quick Dispense filed an application for a temporary restraining order ("TRO"), arguing that it was necessary to prevent the destruction of its business and eliminate the risk of losing more than sixty individual employees. Alternatively, Quick Dispense argued that it demonstrated a likelihood of success on the merits of its claims, and therefore, the balance of equities tip in its favor.

The district court found that Quick Dispense failed to demonstrate that expedited relief was warranted and denied the application for injunctive relief. Specifically, the court found that the six-month waiting period before Quick Dispense filed its complaint illustrated there was no sense of urgency or irreparable harm. The court further reasoned that the nine-month waiting period before Quick Dispense filed its application also supported the notion that the circumstances were the type that did not necessitate *ex parte* relief.

The court then considered the plaintiff's substantive claims. It began by focusing on the claims brought under unfair competition law, CFRA, and CFIL. In its analysis, the court found that Quick Dispense failed to establish that it operated as a franchise under CFRA or CFIL because it never demonstrated that it was required to pay the franchisor a fee. Thus, Quick Dispense failed to demonstrate a likelihood of success on its CFRA or CFIL claims. Additionally, the court found that the unfair competition claim failed because it was predicated upon the existence of a franchise relationship. Lastly, the court found that Quick Dispense failed to demonstrate a likelihood of success regarding its breach of contract claims. The court reasoned that there was no evidence of an existing and active contract between the parties. Instead, the facts establish that Validity complied with the terms of the Agreement and provided adequate notice of its intent to end the relationship. Consequently, the court independently denied plaintiff's application for the injunction on this alternative basis.

CHAPTER 2

Registration and Disclosure

I. Introduction

There were only a handful of reportable cases this year alleging violations of federal and state disclosures requirements and fraudulent or negligent misrepresentations or omissions within or outside a Franchise Disclosure Document ("FDD"). This year's most publicized is likely *United States of America v. Burgerim Group USA, Inc.* where a California district court granted a default judgment in favor of the Federal Trade Commission ("FTC") against franchisor Burgerim Group USA, Inc. *Burgerim* was the result of the first major civil enforcement action against a franchise system by the FTC in over a decade. However, at the state level, there was little success for franchisees during this reporting period alleging violations of state franchise disclosure and relationship laws. In the only two cases of this Chapter 2 addressing violations of state registration or relationship laws, the court dismissed the plaintiffs' cases for failing to state a claim. In the last case of this Chapter 2, *Goldberger v. Scott,* the Tennessee Court of Appeals held that a defendant's announcements regarding a franchise system's alleged violations of the FTC Rule were a matter of public concern requiring protection under the state anti-SLAPP statute.

II. Violations of Registration or Disclosure Requirements

United States of America v. Burgerim Group USA, Inc., No. CV 22-825-DMG, 2024 WL 661189 (C.D. Cal. Jan. 19, 2024). The United States District Court for the Central District of California granted the United States of America's motion for default judgment against a quick-service burger restaurant franchise concept, Burgerim Group USA, Inc., and its owner, after the Federal Trade Commission filed a complaint against the defendants for using misleading sales practices to sell more than 1,500 franchises in violation of the FTC Franchise Rule. The court held that the United States has proved its damages as defendants were paid $57,707,244 in franchise fees from 2015 through July 2019, and of that amount, the defendants only issued $9,230,555 in refunds. The court also found the United States' request for a $5,000 penalty per violation was reasonable as it was far below the amount authorized by the FTC's Rule of Practice. The court granted the United States' request for consumer redress in the amount of $48,747,689 and a civil penalty of $7,750,000. The court also found that a permanent injunction prohibiting the defendants from selling additional franchises was warranted, and an appropriate sanction for their conduct.

Quick Dispense, Inc. v. Vitality Foodservice, Inc., No. 8:23-cv-023322-FWS-ADS, 2024 WL 2925589 (C.D. Cal. June 4, 2024). Plaintiff Quick Dispense, Inc. ("Quick"), a wholesale distributor of Nestlé beverage products, filed a lawsuit against Vitality Foodservice, Inc. ("Vitality") alleging that the distribution agreement entered into between the parties constitutes a franchise under the California Franchise Investment Law ("CFIL"). Quick alleged seven claims against Vitality including violations of the CFIL and wrongful termination or non-renewal under the California Franchise Relations Act ("CFRA"). Vitality argued that Quick Dispense failed to state a claim upon which relief could be granted. The CFIL claims alleged that Vitality failed to provide a franchise disclosure document, sold an unregistered franchise, and made untrue statements or omissions. The court found these claims time-barred by the applicable statute of limitations. Under California law, the statute of limitations for violations related to franchise registration and disclosure is four years from the violation or one year from the discovery of the violation. Quick's claims were based on the agreements executed in November 2020, and the lawsuit was filed beyond the allowable period. With respect to the CFRA violation, the court found Quick failed to allege the necessary elements of a franchise relationship under the CFRA. Specifically, it did not adequately demonstrate that it paid a franchise fee for the right to do business, or that Vitality imposed a marketing plan or system. The court found the allegations regarding excess inventory and weekly payments too conclusory to support the existence of a franchise fee. The court dismissed the CFIL claim without leave to amend, as it was time-barred. However, the court dismissed the CFRA claim with leave to amend, finding that the deficiencies might be curable.

III. Other Misrepresentations or Omissions

Aylin & Ramtin, LLC v. Barnhardt, No. 19 C 3402, 2024 WL 325384 (N.D. Ill. Jan. 29, 2024). In this case, the United States District Court for the Northern District of Illinois granted partial summary judgment in favor of the franchisor of Little Minds Learning Center, LMLC Franchising, LLC ("Franchisor"), a management entity of two franchise locations, LMLC Management, LLC ("LMLC-M"), and the manager Todd Barnhardt ("Barnhardt"). The ruling came at the expense of claims brought by Aylin & Ramtin, LLC ("A&R") and its sole member, an Iranian citizen ("Ramtin"), alleging breach of fiduciary duty and violations of the Illinois Franchise Disclosure Act ("IFDA").

Barnhardt solicited foreign investments through the EB-5 Immigrant Investor Program which allowed lawful foreign investors to become lawful permanent residents. Ramtin learned of the opportunity to invest in Little Mind child-care center franchises. After receiving a franchise disclosure document, he invested in two locations managed by LMLC-M. The venture was unsuccessful and A&R and Ramtin filed suit against Defendants seeking to recover their investment in the franchised centers, alleging that LMCL-M and Barnhardt breached their fiduciary duties and made fraudulent misrepresentations concerning the childcare centers.

The court granted partial summary judgment, rejecting plaintiffs' claims for breach of fiduciary duty, and concluding LMLC-M and Barnhardt did not owe Ramtin any fiduciary duties because Ramtin only interacted with the businesses in his individual capacity as the sole member of A&R. The court also granted summary judgment to all defendants on the IFDA fraudulent practices claim, concluding that opinions or statements relating to future or contingent events, such as future costs, sales, and profitability are not fraudulent practices. Additionally, the portion of claims made after the initial franchise sale were not actionable under the IFDA. The claims for breach of fiduciary duty against Barnhardt, breach of contract, and common law fraudulent misrepresentation, survived the motion for summary judgment.

Goldberger v. Scott, No. M2022-01772-COA-R3-CV, 2024 WL 3339314 (Tenn. Ct. App. July 9, 20224). The Tennessee Court of Appeals reversed the trial court's denial of a petition filed by the defendant, to dismiss the plaintiff's complaint for business disparagement, tortious interference with business relationships, breach of contract, breach of the duty of loyalty, and breach of the duty of care. Plaintiff and defendant were founders and officers of a holding company operating multiple franchised brands. Defendant discovered that his co-owners failed to disclose they had been defendants in previous franchise litigation and also previously settled two state regulatory actions arising out of a failure to comply with state franchise law. All of this history was not disclosed in Item 3 of the franchise disclosure documents. When the defendant uncovered this information, disputes arose between the founders, and the defendant filed a separate lawsuit against plaintiffs. Defendant then contacted several franchise owners to tell them about the lawsuit and posted the ongoing franchising improprieties on the Internet. In response, plaintiffs filed a complaint for business disparagement, among other claims, and moved for an injunction to prevent the defendant from disparaging or defaming plaintiffs. Defendant then moved to dismiss the complaint under the Tennessee Public Participation Act ("TPPA"), Tennessee's anti-SLAPP statute, arguing that he was sued in response to his exercise of the right of free speech in violation of the TPPA. The lower court denied the petition finding that the TPPA did not apply because the claims did not involve issues or matters of public concern as required under the TPPA. The Court of Appeals reversed finding there was prima facie evidence that the plaintiffs commenced their action in response to the defendant's exercise of free speech, and it was a matter of public concern that the franchise systems were continuing to offer and sell without disclosures required under the FTC Rule. The speech qualified as a matter impacting a good, product, or service in the marketplace which qualified for protection under the TPPA. The court found that the regulation of franchises and compliance with franchise regulations is certainly a matter of public concern as they were put in place to protect franchisees.

CHAPTER 3

Industry-Specific Statutes Affecting the Franchising Relationship

I. Introduction

Chapter 3 of this book reminds us that there are myriad state and federal statutes governing the ongoing relationships between trade channel partners. This chapter summarizes cases for this reporting year (2023-2024) involving relationship statutes of general application such as the Wisconsin Fair Dealership Law ("WFDL") as well as state and federal statutes governing the relationship of parties in specific industries, including the Petroleum Marketing Practices Act ("PMPA"), the Automobile Dealer Franchise Act ("ADDCA"), state franchise acts specific to the relationship between manufacturer and dealers of cars, warranty statutes over vehicle sales, laws governing the distribution and sale of alcoholic beverages, and other such particularized statutes.

For practitioners, Chapter 3 reminds us of the value as attorneys of definitions and how the plain words of a statute can determine the outcome on whether statutory protection does or does not exist for a particular channel relationship. While statutes such as the WFDL, and its counterparts in the fifteen states with generalized laws like it, can be powerful weapons for dealers and franchisees seeking protection from unlawful terminations, practitioners can see below how industry specific regulations define the results of terminations and related consequences in those industries affected.

II. Petroleum Marketing Practices Act

Puerto Rico Energy, LLC v. Puerto Rico, No. 20-1591 (ADC), Civil No. 20-1725(ADC), 2024 WL 866326 (D. Puerto Rico, February 28, 2024). The federal district court in Puerto Rico denied the discovery requests of two gasoline wholesalers ("PRE") who filed a lawsuit against Puerto Rico alleging that its "Gasoline Law" ("Gasoline Law") was preempted by the federal the Petroleum Marketing Practices Act ("PMPA"). Puerto Rico's Gasoline Law prohibits gasoline wholesalers from having any control over any non-gasoline service station business that is located on the premises of a gasoline service station. PRE sought declaratory and injunctive relief, plus damages, alleging that enforcement of the Gasoline Law constituted an unconstitutional taking of their property rights. The court consolidated the two actions. In this decision, the court denied the PRE's request for further discovery finding that (1) the frequency and extent of the discovery requested throughout the litigation constituted abuse of the discovery process and (2) based upon the doctrine of legislative privilege of state officials.

Seymour Foodmart, LLC v. Drake Petroleum Co., No. X08-FST-CV-19-6061071-S, 2024 WL 94276 (Conn. Super. Ct. Jan. 2, 2024). Seymour Foodmart, LLC ("Seymour") and Drake Petroleum Company, Inc. ("Drake"), entered into a Convenience Store Lease ("Lease") and a Commissioned Agent Agreement ("Agreement"). Under the Lease, Seymour leased part of the premises to operate a convenience store and sold motor fuel under the CITGO trademark at the location pursuant to the Agreement. Drake was the sole supplier, setting retail prices and paying Seymour commissions on fuel sales and Drake held a gasoline dealer license.

Prior to the expiration of the Lease and Agreement, Drake offered new agreements with a one-year term and increased rent, which Seymour objected to as violating the Connecticut Petroleum Franchise Act ("CPFA"). Seymour eventually signed under protest. Seymour then filed suit against Drake alleging violations of the CPFA and the Connecticut Unfair Trade Practices Act ("CUTPA"). Drake filed a motion for summary judgment on the ground that Seymour was not a franchisee under the CPFA, the relationship was not a franchise, and Drake was not a franchisor.

The court concluded that the relationship between the parties is covered by the CPFA, rejecting Drake's interpretation that commissioned agents are not franchisees under the CPFA. The court considered the legislative history and intent behind the CPFA amendments, focusing on broadening the definitions to cover more gasoline franchises, including consignment dealers, and determined that the CPFA includes both sales and consignment of motor fuel. The court also denied Drake's motion for summary judgment on the CUTPA allegation as well since the allegation was based on the CPFA violation. Because the court determined that the relationship fell under the CPFA, Drake's motion for summary judgment on the two courts was denied and the court found sufficient grounds to proceed with Seymour's claims of violations under CPFA and CUTPA.

3 N Holding Corp. v. LUKOIL North America LLC, No. CV 24-05102 (GC) (TJB), 2024 WL 3355612 (D.N.J. July 9, 2024). Plaintiff franchisee sought a preliminary injunction and temporary restraining order to enjoin a franchisor from terminating the franchise and lease agreement that authorized plaintiff to use, advertise, and sell fuel at a retail gas station. The Petroleum Marketing Practices Act ("PMPA") has a lower threshold for obtaining a preliminary injunction than ordinarily required under the Federal Rules of Civil Procedure. Under the PMPA, a court must grant a preliminary injunction if the franchisee shows (1) that the franchise has been terminated or the franchise agreement has not been renewed; (2) there is a sufficiently serious question going to the merits to make such questions a fair basis for litigation; and (3) the court balances the hardships imposed upon the franchisor by the injunction. Here, the district court granted franchisee's injunction and TRO because all three elements under the PMPA were met. Specifically, the district court held that the franchisee had raised sufficiently serious questions to warrant a preliminary injunction and that the balance of hardships favors the franchisee, all of which favored entry of a preliminary injunction.

Brandford Quick Mart LLC v. Aldin Associates LP, No. NNH CV22-5052782 S, 2024 WL 1172386 (Sup. Ct. Conn., Mar. 14, 2024). The Superior Court of Connecticut held that the plaintiff Quick Mart businesses were not "franchises" within the definition of the Connecticut Petroleum Products Franchises Act ("PPFA") because the plaintiffs were not refiners, distributors or retailers within the meaning of the PPFA. It was the lessor defendant who was engaged in the business of offering and selling the gasoline. The entire entrepreneurial risk was borne by the defendant and the contractual relationship between the parties was not one of "inequitable economic power," and judgment was therefore entered for the defendant.

Marathon Petroleum Co. v. Bulk Petroleum Corp., No. 23-3282, 2024 WL 3339962 (6th Cir. July 9, 2024). The United States Sixth Circuit Court of Appeals affirmed a lower court's decision to enter judgment on behalf of plaintiff, Marathon Petroleum Company ("Marathon") against its former franchisee and jobber, Bulk Petroleum Corporation ("Bulk") for breach of agreements entered into between the parties during Bulk's bankruptcy proceeding. During the term of the parties' relationship, Bulk filed for bankruptcy owing millions to Marathon. The parties then entered into an amendment to their agreement requiring Bulk to pay Marathon $5,135,071.00, purchase minimum amounts of gas, and comply with rebranding requirements. Bulk failed to make the payments and Marathon began setting aside part of the monthly gas payments to satisfy the debt. A year later, Marathon terminated the agreement and the lower court granted Marathon summary judgment on its breach of contract claims. On appeal, the court found that Marathon did not frustrate the purpose of the agreement first by applying part of the gas payments to Bulk's debt and affirmed the decision.

III. Automobile/Motor Vehicle Dealer Laws

DMO Norwood LLC v. Kia America, Inc., No. 22-CV-10470-ADB, 2023 WL 5353744 (D. Mass. Aug. 21, 2023). The district court held that Massachusetts' state law governing the relationship between automobile manufacturers, distributors, and dealers did not limit a dealer's scope of discovery for claims arising out of state law violations. This case is discussed in Chapter 8, Section X.

Ginn Motor Co. v. General Motors, LLC, No. 1:22-cv-03773-WMR, 2023 WL 6536240 (N.D. Ga., Aug. 25, 2023). The Georgia Motor Vehicle Warranty Act ("Warranty Act") contains a "no-cost" provision governing reimbursement of warranty repairs. Under this provision, when a manufacturer furnishes a warranty part at no cost to a dealer, then the manufacturer is required to compensate the dealer by paying the dealer the retail rate markup, less the cost of the warranty part. The Warranty Act also contains several non-waiver provisions, including (1) granting a right to bring a civil action for violations of the statute, notwithstanding any terms, provisions, or conditions of any agreement to which the dealer is a party; (2) a provision nullifying any document with a provision contrary to any section of the Warranty Act; (3) voiding any manufacturer's attempt to nullify any provisions of the statute; (4) preventing a manufacturer from using third parties to evade the statute's requirements; and (5) prohibiting a manufacturer from requiring a dealer to assent prospectively to a release, novation, waiver, or estoppel that would have the effect of relieving any person from liability imposed by the Warranty Act.

Ginn, a GM dealer in Covington, Georgia, brought a putative class action against GM for claimed violations of the Warranty Act arising from GM's program and contractual requirements governing how its dealers obtained warranty reimbursement for expensive electronic parts, such as infotainment systems and lithium-ion batteries used in electric vehicles. Ginn's ordinary retail rate markup for parts was sixty percent of the cost of the part. However, Ginn asserted that for these expensive electronic parts, GM did not pay the retail rate, requiring instead that its dealers obtain such parts through its mandatory Exchange Program. Under the Exchange Program, dealers were contractually obligated to obtain electronic warranty parts from third-party Electronic Service Centers ("ESCs"), which were the sole GM-authorized source for such parts.

Dealers did not pay either GM or the ESCs for any warranty parts. Upon receiving the warranty part from an ESC, the dealer was obligated to return the defective part to the ESC, and if it failed to do so, it was charged a penalty by GM. After completing the warranty repair and complying with the return obligation, GM then paid its dealer for the labor to perform the repair, along with an administrative allowance for the parts. The administrative allowance was a fee, not calculated based on a dealer's retail rates, but a flat-rate fixed fee depending on the type of part involved, from forty-five dollars for an electronic part replacement to $1,120 for lithium-ion batteries. These fixed fees, Ginn claimed, were far lower than the standard sixty percent markup from retail that it charged on parts. For example, the average retail cost of a lithium-ion battery was $6,300, far higher than the fixed administrative allowance paid by GM. Ginn claimed that by refusing to pay anything beyond the fixed administrative allowance, and by not paying a retail rate markup as required by the Warranty Act, GM violated the Act's no-cost provision.

GM asserted four grounds for why Ginn's complaint failed to state a claim upon which relief can be granted, and the court rejected each of them. First, the court ruled that Ginn had not waived its right to sue because it had not demanded retail markup reimbursement within 180 days of the repair, as required by the dealer policies and procedures manual, ruling that multiple non- waiver provisions of the Warranty Act prevented GM from enforcing the manual's requirements on a Fed. R. Civ. P. 12(b)(6) motion.

Second, the court rejected GM's argument that it did not "furnish" the electronic warranty parts to Ginn, as required by the Warranty Act. The court agreed with Ginn that although GM itself did not deliver the replacement parts to dealers under the Exchange Program, it was sufficient for purposes of the statute that GM strictly required that its dealers obtain electronic warranty parts only from the ESCs, and that GM either paid the dealers administrative allowances for installing the warranty parts or penalized them for failing to complete the exchange of replacement for defective parts. The court also ruled that allowing the role of the ESCs to dictate the result of the "furnish" issue would contravene the Warranty Act provision forbidding a manufacturer from violating the Act through a third party.

Third, the court ruled that the electronic warranty parts were furnished at "no cost," because the dealer did not incur any cost during the transaction in which it received the warranty parts, rejecting GM's argument that the penalty imposed on dealers that did not timely return the defective part imposed a "cost" that brought the transaction outside the scope of the Warranty Act. The penalty, the court ruled, had nothing to do with the cost of the replacement part; instead, it was imposed based on failure to return the defective part.

Finally, the court rejected GM's argument that Ginn's compliance with the Exchange Program, including its acceptance of the administrative allowance instead of its ordinary retail markup, barred its claims, holding that enforcing the terms of GM's agreement that were inconsistent with the no-cost requirements of the Warranty Act would have violated several non-waiver provisions of the Act. As a result, the court denied GM's motion to dismiss.

Garrand Brothers, LLC v. America Honda Motor Co., No. 8:22-CV-0924, 2023 WL 5835793 (N.D.N.Y. Sept. 8, 2023). Garrand Brothers, LLC, operated Honda dealerships, under four separate agreements with American Honda Motor Co., Inc. ("Honda"). Honda terminated the agreements on the basis that Garrand abandoned the dealership for failing to operate the premises at the approved locations for seven consecutive days in violation of the dealer agreements, and further, by relocating to an unauthorized location without Honda's consent. Garrand filed suit against Honda alleging breach of contract, breach of the implied covenant of good faith and fair dealing, and claims that Honda violated New York State Franchised Motor Vehicle Dealer Act ("Dealer Act"). Honda filed a motion to discuss for failure to state a claim.

The court granted Honda's motion to dismiss. The court found that Garrand's relocation of the dealership without consent was a breach of the plain language of the dealer agreement as a matter of law, regardless of whether the relocation was out of the control of Garrand. The court similarly dismissed the breach of the implied covenant of good faith and fair dealing claim because it was directly at odds with Honda's express right under the dealer agreement to terminate for abandonment. The court also agreed with Honda that Garrand failed to state a claim for it failing to provide a cure period under the Dealer Act because the Dealer Act only provides a cure to correct certain enumerated performance issues which do not include abandonment. The court granted Honda's motion to dismiss Garrand's complaint.

Mailloux v. American Honda Motor Co., No. 22-CV-171-SM, 2023 WL 6283110 (D.N.H. Sept. 26, 2023). Cynthia Mailloux was the director and president of M&D Cycles, Inc., a dealership that sold and serviced Honda motorcycles, ATVs, multi-purpose utility vehicles, and scooters ("Dealer"). The Dealer decided to sell the underlying property where the dealership operated and contacted American Honda Motor Co., Inc. ("Honda"). Dealer argued that Honda had an obligation to repurchase various parts, specialized tools, and Honda-branded signage under the New Hampshire law governing motor vehicle manufacturers, distributors, and dealers (N.H. Rev. Stat. Ann. 357-C). Honda repurchased certain parts, tools and signage but rejected other requests as untimely, insufficiently documented, or not covered by the statute. Dealer filed suit alleging that Honda failed to satisfy its statutory repurchase obligations. Honda moved for summary judgment. The court denied Honda's motion for summary judgment holding that there were two genuinely disputed material facts: (1) whether Honda was obligated to repurchase all the parts, tools, and signage; and (2) whether Honda made all of the payments that it was obligated to make under the statute.

Tuscaloosa Hyundai, Inc. v. Hyundai Motor America, Inc., No. 7:1-cv-00571-LSC, 2023 WL 6296929 (N.D. Ala. Sept. 27, 2023). A car dealership selling Hyundai and Genesis vehicles filed suit against the manufacturers for implementing new programs that incentivized those dealers who maintained separate sales facilities for the two brands. The dealer alleged twelve claims for violations of the Alabama Motor Vehicle Franchise Act ("AMVFA") and a civil conspiracy claim. The manufacturers moved for summary judgment.

In its decision, the district court dismissed the AMVFA claims alleging that Hyundai and Genesis unlawfully coerced or attempted to coerce the dealer into making substantial alterations to its existing facility or build new standalone facilities because (1) Genesis did not conceal its continuing desire to reduce its network to 100 dealers and any ulterior motives it may have had were irrelevant; (2) the evidence showed that dealer had not been financially harmed; (3)

the incentive programs were efforts to persuade dealers to voluntarily build conforming facilities or not seek renewal of their Genesis distribution agreement, not coercive acts prohibited by the AMVFA. The court further dismissed the claims alleging unlawful price discrimination because there was no dispute that the same incentive programs on the same terms were offered to all dealers. The conspiracy claim was dismissed because Genesis is a wholly owned subsidiary of Hyundai and a corporation cannot conspire with itself under Alabama law. The dealer's request for punitive damages was also rejected because it did not plead tort claims and the AMVFA does not provide for punitive damages.

The only AMVFA claims that survived summary judgment were those based on the alleged arbitrary, unconscionable, unreasonable, or bad faith denial of the dealer's request for an exception to the qualifications of the incentive programs due to the brand new, state-of-the art joint Hyundai/Genesis dealership that the dealer built with the manufacturers' input and express approval a few years before the new incentive programs were announced. The court denied summary judgment, reasoning that the manufacturers had provided insufficient explanation for denying the dealer's request for a variance.

American Honda Motor Co. v. M&N Dealership VI, LLC, No. CIV-24-165-D, 2024 WL 3543465 (W.D. Okla. July 25, 2024). After American Honda filed an action seeking declaratory judgment regarding the parties' rights and duties under a dealership agreement, and Oklahoma statutory law governing auto dealers, distributors, and manufacturers, defendant M&N Dealership filed a complaint with the Oklahoma Motor Vehicle Commission ("OMVC") asking the OMVC to enjoin American Honda from exercising a right of first refusal under the agreement. M&N contemporaneously filed a motion to dismiss and stay the proceedings until the OMVC administrative proceeding was fully and finally adjudicated. M&N argued that the district court should abstain from exercising jurisdiction over the case due to the OMVC action. The court agreed and stayed the case pursuant to the *Colorado River* abstention doctrine. The court analyzed the abstention issue and held that the administrative and court proceedings were parallel because they involved the same parties and issues and the OMVC was operating in a judicial capacity. The court also reviewed the exceptional circumstances that warranted abstention and found the factors weighed in favor of abstention. The court alternatively held that even if abstention were improper, the court could exercise its inherent discretion to stay this case because it would be the prudent course of action.

DMO Methuen, LLC v. FCA U.S., LLC, No. CV 23-10724-GAO, 2023 WL 9228288 (D. Mass. Nov. 21, 2023). An automobile dealer filed suit against a manufacturer for terminating various dealer agreements. The manufacturer-defendant asserted counterclaims against the distributor for breach of contract, conversion, unjust enrichment, and fraud. The manufacturer-defendant also filed a counterclaim under Massachusetts General Laws Chapter 93A Section 11, which regulates business practices between motor vehicle manufacturers, distributors and dealers.

The dealer moved to dismiss all the counterclaims. The magistrate court recommended that the district court grant in part and deny in part the dealer's motion. The magistrate court recommended that the judge grant the dealer's motion to dismiss regarding the manufacturer-defendant's Chapter 93A counterclaim because Chapter 93B already provided an exclusive remedy for the manufacturer-defendant. Since the manufacturer-defendant did not bring a claim under Chapter 93B, the magistrate recommended that the district court allow the manufacturer-defendant to pursue a Chapter 93B claim. Conversely, the magistrate court recommended that the judge deny the dealer's motion for the common law counterclaims, reasoning that nothing in the language of Chapter 93B indicated that the common law claims were barred.

Mercedes-Benz USA, LLC v. J.P. Motors, Inc., No. 23-CV-02281, 2023 WL 8236877 (N.D. Ill. Nov. 28, 2023). Defendant-seller entered into a sale agreement with a third party regarding its ownership interests in three motor vehicle dealerships under different manufacturer brands. Mercedes-Benz attempted to prevent the proposed sale by exercising a contractual right of first refusal for its portion of the three-brand dealership. The trial court granted defendant's motion to dismiss on *Buford* abstention grounds, finding that the unique issues of state law under the Illinois Motor Vehicle Franchise Act ("MVFA") made federal action duplicative and unnecessary, as there was a parallel action pending before the administrative review board which is the designated venue for dispute resolution under the MVFA.

Anderson & Koch Ford, Inc. v. Ford Motor Co., No. 23-CV-0762 (PJS/DTS), 2023 WL 8282060 (D. Minn. Nov. 30, 2023). Plaintiff had operated a Ford dealership for nearly sixty years pursuant to a service-and-sales agreement that included eighteen census tracts surrounding North Branch, Minnesota. Ford removed nine of those tracts, intending to assign them to a new dealership about twenty-seven miles away from North Branch. Plaintiff sued for violations of Minnesota's Motor Vehicle Sale and Distribution Act ("MVSDA"), breach of the implied covenant of good faith and fair dealing and sought a declaratory judgment and injunctive relief. Ford moved to dismiss, which the court granted in part and denied in part.

Plaintiff relied primarily on Section 80E.13(k) of MVSDA, which prohibits a manufacturer from modifying or replacing a "franchise" if the succeeding franchise would "adversely alter the rights of obligations" or "substantially impair[] the sales or service obligations or investments" of the dealer. The court found that this claim was an improper end run around Section 80E.14, which provides that existing dealers can only block new dealerships within ten miles. Moreover, the court noted that Section 80E.03(8) of the MVSDA defined "franchise" as the "written agreement" between the dealer and manufacturer, and the complaint contained no allegations that the wording of Plaintiff's dealership agreement would be modified, so the claim based on Section 80E.13(k) failed. The court also held that while plaintiff was permitted to challenge Ford's change to its Dealer Locality under Section 80E.13(p), that section could not serve as the basis for challenging the creation of a new dealership.

The MVSDA claims and declaratory judgment action were dismissed without prejudice to the extent that they sought to inhibit or prevent creation of a new dealership because the court found they were an attempt to evade the explicit procedures provided by the Minnesota Legislature for challenging a new dealership. Plaintiff's remaining claims, including the claim for breach of the implied covenant of good faith and fair dealing, survived Ford's efforts to have the complaint dismissed.

Racine Car Dealer, LLC v. Hyundai Motor America, Inc., No. 22-CV-322-WMC, 2023 WL 8529832 (W.D. Wis. Dec. 8, 2023). This case arose out of defendants Hyundai Motor America Inc.'s ("HMA") and Genesis Motor America, LLC's ("GMA") motion for summary judgment on plaintiff Racine Car Dealer, LLC's ("RCD") statutory claims and common law claims for breach of contract and tortious interference.

RCD owned and operated an auto dealership in Racine, Wisconsin that sold, promoted, and serviced Hyundai products, including Genesis model vehicles, pursuant to various dealer agreements RCD entered into with HMA which included an exclusivity provision for Hyundai vehicles. Thereafter, HMA announced that it was breaking off its Genesis model vehicles into separate dealerships, forming GMA. After RCD expressed its concern regarding its previous exclusivity requirements, HMA representatives assured RCD that it would still be considered "exclusive," even if it continued to sell both Hyundai and Genesis branded vehicles out of the same location. RCD and HMA never amended the dealer agreement to reflect that agreement and RCD ultimately entered into a separate Genesis dealer agreement. Shortly after, RCD enrolled in HMA's Accelerated Incentive Program ("AIP") in which HMA agreed to provide support for dealers who chose to make improvements to their Hyundai facilities. After several months of correspondence, HMA provided a full list of items that RCD needed to correct at its dealership, without any mention of RCD's ongoing operation of its Genesis dealership in a joint facility with its Hyundai dealership. After HMA gave its approval, RCD began remodeling the joint dealer facility.

RCD then began discussing a $50 million transaction with Zeigler Auto Group about selling its Hyundai and Genesis dealerships as part of a package deal along with other dealerships. The parties agreed in an Asset Purchase Agreement ("APA") that RCD's Hyundai and Genesis franchises would continue to operate in the same facility and that Zeigler would get all the remaining payments from the AIP. The APA was forwarded to HMA and GMA to approve the sale. HMA notified the parties that all Genesis dealer operations had to be moved out of the Hyundai facility for Zeigler to qualify for the AIP moving forward. RCD reluctantly terminated its Genesis franchise and RCD and proceeded with the sale of the dealership with a reduced price of $48 million. As a result, RCD filed suit against HMA and GMA alleging ten separate claims under several provisions of the Wisconsin Motor Vehicle Dealer Law ("WMVDL"), the Federal Automobile Dealer's Day in Court Act ("ADDCA"), and Wisconsin contract law. HMA and GMA moved for summary judgment on all claims.

GMA argued that RCD failed to offer any evidence that GMA had been involved in the conduct complained of. The court agreed with GMA and granted its motion for summary judgment and dismissed GMA as a party. The district court explained that there was not enough evidence to impute liability to GMA for HMA's conduct.

Next, the court addressed HMA's motion for summary judgment. The court began by reviewing RCD's claims under the WMVDL and concluded that there was a genuine issue of material fact that precluded summary judgment on all but one of RCD's claims. First, the court found that RCD presented sufficient evidence for a reasonable jury to conclude that HMA used the AIP as economic leverage to coerce RCD to terminate its Genesis dealer and denied HMA's motion for summary judgment. Second, the court disagreed with HMA's argument that it could not be held liable for indirectly canceling a dealership because the termination was prompted by RCD's own self-interest. The court explained that the genuine issues of material fact with respect to the alleged conduct established that the court could not as a matter of law decide that RCD's termination was voluntary or coerced. Third, the court denied in part and granted in part HMA's motion for summary judgment on RCD's claim regarding timing and procedural requirements in the WMVDL for the dealer's request for approval of a change of ownership. The court found that RCD failed to provide evidence that HMA did not meet the twenty-day requirement in Section 218.0134(a) to respond to the APA. However, the court found that there were still genuine issues of material fact as to when HMA's thirty-day deadline began under Section 218.0134(b). Fourth, HMA argued that the AIP was not considered an agreement under the WMVDL's definition, and therefore, the AIP was not entitled to its protections. The court disagreed and denied HMA's motion for summary judgment. The court explained that Chapter 218 does not require a written instrument for an agreement to be treated as such under the WMVDL. Therefore, a reasonable jury could conclude that HMA modified the AIP agreement based on the alleged conversations between RCD and HMA that gave the impression that RCD had complied with the exclusivity requirements while maintaining the joint facility. Fifth, the court denied HMA's motion for summary judgment of RCD's final WMVDL claim under Section 218.0116(1)(bm). Under Section 218.0116(1)(bm) an agreement is prohibited from waiving a remedy for a dealer and preventing a dealer from bringing an action in a particular forum.

Finally, the court considered HMA's motion for summary judgment on RCD's claim brought under the ADDCA. The court provided background on the ADDCA, stating that the Act "requires actual or threatened coercion or intimidation, which can be inferred from the defendant's course of conduct, but must include a wrongful demand accompanied by the threat of sanctions for noncompliance." Because the parties disputed the specific details surrounding HMA's actions and whether HMA complied with the thirty-day time requirements for a written response, the court denied HMA's motion.

Spitzer Autoworld Akron, LLC v. FCA US LLC, No. 1:22-CV-01755-PAB, 2023 WL 6809935 (N.D. Ohio Oct. 12, 2023). Plaintiff Spitzer Autoworld Akron, LLC ("Spitzer") operated a Chrysler franchise in Akron, Ohio when Chrysler LLC ("Chrysler") filed for bankruptcy protection. During the bankruptcy proceedings, Congress enacted Section 747 of the Consolidated Appropriations Act ("The Act") which required Chrysler and Defendant FCA US, LLC's ("FCA") (the successor in interest to Chrysler), to submit all rejected dealers to arbitration to determine if the dealers should be reinstated as Chrysler brand dealers. Thereafter, Chrysler rejected Spritzer's Chrysler franchise.

FCA and Spritzer went to arbitration, and the arbitrator ordered FCA to reinstate Spritzer as a "new" Chrysler dealer in a different Ohio location. State law required FCA to provide a letter of intent ("LOI") within seven days to all rejected dealers. Before FCA issued the LOI, Fred Martin Motor Company ("Fred Martin") entered into a contractual agreement with Spitzer to "'irrevocably' and 'forever' waive[] its right to protest Spitzer's dealership at both Ohio locations" and to waive "notice of a hearing." Despite the seven-day deadline, FCA did not provide the LOI until several months past the deadline. The LOI contained eight conditions for Spitzer to complete before FCA would issue a Sales and Service Agreement. These conditions were not included in the arbitration decision.

Shortly after FCA issued the LOI, FCA sent notice to Fred Martin of its intent to establish a new Spitzer Dealership, even though FCA knew that Fred Martin had already waived its right to protest Spritzer's dealership. Further, FCA approached Ohio Motor Vehicle Dealers Board ("OMVDB") to assist another dealer, Falls Chrysler, Jeep, Dodge ("Falls") in the filing of a protest. The protest went beyond the fifteen-day filing deadline under Ohio Revised Code § 4517.50. The protest resulted in Spitzer having to halt all construction activities for the new dealership location. Pursuant to state law, FCA was required to participate in the protests and show good cause to establish Spitzer's dealership. FCA continuously reassured Spitzer that they would represent Spitzer's interest throughout the protests. Yet, FCA eventually took a stance in opposition to Spitzer in the protests. FCA colluded with Fred Martin, Falls and their respective attorneys to guarantee that Spritzer's new dealership would never open. Shortly after the protests were dismissed, Spitzer sued FCA for various violations under the Ohio Motor Vehicle Dealers Act ("Dealers Act"). FCA filed a motion to dismiss the complaint.

FCA argued that there was no breach of contract because FCA had fulfilled all of its obligations and the dispute had been resolved once the protests were dismissed. The court disagreed, reasoning that the Dealer's Act does not create such a barrier. Instead, the Dealer's Act permits a franchisor and franchisee to proceed, regardless of the outcome of the protests. Therefore, the court denied FCA's motion to dismiss.

Second, FCA argued that Spitzer failed to state a claim that it had breached its duty of good faith and fair dealing because the LOI did not vest FCA with discretion. FCA thus argued that it did not owe a duty of good faith and fair dealing to Spitzer during the protest. The court agreed and granted FCA's motion to dismiss because nothing in the Dealer's Act explicitly requires a franchisor to demonstrate good cause.

Third, FCA disputed Spitzer's declaratory judgment claim because, according to FCA, it was simply derivative of Spitzer's contract claims. While the court agreed that the declaratory judgment claim was undoubtedly derivative of Spritzer's breach of contract claim, the court already denied FCA's motion to dismiss the breach of contract claim. Consequently, the court also denied FCA's motion to dismiss the declaratory judgment.

Fourth, FCA insisted that Spitzer's breach of fiduciary duty claim be dismissed because Spitzer failed to establish the existence of a fiduciary relationship. The court agreed and granted the motion to dismiss because the Dealer's Act does not establish such a duty.

Fifth, FCA contended that Spitzer's civil conspiracy claim failed because its argument hinged on the breach of contract claim. The court granted the motion to dismiss, reasoning that Ohio state law requires a civil conspiracy claim to be tort-based, and there were no tort claims alleged in the complaint. Similarly, FCA argued that punitive damages were not available because none of the claims are independent tort claims. The court agreed and granted FCA's motion to dismiss.

Liberty Hyundai, Inc. v. Hyundai Motor America, Inc., No. 23-10214, 2023 WL 8828678 (E.D. Mich. Dec. 21, 2023). The United States District Court for the Eastern District of Michigan granted defendants' Hyundai Motor America, Inc. and Genesis Motor America, LLC's ("Genesis") motion to dismiss Liberty Hyundai's ("Liberty") promissory estoppel and fraud in the inducement claims against Genesis. But the court denied defendant' motion to dismiss claims for breach of contract, violations of Michigan's Motor Vehicle Franchise Act, and breach of duty of good faith and fair dealing.

Liberty, a multi-unit franchisee car dealer, filed its lawsuit against Genesis after Genesis denied its relocation request under the dealer sales and services agreements. The court determined that, in viewing the facts most favorable to Liberty, Liberty alleged enough facts to show Genesis strung Liberty along while negotiating with another dealer over the same geographic location, thereby causing Liberty to spend unnecessary time and expense.

Florida Automobile Dealers Association, Inc. v. Ford Motor Co., No. 4:23CV282-MW/MAF, 2024 WL 836384 (N.D. Fla. Jan. 25, 2024). Florida Automobile Dealers Association, Inc. ("FADA") challenged Ford Motor Company's ("Ford") "Model e EV Certification Program" on grounds that it violated the Florida Motor Dealer Act. Ford moved to dismiss the complaint, arguing that FADA lacked standing because it was not a "motor vehicle dealer" within the statutory meaning of the Florida Motor Dealer Act. In granting the motion, the court found that the statute was not broadly applicable to grant statutory standing by association.

Frye v. American Honda Motor Co., No. 23AP-490, 2024 WL 1741040 (Ct. App. Ohio Apr. 23, 2024). The Ohio Tenth District Court of Appeals affirmed the lower court's decision to affirm an order of the Ohio Motor Vehicle Dealers Board ("Board") finding American Honda Motor Co., Inc. ("Honda") had good cause to refuse to approve the transfer of a dealership to Sunnyside Automotive, Inc., owned by appellee, Kirtlund C. Frye ("Sunnyside"). Honda rejected a transfer of one dealership to Frye, citing Sunnyside's poor sales performance and non-compliance with Honda's Dealer Agreement, including service retention issues and facility requirements. Sunnyside filed a protest under the Ohio Motor Vehicle Code Section R.C. 4517.56(C). The Board decided to uphold Honda's denial, and Sunnyside then appealed to the common pleas court which affirmed the Board's decision. The appeals court then concluded that reliable, probative, and substantial evidence supported the Board's original order. Honda's adjusted metrics demonstrated good cause for refusing the transfer due to Sunnyside's historical inability to meet sales performance requirements, and the court found that Honda complied with R.C. 4517.56(A) that requires franchisors to evaluate a proposed transferee's qualifications based on reasonable and objective criteria.

IV. Beer and Wine Laws

Jean-Paul Weg., LLC v. Graziano, No. 19-14716(JXN)(LDW), 2023 WL 5370522 (D.N.J. Aug. 22, 2023). Plaintiffs filed a civil rights action alleging that New Jersey's laws and regulations ("NJ Law") governing the sale and distribution of alcoholic beverages was unconstitutional because it discriminates against wine retailers located outside New Jersey who are engaged in interstate commerce. Specifically, plaintiffs alleged that the NJ Law prohibits out-of-state wine retailers from taking telephone and internet wine orders from New Jersey consumers and selling, shipping, and delivering to New Jersey customers from their out-of-state business locations. Plaintiffs requested a declaratory judgment that the NJ Law violated the Commerce Clause of the United States Constitution and injunction prohibiting the defendants from enforcing the law against plaintiff and similar out-of-state wine retailers like Plaintiffs, among other relief. The court disagreed with plaintiff's argument that the NJ Law violated the Commerce Clause because it was not a valid exercise of the state's power under the Twenty-First Amendment. Under the Twenty-First Amendment, states have virtually complete control over the importation and sale of liquor and the structure of the liquor distribution system. In applying the "Granholm Test," the court held that the NJ Law was a valid exercise of New Jersey's power under the Twenty-First Amendment and is justified by the legitimate non-protectionist ground of promoting public health and safety, which could not be adequately served by reasonable nondiscriminatory alternatives. The court denied plaintiff's motion for summary judgment and their commerce clause claim was dismissed with prejudice.

Ste. Michelle Wine Estates, LLC v. Tri County Wholesale Distributors, Inc., No. 4:22 CV 1702, 2023 WL 605114 (N.D. Ohio Sept. 18, 2023). A wine manufacturer ("Michelle Wine") terminated its distribution agreement with its distributor ("Tri County"). Under Ohio's Alcoholic Beverages Franchise Act (the "Act"), Michelle Wine was permitted to terminate the agreement upon a change of control but was required to compensate Tri County on the diminished value, resulting from the loss of the brands. The parties could not agree on the calculation of the diminished value so Michelle Wine brought a case seeking a judicial determination of the amount. Michelle Wine then filed a motion to exclude plaintiff's expert report and Tri County filed a motion to exclude certain opinions of plaintiff's expert. The court denied both motions holding that it was entirely capable of evaluating the reliability of the data and deciding what information from the experts to accept or reject and a wholesale exclusion of the report and testimony was not warranted.

Shady Knoll Orchards & Distillery LLC v. Postman, No. 1:23-CV-3093-TOR, 2023 WL 7004422 (E.D. Wash. Oct. 24, 2023). Plaintiffs in this case were (1) Shady Knoll Orchards and Distillery LLC ("Distillery"), a small distillery headquartered in New York operating an online marketplace selling and shipping directly to consumers; and (2) two Washington State consumers who enjoy Distillery's products (together with Distillery, the "Plaintiffs"). Plaintiffs filed an action against defendant, the Washington Liquor and Cannabis Board ("Defendant"), requesting a declaratory judgment affirming that Washington State's restrictions on the direct sale and shipment of liquor by out-of-state distilleries (like Distillery) to Washington consumers unlawfully discriminated against interstate commerce in violation of the dormant Commerce Clause, and an injunction preventing Defendant from enforcing the laws. Due to Washington state's physical presence requirement, out-of-state distilleries may not make direct shipments to online Washington consumers. Defendant brought a 12(b)(6) motion to dismiss and the court denied it. The court cited to precedent holding that a state law which facially discriminates against interstate commerce is per se invalid. However, a presumptively invalid discriminatory law may survive if the state shows that the law serves a legitimate local purpose, and that the purpose could not also be served by available nondiscriminatory means. In ruling on the motion, the court found the regulations permitting Washington distilleries to retail their products directly to online consumers while prohibiting out-of-state distilleries from doing the same was facially discriminatory. Second, the court rejected Defendant's argument that the Supreme Court has recognized many legitimate areas of concern under the Twenty-First Amendment outside of economic protectionism, including "a state's interest in preserving its three-tier system" as sufficient to dismiss the case at this posture. The court looked to the Supreme Court case, *Granholm v. Heald*, where producers and consumers challenged Michigan and New York's restrictions on out-of-state shipments of wine. Both states, which had adopted a three-tier structure similar to Washington's, permitted direct shipments from in-state wine producers to instate consumers, but restricted out-of-state wineries from making similar direct shipments. Michigan banned out-of-state direct shipments altogether, whereas New York required out-of-state wineries to establish an in-state distribution operation before they could directly ship to in-state consumers. In *Granholm*, the Supreme Court concluded that Michigan's total ban as well as New York's physical presence requirement discriminated against interstate commerce. The court denied the motion to dismiss considering (1) the Supreme Court precedent on similar state bans; and (2) the split at the court of appeals level over the use of similar "three-tier systems" by states. Even accepting Defendant's claims that some post-*Granholm* authority exists which would support a discriminatory in-state physical presence requirement, the existence of a circuit split supported denying the motion to dismiss. At this stage, the court found Defendants did not show that Plaintiffs' allegations, if proven true, failed to state a plausible claim to relief.

Cavalier Distributing Co. v. Lime Ventures, LLC, No. 23-3283, 2023 WL 8924279 (6th Cir. Dec 27, 2023). The Sixth Circuit Court of Appeals affirmed the district court's denial of an Ohio beer distributor's preliminary injunction request to halt the importer of the beer from entering into a distribution agreement with a competitor distributor. Cavalier Distributing Company, Inc. ("Cavalier") distributed a certain lambic beer produced by two Belgian microbreweries under an agreement with the breweries' importer, Shelton Brothers.

Under Shelton Brothers' agreement with the breweries, it acquired the right to use the brands, and to purchase and import the beer into the United States. Shelton Brothers promoted and advertised the unknown beers in the United States, making all marketing and distribution decisions without input from the breweries. Shelton Brothers entered into an exclusive distribution agreement with Cavalier. When Shelton Brothers filed for bankruptcy, the breweries stopped selling beer to Cavalier. Defendant, Lime Ventures, Inc. ("Lime") purchased the remaining inventory in bankruptcy and eventually acquired the importer distribution rights for the brands. After negotiations for a new distribution agreement broke down between Lime and Cavalier, Lime entered into an agreement without a different distributor in Ohio.

Cavalier sought a preliminary injunction to bar Lime from selling beer to other distributors in Ohio claiming that Lime terminated Cavalier's franchise with the breweries in violation of the Ohio Alcoholic Beverage Franchise Act ("Franchise Act"). The district court denied the motion for preliminary injunction finding Cavalier was unlikely to prevail on the merits.

The court disagreed with Cavalier's assertion that it entered into a franchise agreement with the breweries and the termination of the franchise agreement through Lime was a violation of the Franchise Act's for-cause termination restrictions. Instead, the court found that the parties created a franchise under the Franchise Act, as Shelton Brothers was the party that controlled the beer brand in Ohio. This conclusion was reinforced by case law consistently holding that, when applying the Franchise Act to a change in U.S. importers, a franchise applies to the party that owns and controls the beer brand in Ohio. As Shelton Brothers designed the product labels, exclusively controlling marketing in the United States, gave input on recipes, and maintained exclusive control over distribution in the United States. Although the breweries did retain some control, the focus was not on the party that actually brews the beer but on "who controls the physical product as it moves through the market in Ohio." The agreement requiring protection was between Shelton Brothers and Cavalier. Therefore, the court found that if Cavalier did not have a franchise agreement with the breweries, then Lime could not have wrongfully terminated the franchise agreement. Since Cavalier was unlikely to succeed on the merits, the motion for preliminary injunction was denied.

City Beverages LLC v. Crown Imports LLC, No. 3:22-CV-05756-DGE, 2023 WL 7412835 (W.D. Wash. Nov. 9, 2023). The United States District Court for the Western District of Washington denied plaintiff's second motion for a temporary restraining order because plaintiff City Beverages (operating under the name "Olympic Eagle") failed to establish a likelihood of success on the merits. Constellation brands terminated Olympic Eagle's distribution rights for Modelo beer in favor of another distributor (Columbia). Olympic Eagle sought to impede the termination pending an arbitration over the value of the distribution rights, but the district court determined that irreparable harm was distinct from the harm caused by the termination of the Distribution Agreement, which could be remedied by money damages. The district court further concluded that enjoining the termination was not in the public interest.

JRC Beverage, Inc. v. K.P. Global, Inc., 2024 N.Y. Slip Op. 00067, 2024 WL 104855 (Sup. Ct. N.Y. Jan. 10, 2024). In this case, the Supreme Court of New York held that protections afforded to beer wholesalers under Alcoholic Beverage Control Law ("NY ABC Law") obligate an importer to honor a wholesale distribution agreement entered into by the prior importer of the same brand, even where there was no relationship or privity of contract between the prior importer and the new importer.

JRC Beverage, Inc. ("JRC") was a beer wholesaler who purchased and resold beer to retailers. JRC entered into an exclusive distribution agreement with BWS Group Co. ("Prior Importer"), the U.S. importer of beer brands produced by Oriental Brewery Company ("Brewer"), a South Korean brewery. Brewer terminated its agreement with Prior Importer due to alleged breach of terms and subsequently appointed defendant, K.P. Global, Inc. ("KP"), as the new importer. KP then designated defendant, Northern Beverage, Inc. ("Northern"), as the exclusive distributor for Brewer's beer in New York. JRC then filed a complaint against KP and Northern alleging violations of NY ABC Law, tortious interference with contract, and unfair competition, as they were the exclusive distributor of Brewer's beer in New York per their agreement with the Prior Importer.

The lower court granted KP and Northern motion for summary judgment to dismiss the complaint. JRC appealed the dismissal of its claim under the NY ABC Law. The Supreme Court of New York reversed, concluding that under the specific language of the NY ABC Law, the defendant importer, KP, was a "successor to a brewer" within the meaning of the NY ABC Law, and JRC demonstrated as a matter of law that KP failed to honor, without good cause, the wholesale distribution agreement entered into by JRC and the Prior Importer.

The court analyzed the definition and scope of "Successor to a Brewer" under the NY ABC Law. The critical issue was whether KP, as the new importer acquiring rights directly from the Brewer, constituted a "successor to a brewer" under the NY ABC Law. JRC argued that KP acquired the business or beer brands of a brewer in a transaction, fulfilling the statutory definition of a successor. The defendants contended that KP couldn't be considered a successor as there was no privity of contract with the Prior Importer or JRC.

The court analyzed the legislation's purpose to protect beer wholesalers against arbitrary termination by larger manufacturers and importers. The amendments and legislative history highlighted efforts to maintain a balance of power in the beer industry, favoring small family-owned businesses and preventing market domination by large entities. The court held that the statute's language did not require contractual privity between the successor and the entity being succeeded. The definition of "successor to a brewer" was interpreted broadly to include any entity acquiring the beer brands or business of a brewer in any transaction. The court rejected the defendants' argument that KP was not a successor since it did not acquire the rights from the Prior Importer.

The court held that the lower court erred in dismissing JRC's claim under the NY ABC Law and in denying its cross-motion for summary judgment on the issue of liability because JRC demonstrated that KP, as a successor to a brewer, failed to honor the wholesale distribution agreement entered by the Prior Importer and JRC without good cause. The court affirmed the dismissal of JRC's claims for tortious interference with contract and unfair competition. The order was modified to (1) deny defendants' motion for summary judgment on the NY ABC Law violation and (2) grant JRC's cross-motion for summary judgment on the issue of liability under the NY ABC Law. The order was affirmed in other respects.

Dwinell, LLC v. McCullough, No. 2:23-CV-10029-SB-KS, 2024 WL 3009300 (C.D. Cal. May 17, 2024). Plaintiffs, who are winegrowers operating wineries in Washington and Colorado, sued the Director of the California Department of Beverage Control and California's Attorney General for violations of the Alcoholic Beverage Control Act. Defendants moved to dismiss plaintiffs' claim for lack of standing and failure to state a claim. The district court granted the motion to dismiss because the plaintiffs failed to adequately allege that they had suffered an injury in fact based on a concrete plan to violate the law. The court granted the plaintiffs leave to amend the complaint. However, prior to amending the complaint, the court ordered that the parties meet and confer to thoroughly discuss the constitutionality of the complaint to avoid any future disputes or amendments. The court directed that plaintiffs' amended complaint must identify every provision they contend is unconstitutional and the reason for its unconstitutionality.

Dichello Distributors, Inc. v. Anheuser-Busch, LLC, No. 3:20-cv-01003-MPS, 2024 WL 473661 (D. Conn. Feb. 7, 2024). Under Connecticut's Liquor Control Act ("CT Act"), Connecticut adopted a three-tier system for alcohol distribution, in which out-of-state shippers and manufacturers sell to wholesalers, wholesalers to retailers, and retailers to consumers. To maintain this system, the CT Act and underlying regulations prohibit businesses in any tier from controlling businesses in any other tier. In this case, Dichello Distributors, Inc. ("Dichello"), a licensed beverage wholesaler, filed a claim against its beer supplier, out-of- state shipper Anheuser-Busch, LLC ("AB"), that it violated the CT Act, the Connecticut Unfair Trade Practices Act ("CUTPA"), and tortiously interfered with its business relationships with two of its employees by exercising excessive control over it. The court granted AB's motion for summary judgment on the Plaintiff's CUTPA and tortious interference claims and partially granted AB's motion for summary judgment on its breach of contract counterclaims. Under the agreement between Dichello and AB, AB had approval rights over its wholesalers' manager appointments. AB required each manager to meet certain standards, successfully complete training, and own an equity interest in the wholesaler to which it managed. Dichello alleged that AB pushed it to accept a former AB-aligned employee to the manager position, requiring Dichello to sell equity at a reduced rate. Dichello then alleged the new manager disclosed confidential information to AB and implemented management policies in the best interest of AB, not Dichello. Eventually Dichello terminated the manager and attempted to hire a replacement which AB declined to approve. The court found that while the agreement between AB and Dichello did contain certain rights for AB to control certain aspects of the business relationship, AB was not exercising control in the way prohibited under the CT Act and there was no potential for a jury to determine AB breached its agreement with Dichello.

Eskimo Hut Worldwide, Ltd. v. South Plains Sno, Inc., No. 07-22-00259-CV, 2024 WL 791004 (Ct. App. Tex. Feb. 26, 2024). On a permissive appeal, the Texas Court of Appeals determined whether certain terms of a franchise agreement requiring the defendant, South Plains Sno, Inc. ("South Plains"), a multi-unit franchisee of Eskimo Hut Worldwide, Ltd. ("Franchisor"), to purchase and use only specified non-alcoholic and alcoholic base mixes and flavorings for their frozen drinks, violated section 109.53 of the Texas Alcoholic Beverage Code ("Texas Code"). In 2019, the trial court granted a temporary injunction in favor of the Franchisor affirming that South Plains was not complying with the franchise agreement's terms, which South Plains contested, alleging it violated section 109.53 of the Texas Code prohibiting a scheme that surrenders control concerning the sale and storage of alcoholic beverages to another entity, in this case, the Franchisor. The court determined that the franchise agreement's terms do not violate section 109.53 of the Texas Code, as they do not directly control the alcoholic beverages sold and reversed the trial court's ruling that partially favored South Plains.

V. Relationship Statutes of General Application

Brava Salon Specialists, LLC v. REF North America, Inc., No. 22-cv-695-wmc, 2023 WL 7709310 (W.D. Wis. Nov. 15, 2023). The United States District Court for the Western District of Wisconsin previously granted a preliminary injunction in favor of an exclusive distributor of REF haircare products, Brava Salon Specialists, LLC ("Brava") with territory in Wisconsin, Minnesota, Iowa, and North Dakota against the defendant manufacturer, REF North America, Inc. ("REF") requiring REF to take certain steps to protect Brava's exclusivity. REF then filed a motion to amend the injunction to permit REF to contract with Amazon which would result in encroachment by REF within Brava's exclusive territory. The court denied REF's motion on two grounds. First, REF failed to abide by the Wisconsin Fair Dealership Law ("WDFL") requirement that manufacturers provide notice to its distributors before making changes that would materially modify the parties' business contract. Second, even if REF compiled with the notice requirements under the WDFL, REF did not meet the "good cause" standard that would permit REF to modify the agreement. The "good cause" standard under the WDFL is only satisfied if the distributor can demonstrate: (1) an objectively ascertainable need for the change; (2) a proportionate response to the need; and (3) a nondiscriminatory action. Although REF argued that maintaining a storefront on Amazon was essential to protect its brand from unauthorized online sellers and benefit REF and all of its distributors and the public interest from ensuring only authentic products were sold, REF did not submit actual evidence to the court to support the assertions. To support a "good cause" showing under the WDFL, REF needed to provide evidence showing actual reputational or financial harm. Since REF was unable to establish its compliance with the notice requirement and good cause, REF's motion was denied.

DET Beverages, LLC v. Kentucky Bourbon Distillers, Ltd., No. 3:23-CV-00363, 2024 WL 55480 (M.D. Tenn. Jan. 4, 2024). This dispute arose out of a distributor's failure to provide the statutorily required notice under Tennessee law to a liquor manufacturer prior to transferring its distribution business to another company. DET Distributing Company ("DET") entered into two separate agreements with defendant Kentucky Bourbon Distillers, Ltd. d/b/a Willet Distillery ("Willet"). Both agreements assigned DET as the sole distributor and wholesaler of Willet Whiskey throughout various Tennessee counties. Both agreements awarded distribution rights to DET in the specified counties "in perpetuity." The parties operated under the agreement for nearly five years without any issues. Thereafter, DET drafted an Asset Purchase Agreement ("APA") with plaintiff DET Beverages, LLC ("DBLLC") in which DBLLC agreed to acquire all of DET's assets. Prior to signing the

APA, DBLLC and DET requested written approval of the transfer from Willet, multiple times. Willet responded that it had no intention of consenting to the transfer. Thus, DBLLC filed suit alleging that Willet violated Tennessee state law by failing to consent.

The court granted Willet's motion to dismiss. It cited Tenn. Code Ann. Section 47-25-1508, which governs the conveyance of liquor distribution franchises, and found that Willet's consent was never triggered because DBLLC never provided Willet the statutorily required notice under Tennessee law. Therefore, Willet never had an obligation to respond to DBLLC's request. The court used the same line of reasoning to grant Willet's motion to dismiss for the breach of contract claim, finding that a binding contract never existed between DBLLC and Willet because there was never a valid transfer.

Sour Grapes, LLC v. Vinum USA, Inc., No. 1:22-cv-203-MOC-WCM, 2024 WL 561118 (W.D.N.C. Feb. 12, 2024). The United States District Court for the Western District of North Carolina denied defendant's motion for summary judgment and stayed the case following a policy of abstention until the governing North Carolina agency or state courts interpreted whether the defendant met the definition of a "winery" under the North Carolina Wide Distribution Agreement Act.

The Homesteader's Store, Inc. v. Kubota Tractor Corp., No. 24-cv-23-jdp, 2024 WL 1701706 (W.D. Wis. Apr. 19, 2024). The Homesteader's Store, Inc. ("Plaintiff") operated a recreational land equipment business operating out of multiple retail locations. Plaintiff was also an authorized dealer of Kubota Tractor Corporation ("Kubota"). Plaintiff sold Kubota tractors at its locations under a Dealer Sales and Service Agreement ("Dealer Agreement") that allowed the sale of specific Kubota products, and set sales goals based on market share within its designated market area. After multiple notices of default from Kubota regarding underperformance, Kubota issued a notice of termination to

Plaintiff, citing failures to meet sales goals and other standards. Plaintiff challenged the termination under the Wisconsin Fair Dealership Law ("WFDL") and sought a preliminary injunction to prevent the termination, arguing (1) that it was impossible to meet the sales targets due to inventory issues; (2) Kubota applied the metrics in an discriminatory manner against underperforming dealers and that Kubota's market share metric was unreasonable and arbitrarily enforced; and (3) it was not an essential requirement of the Dealer Agreement. The court decided that Plaintiff made an adequate showing of a likelihood of success in challenging the termination under the WFDL which requires good cause and adequate notice for termination. Plaintiffs' argument that Kubota's use of market share as a performance metric was arbitrary, particularly since it did not reflect actual market conditions or dealer efforts, was sufficient to meet the burden. The court determined that Plaintiff faced irreparable harm if the injunction was not granted, as the loss of Kubota's dealership would significantly impact its business operations and financial health. The court balanced this against the harm to Kubota from delaying the termination, noting that Kubota's calculated potential losses were not credible, and did not outweigh the harms to Plaintiff.

Roadbuilders Machinery Supply Co. v. Sandvik Mining & Construction USA, LLC, No. 2:22-CV-02331-HLT, 2024 WL 1116079 (D. Kan. Mar. 14, 2024). The parties filed cross-motions for summary judgment. The court granted summary judgment to Plaintiff finding that the Kansas Outdoor Power Equipment Dealership Act ("KOPEDA") governed the case, and that the facts demonstrated that Defendant had violated the KOPEDA when it terminated the plaintiff's dealership agreement without good cause, proper notice, and required opportunity to cure. The court denied summary judgment to the defendant on the liability issues and rejected the ability to decide whether the plaintiff had properly mitigated its damages, leaving that issue for trial.

Altomare Auto Group, LLC v. Volkswagen Group of America, Inc., No. A-1753-20, 2023 WL 6930316 (N.J. Super. Ct. App. Div. Oct. 19, 2023). In an unpublished appellate opinion, the Superior Court of New Jersey considered whether (1) the circuit court imposed an appropriate sanction in precluding lost profits damages for a five-year period during which Plaintiff failed to preserve their car dealerships' general ledger, and granting an adverse inference charge at trial related to that spoiled part of the ledgers; and (2) whether summary judgment was appropriate against Plaintiffs on their claims that Volkswagen Group of America (VWOA) were provided insufficient (and less than promised) vehicle inventory upon opening to ensure the dealership's success.

Anthony Altomare (owner of Altomare Auto Group, LLC) (collectively ("Altomare")), a businessman with almost twenty years' experience operating a successful Volkswagen dealership, entered into a new agreement with VWOA to open a dealership in Union, New Jersey. Over the course of the next several years, the new dealership suffered financial trouble—eventually resulting in its bankruptcy. Altomare filed suit, alleging violations of the New Jersey Franchise Practices Act, fraudulent inducement, and breach of contract (alongside related claims) blaming his financial losses on VWOA's failure to fairly allocate new vehicle inventory to the Union Dealership, and alleging that VWOA had misrepresented the anticipated sales and profit forecast, along with the inventory required to reach those projected sales. Although Altomare testified that he believed he "would be provided inventory sufficient . . . [to] maintain[] 300 cars on the lot to begin each month" he admitted that VWOA never made any specific inventory commitment—only assuring him that he would have "more than enough" vehicle inventory by the time the Union Dealership opened. The dealer agreement, too, only provided that VWOA would make "a fair and equitable allocation and distribution" based on supply, demand, and shortages. VWOA testified that its goal was to provide dealers with a "sixty-day supply of cars," a number based on planning volume, anticipated sales, and inventory availability. While VWOA provided sales estimates—these were prefaced as estimates, not guarantees.

Ultimately, the court of appeals affirmed the circuit court's summary judgment decision, holding that the record demonstrated that VWOA's goal of providing a 60-day supply of inventory was met or exceeded, that it was "more than sufficient to satisfy demand" and met industry inventory guidelines, despite Altomare's dissatisfaction with the number and mix of vehicles provided. The court also affirmed judgment on the inducement claim based in part on Altomare's own admissions that the rosy projections made to him were the product of "euphoria and excitement over the new dealership," because they were premised as projections, and because Altomare actually fell within the low end of the range of projected sales. Because the court affirmed the court's summary judgment decision on liability, it did not address the circuit court's spoliation decision prohibiting Altomare from presenting evidence on lost profits for those years where it had failed to preserve its general ledger. It also did not address the circuit court's grant of an adverse inference charge at trial.

Nilo Watch Parts, Inc. v. Rado Watch Co., No. 23-1085 (CVR), 2023 WL 5814264 (D. P.R. Sept. 7, 2023). Rado, a well-known maker of luxury watches within the Swatch family of companies, appointed Nilo its sole distributor of Rado watches in Puerto Rico. Rado provided Nilo with specific marketing and sales guidelines to ensure consistent messaging and sales around the world. In 2008, Rado became concerned about Nilo's decreasing sales and required Nilo to make marketing changes designed to improve the Rado image in Puerto Rico, fit within Rado's global marketing strategy, and increase sales. Nilo attempted to make some of the required changes, but pushed back against others. In the end, Nilo's sales decreased from 2006-2022. Even considering the effects of Hurricane Maria in 2017 and the COVID-related shutdowns in 2020, a clear downward trend in sales emerged. That trend, combined with Nilo's refusal to update its marketing and retails concepts consistent with Rado's global standards, caused Rado to terminate the relationship, with over six months' notice. Rado offered to support Nilo in a transition from a distributorship relationship to a retailer model, but Nilo ultimately declined to sign Rado's retailer agreement. Nilo filed suit alleging wrongful termination of a distributorship and sought a preliminary injunction to preserve the status quo pending the litigation. The district court held an evidentiary hearing on the injunction motion.

The court analyzed the four elements Nilo bore the burden of proving to show why the injunction should issue (likelihood of success, irreparable harm, balancing of equities, and effect on public interest), but noted that this framework should be liberally applied in dealership cases to ensure adherence to the public policy goals underlying the dealership law. The fundamental public policy of the dealership law is to prevent termination of dealerships without "just cause." The court found that Nilo was not likely to prove a lack of just cause due to evidence of its (1) poor sales performance; (2) resistance to marketing suggestions from Rado that could have improved sales; (3) failure to adopt Rado marketing strategies; and (4) challenges to Rado's global strategies. The district court next found Nilo failed to prove irreparable harm because one of its witnesses admitted on cross-examination that monetary damages would suffice and because Nilo continued to operate its business and sell different watches under the Swatch brand. The third factor also favored Rado because the court found that requiring Rado to continue the relationship with Nilo would further erode Rado's brand and reputation in Puerto Rico and would prevent the implementation of Rado's marketing campaign it was waiting to launch. Finally, the court found an injunction would not serve the public interest because the evidence showed that Rado did not act in bad faith or attempt to take advantage of a favorable market created by Nilo. The district court specifically found that the dealership law "was not intended to prevent termination of unworkable relationships, but only to prevent arbitrary terminations."

Air-Con, Inc. v. Daikin Applied Latin America, LLC, No. CV 18-1800 (RAM), 2024 WL 1016184 (D.P.R. Mar. 8, 2024). In this case a dealer pursued claims under the Puerto Rico Dealer's Act for a manufacturer's alleged impairment of the dealer's contractual rights, and the defendant manufacturer asserted counterclaims for the collection of unpaid sums and declaratory relief. On summary judgment, the trial court dismissed the dealer's claims as time barred, dismissed the manufacturer's request for declaratory relief on ripeness grounds, and allowed the manufacturer's collection claim to proceed.

Meta Med, LLC v. Insulet Corp., No. CV 23-1546 (CVR), 2024 WL 1763610 (D.P.R. Apr. 23, 2024). Plaintiff-distributor pursued claims under the Puerto Rico Dealer's Contract Act against two distributors and a manufacturer. The trial court granted the two distributor defendants' motions to dismiss because the Puerto Rico Dealer's Act was inapplicable. The Act only applies to principals or grantors, and the distributor defendants were neither. The court also granted the manufacturer's motion to dismiss because plaintiff failed to overcome the presumption that the forum selection and choice of law clause in the contract was invalid, overreaching, unreasonable, or unjust.

Sany America, Inc. v. The G.W. Van Keppel Co., No. 1:23-CV-03532-JPB, 2024 WL 3402528 (N.D. Ga. July 12, 2024). A supplier of heavy construction equipment filed a breach of contract claim against one of its dealers. The dealer counterclaimed, alleging that the supplier failed to provide notice and opportunity to cure the breaches as required by the Arkansas Franchise Practices Act. The court denied the supplier's motion to dismiss the counterclaim, holding that the termination notice did not provide the dealer an opportunity to cure any of the alleged deficiencies in the dealer's performance giving rise to the termination by the supplier. Further, even after the dealer provided data to the supplier that it was on track to meet the performance requirements, the supplier specifically indicated it would not reconsider its position or provide the dealer an opportunity to cure.

Brava Salon Specialists, LLC v. REF North America, Inc., No. 22-cv-695-wmc, 2024 WL 3443799 (W.D. Wis. July 16, 2024). The United States District Court for the Western District of Wisconsin denied a motion for summary judgment filed by a dealer ("Brava") of defendant, REF North America, Inc. ("REF"). Brava alleged that REF breached its distributor agreement and violated the Wisconsin's Fair Dealership Law ("WFDL") by permitting another dealer to sell REF products online, and in plaintiff's exclusive territories, and by imposing additional obligations on plaintiff without proper notice or justification. Brava and REF's distributor agreement covered territory in Wisconsin. The parties were in discussion regarding Brava's expansion into Florida. However, the evidence showed that Brava failed to provide a business plan and other information requested by REF. As a result, REF engaged in a relationship with Amazon and other parties. In denying the motion for summary judgment, the court determined that there was a question as to whether the WFDL extended geographically to Florida.

CHAPTER 4

Disputes Regarding Performance, Termination, and Transfers

I. Introduction

As one of the longest Chapters in Annual Developments each year, there was no shortage of cases relating to aspects of the franchisor and franchisee relationships. Courts routinely enforced the language of the franchise agreement in breach of contract claims asserted by franchisees against the franchisor. In this reporting period, courts: enforced an entire agreement clause in a breach of contract claim based on language in an FDD *(Park 80 Hotels, LLC v. Holiday Hospitality Franchising, LLC)*; dismissed breach of contract claims as time barred, enforcing a one year statute of limitation in the franchise agreement (*Bigelow Corporation v. Hounds Town USA, LLC);* and denied summary judgment in favor of a franchisee on a breach of contract claim finding liquidated damages in a franchise agreement were not an unenforceable penalty *(NGM Mgmt. Grp., LLC v. Bareburger Grp., LLC).* In a series of interesting distributor breach of contract cases, courts showed an openness to finding enforceable agreements even where a formal contract was not executed (*Shanghai Weston Trading Co.*

v. Tedia Co. and *Sundrop Bottling Co. v. Fiji Water Co.).* One of the most noteworthy decisions in this Chapter was the Tenth Circuit vacating a $792,239 judgment in favor of a KFC franchisee and remanding for judgment in favor of the franchisor finding that there was no breach of the covenant of good faith and fair dealing to expand protections against encroachment beyond the terms of the franchise agreement.

Franchisors attempting to enforce non-competition and non-solicitation covenants was also an active area during this reporting period with courts being reluctant to grant preliminary injunctions particularly where geographic restrictions were broadly defined (*Cookie Dough Bliss Franchising, LLC v. Feed Your Soul Minnesota, LLC* and *HOA Franchising, LLC et al. v. MS Foods, LLC*). In a win for a franchisor, the District Court of Arizona granted LeTip World Franchise an injunction against a former franchisee who continued to operate in its territory after termination with a new venture. The franchisee further violated post-termination provisions by modifying the LeTip logo by adding the word "Just" before the trademark to market its competing business. Finally, in an interesting case of first impression, the New York Supreme Court rejected that agreed upon contractual limitations of damages should limit recovery against tortfeasors in *Liberty Petroleum Realty, LLC v. Gulf Oil, LP.*

A. BREACH OF CONTRACT

Travelodge Hotels, Inc. v. Huber Hotels, LLC, No. 219CV20571BRMJSA, 2022 WL 44634 (D.N.J. Jan. 5, 2022). The district court denied franchisor Travelodge Hotel, Inc.'s ("Travelodge") motion for summary judgment for liquidated damages and past-due franchise fees against a franchisee that shut down and transferred ownership of their hotel after seven months, when Travelodge delayed six months in adding that franchisee to their reservation system. To the court, this raised questions of material fact as to whether Travelodge materially breached the agreement, excusing the franchisee's subsequent breach.

Bigelow Corp. v. Hounds Town USA, LLC, No. CV-00134-FDW-SCR, 2023 WL 4939386 (W.D.N.C. Aug. 2, 2023). Franchisee, Bigelow Corporation brought claims against franchisor, Hounds Town USA, LLC for (1) breach of contract, (2) unjust enrichment, (3) punitive damages, (4) unfair and deceptive trade practices, (5) piercing the corporate veil, alter ego, and mere instrumentality, (6) fraud, (7) negligent misrepresentation, (8) negligence, and (9) negligent infliction of emotional distress after franchise location opening was delayed for two years. Franchisee claimed the failure to open on time was the result of construction issues, including permit problems, overpricing, and delays caused by the franchisor recommended contractor. The court found that the breach of contract and other claims were time-barred by the one year statute of limitations provision in the franchise agreement and granted the franchisor's motion to dismiss for failure to state a claim under Rule 12(b)(6).

360 Painting, LLC v. R. Sterling Enterprises, Inc., No. 20 C 4919, 2024 WL 2113035 (N.D. Ill. May 10, 2024). The district court denied cross motions for partial summary judgment filed by the franchisor and franchisee because both the franchise agreement and its addendum were ambiguous and both parties offered reasonable interpretations of what the parties intended. The court also granted plaintiff's uncontested summary judgment motion on the affirmative defense of fraudulent inducement.

Park 80 Hotels, LLC v. Holiday Hospitality Franchising, LLC, No. 1:21-CV-04650-ELR, 2023 WL 5523617 (N.D. Ga. Aug. 4, 2023). The plaintiffs purchased six hotels from the defendant franchisor, Holiday Hospitality Franchising LLC, ("Holiday"), and in connection with the purchase, Holiday provided a new franchise disclosure document ("FDD") to the plaintiffs. At the closing of the purchase, the plaintiffs entered into new franchise agreements for the hotels. Each franchise agreement contained an "entire agreement" clause stating that the franchise agreement was the entire agreement between the parties and that it superseded prior discussions, but did not disclaim representations made in the FDD.

The plaintiffs brought suit for breach of contract, and the court dismissed all of the breach of contract claims against the defendants that were based on the FDD. The court found that the franchise agreement terms supersede the FDD, and the FDD is therefore, not part of the contact between the parties. The language stating that the franchise agreement did not disclaim representations made in the FDD was only intended to clarify that the franchisee was not prohibited from asserting a fraud claim based on FDD misstatements. The court denied the motion for reconsideration confirming its conclusion that the FDD was not part of the franchise agreement and plaintiffs could not base a breach of contract claim on statements in the FDD.

Mayville Engineering Co. v. Peloton Interactive, Inc., 226 A.D.3d 482, 210 N.Y.S.3d 373 (2024). In this case, the parties cross-appealed a New York trial court's decision denying a distributor's motion to compel discovery and motion to dismiss a breach of contract claim brought by Peloton and granting the distributor's motion to dismiss Peloton's claim for breach of the implied duty of good faith and fair dealing. The appellate division affirmed the trial court's decision after finding that the contract contained ambiguities not resolvable on a motion to dismiss.

NGM Management Group, LLC v. Bareburger Group, LLC, 224 A.D.3d 600, 206 N.Y.S.3d 267 (2024). Franchisor appealed a trial court's denial of summary judgment on franchisor's claims for breach of contract and rescission and franchisee's counterclaims for breach of contract, liquidated damages, and professional fees. The court granted the franchisor's motion for summary judgment as to the franchisee's counterclaim for breach of contract. The court reasoned that the franchisee had failed to demonstrate its entitlement to judgment as a matter of law and that the liquidated damages provision at issue did not constitute an unenforceable penalty as asserted by the franchisee.

Kennynick, LLC v. Standard Petroleum Co., 222 Conn. App. 234 (2023). Plaintiff Kennynick LLC, in a class action, alleged that franchisor Standard Petroleum Company had breached the parties' dealer supply agreement, overcharging them for gasoline by (1) failing to apply the federal volumetric ethanol excise tax credit; and (2) improperly charging Plaintiff for the Connecticut gross receipts tax. Ultimately, the Connecticut Superior Court determined that Standard Petroleum was liable for failing to properly apply the credit and tax–but ruled in the Defendant's favor on Plaintiff's other claims brought under various Connecticut state protection statutes. The Connecticut Appellate Court considered cross-appeals from both parties, but ultimately affirmed the Superior Court's decision, adopting its memorandum in full.

Mall Chevrolet, Inc. v. General Motors LLC, 99 F.4th 622 (3d Cir. 2024). In this case, the Third Circuit Court of Appeals affirmed a district court decision granting summary judgment to General Motors. It held there was no genuine dispute of material facts, specifically that the dealership failed to substantially comply with dealership agreement's fundamental requirements, and that the manufacturer was thus rightly entitled to judgment as a matter of law on each appealed claim.

Hess v. Biomet, Inc., 105 F.4th 912 (7th Cir. 2024). Hess, one of six sales distributors, filed suit against medical device manufacturer Biomet for breach of a distributorship agreement for failing to pay long-term commissions after retirement. The court granted the defendant's motion to dismiss two of the three claims for failure to state a claim, and denied cross motions for summary judgment on the third claim because the agreement was deemed ambiguous. At trial, the jury returned a split verdict, finding that Biomet owed long-term commissions on some products but not others. Biomet pursued judgment as a matter of law after the verdict pursuant to Fed. R. Civ. P. 50, arguing that the jury acted unreasonably, which the district court denied. Biomet then appealed the denial of its summary judgment and Rule 50 motions. The Seventh Circuit affirmed the district court's decision holding that the commission agreement was ambiguous and that the jury properly decided whether specific categories of products were subject to long-term commissions. The court of appeals also affirmed the denial of Biomet's Rule 50 motion concluding that the trial record provided a sufficient basis for a rational jury to support the verdict.

Compass Tax Services LLC v. Karki, No. 22CVS001021-670, 2024 WL 2273416 (N.C. Super. Ct. May 20, 2024). Plaintiff moved for summary judgment on four of defendant's counterclaims: fraud, breach of fiduciary duty, constructive fraud, and the North Carolina Unfair and Deceptive Trade Practices Act ("UDTPA"). Defendant moved for summary judgment on plaintiff's breach of contract and breach of fiduciary duty claims and on his own breach of contract counterclaim. The court granted plaintiffs' motion as to breach of fiduciary duty and constructive fraud because the claims relied on the same insufficient and undisputed facts. The court also granted the defendant's motion because no condition precedent existed that relieved plaintiffs of their obligation to pay under the franchise agreement. The remaining claims were to proceed to trial because there were genuine issues of material fact in dispute.

Brow Art Management, LLC v. Idol Eyes Franchise, LLC, No. CV 23-11434, 2024 WL 1348357 (E.D. Mich. Mar. 29, 2024). The court granted in part and denied in part defendants' motion to dismiss all but one of plaintiff's claims for failure to state a claim. The court granted defendants' motion to dismiss plaintiff's claims for injunctive and declaratory relief because the claims are forms of relief, not claims for which relief is granted. The court also granted defendants' motion to dismiss plaintiff's breach of contract and tortious interference claims because both counts lacked a necessary element to state a claim, specifically the element of a valid contract. The court dismissed plaintiff's breach of fiduciary duty claim because no fiduciary duty attached to the defendant employees in their employment as eyebrow threaders. The court denied defendants' motion to dismiss the plaintiff's tortious interference with a prospective business advantage and civil conspiracy because the claims were adequately stated and plausibly pled under *Twombly*.

Kings Autoshow, Inc. v. Mitsubishi Motors of North America, Inc., No. 22-CV-07328, 2023 WL 5200398 (E.D.N.Y. Aug. 14, 2023). Kings Autoshow, Inc. ("Kings") was a car dealer of Mitsubishi Motors of North America, Inc. ("Mitsubishi"). While in business as one of Mitsubishi's dealers, Kings entered into a Consent Order with the New York City Department of Consumer and Worker Protection, pled guilty to 13 counts of violating New York City consumer protection laws, and paid $500,000 in civil penalties and $304,901.54 in restitution. As part of the Consent Order, Kings was also prohibited from selling used cars for one week. When Mitsubishi learned of the Consent Order, it sent a notice of termination to Kings. Kings argued (1) the franchise agreement did not cover "used" cars; and (2) the breach was immaterial and Mitsubishi lacked good cause to terminate. The court found no support for Kings' argument that there was no technical breach of the franchise agreement simply because it failed to explicitly cover "used" automobiles. The agreement language clearly applied to *all* dealer customers because it prohibited Kings from engaging in deceptive or misleading practices relating to *any* vehicle sale. The court also rejected Kints' argument that the breach was immaterial because Mitsubishi did not discover the Consent Order and send the termination notice until after New York's sale license suspension was lifted. The court granted Mitsubishi's motion for summary judgment, finding that Kings materially breached the dealer agreement by engaging in deceptive business practices, the breaches caused reputational harm that was incurable, and Mitsubishi acted in good faith in terminating the agreement.

KVC Waffles Ltd. v. New Carbon Co., No. 22-1746, 2023 WL 7688304 (4th Cir. Nov. 15, 2023). Court affirmed the district court's decision to grant defendant New Carbon Company, LLC's motion for summary judgment on breach of contract claim because the claim was barred by Maryland state law. This case is discussed in Chapter 4, Section I, Subsection C.

J.R. Enterprises LLC v. Hartman Snack Group Inc., No. 75-MDA-2023, 2023 WL 8440863 (Pa. Super. Ct. Dec 5, 2023) Affirming the trial court's decision that there was no breach of contract where the supplier sent a termination letter to the distributor offering to pay a two percent increase for the remaining transactions and the distributor complied with the terms of the letter by forwarding updated account information.

Racine Car Dealer, LLC v. Hyundai Motor Am., No. 22-CV-322-WMC, 2023 WL 8529832 (W.D. Wis. Dec. 8, 2023). The district court denied defendant Hyundai Motor America's motion for summary judgment on dealer's breach of contract claim because there was a genuine issue of material fact. This case is discussed in Chapter 3, Section III.

CBD Franchising, Inc. v. Dres, No. 822CV00313FWSJDE, 2023 WL 9687348 (C.D. Cal. Dec. 11, 2023). The court granted Plaintiff's motion to dismiss Defendants' crossclaim for breach of contract because Defendants failed to allege that they performed their contractual obligations or had an excuse for nonperformance and that Plaintiff breached the agreement. This case is discussed in Chapter 4, Section I, Subsection C.

Action Rentals Holdings, LLC v. Wacker Neuson America Corp., No. 22-CV-777, 2023 WL 8654002 (E.D. Wis. Dec. 14, 2023). The district court upheld plaintiff's counterclaim for breach of contract, unjust enrichment, and breach of guarantee against defendant distributor's motion to dismiss on the basis that defendant's assertions against the claim were not central to plaintiff's allegations.

Dry Tech 24/7, Inc. v. The Clorox Co., No. 22-61291-CIV, 2023 WL 9064671 (S.D. Fla. Dec. 18, 2023). Dry Tech 24/7, Inc. ("Dry Tech") was an authorized distributor of The Clorox Company's ("Clorox") electrostatic machines and chemicals for mold remediation, pursuant to a distributor access agreement entered into with Clorox in November 2019 ("Distributor Agreement"). Under the Distributor Agreement, Dry Tech was to purchase products from Essendant, Co. ("Essendant"), Clorox's national distributor, with a minimum monthly purchase requirement. During the COVID-19 epidemic, demand for Clorox machines increased for disinfection purposes. Dry Tech alleged Clorox unilaterally chose to allocate machines to Home Depot and other national retailers and refused to permit Essendant to fill its orders. Dry Tech filed suit for breach of implied covenant as a result of Clorox failing to supply Dry Tech with sufficient products to meet its monthly minimum purchase requirement (Count 1); breach of covenant of good faith and fair dealing (Count II): detrimental reliance (Count III); tortious interference with business relations (Count IV); unjust enrichment (Count V); and a breach of contract claim against Essendant (Count VI) as a result of defendant's' failure to supply the ordered machines and chemicals which Dry Tech alleged caused it to lose customers and sales staff. Clorox and Essendant each filed motions to dismiss Dry Tech's complaint and the court recommended the granting of Clorox's and Essendant's motions to dismiss be granted.

The court held that: (1) Dry Tech failed to establish an implied-in-fact contract to sustain Count I as there was no requirement that Clorox allocate product to Dry Tech; (2) without a without a breach of an express contract term, Dry Tech could not maintain Count II; (3) Dry Tech failed to demonstrate Clorox made a specific promise regarding product allocation to plead a promissory estoppel claim; (4) Dry Tech's tortious interference claim was barred by Florida's independent tort doctrine as it is not distinct from the breach of contract claim; (5) the equitable claim of unjust enrichment was not viable since there was no direct benefit conferred on Clorox by Dry Tech; and (6) Dry Tech failed to establish a contractual relationship with Essendant to plead its breach of contract claim since Dry-Tech never alleged Essendant was party to the Distributor Agreement. The court recommended that Counts I-V be dismissed with prejudice and Count VI was dismissed without prejudice, giving Dry Tech a limited opportunity to establish a breach of contract claim against Essendant.

M.A. Silva Corks USA, LLC v. M.A. Silva Holdings, Inc., No. 22-CV-04345-AMO, 2024 WL 1180999 (N.D. Cal. Mar. 18, 2024). In a contract dispute between the parties to a distribution agreement over the exclusive sale and distribution of corks from Portugal used in the wine industry, the United States District Court for the Northern District of California denied the cork supplier's motion for leave to file a counterclaim because defendants failed to show good cause to amend the scheduling order. Specifically analyzing Fed. R. Civ. P. 15(a), the district court found that the plaintiff would be prejudiced in having to defend the counterclaim so late in the litigation. It also found that defendants had engaged in undue delay in bringing the amendment to the court's attention. The district court also partially granted the plaintiffs' motion for summary judgment, concluding that no genuine issue of material fact existed regarding the claim that defendants had breached the distribution agreement by selling corks to a competitor of the plaintiffs in the United States. Because the distribution agreement gave plaintiffs exclusive rights to the Cortigas corks from Portugal, it granted judgment to the plaintiffs. Notwithstanding the decision, the district court denied plaintiff's summary judgment as to the breach of contract claim for supplier Cortigas' delayed and poor-quality cork and associated liability under an alter ego theory. The district court reserved that claim for trial.

Shanghai Weston Trading Co. v. Tedia Co., No. 1:23-cv-117, 2023 WL 8787235 (S.D. Ohio Dec. 19, 2023). The United States District

Court for the Southern District of Ohio denied defendant Tedia Company, LLC's ("Tedia") motion to dismiss breach of contract claim by distributor, Shanghai Weston Trading Co., Ltd. ("Shanghai") but granted dismissal of the distributor's fraud claim. Shanghai was a distributor of Tedia's products. Periodically throughout the business relationship, Tedia would issue certificates on letterhead appointing Shanghai as its "exclusive distributor" for a period of time. Tedia then abandoned the relationship prior to the end of the term designated in the last certificate, and Shanghai brought a breach of contract action against Tedia. The court denied Tedia's motion to dismiss on the basis that the agreement was unenforceable due to (1) lack of necessary terms; and (2) lack of consideration, making it illusory. Rather, the complaint alleged an enforceable contract that Tedia allegedly breached. The court did dismiss the fraud claim finding that there was no duty for Tedia to disclose the sale of its interest to a third party.

Remy Holdings International, LLC v. Fisher Auto Parts, Inc., 90 F.4th 217 (4th Cir. 2024). Remy Holdings International, LLC ("Remy") sold automotive parts to Fisher Auto Parts, Inc. ("Fisher") under various agreements. After Fisher terminated the relationship with Remy, alleging Remy failed to perform under the contracts, Fisher entered into a relationship with a different manufacturer selling its core inventory to the new manufacturer. Remy then filed a suit against Fisher, claiming breaches of contract, unjust enrichment, and conversion in connection with the sale of the core inventory, arguing that the core inventory was Remy's property. Fisher counterclaimed for breach of contract due to Remy's poor performance. The district court granted summary judgment in favor of Fisher on all claims and counterclaims except for Remy's conversion claim. That claim, and the amount of Fisher's damages flowing from the claims determined on summary judgment, proceeded to trial, resulting in a verdict favoring Fisher and awarding Fisher substantial damages. The district court found that Remy failed to keep Fisher competitive, as required by their agreements, which was a material breach. Under the first material breach doctrine, Fisher was not liable for any alleged breaches. Fisher was awarded over $1.8 million in damages for its breach of contract claim. Remy appealed and the Fourth Circuit Court of Appeals affirmed the lower court's decision resolving all claims in favor of Fisher.

Burger King Co. v. Consolidated Burger Holdings, LLC, No. 24-20178-CIV, 2024 WL 3455407 (S.D. Fla. July 18, 2024). In this franchise dispute, the district court denied the defendants' motion for summary judgment because the parties disagreed on the intent of the franchise agreements' terms, offered differing interpretations of the terms in dispute, and because the court deemed the agreements ambiguous. In so doing, the court concluded that disputed issues of material fact precluded the entry of summary judgment.

Revel Systems, Inc. v. Frisch's Restaurants, Inc., No. 1:23-CV-507, 2024 WL 1406107 (S.D. Ohio Apr. 2, 2024). Franchisor moved to dismiss its payment software company's first amended complaint arguing that the court lacked subject-matter jurisdiction and that the complaint failed to state a claim for relief. The court denied franchisor's motion to dismiss because franchisor's interpretation of the agreement regarding damages was not a jurisdictional issue but rather about the claim's merits, and because franchisor's reading of the agreement would defeat the purpose of the contract.

Smart Shoppers NY LLC v. Tylers Coffee LLC, No. 22 CIV. 4969 (NSR), 2024 WL 113731 (S.D.N.Y. Jan. 10, 2024). Smart Shoppers NY LLC ("Smart Shoppers") filed an action against two individuals, Ornstein and Harding, and the various companies that they owned and operated (together, "defendants"). The defendants entered into an agreement with Smart Shoppers and two other third-party distributors whereby they agreed to sell defendants' coffee products on Amazon. Shortly after, one of the third-party distributors unexpectedly lowered the price of defendants' product on Amazon. Smart Shoppers contacted Ornstein and Harding seeking exclusive distribution rights of the coffee products. At that time, Ornstein and

Harding requested that Smart Shoppers invest into two new companies that they were in the process of organizing. Smart Shoppers conditioned their willingness to invest on the fulfillment of an exclusive agreement. Ornstein and Harding agreed to make Smart Shoppers the exclusive distributor of defendants' coffee products. Thereafter, Smart Shoppers agreed to invest $100,000.00 over a period that would function as a loan and eventually convert to an investment once the partnership was finalized; however, a formal agreement was never executed.

Subsequently, Smart Shoppers placed an order for $250,000.00 worth of defendants' coffee products, in which it paid a total of $220,000.00 in advance. After several delays in the shipment, defendants requested that Smart Shoppers pay the remaining balance. Smart Shoppers complied with the request. Eventually, defendants halted all communication with Smart Shoppers. Later, defendants informed Smart Shoppers that they no longer had intentions of continuing the business relationship. Smart Shoppers counsel contacted defendants' counsel and requested that defendants return all the money owed. Defendants' counsel responded that Smart Shoppers owed the defendants money. Smart Shoppers's money was never returned, nor were the orders ever fulfilled. Smart Shoppers filed suit alleging breach of contract, unjust enrichment, and fraud. In response, defendants filed a motion to dismiss.

In support of its motion to dismiss the breach of contract claim, defendants argued that there was never an enforceable contract that required it to perform. The court agreed and granted defendants' motion to dismiss the breach of contract claim. The court found that Smart Shoppers failed to establish that the exclusivity agreement identified any major terms, such as how the performance would be carried out or the duration of performance. Further, the court found that Smart Shoppers failed to sufficiently allege there was a partnership agreement because there was never any indication that there was meeting of the minds. The court also found that there was never any breach for the loan agreement because Smart Shoppers never indicated the terms of the loan agreement. The court granted the defendants' motion to dismiss for the remaining claims for similar reasons.

O'Neal v. American Shaman Franchise System, LLC, No. 8:20-CV-936-KKM-AAS, 2024 WL 340767 (M.D. Fla. Jan. 12, 2024). A magistrate recommended that the district court grant in part and deny in part defendant franchisee's motion for summary judgment on its counterclaim. Specifically, the magistrate judge recommended that the franchisee's motion be granted for its breach of contract claim related to a prior release the parties signed. The magistrate judge recommended that the court award reasonable attorneys' fees and expenses as damages. Conversely, the magistrate judge recommended that the district court deny the franchisee's request that court impose sanctions against opposing counsel, finding that the attorney was entitled to a hearing pursuant to 28 U.S.C. § 1927. Further, the magistrate judge also recommended that the court grant in part plaintiff's motion with respect to the franchisee's counterclaim for declaratory judgment regarding the settlement agreement's enforceability.

Boswell v. Pappy's Pet Lodge Group, LLC, No. 05-23-00040-CV, 2024 WL 396621 (Tex. Ct. App. Feb. 2, 2024). This dispute arose out of an agreement between two parties where the plaintiff agreed to act as a franchise consultant for defendants. The agreement contained a provision that awarded a percentage of each franchised location's gross revenue to the plaintiff each month, and an additional hourly pay for their services. Nearly one year after signing the agreement, defendants informed plaintiff that they wanted to end the relationship because they were not going to be franchising the business anymore. Several years later, plaintiff learned that defendants had sold the franchise system, and plaintiff sought royalties under the agreement. Thereafter, plaintiff filed suit for breach of contract, fraud, fraud by nondisclosure, and promissory estoppel. The trial court granted the defendants' motion for summary judgment on all claims.

On appeal, plaintiff contended that it produced sufficient evidence to raise genuine issues of material fact on all four claims. The court of appeals affirmed the trial court's judgment in part and reversed in part. First, the court agreed with the plaintiff regarding the breach of contract claim and fraudulent inducement claim, finding that the parties disagreed about what services the plaintiff was required to perform under the agreement. However, the court affirmed the trial court's judgment for the remaining claims because plaintiff failed to state an adequate injury that went beyond the breach of contract claim.

Honey Dew Associates, Inc. v. Kennedy, No. 23-P-259, 2024 WL 630228 (Mass. App. Ct. Feb. 15, 2024). The Appeals Court of Massachusetts concluded that there were material facts in dispute between a former franchisee and its franchisor regarding the alleged violations of a franchise agreement that caused franchisor to terminate franchisee, and the court vacated the summary judgment granted in favor of the franchisor and remanded the case.

At the trial court level, Honey Dew Associates, Inc. ("Honey Dew"), was awarded the sum of $83,027 on its breach of contract claim alleging that franchisee, John F. Kennedy ("Kennedy"), violated the franchise agreement by abandoning his donut shop without Honey Dew's written permission. Kennedy's argument on appeal, as it was in his opposition to the motion for summary judgment in the superior court, was that he did not "abandon" his franchise agreement with Honey Dew donut shop, but instead that it was impossible for him to open and operate the donut shop in compliance with the COVID-19 state order issued by Massachusetts governor which required certain mitigation and distancing requirements that were not feasible with the layout of the location. The appeals court agreed, and reversed.

Chicago Franchise Systems, Inc. v. Dominique, No. 22-cv-2396, 2023 WL 756806 (N.D. Ill. Feb. 23, 2024). The United States District Court for the Northern District Court of Illinois granted Chicago Franchise System's (the "Franchisor") motion to dismiss the defendant's counterclaims. After the Franchisor brought suit against the former franchisee for trademark infringement and dilution, the franchisee counterclaimed for fraudulent misrepresentations, breach of contract, and breach of an implied contract in connection with the Franchisor's refusal to certify an SBA loan. The court found that defendant's allegation that the Franchisor used the brand fund to defray operating costs in violation of the franchise agreement was based only on suspicions and that there was no obligation under the franchise agreement for the Franchisor to certify the SBA loan.

NGM Management Group, LLC v. Bareburger Group, LLC, No. 2023-01081, 1024, 2024 WL 781669 (N.Y. Sup. Ct. Feb. 27, 2024). The plaintiff, NGM Management Group, LLC ("Franchisee") operated five restaurants in Manhattan under franchise agreements with defendant, Bareburger Group, LLC ("Bareburger"). The restaurants encountered financial issues and Bareburger and Franchisee entered into a step-in-rights agreement. Plaintiff filed complaints against defendants alleging breaches of the franchise agreement, step-in-rights agreements and defendant filed a motion for Summary Judgment and counterclaims. In this case, the court granted, in part, the defendants' motion for summary judgment, dismissing plaintiffs' causes of action related to breach of franchise agreements through misuse of brand fees and failure to advance funds. The court also granted summary judgment to Bareburger on liability for certain counterclaims concerning breach of franchise agreements, unpaid royalties, interest on overdue payments, and liquidated damages against the Franchisee. The court also found that the liquidated damages provision was enforceable and not a penalty, as it bore a reasonable proportion to probable loss. Bareburger was also granted summary judgment on its counterclaim regarding the no-challenge provision, which plaintiffs had violated by contesting Bareburger's ownership of trademarks. However, the court declined to award Bareburger professional fees and struck its demand for punitive damages.

Wine Country Gateway Recreational Vehicle Park, LLC v. Eagle Energy, Inc., No. 2D CIV. B322766, 2024 WL 833422 (Cal. Ct. App. Feb. 28, 2024). The California Court of Appeals reviewed a trial court decision granting summary judgment on Eagle Energy, Inc.'s ("Eagle") cross-complaint for breach of contract against Plaintiff Wine Country Gateway Recreational Vehicle Park, LLC ("Wine Country"), Letters, Inc., and its principal John Letters (together, "Letters"). Eagle was a gasoline distributor that purchased wholesale gasoline from ConocoPhillips. Wine Country and Letters each owned independent service stations. Eagle entered into two agreements with Wine Country and Letters separately, a purchase contract and letter of intent.

Wine Country and Letters sued Eagle, arguing that Eagle breached the contracts by charging $0.03 per gallon more than the agreed upon price. The lower court granted summary judgment in favor of Eagle and concluded that the prices were reasonable and set in good faith. Nevertheless, Wine Country and Letters stopped purchasing fuel from Eagle. Thus, Eagle filed a cross complaint against Wine Country and Letters for breach of contract. The lower court relied on its previous decision and granted summary judgment in favor of Eagle.

On appeal, Wine Country and Letters argued that the contracts were ambiguous. Specifically, their position was that the parties never intended to agree to a markup price since Eagle was not charging a markup price for several years prior. The appellate court disagreed and affirmed the lower court's decision. The court found that the contracts contained an open price provision. Therefore, Eagle could charge any price that was reasonable and set in good faith.

Sundrop Bottling Co. v. Fiji Water Co., No. 1:19-cv-0039, 2024 WL 898200 (M.D. Tenn. Mar. 1, 2024). Plaintiff, Sundrop Bottling Company, Inc. ("Sundrop") a distributor of beverage products in Tennessee, had an oral agreement with Fiji Water Company, LLC ("Fiji") since 2003 to be the exclusive distributor of Fiji water in certain Tennessee counties. Sundrop distributed Fiji water under the oral agreement until 2018 dealing with national, regional, and independent retailers. The oral agreement lacked written specifications regarding its termination, and there was no prior discussion on this matter between Sundrop and Fiji. After Fiji terminated the oral agreement in 2018 with 29-day notice, Sundrop filed suit, alleging that Fiji breached the agreement by not providing reasonable notice before termination, and alleging Fiji tortiously interfered with Sundrop's business relations concerning their interactions with national retailers. Sundrop argued that industry norms and their operational practices necessitated a longer notice period to adjust and prevent business disruption. After a bench trial, the court found Fiji in breach of contract for not providing a 90-day termination notice as deemed reasonable based on industry norms, the parties' course of performance, and the specific circumstances of their business relationship. Sundrop was entitled to damages calculated based on its net margin from Fiji water sales during the notice period that was not provided. The court dismissed Sundrop's claim for tortious interference, concluding that Sundrop didn't demonstrate a direct business relationship with the national retailers that Fiji could interfere with. Fiji's engagement with these retailers was independent of the distribution relationship with Sundrop. The court awarded Sundrop $30,244.41 in damages, reflecting the lost net margin from the insufficient notice period. However, Sundrop's tortious interference claim was dismissed, and no damages were awarded for loss of goodwill, as Sundrop effectively mitigated its losses by adopting new business strategies post-termination, when it started promoting a competing brand, CORE water, and commenced distributing another premium water brand, Evian.

Hydroflow USA, LLC v. ECO Integrated Technologies, Inc., No. 2:23-cv-01317-TL, 2024 WL 104999 (W.D. Wash. Mar. 11, 2024). Plaintiff, Hydroflow USA, LLC ("Hydroflow"), the exclusive distributor in the USA and Mexico of Hydroflow water conditioners, entered into a distribution agreement in July 2021 with defendant ECO Integrated Technologies, Inc. ("ECO") under which ECO was a sub-distributor of the products. In June 2023, Hydroflow terminated the distribution agreement. ECO then began selling a competitive product through its own network of affiliates and dealers at a lower cost point. Hydroflow responded by filing a lawsuit against ECO alleging it breached the distribution agreement between the two parties, breached the implied duty of good faith and fair dealing, and engaged in unfair competition and conspiracy to wrongfully compete against Hydroflow. ECO moved to dismiss the lawsuit. The court granted the motion to dismiss the breach of contract claim, finding that there was no violation of the non-compete in the distribution agreement since it only applied in the event ECO terminated the agreement. However, it denied ECO's motion with respect to the breach of the duty of good faith and fair dealing claim, finding that Hydroflow alleged enough facts to plead that ECO set the plan to compete in motion during the term of the distribution agreement thus potentially violating the in-term non-compete.

Popeyes Louisiana Kitchen, Inc. v. Florida Pop, LLC, No. 1:23-cv-23955-KMM, 2024 WL 1430446, (S.D. Fla. Mar. 18, 2024). Popeyes Louisiana Kitchen, Inc. ("Popeyes") brought an action against a multi-unit franchisee ("Franchisee") alleging trademark infringement in violation of the Lanham Act, false designations of origin in violation of the Lanham Act, common law trademark infringement, common law unfair competition; and breach of contract, after the Franchisee failed to close its Popeyes restaurants after termination of a franchise agreement and subsequent limited license agreement ("LLA"). Popeyes had provided Franchisee an additional period under the LLA in which to operate the restaurants after termination with the purposes of allowing Franchisee to market and sell the locations, but Franchisee failed to bring a legitimate buyer to Popeyes to approve before the deadline under the LAA. Franchisee counterclaimed for (1) breach of contract; (2) breach of the duty of good faith and fair dealing; (3) tortious interference with contractual relations; and (4) violation of Florida Deceptive and Unfair Trade Practices Act ("FDUTPA"). Popeyes moved to dismiss the counterclaims. The court dismissed all of Franchisee's counterclaims refusing to read an implied duty to extend the period under the LLA as argued by Franchisee and found there to be no basis for Franchisee's claim of lost profits from a potential sale under the FDUTPA.

CajunLand Pizza, LLC v. Marco's Franchising, LLC, No. 3:20-CV-536, 2024 WL 1014028 (N.D. Ohio Mar. 8, 2024). The United States District Court for the Northern District of Ohio denied a franchisor's motion for summary judgment seeking to dismiss its franchisees' claims for breach of contract based on franchisor's rescission of its approval of franchisees' sale of their stores to another existing Marco's Pizza franchise owner, and its wrongful refusal to approve the sale.

B. BREACH OF COVENANT OF GOOD FAITH AND FAIR DEALING

Kazi v. KFC US, LLC, 76 F.4th 993 (10th Cir. 2023). The Tenth Circuit Court of Appeals vacated a $792,239 judgment by the lower district court in favor of a Kentucky Fried Chicken franchisee ("Franchisee") and remanded for entry of judgment in favor of franchisor, KFC US, LLC ("KFC"). Franchisee originally owned four Kentucky Fried Chicken restaurants in Pueblo, Colorado, but at the time of the lawsuit, owned a single location. It filed a lawsuit against KFC for breach of contract, breach of the implied covenant of good faith and fair dealing (bad faith), promissory estoppel, and unjust enrichment after KFC allegedly failed to follow its impact-study guidelines when it approved the new restaurant in north Pueblo. The district court narrowed the claims, and the trial court heard only the bad faith claim. The jury found in Franchisee's favor and KFC moved under Fed. R. Civ. P. 50(b) and 59 arguing that Franchisee failed to prove bad faith.

Applying Kentucky law, the court found that the implied covenant of good faith and fair dealing does not act to prevent a party from exercising contractual rights where an allegation of bad faith was not tied to the terms of the contract. The court interpreted that prior holding by the Kentucky Supreme Court to mean that a court does not have the power to revise a contract to make it fair. To prevail on a claim of bad faith, a plaintiff must identify a specific expectation with respect to an agreement that the other party defeated in bad faith. The franchise agreement between KFC and Franchisee only prohibited KFC from granting a new franchise within the 1.5-mile protected area around Franchisee's restaurant and there was no provision restricting KFC's ability to grant licenses to other franchisees outside that mile and a half radius. Further, under the franchise agreement, the Franchisee only had exclusivity with respect to the 1.5-mile territory which implied that there was no exclusivity outside that area. Finally, the court pointed to a section in the contract stating that Franchisee had a right to negotiate conditionally for a franchise approved restaurant if he had the licensed restaurant closest to the proposed new location. This showed that the parties had a process under the franchise agreement for addressing new locations outside Franchisee's exclusive territory and there was no reasonable expectation of further protection.

The court also cited additional good faith and fair dealing questions in other circuit courts holding that a franchisee cannot invoke the covenant of good faith and fair dealing to expand protections against encroachment beyond the terms of the contract. Because Franchisee could not show that he had an expectation of protection beyond the exclusive radius under the franchise agreement, he did not have, as a matter of law, a claim for breach of the implied covenant.

Cognex Corp. v. Air Hydro Power, LLC, No. CV 22-10051-NMG, 2023 WL 5833112 (D. Mass. Sept. 8, 2023). The United States District Court for the District of Massachusetts found no breach by a manufacturer of the covenant of good faith and fair dealing by not compensating its distributor upon nonrenewal for unsold demonstration equipment because there was no expectation under the agreement for reimbursement. This case is discussed in Chapter 1, Section II.

Garrand Brothers, LLC v. America Honda Motor Co., No. 8:22-CV-0924, 2023 WL 5835793 (N.D.N.Y. Sept. 8, 2023). The court granted American Honda Motor Co., Inc. ("Honda") motion to dismiss a dealer's claim for breach of the implied covenant of good faith and fair dealing after Honda terminated the dealer for failing to open for seven consecutive days because the claim would create a duty that negates Honda's express right under the dealer agreement to terminate for abandonment. This case is discussed in Chapter 3, Section III.

Windy Cove, Inc. v. Circle K Stores, Inc., No. 21-cv-1416-MMA-DEB, 2023 WL 6284466 (S.D. Cal. Sept. 7, 2023). Defendant Circle K distributed gasoline to plaintiff dealers. The relevant purchase agreements all had an open price term. Plaintiffs believed Circle K was charging unreasonably high prices for the gasoline and filed suit alleging breach of the covenant of good faith and fair dealing and unfair business practices. Circle K asserted a Counterclaim seeking a declaratory judgment that it set its prices in good faith. The parties cross-moved for summary judgment and also moved to exclude each other's experts.

Defendants' challenged expert, Dr. John Umbeck, held a Ph.D. in Economics from the University of Washington and was teaching Economics in the Krannert School of Management at Purdue University. He opined that the defendants' prices were within the range of prices offered by other suppliers and therefore were reasonable. He relied in part on industry reports known as Lundberg

Surveys, which collected daily information regarding wholesale gasoline prices of each major brand. Plaintiffs challenged his qualifications and methodology. The court rejected all challenges to Dr. Umbeck, finding him qualified, holding that reliance on the Lundberg Surveys was not a basis to exclude his opinion, and holding that he did not rely on an improper legal standard. The court, however, did exclude portions of the report of Plaintiff's expert, Donald Maday. Specifically, the court excluded opinions relying on a legal standard that prices be "in the middle of the pack" rather than "in the range." Additionally, the court excluded opinions related to subjective bad faith because the proper standard is objective bad faith. Opinions regarding reasonableness of defendants' pricing methodology were also excluded because that is not relevant to an objective bad faith inquiry.

On summary judgment, the court found as a matter of law that Circle K did not violate the covenant of good faith and fair dealing in setting the prices charged to plaintiffs. A safe harbor in the UCC § 2305, cmt. 3 provided safe harbor presumption of good faith when the seller charged the "regularly posted price." Plaintiffs attempted to rebut this presumption with evidence allegedly showing that defendants' prices were not commercially reasonable and that defendants engaged in price discrimination. Plaintiffs argued that because other companies used a different pricing formula than defendants, the prices charged were commercially unreasonable. The court rejected this argument, holding that "pricing methodology is not relevant to an objective bad faith inquiry; the relevant inquiry for assessing commercial reasonableness . . . is whether . . . prices fall in the range of prices charged by other competitors" in the relevant market. The undisputed evidence demonstrated that Circle K's prices were, in fact, within the range of those charged by others. Plaintiffs also contended that Circle K engaged in price discrimination because it set a sales price for its own stores that was lower than the price charged to plaintiffs. This position failed as a matter of law because the plaintiff offered no evidence to support it. Based on its analysis of plaintiff's arguments, the court granted

Circle K's motion for a judgment declaring that it was setting its prices in good faith.

CBD Franchising, Inc. v. Dres, No. 822CV00313FWSJDE, 2023 WL 9687348 (C.D. Cal. Dec. 11, 2023). The district court granted Plaintiff's motion to dismiss Defendants' crossclaim for breach of the implied covenant of good faith and fair dealing because Defendants failed to allege that Plaintiff breached the express terms of the related franchise agreement or allege that one of the named Plaintiffs was a party to the agreement. This case is discussed in Chapter 4, Section I, Subsection C.

Hydroflow USA, LLC v. ECO Integrated Technologies, Inc., No. 2:23-cv-01317-TL, 2024 WL 104999 (W.D. Wash. March 11, 2024). Plaintiff, Hydroflow USA, LLC ("Hydroflow"), the exclusive distributor in the USA and Mexico of Hydroflow water conditioners, entered into a distribution agreement in July 2021 with defendant ECO Integrated Technologies, Inc. ("ECO") under which ECO was a sub-distributor of the products. In June 2023, Hydroflow terminated the distribution agreement. ECO then began selling a competitive product through its own network of affiliates and dealers at a lower cost point. The court found that Hydroflow alleged enough facts to plead that ECO set the plan to compete in motion DURING the distribution agreement thus potentially violating the during term non-compete and establishing a claim for breach of the duty of good faith and fair dealing. This case is discussed in Chapter 4, Section I, Subsection A.

Pacific Office Automation, Inc. v. Pitney Bowes, Inc., No. 3:20-cv-651-AR, 2024 WL 3415894 (D. Or. July 15, 2024). The United States District Court for the District of Oregon granted summary judgment in favor of Pitney Bowes Inc. ("Pitney") against one of its authorized dealer's ("Dealer") claims for breach of contract and violations of the Connecticut Unfair Trade Practices Act

("CUTPA"). The court found that there was no genuine dispute of fact as to whether Pitney's alleged conduct harmed the Dealer.

Dealer and Pitney entered into a three-year agreement, and when the relationship soured, Dealer allege that Pitney violated the express incorporation of the covenant of good faith and fair dealing and the CUTPA by making substantial changes to the dealer compensation plan, using Dealer's confidential customer information to compete against Dealer, interfering with Dealers's ability to sell to Pitney's existing customers, and refusing to renew the agreement under fair and equitable terms. The court found that Pitney was able to establish uncontested evidence that Pitney sales team had no access to Dealer's customer information and therefore, could not misuse it. The court also found that Pitney negotiated in good faith for a new agreement once the current dealer agreement expired, and there was no evidence that it failed to do so, or that Pitney had an obligation to renew the agreement on the terms demanded by Dealer. Finally, Dealer was unable to establish the new dealer compensation plan was unreasonable and the breach of covenant and good faith and fair dealings and CUTPA claims failed.

C. TORTIOUS INTERFERENCE

Cognex Corp. v. Air Hydro Power, LLC, No. CV 22-10051-NMG, 2023 WL 5833112 (D. Mass. Sept. 8, 2023). The United States District Court for the District of Massachusetts dismissed a counterclaim brought by a distributor against its supplier of tortious interference with a business relationship. The court found the distribution agreement expressly permitted the supplier to transfer sales leads within a territory, so the distributor could not establish the conduct was improper, an essential element to state a claim. This case is discussed in Chapter 1, Section II.

KVC Waffles Ltd. v. New Carbon Co., No. 22-1746, 2023 WL 7688304 (4th Cir. Nov. 15, 2023). Court affirmed the district court's decision to grant defendant New Carbon Company, LLC's motion for summary judgment on a tortious interference claim because the plaintiff, KVC Waffles Ltd., failed to show that the defendant caused its injuries or that it incurred damages as a result of such conduct. This case is discussed in Chapter 4, Section I, Subsection A.

Racine Car Dealer, LLC v. Hyundai Motor America, No. 22-CV-322-WMC, 2023 WL 8529832 (W.D. Wis. Dec. 8, 2023). The district court granted defendant Hyundai Motor America's motion for summary judgment for an intentional interference with contract claim regarding a dealer's Asset Purchase Agreement with a third party, finding that the claim was duplicative of an independent claim, unnecessary, and would potentially be confusing for a jury. This case is discussed in Chapter 3, Section III.

Reecon North America, LLC v. Enerco Group, Inc., No. 2:23-CV-890, 2023 WL 8529131 (W.D. Pa. Dec. 8, 2023). Plaintiff, Reecon North America, LLC ("Reecon"), filed a complaint against defendant, Enerco Group, Inc. ("Enerco"), alleging Enerco tortiously interfered with an exclusive supply agreement ("ESA") it had in place with a manufacturer ("M&E"). Enerco and Reecon entered into acquisition discussions and Enerco learned of the ESA during due diligence. While Reecon's EDA was still in effect, Enerco started to develop a relationship with M&E and the two companies eventually entered into their own distribution agreement during the exclusivity period under the ESA. Reecon discovered the relationship after M&E filed a separate lawsuit against Reecon alleging it breached the ESA ("M&E Lawsuit"). Enerco argued that Reecon failed to meet the elements to state a claim for tortious interference because there was no enforceable contract between M&E and Enerco. The court disagreed, noting that the argument was premature because the M&E Lawsuit was still ongoing, and M&E's complaint that the contract was not enforceable was simply an allegation. The court also disagreed with Enerco's argument that it was privileged to interfere with the relationship because it is in competition with Reecon. The court found Reecon was in a non-terminable at will existing contract so its claim of privilege failed.

The United States District Court for the Western District of Pennsylvania therefore denied Enerco's motion to dismiss.

CBD Franchising, Inc. v. Dres, No. 822CV00313FWSJDE, 2023 WL 9687348 (C.D. Cal. Dec. 11, 2023). Plaintiff and Cross-Defendants CBD Franchising Inc, and Closets by Design, Inc. (together, "Plaintiff") filed a motion to dismiss Defendants' counterclaim for intentional interference with prospective business advantage and negligent interference with prospective business advantage claims.

Under California law, a claim for interference with prospective economic advantage is established if the following elements are met: "(1) the existence, between the plaintiff and some third party, of an economic relationship that contains the probability of future economic benefit to the plaintiff; (2) the defendant's knowledge of the relationship; (3) intentionally wrongful acts designed to disrupt the relationship; (4) actual disruption of the relationship; and (5) economic harm proximately caused by the defendant's action." Plaintiff argued that Defendants' claim for intentional interference with prospective business advantage failed because Defendants' allegations did not meet the first and third elements. The court concluded that Defendants sufficiently established the first element by alleging that it had secured an interested third-party to take over the franchise and Plaintiff refused to consent to the transfer. However, the court found that Defendants' allegation that the acts were wrongful because they were "intentional, malicious, and in bad faith"' failed to satisfy the third element because Defendants failed to allege why Plaintiff's actions were not prescribed by law. The court granted the motion on the interference claims.

Next, Plaintiff argued that Defendants failed to establish that an economic relationship existed between Defendants and a third-party which contained a reasonably probable future economic benefit or advantage to Defendants. The court disagreed and found that Defendants adequately alleged an interference with an existing relationship with a specific party. As a result, the court denied Plaintiff's motion to dismiss this claim.

DSG Commercial ECO Cleaning Systems, Inc. v. DHL Express (USA), Inc. No. 2:23-cv-02093-MSN-tmp, 2024 WL 532329 (W.D. Tenn. Feb. 9, 2024). The United States District Court for the Western District of Tennessee granted defendant, DHL Express (USA) Inc.'s, motion to dismiss claims made by plaintiff, DGS Commercial ECO Cleaning Systems, Inc. ("DSG"), a Jan-Pro janitorial franchisee. Defendant was a business customer of DSG who became unhappy with the pricing of a COVID-19 deep clean serviced by plaintiff. Defendant contacted the franchisor, Jan-Pro, to complain and negotiate a discount to the invoices while at the same time negotiating the pricing with the franchisee. Jan-Pro subsequently sent notice to DHL that DSG was being replaced and then terminated DSG's franchise agreement. DSG then filed a complaint against DHL alleging defamation, tortious and intentional interference with business relations and prospective business relations, and breach of contract. The court granted DHL's motion to dismiss all counts. The court held that the statements made by DHL were not sufficiently defamatory to hold DSG up to public hate, contempt or ridicule and dismissed the defamation claim. The court found that DSG failed to plead facts sufficient to show the improper motive necessary to state a claim of tortious interference. Finally, the breach of contract claim failed as DSG was unable to plead facts showing that DHL had any intention of inducing the franchisor to breach the franchise agreement or that the franchise agreement was breached.

Ecochem Australia Pty Ltd. v. CST Systems Inc., No. 1:22-CV-4908-TWT, 2023 WL 6276354 (N.D. Ga. Sept. 26, 2023). This case involved a written dealership agreement between the parties that CST claimed had been breached by Ecochem. The relationship deteriorated further when Ecochem established a U.S. presence, creating the business Clean Print and Dicar to service the market in the United States, which CST brought into the case after being sued for breach by Ecochem. Clean Print and Dicar filed a motion to dismiss CST's third-party claims for failure to state a claim. The district court denied the motion because CST plausibly alleged causation and a claim for tortious interference by Clean Print and Dicar.

D. FRAUD

The Learning Experience System, LLC v. Collins, No. 20-CV-2504 (MLB), 2023 WL 5835034 (E.D.N.Y. Sept. 8, 2023). Plaintiffs, franchisor The Learning Experience Systems, LLC and The Learning Experience at Queens-Long Island City, LLC (together "TLE"), commenced several actions against a former franchisee, its owners and executive director, claiming breaches of representations and warranties, common law fraud, fraudulent inducement, conspiracy to commit fraud, indemnification, breach of the duty of good faith and fair dealing, negligence, negligent supervision, and breach of the franchise agreement after discovering fabricated and doctored background checks and medical clearance forms for the childcare center staff.

The defendant, Brite Tikes LLC ("Brite Tikes") and its owners, Jubran C. Jubran ("Jubran") and Jubran's daughter Nicole Collins ("Collins"), operated a franchised child learning and care center in New York (the "Center"). During Brite Tikes' ownership and operation of the Center, the Center had a positive reputation in the community, a strong client base, and expanding growth. It was one of the highest grossing franchises in the country. On December 31, 2018, Brite Tikes sold the center to TLE and in connection with the sale, the franchise agreement was terminated.

After closing, TLE discovered fraudulent documents and received their first DOH violation. TLE argued that the Brite Tikes' executive director, Ara Pasaoglu ("Pasaoglu") was involved in falsifying or altering some of the supporting documents for the required licenses or permits, which happened pre-closing during Brite Tikes' ownership.

The court denied TLE's motion for summary judgment in its entirety. The court determined there were disputed issues of fact regarding whether defendants breached the representations and warranties in the purchase agreement, so the court denied both TLE and defendants' motions for summary judgment on the breach of purchase agreement claim. The court granted Brite Tikes's motion for summary judgment as to TLE's claims for fraud, fraudulent inducement, conspiracy to commit fraud, negligent misrepresentations and omissions, indemnification, breach of the covenant of good faith and fair dealing, general negligence, negligent supervision, and breach of the franchise agreement (because TLE failed to present any evidence that the Franchise Agreement survived the closing of the sale of the Center, they did not show that the Brite Tikes defendants breached the Franchise Agreement). The Court granted Pasaoglu's motion for summary judgment in its entirety as any reliance by TLE on the employee Pasaoglu was unreasonable since he was not party to any agreement with them.

Migdal 1, LLC v. Hyundai Motor America Corp., No. 1:22-cv-01088, 2023 WL 6214528 (N.D. Ohio Sept. 25, 2023). A car dealership sued Hyundai and Genesis for fraud, alleging that the manufacturers should have disclosed 2020 incentive programs requiring separate facilities for Hyundai sales versus Genesis sales when "pressur[ing]" the dealership to build a new dual facility with separate spaces for Hyundai and Genesis vehicles in 2018. The dealership claimed that it faced a significant competitive disadvantage by choosing not to remodel for the second time in two years. The court dismissed the dealer's fraud claim because: (1) future conduct cannot serve as basis for fraud absent a promise from the alleged tortfeasor that they never intended to keep; and (2) the proposed amended complaint lacked required specificity to sustain fraud claim such that it was futile.

Shanghai Weston Trading Co. v. Tedia Company, LLC, No. 1:23-cv-117, 2023 WL 8787235 (S.D. Ohio December 19, 2023). The District Court for the Southern District of Ohio granted defendant's, Tedia Company, LLC ("Tedia") motion to dismiss the fraud claim by distributor, Shanghai Weston Trading Co., Ltd. ("Shanghai") finding that there was no duty for Tedia to disclose the sale of its interest to a third party. This case is discussed in Chapter 4, Section I, Subsection A.

Tryp Hotels Worldwide, Inc. v. Sebastian Hotel, LLC, No. CV2111557MEFJSA, 2024 WL 1327311 (D.N.J. Mar. 28, 2024). The district court granted the franchisor's summary judgment motion regarding the franchisees' counterclaims for fraud and breach of contract. Statements of opinion and future predictions are not negligent misrepresentations or a sufficient factual basis to assert a claim for fraudulent inducement of a contract. The court denied franchisor's motion seeking damages and attorneys' fees because genuine issues of material fact existed on the damages claims, and the issue of attorneys' fees was not yet ripe for resolution.

Shah v. General Motors LLC, No. 23-CV-04319-SI, 2023 WL 8852491 (N.D. Cal. Dec. 21, 2023). Plaintiff purchased a new 2019 Chevrolet Bolt from an authorized dealer and agent of General Motors ("GM") in California. As part of the sale, GM provided an express warranty that the vehicle was free from defects in materials, nonconformities, or workmanship during an extended period. If there were defects, GM agreed to repair them during the period. Shortly after, Plaintiff learned that the vehicle's battery may ignite when they are fully charged, and it could not be parked inside overnight due to fire risk. Accordingly, Plaintiff filed a complaint against GM and other affiliated parties, alleging a cause of action under the Song-Beverly Consumer Warranty Act, a cause of action for fraud and a cause of action for violations of California's Unfair Competition. After the court granted GM's motion to dismiss the last two causes of action, Plaintiff filed an amended complaint. GM filed a motion to dismiss again, arguing that the amended complaint did not remedy the issues in the original one. The court agreed with GM, finding that Plaintiff only presented conclusory allegations for both causes of action. The court noted that the Plaintiff failed to sufficiently plead facts for fraudulent misrepresentation because it failed to address GM's knowledge and intent. Based on the lack of specificity, the court did not consider the disputed elements of California's Unfair Competition. Thus, the court granted GM's motion to dismiss.

Bustos v. Invierte en Texas, LLC, No. 4:22-CV-02690, 2024 WL 3364039 (June 3, 2024). The United States Magistrate Judge recommended the court dismiss plaintiff's claims alleging RICO violations, common law fraud, fraudulent inducement, violation of the Texas Deceptive Trade Practices Act, fraudulent transfer, and civil conspiracy against defendants involved in a purported scheme to market RhinoPro franchise opportunities to foreign nationals for the purpose of obtaining visas for permanent residency. The judge found that the complaint failed to state a claim. Specifically, the plaintiffs failed to explain how or why any alleged representations about the license vs. franchise business structure, the potential rates of return, and other descriptions of the franchise business, were fraudulent when made by the defendants to support the fraud claim.

E. UNFAIR AND DECEPTIVE TRADE PRACTICES

NVL, Inc. v. Volvo Car USA LLC, No. A-0640-22, 2024 WL 657202 (N.J. Super. Ct. App. Div. Feb. 15, 2024). The court reviewed the trial court's decision granting summary judgment to Volvo Car U.S. LLC ("Volvo") for all of the claims brought against it by NVL, Inc. and Hooman Nissani ("Nissani"). The parties executed two separate Letter of Intent agreements between 2014-2016 to construct a new Volvo dealership in Long Beach, California. The most recent LOI was signed in 2016 and defined specific deadlines for the project. Despite Volvo's numerous attempts to push the project forward, Nissani failed to meet the construction deadlines put forth in the 2016 LOI. Thereafter, Volvo provided notice to Nissani of its intent to terminate the parties' agreement. Nissani brought claims for unconscionability, violations of the New Jersey Consumer Fraud Act ("CFA"), and unjust enrichment.

On appeal, Nissani's first argument was that the 2016 LOI covenant not to sue clause was unconscionable and unenforceable. Although the court agreed with Nissani that there was an adhesion contract, it still found Nissani failed to establish it was unconscionable. The court reasoned that both of the parties were experienced and sophisticated when they agreed to the 2016 LOI's terms, and that they both had equal opportunity to have legal counsel review the document before signing it. Second, Nissani argued that there were still issues of material fact as to whether Volvo terminated the 2016 LOI in bad faith, and with wrongful intent, which prevented summary judgment. The court rejected this argument because there was evidence that Volvo extended the deadlines multiple times in an attempt to try to work with Nissani. It was only after Nissani failed to meet the extended deadlines that Volvo terminated the agreement. Third, the court rejected Nissani's argument that the lower court judge erred when it found that the proposed dealership was not covered under the CFA. The court reasoned that the CFA only applies to merchandise that is offered to the public. Finally, the court rejected Nissani's argument in connection to its unjust enrichment claim because it considered the 2016 LOI an express contract.

Torres v. Botanic Tonics, LLC, No. 23-CV-01460-VC, 2023 WL 8852754 (N.D. Cal. Dec. 21, 2023). Plaintiffs filed suit against the manufacturer of a drink called Feel Free, and two retailers who sold Feel Free, alleging violations of California's Unfair Competition Law. One of the named defendants was 7-Eleven, whose store sold the drink to plaintiff Romulo Torres ("Torres"). In support of its motion to dismiss, 7-Eleven argued that it did not have a duty to disclose information to Torres under the unfair-practices prong of California's Unfair Competition Law because there was no preexisting duty to disclose the relevant information from any other source of law. The court rejected this argument, and instead held that a party may have a duty to disclose under the unfair-practices prong even if no other source of law already imposes such a duty. The court noted that there has never been a prerequisite for a court to find a violation of a duty to disclose in common law or statutory law to aid in its analysis regarding the duty under the unfair-practices prong.

F. NEGLIGENCE

General Security Indemnity Co. of Arizona v. Felix F. Callari, Inc., No. FST-CV-22-6056679-S, 2023 WL 5928083 (Super. Ct. Sept. 7, 2023) (Court denied franchisor's motion to dismiss because the franchisee met the applicable burden for establishing a negligence claim in its amended complaint).

G. OTHER CLAIMS

Carolina Beverage Corp. v. FIJI Water Co., 102 Cal.App.5th 538, 321 Cal.Rptr.3d 647 (May 30, 2024). A bottled water manufacturer and its distributor each timely appealed after a jury found for the plaintiff distributor on its breach of contract and breach of the implied covenant of good faith claims, awarding damages of $1,993,670. The jury rejected the plaintiff's fraudulent concealment claim. Before the court entered judgment, manufacturer FIJI moved for judgment notwithstanding the verdict ("JNOV"), which the trial court denied. The court also issued an order awarding distributor Carolina Beverage $4,343,712 in attorneys' fees and costs. There were three issues on appeal: (1) whether constructive termination was a viable theory for recovery; (2) whether the trial court erred in two evidentiary rulings; and (3) whether the trial court abused its discretion in awarding attorneys' fees and costs in this amount. The court of appeals held constructive termination was not a viable theory for recovery because it is not a viable theory under California common law, the agreement didn't contain a constructive termination provision, and Carolina Beverage continued under the contract and did not treat the agreement as terminated. The court thus reversed the trial court's denial of a JNOV on the jury's verdicts on the breach of contract and breach of implied covenant claims and directed the trial court to enter judgment for FIJI on those claims.

City Calibration Centers Inc. v. Heath Consultants Inc., No. 22-CV-7845 (JS)(ST), 2024 WL 1345330 (E.D.N.Y. Mar. 29, 2024). City Calibration Centers, Inc. ("Distributor") brought action against a developer of calibration devices, Health Consultants Inc. ("Developer") alleging Developer began advertising and selling the products directly to consumers in area served by Distributor, and asserting claims for breach of contract, promissory estoppel, fraudulent inducement, unfair competition, and tortious interference with economic advantage. Developer filed a motion to dismiss for failure to state a claim. The court found that Distributor failed to state a claim for fraudulent inducement, tortious interference and unconscionable injury to support its promissory estoppel claim. However, Distributor sufficiently alleged applicability of merchant exception to statute of frauds, formation of distribution agreement, and its claim for unfair competition by Developer. The court found that Distributor plausibly alleged a valid and enforceable contract with a confirmatory email, and further, if the agreement was enforceable, that would support a finding that Developer misappropriated any advantage by entering Distributor's market and unfairly competing.

H. PROMISSORY ESTOPPEL

Dry Tech 24/7, Inc. v. The Clorox Co., No. 22-61291-CIV, 2023 WL 9064671 (D. Fla. December 18, 2023). The District Court of the Southern District of Florida recommended the dismissal of a distributor's promissory estoppel and detrimental reliance claim against The Clorox Company's ("Clorox") after the distributor alleged Clorox failed to supply distributor with sufficient products to meet its monthly minimum purchase requirement since the distributor was unable to establish a definitive promise by Clorox to supply a specific quantity of product. The only promise made by Clorox was to grant Dry Tech distributor rights, which promise was fulfilled. This case is discussed in Chapter 4, Section I, Subsection A.

Branches Co. v. Wilkinson, No. 23-cv-02576-GPG-STV, 2024 WL 3402710 (D. Colo. Apr. 30, 2024). Franchisor, Footprint Floors, LLC ("Franchisor") filed an action seeking a permanent injunction against a franchisee and its affiliate and their respective owners (collectively "Viking Floors"), after they founded and opened a competing business allegedly using Franchisor's confidential information. The parties entered into a stipulation for entry of permanent injunction enjoining Viking Floors from operating competing businesses in the area restricted in the franchise agreement, and requiring the return of all confidential information. The Franchisor then filed a motion for attorneys' fees against all Viking Floors. The Magistrate Judge recommended that the court grant Franchisor's motion for attorneys' fees against its franchisee and owner, but deny it with respect to the affiliate, on the basis that the affiliate was not a signatory or party to the franchise agreement containing the attorneys' fee shifting provision. The Magistrate Judge found no merit in the estoppel argument since the Franchisor could not establish how it relied on the affiliate when entering into the franchise agreement, especially since the affiliate did not exist at the time the parties entered into the franchise agreement. This case is discussed in Chapter 4, Section VI.

II. Non-Compete, Non-Solicitation Covenants

Cookie Dough Bliss Franchising, LLC v. Feed Your Soul Minnesota, LLC, No. CV 23-1552 (JWB/TNL), 2023 WL 4901292 (D. Minn. Aug. 1, 2023). The United States District Court for the District of Minnesota considered whether to grant a temporary injunction in favor of Cookie Dough Bliss Franchising ("Cookie Dough Bliss") against a former franchisee for violating the non-compete clause in a franchise agreement when it opened a new cookie-dough business in the same location but with a new recipe and updated signage. The new location was dubbed "UnBakeable."

In considering whether irreparable harm was likely to exist in the absence of an injunction, the district court first determined that Cookie Dough Bliss had not established the existence of any consumer confusion, in part because Cookie Dough Bliss's own website contributed to any confusion by still including references to its former franchise location. Although Cookie Dough Bliss argued that its ability to re-franchise was frustrated by UnBakeable's competition, the district court found that because Cookie Dough Bliss was not yet registered to sell franchises in the State of Minnesota, and its closest location was more than 1,000 miles away, that any potential harm was speculative, uncertain, and not immediate. The court further dismissed Cookie Dough Bliss's concern that other franchisees would disregard the terms of their agreements as speculative, and unable to support a finding of irreparable harm. Finally, because the franchise agreement provided for liquidated damages in the amount of $100,000 for a breach of the non-compete provision, the district court rejected the concept that money damages would be inadequate to compensate for the harm.

As to whether a likelihood of success on the merits existed, the court focused on whether the noncompete covenant was enforceable. The covenant here was defined as being within a radius of thirty miles of the "Location", but the "Location" was defined as the area within 100 miles of Minneapolis, Minnesota—effectively setting out a 130-mile non-compete radius around Minneapolis. The court concluded that it was unclear whether the non-compete provision served a legitimate purpose, both because Cookie Dough Bliss was not registered to sell franchises in Minnesota and because it was not likely the scope of the non-compete provision was reasonable. Finally, the district court determined that the impact on the former franchisee's would have been definite and significant, making the balance of harms weigh in their favor, and that public interest considerations were neutral—ultimately denying the injunction.

Deslandes v. McDonald's USA, LLC, 81 F.4th 699 (7th Cir. 2023), cert. denied, No. 23-562, 2024 WL 1143666 (S. Ct. Mar. 18, 2024). The Seventh Circuit Court of Appeals vacated an order dismissing antitrust claims that non-compete provisions in McDonald's franchise agreements constituted antitrust violations. This case is discussed in Chapter 6, Section II.

Baldwin v. Express Oil Change, LLC, No. 119859, 2023 WL 8445825 (N.D. Ga. Dec. 6, 2023). Plaintiff worked as an employee for various franchisees of defendant Express Oil Change, LLC ("LLC") for more than two decades. Plaintiff was ultimately promoted to a senior managerial role where he was tasked with overseeing the operations of eighteen stores. Eventually, Express sought to buy out the LLC's stores and convert the franchised stores into corporate stores. The owners of the LLC approached Plaintiff and proposed an offer in exchange for the Plaintiff signing two contracts. One contained a restrictive covenant, and the other was an asset purchase agreement for Plaintiff's stock in another LLC. The owners told Plaintiff they could not review the agreements prior to consenting. After pushing back, the Plaintiff eventually signed the agreements. Express and Plaintiff were unable to reach an agreement on Plaintiff's salary, which led to the Plaintiff resigning from their position. Thereafter, the Plaintiff considered starting an independent repair shop in violation of the restrictive covenant.

Express sought to enforce the covenant. As a result, plaintiff filed suit in Georgia seeking a declaration that the restrictive covenant was unenforceable under the Georgia Restrictive Covenants Act ("GRCA"). Plaintiff argued that the terms of the covenant had unreasonable restrictions in terms of time, geography and scope. The trial court agreed and granted a preliminary injunction and identified the sections of the agreement that were unreasonable. The trial court revised the relevant sections of the agreement to reduce its scope through "blue penciling." On appeal, Express argued that the time and geographic scope of the original covenant was reasonable and that the trial court exceeded its authority when it revised the agreement.

The appellate court first considered the enforceability of the geographic restrictions by applying Georgia law. Section 13-8-56(2) of the GRCA creates a presumption that the geographic territory is reasonable if one of the following subsections is satisfied: (A) the total distance of the provision is also reasonable; (B) the agreement lists particular competitors as prohibited employers for a specified time after the term of employment or a business or commercial relationship; or (C) both (A) and (B) are satisfied. The court focused on subsection (A) in its analysis. The court held that the trial court did not abuse its discretion when it found that subsection (A) was not satisfied. Express failed to establish a legitimate business interest for restricting Plaintiff's activities beyond its prior service area.

The appellate court then considered the reasonableness of the time restriction under Georgia law. The GRCA provides rebuttable presumptions for a court to apply when determining the reasonableness of time for a restrictive covenant. The trial court applied Section 13-8-57(b) which provides that any restraint of more than two years against a former employee is presumed unreasonable. Express argued on appeal that the trial court should have applied Section 13-8-57(d) which states that a restriction of five years or more in the context of a covenant being enforced against the owner or seller is presumed unreasonable. The appellate court agreed with Express because it considered Plaintiff a "seller" as defined by the GRCA and partly vacated the preliminary injunction to the extent that it altered the duration of the agreement. The court held that Section 13-8-57(d) applies to "an executive employee of the business who receives, at a minimum, consideration in connection with a sale of all or a material part of one of the five enumerated interests."

JTH Tax LLC v. Foster, No. 23-00005, 2023 WL 5938983 (W.D. Pa. Sept. 12, 2023). The United States District Court for the Western District of Pennsylvania dismissed plaintiff franchisor, Liberty Tax Service's ("Liberty") complaint pursuant to Rule 12(b)(6). Specifically, the court dismissed with prejudice Liberty's request for injunctive relief to enforce a non-competition and non-solicitation covenant. However, the court denied the franchisee's motion to dismiss Liberty's breach of contract claim as time-barred—and whether a laches defense applies with respect to Liberty's request for the return of its materials, holding that these were questions of fact that could not be decided at the dismissal stage.

The defendant franchisee entered into the relevant franchise agreement with Liberty in September 2015. Upon termination of the franchise agreement, franchisee agreed to a covenant not to compete against Liberty or to solicit Liberty customers, as well as a promise "to refrain forever" from interfering or attempting to interfere with Liberty's business relationships and from using or disclosing Liberty's confidential information and trade secrets.

Liberty terminated the franchise agreement with franchisee on June 9, 2020, for failure to cure both monetary and non-monetary breaches. Liberty discovered that the franchisee began operating a competing tax service under the name "Foster Tax Services," and openly soliciting Liberty's clients while she was still a Liberty franchisee. Liberty asserts that Foster Tax submitted more tax returns in 2021 than the franchisee had submitted in the 2020 tax season and that Foster Tax continued to operate out of the same Grove City location in 2022, with the same telephone number, advertising on its website that it has serviced customers "for nearly five years" and "offers the same friendly and accurate service" despite its name change.

Liberty sought to enjoin defendant's tax preparation services, diversion of business, soliciting customers and using confidential information and trade secrets. Liberty also sought an order requiring delivery of all originals and copies of the Operation Manual, customer lists and contact information, customer tax returns and related files.

The court held that under the Virginia choice of law contained in the franchise agreement, prospective enforcement of the two-year non-compete would not be granted because enforcement was two years seven months beyond the contractual rights, and the delay was entirely within Liberty's control. The court held that the delay reflects Liberty's lack of due diligence in monitoring and enforcing its contractual rights.

The court did not immediately reject, however, Liberty's claim for return of property under Pennsylvania state law. The court held that this was an equitable claim, subject to the defense of laches, which was a rebuttable defense which could not be resolved on the face of the complaint. The court's also confirmed that it had jurisdiction under the Defense of Trade Secrets Act of 2016. The court concluded that Liberty Tax had properly alleged that there was a direct nexus between its confidential information and trade secrets and interstate commerce through its national network of tax preparation centers.

HOA Franchising, LLC v. MS Foods, LLC, No. 1:23-CV004096-ELR, 2023 WL 9692401 (N.D. Ga. Dec. 20, 2023). The United States District Court for the Northern District of Georgia granted, in part, HOA Franchising, LLC ("Hooters") motion for preliminary injunction against a former franchisee, MS Foods, LLC ("Franchisee") after the Franchisee was terminated for repeated defaults, including failing to meet operational standards, failing to pay amounts due as a result of Franchisee's indemnification obligations under the franchise agreement, and engaging in an unauthorized transfer. The court granted Hooter's request to enjoin the Franchisee from operating a Hooters restaurant, using the Hooters marks, operating any competitive business within a three-mile radius, and making any representations about being associated with Hooters. But the court "blue-penciled" the portion of the post-term non-competition provision in the franchise agreement to the extent that it prohibited the former Franchisee from operating any competitive business in any "any other territory of Plaintiffs' franchisees or affiliates." The court found that Hooters had established a substantial likelihood of success on the merits of its cases given the large amount of uncontroverted evidence in support of the multiple contract breaches. The court also found that Hooters had a legitimate business interest in enforcing the non-compete and it was reasonable in scope and duration. The court, however, rejected Hooter's assertion that the non-compete was reasonable in geographic scope. First, Hooter's non-compete failed to specify the other franchisees or affiliates whose territories protected by the restriction, in other words, it failed to contain language restricting the provision to only those franchisees or affiliates in existence at the time of the termination of the franchise agreement). Further, the provision failed to define the size of the protected territory of any other franchisee or affiliate. Because the court was unable to accurately assess whether the total distance encompassed by the provisions of the non-compete covenant was reasonable, the court "blue-penciled" the provision and excised this geographic restriction before otherwise granting the preliminary injunction against the franchisee.

SpeeDee Worldwide, LLC v. Toppa, No. 24-CV-10274, 2024 WL 1558386 (D. Mass. Apr. 10, 2024). The district court granted franchisor-plaintiff's motion for preliminary injunction and entered an injunction because plaintiff established (1)likelihood of success on the merits; (2) that it would suffer irreparable harm in the absence of preliminary relief; and (3) the public's interest in enforcing non compete covenants outweighed the interest of defendant-franchisee's hardships in the face of evidence showing that the franchisee knowingly breached the franchise agreement and non compete covenant.

Smoothie King Franchises, Inc. v. Best Smoothie, Inc., No. 1:21-cv-04402-WMR, 2024 WL 67187 (N.D. Ga. Jan. 12, 2024). The United States District Court for the Northern District of Georgia denied defendants' motion for summary judgment finding there were genuine issues of facts and issues of credibility as to whether defendants were in active concert with a former Smoothie King franchisee to violate a franchise agreement's post-term restrictive covenant. There was a dispute as to whether the defendants had worked together to open a competing location after defendants were not approved by the franchisor to purchase the defaulting franchisee's location.

LeTip World Franchise LLC v. Long Island Social Media Group LLC, No. CV-24-00165-PHX-SMB, 2024 WL 380985 (D. Ariz. Feb. 1, 2024). The United States District Court for the District of Arizona granted franchisor, LeTip World Franchise LLC ("LeTip") a temporary restraining order against a former franchisee ("Franchisee") who violated its post-term non-compete by starting a networking and lead generation business that directly competed against LeTip. The Franchisee was terminated after failing to comply with a trademark cease and desist in response to the Franchisee affixing the word "Just" after the LeTip mark on his boat and publicizing the modified mark on social media. LeTip stated that the phrase was "deliberately infused with vulgar and sexual innuendo" in violation of the franchise agreement and brand standards. After termination, the Franchise then started its own competitive business and scheduled its "launch party" immediately prior to the start of a LeTip Chapter meeting in the same location with the intention of soliciting LeTip members to its new business networking group. The court found that LeTip met the standards for a preliminary injunction and was able to show that: (1) it was likely to succeed on the merits; (2) it was likely to suffer irreparable harm without an injunction; (3) the balance of equities tipped in its favor; and (4) an injunction was in the public interest. The restrictive covenants were found to be narrowly tailored and likely enforceable.

Defendants' creation of a new business venture in the same geographic territory seeking the same customers was causing irreparable harm, and likely to cause LeTip to lose current and prospective customers and good will. Additionally, in signing the Franchise Agreement, Franchisee acknowledged that any breach of the covenants would cause irreparable harm, for which there was no adequate remedy at law. The only means of effectively enforcing the provisions was injunctive relief. The court imposed the restraining order pending an evidentiary hearing on the request for a preliminary injunction.

LeTip World Franchise LLC v. Long Island Social Media Group, LLC, No. CV-24-00165-PHX-SMB, 2024 WL 1285621 (D. Ariz. Mar. 26, 2024). After the district court's earlier decision on February 1, 2024, it granted plaintiff's preliminary injunction after an evidentiary hearing because defendant did not have permission to modify the logo at issue and such modifications violated the franchise guidelines. The court also granted the injunction because the defendant had failed to follow the reasonable post-termination restrictive covenants when it created a new business venture that directly competed with the plaintiff in the same geographic territory seeking the same customers.

Eastern Wholesale Fence LLC v. Tucker, No. 323CV00280RJCSCR, 2024 WL 1009541 (W.D.N.C. Jan. 31, 2024). Court denied former employee's motion to dismiss complaint seeking enforcement of covenants not to compete, on grounds that further factual development was necessary to evaluate enforceability of noncompete agreement.

Clean Juice Franchising, LLC v. Charleston Juicing, LLC, No. 3:23-cv-00894-RJC-SCR, 2024 WL 2032947 (W.D.N.C. May 7, 2024). The United States District Court for the Western District of North Carolina granted a franchisee's motion for a limited evidentiary hearing to call a franchisor's corporate representatives to testify about alleged irreparable harm suffered by Plaintiff in the enforcement of noncompetition agreements with other franchisees and its history of permitting other Clean Juice franchisees to violate their non-compete agreements. The motion arose in the context of a request for a preliminary injunction filed by the franchisor, Clean Juice Franchising, LLC against its former franchisee, Charleston Juicing, LLC. The court recognized that where the franchisor has an history of permitting other franchisees to violate their non-competes without action, then franchisor's arguments for enforcing it are undermined, and the court ordered that the parties be permitted to present testimony at a hearing, and further, that the franchisor must produce at the hearing copies of any and all agreements entered into with its franchisees within the last two years where the franchisor expressly waived or limited its non-compete clauses contained within its franchise agreements.

III. Transfer Disputes

Wirtgen America, Inc. v. Hayden-Murphy Equipment Co., No. 3:22-cv-00308, 2023 WL 591704 (M.D. Tenn. Sept. 11, 2023). A Tennessee-based supplier filed an action seeking a declaratory judgment approving the termination of a Minnesota dealer based on transfer of ownership and loss of key employees, including its CEO, in violation of terms of distribution agreement. The Dealer asserted waiver, arguing that the changes occurred three years prior to the lawsuit and asserted a counterclaim for violations of Tennessee and Minnesota relationship statutes, breach of contract for selling to other Minnesota dealers, and violations of the implied covenant of good faith and fair dealing. The parties filed various motions, including one to strike the defense of waiver, to dismiss the counterclaim, for judgment on the pleadings, and for leave to amend the complaint.

The dealer's motion to strike the defense of waiver argued that the anti-waiver clause in the distribution agreement only applied to later violations, not belated action on the original violations. The trial court denied the motion, finding the anti-waiver clause broad enough to cover both circumstances. The supplier's motion to dismiss the counterclaim based on ripeness because termination had not actually occurred was denied because the court reasoned that seeking injunctive relief considering pending termination was both statutorily permitted and ripe. The court denied the motion for judgment on the pleadings, in part, because alternatively alleging violations of both Tennessee and Minnesota law was permissible at the pleading stage. The court also granted the motion in part because, while the distribution agreement prevented direct sales to consumers in the dealer's territory, the dealer conceded it was a non-exclusive dealer and therefore the supplier's sales to other Minnesota dealers were allowed under the agreement. The supplier's motion to amend was also granted because (1) contract statutes of limitation did not apply to a declaratory judgment action seeking to exercise supplier's right to termination under the distribution agreement; (2) the distribution agreement allowed for termination based on changes in ownership "or" control (not both); and (3) whether ownership changes were substantial was a fact question that did not prevent repleading.

Oakland Family Restaurants, Inc. v. American Dairy Queen Corp., No. 221CV12530TGBEAS, 2024 WL 1396258 (E.D. Mich. Mar. 31, 2024). Franchisee Oakland Family Restaurants and Franchisor Dairy Queen filed cross-motions for summary judgment on the issue of whether Franchisor could deny Franchisee's proposed ownership transfer. Franchisor had denied the transfer request based on the transferee's refusal to enter into Franchisor's new standardized franchise agreement, which included grandfathered provisions from previous agreements. The court denied Franchisee's motion for summary judgment and granted Franchisor's motion because Franchisee failed to present a genuine issue of fact concerning whether a breach occurred, failed to show it was entitled to declaratory judgment. The court also dismissed the promissory estoppel claim because there was an express contract between the parties. The court also held that Franchisor did not violate the Michigan Franchising Investment Act ("MFIL") by prohibiting restrictions on transfer of ownership without good cause because Franchisor presented ample evidence for its decision to not approve of proposed transfer without signing a new franchise agreement, including Franchisor's desire to modernize and standardize its franchise agreements across its entire franchise system, adapt to recent legal and regulatory changes, and remain competitive in the shifting economic landscape.

IV. Injunctive Relief

Autobar Systems of New Jersey v. Berg Liquor Systems, LLC, No. 23-3790 (MAS)(JBD), 2023 WL 5311499 (D.N.J. Aug. 17, 2023). Court denied motion for preliminary injunction, finding that Autobar had not established irreparable harm following a franchisor's termination of the franchise agreement, despite evidence that sales of Berg products accounted for eighty-five percent of Autobar's revenue. Fifteen percent of its sales came from other sources, so the business could continue operating, and the termination did not result in irreparable harm.

Vocelli, LLC v. JAF3, Inc., No. 1:23-cv-1284, 2023 WL 9105453 (E.D. Va. Sept. 20, 2023). The United States District Court for the Eastern District of Virginia granted a preliminary injunction in favor of pizza restaurant franchisor, Vocelli, LLC ("Vocelli") finding it met its burden of establishing that it (1) is likely to succeed on the merits; (2) is likely to suffer irreparable harm in the absence of relief; (3) the balance of equities tips in its favor; and (4) an injunction would be in the public interest. The court then ruled on supplemental briefings regarding the appropriate bond amount to be posted by Vocelli, rejecting defendant's request for a $650,000 bond based on its initial investment. The court found no correlation between the initial investment of the defendant and potential damages if the plaintiff is found to be wrongfully enjoined and instead found that the parties waived the bond requirement through the operative terms of the franchise agreement.

3 N Holding Corp. v. LUKOIL North America LLC, No. CV 24-05102 (GC) (TJB), 2024 WL 3355612 (D.N.J. July 9, 2024). The district court granted a preliminary injunction and temporary restraining order under the lower threshold of the Petroleum Marketing Practices Act ("PMPA"). The court found that the franchisee met the required elements. This case is discussed in Chapter 3, Section II.

Baskin-Robbins Franchising LLC v. Blu Moo Ice Cream Inc., No. 1:24-CV-00293-JRS-CSW, 2024 WL 2730252 (S.D. Ind. May 7, 2024). Baskin-Robbins moved for a preliminary injunction and default judgment against franchisee Blu Moo because defendants breached the franchise agreement and failed to remove Baskin-Robbins' proprietary marks after termination. The magistrate judge recommended entering the preliminary injunction and granting default judgment to Baskin-Robbins because defendants failed to appear or respond despite being served a copy of the pleadings. The court adopted these recommendations in ***Baskin-Robbins Franchising LLC v. Blu Moo Ice Cream Inc.***, No. 1:24-CV-00293-JRS-CSW, 2024 WL 2722900 (S.D. Ind. May 28, 2024).

More Automotive Products, Inc. v. Dollar Rent A Car, Inc., No. 2:22-CV-457-SPC-KCD, 2024 WL 3103604 (M.D. Fla. May 21, 2024). Plaintiff ran a Dollar Rent-A-Car franchise in Puerto Rico for decades. After franchisor Dollar Rent a Car terminated the franchise agreement, plaintiff sued in the U.S. District Court for the District of Puerto Rico, asserted a claim for unlawful termination of the franchise, and moved for a preliminary injunction and expedited hearing to enjoin the termination. Plaintiff then voluntarily dropped that case and filed a new action in the United States District Court for the Middle District of Florida and again moved for temporary and preliminary injunctive relief. The district court granted plaintiff's motion for an expedited injunction hearing because plaintiff had been pursuing temporary injunctive relief for the previous two months with the franchisor's knowledge and was entitled to be heard on an expedited basis.

Redbox+ International, LLC v. Waste Management Solutions, Inc., No. 8:23-cv-393-CEH-SPF, 2023 WL 8438571 (M.D. Fla. Oct. 5, 2023). Franchisor, Redbox+ International, LLC ("RedBox") filed a lawsuit against a former multi-unit franchisee of Redbox ("WMS") for breach of post-termination obligations under the franchise agreement, along with Lanham Act violations. After entering into the franchise agreements, the defendant franchisee failed to make payments for purchased equipment and was declared in default. The following month the franchise agreements were terminated due to WMS's breaches. WMS continued to operate its RedBox+ franchises, responding to RedBox that there was "nothing [franchisor] could do about it." During this time of operation, RedBox received complaints that the defendant engaged in a hit-and-run accident and released the contents of its dumpsters on private property. The could found that (1) under Pennsylvania law, the elements of a breach of contract were satisfied, and the termination of the franchise agreements was justified; (2) WMS breached its post-termination obligations under the franchise agreements and infringed on RedBox's trademarks and trade dress; and (3) WMS's unauthorized use of RedBox's mark and trade dress was likely to cause consumer confusion. The court granted RedBox's motion for a default judgment in part, ordering a permanent injunction against WMS, barring it from operating in the territories covered by the franchise agreements and from using Redbox's trademarks and trade dress.

TotalEnergies Marketing Puerto Rico Corp. v. Rivera-Robles, No. CV 23-1566 (ADC), 2024 WL 1831166 (D.P.R. Apr. 26, 2024). The district court adopted the magistrate judge's report and recommendation to issue a preliminary injunction in favor of plaintiff over defendants' objections because the defendants' objections simply rehashed arguments previously considered by the magistrate and because the injunction request was factually unopposed by the defendants. The court also held that the federal claims gave the court federal jurisdiction to decide the matter.

HP Holding LLC v. Red Roof Inns, Inc., No. CV 23-20907 (RBK/MJS), 2024 WL 2720463 (D.N.J. May 28, 2024). The United States District Court for the District of New Jersey granted a hotel franchisor's motion to dismiss plaintiffs' tortious interference and breach of contract claims with prejudice because they were time barred under New Jersey's six-year statute of limitations and the three-year limitation period in the parties' franchise agreement. The court also granted defendants' motion to dismiss plaintiffs' claim under the New Jersey Franchise Practices Act ("NJFPA") without prejudice because the allegations fell short of the $35,000 threshold required to state a claim under the statute. The court granted plaintiffs' motion to amend its complaint provided it did not re-raise claims the court dismissed with prejudice.

Muffler Man Supply Co. v. TSE Auto Service, Inc., No. 2:24-CV-11706, 2024 WL 3493461 (E.D. Mich. July 3, 2024). The United States District Court for the Eastern District of Michigan granted a franchisor plaintiff's ex parte motion for a temporary restraining order ("TRO") alleging claims under the Lanham Act and the Anti--cybersquatting Consumer Protection Act. The court granted the motion because TSE, a franchisee of automotive parts supplier Muffler Man, planned to open a competing business close to its Muffler Man franchise location and continued to use Muffler Man's trademarks and social media to advertise. The district court held that franchisor Muffler Man sufficiently demonstrated entitlement to an ex parte TRO because all the relevant factors weighed in Muffler Man's favor. Muffler Man sufficiently alleged likelihood of success on the merits of its claims, that Muffler Man would suffer irreparable injury without the TRO, that franchisee TSE willfully incurred the risk of the non-compete agreement enforcement, and enforcement of contractual duties was in the public interest.

Because TSE was not present to explain the proper amount of a bond, the court did not require one, but reserved the right to revisit the issue.

Hyundai Construction Equipment Americas, Inc. v. Southern Lift Trucks, LLC, No. SC-2023-0109, 2023 WL 7266935 (Ala. S. Ct., Nov. 3, 2023). In this case, the trial court entered a temporary restraining order and preliminary injunction prohibiting Hyundai from allowing its dealers to sell certain equipment in its franchisee Southern's designated territories, or to otherwise advertise that other dealers were authorized to sell in those territories. Southern believed that another dealer was advertising and selling in violation of the court's orders and filed a motion for contempt, including a reply brief and additional affidavits filed less than 30 minutes before the contempt hearing. The trial court granted the contempt motion and Hyundai appealed. The Alabama Supreme Court reversed, holding that the reply filed shortly before the hearing, which relied solely on new affidavits and documentary evidence rather than live testimony at the hearing, violated Hyundai's due process rights, and prevented Hyundai from fully defending itself in the contempt proceeding.

Oakberry SD UTC, LLC v. Oakberry Acai, Inc., No. 3:23-CV-01883-BEN-MSB, 2023 WL 7508163 (S.D. Cal. Nov. 13, 2023). The district court denied plaintiff's *ex parte* Application for a Temporary Restraining Order seeking injunctive relief preventing a compelled arbitration. In doing so, the court rejected the plaintiff's argument that it would suffer irreparable harm if it were forced to participate in the arbitration. The court distinguished the facts of this case from precedent that found irreparable harm for compelling an arbitration proceeding by noting that the plaintiff voluntarily entered into the licensing agreement which contained the arbitration clause at issue.

L.A. International Corp. v. Prestige Brands Holdings, Inc., No. 18-6809-MWF (MRWX), 2024 WL 2272384 (C.D. Cal. May 20, 2024). Plaintiff filed suit against defendants for unlawful price discrimination and unfair competition in violation of the Robinson-Patman Act ("RPA"), California's Unfair Practices Act ("UPA"), and California's Unfair Competition Law ("UCL"). A jury found in favor of plaintiffs on their RPA and UPA claims. The court entered judgment after deciding the remaining claim for injunctive relief under the UPA and UCL. In response, the defendants moved for a new trial and the plaintiffs moved for permanent injunction. The court denied defendants' motion for a new trial because the trial court did not err in instructing the jury as argued by the defendants. The court granted four of the five proposed terms of plaintiffs' motion for permanent injunctive relief.

Spimerica Access Solutions, LLC v. Palazzani Industrie, S.P.A., No. 23-23222-Civ-Scola, 2023 WL 7545325 (S.D. Fla. Nov. 14, 2023). The United States District Court for the Southern District of Florida denied distributor's *ex parte* application for a preliminary injunction against its former manufacturer because the distributor ("Spimerica") was unable to establish its burden of showing a substantial likelihood of success on the merits. Spimerica and defendant entered into an exclusive distribution agreement ("EDA") under which Spimerica became the exclusive distributor of Palazzani lift machines in North America. Two years into the EDA, Palazzani threatened to terminate the EDA and begin selling products to customers directly unless Spimerica undertook cure procedures that Spimerica alleged were practically impossible to meet. At the hearing, neither party was more credible than the other and each set forth a narrative where either party could be responsible for multiple breaches of the EDA. The court therefore denied the preliminary injunction motion.

HouseMaster SPV LLC v. Burke, No. CV2113411MASTJB, 2024 WL 493272 (D.N.J. Feb. 8, 2024). District court granted franchisor's voluntary motion to dismiss, agreeing with the franchisor that the court's preliminary injunction and enforcement of a franchise agreement's restrictive covenants provided a sufficient remedy against a former franchisee.

InterRad Medical, Inc. v. Aquilant Ltd., No. 23-CV-3709 (ECT/DTS), 2024 WL 913343 (D. Minn. Mar. 4, 2024). The court denied plaintiff's motion for a preliminary injunction for a breach of contract claim where the former exclusive distributor failed to cease selling plaintiff's product after terminating the distribution agreement because that specific task was not included in the post-termination obligations.

EYM Pizza of Georgia LLC v. Pizza Hut LLC, No. 3:24-cv-0646-x, 2024 WL 1444992 (N.D. Tex. Apr. 2, 2024). The United States District Court for the Northern District of Texas denied a multi-unit Pizza Hut restaurant franchisee's ("Franchisee"), motion for a preliminary injunction to enjoin its franchisor, Pizza Hut LLC ("Pizza Hut") from terminating Franchisee's ability to operate its restaurants. The Franchisee began struggling to operate its 142 restaurants starting in 2022 when hyperinflation eroded margins. The Franchisor sent multiple notices of concern and default throughout 2022 and 2023 and Pizza Hut agreed to enter into a forbearance agreement with the Franchisee instead of terminating the franchise agreements. The court found that the Franchisee did not show a substantial likelihood of success on the merits as Pizza Hut was within its right to terminate the forbearance agreement under the unambiguous conditions for forbearance. Pizza Hut also did not tortiously interfere with Franchisee's contracts and prospective relations or sabotage Franchisee by speaking with Franchisee's lenders as Pizza Hut was permitted to do under the forbearance agreement.

Honest Abe Roofing Franchise, Inc. v. DCH & Associates, LLC, No 2:22-cv-00387-JRS-MG, 2024 WL 3161264 (S.D. Ind. April 4, 2024). Court denied in part motion for preliminary injunction on noncompete that was nearly expired. This case is discussed in Chapter 8, Section XI.

Popeyes Louisiana Kitchen, Inc. v. Florida Pop, LLC, No. 1:23-cv-23955-KMM, 2024 WL 1564668 (S.D. Fla. Apr. 4, 2024). The

United States District Court for the Southern District of Florida granted franchisor, Popeyes Louisiana Kitchen, Inc. ("Popeyes") a preliminary injunction against a multi-unit Popeyes franchisee ("Franchisee") that continued to operate under the Popeyes brand without authorization after the termination of franchise agreements. The defendant had operated fifty-two Popeyes restaurants in Florida. Popeyes terminated the franchise agreements for multiple breaches but entered into a limited license to allow Franchisee an opportunity to sell the franchises. The magistrate judge recommended granting the preliminary injunction, concluding Franchisee did not meet the critical deadlines set forth in the limited license agreement between the parties, including the requirement to finalize a sale of the restaurants by the agreed upon dates. The court disagreed with the defendant's argument that the submission of a last-minute asset purchase agreement tolled the expiration of the limited license agreement and continued operation under the Popeyes name, which likely caused customer confusion and damage to Popeyes' brand reputation. The court found that the harm to Popeyes from non-action would outweigh any harm to the defendants from the injunction.

Vital Distributions, LLC v. Pepperidge Farm, Inc., No. 2:22-cv-00319-MCE-CKD, 2024 WL 1484198 (E.D. Cal. Apr. 6, 2024). Plaintiff, Vital Distributions, LLC ("Vital"), entered into a Consignment Agreement ("Agreement") with Defendant, Pepperidge Farm, Inc. ("Pepperidge Farm"), granting Vital the exclusive right to distribute Pepperidge Farm's products within a defined territory. The Agreement included provisions regarding commissions earned by Vital on sales and distribution of consigned products to retail stores. Pepperidge Farm attempted to get Vital to acknowledge "retail stores" did not include e-commerce prior to signing the Agreement, but Vital refused. However, the parties moved forward with the Agreement. During the COVID-19 pandemic, demand for consigned products surged, but Pepperidge Farm allegedly allocated products disproportionately, favoring e-commerce sales over distribution to Vital, and then refused to pay commissions to Vital for e-commerce sales fulfilled through Amazon facilities within its defined territory. Vital filed a lawsuit against Pepperidge Farm, alleging breach of contract, breach of the implied covenant of good faith and fair dealing, an accounting, and declaratory relief. Pepperidge Farm moved to dismiss the claims, but the court denied the motion, finding the term "retail stores" ambiguous and concluding that Vital had sufficiently pleaded its claims. Shortly before the hearing on the motion for a preliminary injunction, Pepperidge Farm exercised a buyback provision in the Agreement seeking to repurchase the distributorship from Vital at reduced value, triggering Vital's request for a temporary restraining order. The court found that the term "retail stores" in the Agreement was ambiguous and could reasonably include e-commerce sales fulfilled through brick-and-mortar locations within Vital's territory. Pepperidge Farm's actions, including the exercise of the Buyback Provision, and withholding of commissions, were deemed potentially harmful to Vital's interests. The court granted Vital's motion for a preliminary injunction, enjoining Pepperidge Farm from further interference with Vital's operations and ordering Pepperidge Farm to continue paying commissions to Vital.

AAMCO Transmissions, LLC v. Gleason and Dannicole, LLC, No. 2:24-cv-00300, 2024 WL 2231361 (E.D. Pa April 9, 2024). The United States District Court for the Eastern District of Pennsylvania granted a preliminary injunction in favor of plaintiff franchisor AAMCO Transmissions against its former franchisee. The preliminary injunction was warranted to prevent the former franchisee from operating a transmission repair business at the location of its former franchised AAMCO location under the AAMCO trademark despite the termination of its franchise agreement for cause.

JTH Tax, LLC v. Samb, No. 3:24-cv-102, 2024 WL 1704537 (S.D. Ohio Apr. 19, 2024). The United States District Court for the Southern District of Ohio granted plaintiff, Liberty Tax Service ("Liberty"), a preliminary injunction against a former franchisee after previously granting Liberty a temporary restraining order prohibiting defendants from: (1) offering tax preparation services within a certain area; (2) using Liberty's confidential information and trade secrets; (3) using Liberty's trademarks; and (4) using the telephone number previously associated with the former Liberty franchise.

Martin Saturn of Ontario, Inc. v. Subaru of America, Inc., No. ED CV23-00853 JAK, 2024 WL 3305773 (C.D. Cal. June 7, 2024).

In this case, the Federal District Court for the Central District of California dismissed two counterclaims made by a defendant motor vehicle distributor, Subaru of America, Inc. ("Subaru") against one of its authorized dealers ("Dealer") for declaratory relief and for damages resulting from state motor vehicle law violations. The court granted Dealer's motion to dismiss the declaratory relief cause of action on the basis that Subaru was not able to state why the claim for declaratory relief would allow a remedy that is otherwise unavailable through Subaru's cause of action for breach of contract and breach of the implied covenant of good faith and fair dealing. The court concluded that declaratory relief requires an actual, present controversy and operates prospectively to relieve uncertainty and prevent future harm. Declaratory relief was unnecessary in this case when the alleged controversy had already ripened into a dispute that could be remedied through other causes of action. The court also dismissed Subaru's claim for damages resulting from Dealer's violations of certain California motor vehicle laws as the statute did not provide a private cause of action.

Real Property Management SPV, LLC v. Truitt, No. 2:24-cv-00184-DAK, 2024 WL 3567866 (D. Utah July 29, 2024). The United States District Court for the District of Utah granted a franchisor's motion for a preliminary injunction against a franchisee who unliterally terminated a franchise agreement in violation of the franchise agreement terms and immediately began a competing business. The court found that the franchisor established a substantial likelihood of success on the merits as the non-compete was valid and enforcement as written, the non-compete was supported by adequate consideration and entered into in good faith, the non-compete was necessary to protect the goodwill of the franchise system and other franchisees, the terms were reasonable, and the franchisor faced real on-going potential harm which outweighed any potential harm to the former franchisee defendant.

V. Damages

Little Caesar Enterprises, Inc. v. S&S Pizza Enterprises, Inc., No. 21-11776, 2023 WL 5489021 (E.D. Mich. Aug. 24, 2023). In this case, the United States District Court for the Eastern District of Michigan granted an unopposed motion for summary judgment awarding liquidated damages and counsel fees to the franchisor, Little Caesar Enterprises, Inc. The defendant franchisee entity and its two key person obligors breached their franchise agreements by failing to address multiple notices to cure and unilaterally closing their locations. The court noted that Michigan law did not define "good cause" for termination, but the court held that the facts supported good cause for termination, that the liquidated damages clause was reasonable, and that counsel fees under the contract should be awarded to compensate the franchisor for the financial burden of proving good cause for termination.

M&D Cycles, Inc. v. American Honda Motor Co., No. 22-cv-172-SM-AJ, 2023 WL 7182107 (D.N.H. Sept. 29, 2023) Plaintiff was a terminated dealer whose damages expert's testimony was excluded under Federal Rule of Evidence 702 and *Daubert* in a case involving motor vehicle manufacturer's obligations to repurchase certain tools, equipment, and other materials after termination. This case is discussed in Chapter 8, Section X.

JTH Tax LLC v. Sanchez d/b/a Triple J, No. 22-CV-6160, 2023 WL 6798456, 2023 WL 6813449 (S.D.N.Y. Oct. 16, 2023). The plaintiff franchisor, Liberty Tax Service ("Liberty"), brought an action against the defendant franchisee and its owners for breaches of a franchise agreement. The dispute was settled with all defendants, except Don Varghese ("Varghese"). Liberty obtained a default judgment after Varghese failed to appear in court and sought $554,834.41 in damages. The damage calculation included amounts due under a promissory note related to the purchase of the franchised locations, interest at the rate of twelve percent, accounts receivable under a guaranty agreement and attorneys' fees and costs. The court found that Liberty had established its damage claims with reasonable certainty, based on the declarations of its regional directors, and that Varghese was not entitled to a set-off of the damages against the settlement amount paid by the other defendants because he failed to raise it as an affirmative defense. Varghese chose not to participate in the litigation by failing to appear and awarding him the right to set-off could incentivize others to ignore lawsuits brought against them. The court did reduce the amount of attorneys' fees requested by Liberty because all the timekeeper entries did not distinguish between work expended in plaintiff's claims against Varghese versus the other defendants.

Liberty Petroleum Realty, LLC v. Gulf Oil, LP, 2023 N.Y. Slip Op. 23353, 2023 WL 7599125 (N.Y. Sup. Ct. Nov. 14, 2023). Franchisor Liberty Petroleum Realty, LLC ("Liberty") filed a claim for tortious interference with contract against Gulf Oil, LP ("Gulf") alleging that Gulf induced Liberty's multi-unit gas station franchisee, Go-Green, to breach its franchise agreements and purchase gas from Gulf instead of Liberty. Gulf moved in limine for an order excluding lost profits and other damage testimony arguing that because Liberty already collected liquidated damages from Go-Green, it should not be allowed recovery against Gulf in an amount in excess of the contractual liquidated damages. Additionally, Go-Green agreed to indemnify Gulf for any claims made by Liberty against Gulf to induce Gulf to sell Go-Green gasoline. Gulf argued that allowing recovery against Gulf, which would ultimately be identified by Go-Green, defeats the bargain made by the franchisee under the franchise agreement.

In a case of first impression, the court rejected the argument that an agreed upon contractual limitation of damages should in any way limit potential recovery of damages against tortfeasors. The court was also not persuaded that Go-Green's decision to indemnify the party that allegedly committed the tortious interference should defeat a plaintiff's right to recovery. According to the court, tortfeasors should not enjoy contractual limitations of damages from the contract they were alleged to have tortiously induced a breach. Gulf's motion was denied.

Suh v. Pak, No. B320737, 2024 WL 768839 (Cal. Ct. App. Feb. 26, 2024). The California Court of Appeals affirmed a trial court's damages award in a franchisee's favor for lost profits based on the franchisor's failure to adhere to the non-compete provision in a purchase agreement which gave the franchisee exclusive rights to a specific territory. The court also affirmed the district court's decision to deny the franchisee any damages award for anticipated reverse royalties, finding that the expert witness that the franchisee presented at trial based its calculations on pure speculation and an insufficiently supported factual basis.

NGM Management Group, LLC v. Bareburger Group, LLC, No. 2023-01081, 1024, 2024 WL 781669 (N.Y. Sup. Ct. Feb. 27, 2024). The plaintiff, NGM Management Group, LLC ("Franchisee") operated five restaurants in Manhattan under franchise agreements with defendant, Bareburger Group, LLC ("Bareburger"). The restaurants encountered financial issues and Bareburger and Franchisee entered into a step-in-rights agreement. Plaintiff filed complaints against defendants alleging breaches of the franchise agreement, step-in-rights agreements and defendant filed a motion for summary judgment and counterclaims. The court granted summary judgment to Bareburger on liability for certain counterclaims and found that the liquidated damages provision was enforceable and not a penalty, as it bore a reasonable proportion to probable loss. This case is discussed in Chapter 4, Section I, Subsection A.

Wine Country Gateway Recreational Vehicle Park, LLC v. Eagle Energy, Inc., No. 2D CIV. B322766, 2024 WL 833422 (Cal. Ct. App. Feb. 28, 2024). The California Court of Appeals reversed a trial court's damages award for lost profits on a breach of contract claim, reasoning that the purchase contract clearly precluded lost profits as damages for early termination. This case is discussed in Chapter 4, Section I, Subsection A.

Carolina Beverage Corporation v. FIJI Water Company, LLC, 102 Cal.App.5th 538 (May 30, 2024). Carolina Beverage Corporation ("Distributor") brought an action against Fiji Water Company, LLC ("Fiji") alleging Fiji invaded around 85% of Distributor's territory without negotiating with Distributor as required by distribution agreement, and asserting claims for breach of contract, constructive termination, breach of the implied covenant of good faith and fair dealing, and concealment. Fiji appealed a jury verdict in favor of Distributor and denial of Fiji's motion for judgment notwithstanding the verdict, and granted distributor attorney fees and costs. The court found that that (1) the general rule under California common law is that a party may not seek contractual recovery on the basis of constructive termination; (2) distribution agreement did not contain constructive termination provision that could render distributor eligible for termination payment; (3) assuming constructive termination was viable theory under common law or distribution agreement, Distributor could not prevail on such theory to support contract claims; (4) manufacturer did not breach implied covenant of good faith and fair dealing; (5) any breach by manufacturer of covenant of good faith and fair dealing would not entitle distributor to termination payment; and (6) remand with direction for trial court to enter judgment in favor of Fiji on contract claims, rather than remand for new trial so that Distributor could pursue alternative measures of damages, was appropriate.

Bank United N.A. v. GC of Vineland, LLC, No. 18cv12879 (EP) (CLW), 2024 WL 1299024 (D.N.J. Mar. 27, 2024). In an unpublished decision, the United States District Court for the District of New Jersey held that franchisor, Golden Corral, was entitled to consequential damages of $1,168,368 in connection with the termination of a New Jersey Golden Corral restaurant franchise. The court found that Golden Corral lost profits when franchisees closed their restaurant and stopped paying royalties and marketing fund fees. The court also found that the franchisee failed to establish that Golden Corral acted unreasonably to trigger a violation of the New Jersey Franchise Practices Act.

Martin Saturn of Ontario, Inc. v. Subaru of America, Inc., No. ED CV23-00853 JAK (SHKx), 2024 WL 3305773 (C.D. Cal. June 7, 2024). In this case, the Federal District Court of Central California dismissed two counterclaims made by a defendant motor vehicle distributor, Subaru of America, Inc. ("Subaru") against one of its authorized dealers ("Dealer") for declaratory relief and for damages resulting from state motor vehicle law violations. The court granted Dealer's motion to dismiss the declaratory relief cause of action on the basis that Subaru was not able to why the claim for declaratory relief would allow a remedy that is otherwise unavailable through Subaru's cause of action for breach of contract and breach of the implied covenant of good faith and fair dealing. The court analyzed that declaratory relief requires an actual, present controversy and operates prospectively to relieve uncertainty and prevent future harm. Declaratory relief was unnecessary in this case when the alleged controversy has already ripened into a dispute that can be remedied through other causes of action. The court also dismissed Subaru's claim for damages resulting from Dealer's violations of certain California motor vehicle laws as the statute did not provide a private cause of action.

VI. Attorneys' Fees

G.P.P., Inc. v. Guardian Protection Products, Inc., No. 1:15-cv-00321-SKO, 2023 WL 7723234 (E.D. Cal. Nov. 15, 2023). The court granted plaintiff's motion for attorney's fees and denied defendant's motion for attorneys' fees citing ***Frog Creek Partners, LLC. v. Vance Brown, Inc.***, 206 Cal. App. 4th 515, 520 (2012) for the proposition that there can only be one prevailing party on a single contract under the California Civil Code Section 1717 governing the recovery of attorney's fees pursuant to an underlying contract. The court determined plaintiff succeeded on the pervading question and gravamen of the lawsuit and was the "prevailing party" successfully defending and prosecuting eight claims to the defendants, five claims and four claims, respectively.

Creative Management, Inc. v. 7514 Tonnelle Avenue, LLC, No. A-3050-20, 2023 WL 8450777 (N.J. Super. A.D. Dec. 6, 2023). Appellate court affirmed the district court's decision to award pre-judgment interest and attorneys' fees to the seller in proceeding against the buyer to enforce a credit agreement in New Jersey. This case is discussed in Chapter 8, Section XIX.

Sonesta RL Hotels Franchising, Inc. v. Patel and Lotus Sky, LLC, No. 1:23-cv-12548-JEK, 2024 WL 457046 (D. Mass. February 6, 2024). In this case, the court granted plaintiff franchisor Sonesta RL Hotels Franchising, Inc.'s ("Sonesta") motion for default judgment against the defendant franchisee for breach of contract and breach of the implied covenant of good faith and fair dealing, holding that Sonesta was entitled to damages and litigation costs. However, the court found that Sonesta's request for $27,957 in attorneys' fees and costs was not "reasonable" as required under the franchise agreement between the parties. Sonesta has failed to produce the required time and billing records. It had merely submitted an affidavit declaring the number of hours worked by four attorneys (2.4, 16.2, 38.6, and 15.1 hours) and one paralegal (3.6 hours) as well as their respective rates. The plaintiff was unable to establish to the court's satisfaction why it would take over 75 hours to file a complaint, serve defendants, file a motion for an entry of default, and file a motion and reduced the requested attorneys' fees to $20,800.

Trade Links, LLC v. Bi-Qem SA de CV, No. 3:19-CV-00308 (KAD), 2024 WL 198024 (D. Conn. Jan. 18, 2024). After obtaining a jury verdict in its favor, plaintiff Trade Links, a sales representative working under a written sales commission agreement with defendant Bi-Qem, sought an award of attorneys' fees and costs. Plaintiff sought to recover $1,750,054.79 incurred in connection with litigation. The district court noted that the litigation was marred by excessive and unreasonable litigation strategies by all parties and found that six of plaintiff's original ten claims had either been dismissed or abandoned before trial. For these reasons, the district court applied a straight percentage reduction in the amount of attorneys' fees being pursued. In so doing, the court reduced the award by fifty percent, awarding plaintiff $712,303.27 in attorneys' fees. The court also reduced the amount of costs plaintiff sought for similar reasons, reducing the recoverable amount to $67,950.80. In total, the district court awarded the plaintiff $775,844.27 because it had prevailed on its remaining claims before the jury.

CajunLand Pizza, LLC v. Marco's Franchising, LLC, No. 3:20-CV-536, 2024 WL 1014027 (N.D. Ohio Mar. 8, 2024). Former Louisiana pizza shop franchisees moved for reconsideration of an order granting attorneys' fees to a franchisor based on recent decisional law regarding Ohio's interpretation and enforceability of unilateral attorneys' fees provisions under Ohio law. The court held that the case was not controlling, denied the motion for reconsideration, and awarded most of the fees that the defendant sought.

Branches Company, LLC f/k/a Footprints Floors, LLC v. Wilkinson, No. 23-cv-02576-GPG-STV, 2024 WL 3402710 (D. Colo. April 30, 2024). Franchisor, Footprint Floors, LLC ("Franchisor") filed an action seeking a permanent injunction against a franchisee, its owner and an affiliate of franchisee ("Viking Floors") and its owner after they founded and opened Viking Floors, a competing business allegedly using Franchisor's confidential information. The parties entered into a stipulation for entry of permanent injunction enjoining the franchisee, its owner and Viking Floors from operating competing businesses in the area restricted in the franchise agreement and requiring the return of all confidential information. The Franchisor then filed a motion for attorneys' fees against all three defendants. A US Magistrate Judge recommended that the court grant Franchisor's motion for attorneys' fees against its franchisee and owner, but deny it with respect to Viking Floors on the basis that Viking Floors was not a signatory or party to the franchise agreement containing the attorneys' fee shifting provision. The Magistrate Judge rejected Franchisor's argument that Viking Floors was a "closely related defendant-signatory" or successor company. Further, the judge declined to expand these doctrines beyond determining the enforceability of a contract's forum selection clause. Finally the Magistrate Judge found no merit in the estoppel argument since the Franchisor could not establish how it relied on Viking Floors when entering into the franchise agreement, especially since Viking Floors did not exist at the time the parties entered into the franchise agreement. This case is discussed in Chapter 4, Section II, Subsection H.

Baymont Franchise Systems, Inc. v. Bernstein Co., No. 18CV620 (EP) (AME), 2024 WL 2318934 (D.N.J. May 22, 2024). After the United States District Court for the District of New Jersey granted summary judgment in favor of the plaintiff franchisor and determined that attorneys' fees were warranted under the fee provision in the parties' franchise agreement, the plaintiff sought by motion $117,301.21 in attorneys' fees and costs, which was comprised of a fixed fee amount and hourly fees. The court granted the request of $104,701.21 in attorneys' fees. The court denied the fixed fee amount but granted the hourly fees.

Roman v. Jan-Pro Franchising International, Inc., No. 3:16-cv-05961-WHA, 2024 WL 2412387 (N.D. Cal. May 23, 2024). The United States District Court for the Northern District of California granted the plaintiffs' motion for final approval of settlement and attorneys' fees, costs and expenses in a wage-and-hour misclassification class action, finding that in calculating counsel fees, it would approve an amount of the total settlement fund equal to one third of the fees instead of the twenty-five percent benchmark. The court weighed the strong result achieved for the class in making the determination. This case is discussed in Chapter 8, Section IX.

McLaren v. Smash Franchise Partners, LLC, No. 376, 2024 WL 2956899 (Del. Sup. Ct. June 12, 2024). Plaintiff McLaren appealed a Court of Chancery's order and final judgment arguing that the trial court erred in failing to address McLaren's request for attorneys' fees and costs in the judgment, and that the court erred in denying its discovery protective order. The appellate court affirmed the court of chancery's rulings because the judgment explicitly and implicitly addressed McLaren's request for attorneys' fees and because the trial court's decision to deny the discovery ruling was based on conscience and reason.

VII. Other Issues

Reach Cos. v. Newsert, LLC, 94 F.4th 712 (8th Cir. 2024). The Eighth Circuit Court of Appeals held that the lower court did not err by denying a motion for a new trial filed by Reach Companies, LLC, a hand sanitizer distributor ("Reach"). During the trial a jury found that Reach breached its agreement to ship product to Newsert, LLC, a wholesaler engaged in the distribution of hand sanitizer to retailers ("Newsert"). At trial, a jury awarded Newsert about $1.2 million in damages. On appeal, Reach raised three arguments for a new trial (1) jury instruction error; (2) sufficiency of the evidence Newsert provided about its lost profits; and (3) an evidentiary ruling admitting evidence for impeachment purposes of old criminal convictions against a Reach executive. The Eighth Circuit found the district court did not make any jury instruction error based on its determination that there was no ambiguity in their written agreement. It also rejected Reach's assertion that the record at trial was insufficient to prove Newsert's lost profits with reasonable certainty. Finally, the trial court did not abuse its discretion when it found there were exceptional circumstances to allow old convictions for forgery to impeach a Reach executive witness.

CHAPTER 5

Intellectual Property Disputes

I. Introduction

As we discuss in Chapter 1, one of the requirements for franchise protection under state and federal law is establishing that the franchisor, manufacturer, or other trade partner authorized the franchisee's use of its trademarks and other intellectual property during the relationship. Every franchise agreement in the United States implicates the use of the franchisor's intellectual property and fights most often ensue over the use of such property at the end of a relationship. Many of the cases from the reporting period (2023-2024) focus on alleged infringement of trademark rights in this setting and the protections afforded trademark owners under the Lanham Act. We also report on cases involving the misappropriation of trade secrets by competitors and the misuse of patent and copyrights. Often these cases implicate applications for injunctive relief and so we dedicate some of Chapter 5 to cases granting and denying injunctive relief in this context.

II. Unauthorized Use of Trademarks

Toyota Motor Sales, U.S.A., Inc. v. Allen Interchange LLC, No. 22-cv-1681, 2023 WL 5207389 (D. Minn. Aug. 14, 2023). Toyota

Motor Sales, U.S.A., Inc. ("Toyota USA"), the exclusive authorized importer of Toyota-branded parts in the United States, filed a trademark action under the Lanham Act and Minnesota state law against Allen Interchange, LLC ("Allen Interchange"). Toyota USA accused Allen Interchange of selling Toyota-branded parts that differ materially from those distributed by Toyota USA and falsely advertising them as covered by a manufacturer's warranty. Allen Interchange filed a motion for partial dismissal of Toyota USA's claims and requested joinder of Toyota Motor Corporation ("Toyota Japan") in the lawsuit.

The court found Toyota USA lacked standing to raise federal and state statutory trademark dilution claims, as well as its common law infringement claim, because it was not the owner of the trademarks at issue. The court granted Allen Interchange's motion in part, dismissing these without prejudice due to Toyota USA's lack of standing. The court denied Allen Interchange's motion for joinder concluding that Toyota Japan was not a necessary party for the remaining claims, as these claims were about unfair competition, not direct trademark infringement.

AAMCO Transmissions, LLC v. Up to Parr, LLC, No. 22-3212-PJM, 2023 WL 5510081 (D. Md., Aug. 25, 2023). After a default judgment was granted to a franchisor in a trademark misappropriation case, the court made an "exceptional case" finding supporting award of attorneys' fees and costs, awarding $25,000 of claimed $41,410.08 expense.

Endo Fitness LL, LLC v. F-19 Holdings, LLC, No. 2:22-cv-03124-MEMF-JC, 2023 WL 8825670 (C.D. Cal. Dec. 1, 2023). Defendant F-19 Holdings, LLC owned the trademark rights to "Fitness 19" which it licensed to its affiliate, F-19 Franchising, LLC ("F19"). F19 sublicenses the trademark to franchisees to operate gym locations. Plaintiff, Endo Fitness LL, LLC ("Endo") initially sought to enter into a franchise agreement with F19 but when negotiations soured, it opened a gym under the Fitness 19 name and initiated a lawsuit for a declaration that F19, through naked licensing, abandoned the Fitness 19 mark. The court granted defendant's motion for summary judgment finding that there was no genuine dispute that F19 exercised control over its franchisees and did not engage in naked licensing.

The court cited the Ninth Circuit Court of Appeals three-prong test to determine whether a licensor exercises adequate control over its marks: (1) whether the license contained an express contractual right on the part of the licensor to inspect and supervise the licensee's operations; (2) whether the licensor exercised actual control over the licensee's operations; and (3) whether the licensor reasonably relied on the licensee to maintain quality control.

The court found no dispute that the license agreement between F-19 Holdings, LLC and F19 and the form of franchise agreements between F19 and its franchisees contained an express right to inspect the operations of the locations and permitted termination in the event of a material breach or default. The court also found no facts in dispute that F19 conducted investigations and quality control inspections. Although Endo argued that the inspections were of a form below the industry standard, the court found no binding authority to require F19 to act in accordance with best practices to meet the Ninth Circuit test. The court also rejected Endo's claim that F19 failed to exercise actual control by presenting minor inconsistencies across Fitness 19 unit locations in various geographic territories. The court found that it was undisputed that "despite any inconsistencies across the franchise, the quality was equally high across all of the franchise." The court focused its analysis on quality control, not consistency in conducting the analysis for the third prong of the test. Because F19 met the Ninth Circuit three-prong test and Endo was unable to establish any genuine issue of dispute to adequately assert a "naked licensing" claim, the court granted F19's motion for summary judgment.

Ledo Pizza Systems, Inc. v. Ledo's Inc., No. 20 CV 7350, 2024 WL 1013897 (N.D. Ill. Mar. 7, 2024). This case involved a trademark dispute between Ledo Pizza System, a franchisor with 100 stores nationally, in business since 1955 and holding trademark registration since 1988, and Ledo's, a pizza restaurant in Countryside, Illinois, that opened for business in 1961. On cross-motions for summary judgment, the district court rejected most of the defendant's counterclaims over the name but granted Ledo's Inc. summary judgment on its claim that it was an intermediate junior user entitled to continue using Ledo's mark over a geographic area to be determined in later proceedings.

Penn Engineering & Manufacturing Corp. v. Peninsula Components, Inc., No. CV 19-513, 2023 WL 9051998 (E.D. Pa. Dec. 28, 2023) The United States District Court for the Eastern District of Pennsylvania denied both plaintiff Penn Engineering & Manufacturing Corp.'s ("PEM") and defendant Peninsula Components, Inc.'s ("Peninsula") motion for summary judgment because a genuine factual dispute remained regarding whether Peninsula's visible use of the PEM keywords in advertising results to sell its own fastener product online created customer confusion. Further, the court held that Peninsula's website search tool constituted "use" under the Lanham Act because Peninsula included PEM's marks in its meta tags and then directed consumers to purchase Peninsula products.

Florida Virtual School v. K12, Inc., No. 6:20-CV-2354-GAP-EJK, 2024 WL 22039 (M.D. Fla. Jan. 2, 2024). Plaintiff Florida Virtual School ("FVS") sued its competitors in the online education market, defendants K12, Inc. and K12 Florida, LLC (together, "K12"), for using the mark, "Florida Online School" and the associated acronyms to FVS's online school program. In 2015, FVS and K12 entered into an agreement requiring K12 to stop using the words "Florida" and "Virtual" together in a mark. About three years later, K12 launched "Florida Online School" under a third-party contract. As a result, FVS demanded that K12 stop using that mark, and K12 acquiesced by changing its new name to "Digital Academy of Florida." However, FVS still filed suit, seeking a portion of the profits K12 earned during the period it used the name "Florida Online School." The court granted judgment in favor of K12, finding that FVS failed to establish that K12's use of the marks created actual confusion for consumers because the marks had different visual appearances and marketing strategies. The court further explained that K12 started the process of changing its marks immediately after FVS made the demand. Therefore, there was no evidence that K12 adopted the Florida Online School mark with intent to play off the goodwill of FVS's marks.

CHHJ Franchising LLC v. Spaulding, No. 823CV01979WFJAAS, 2024 WL 229406 (M.D. Fla. Jan. 22, 2024). Plaintiff College Hunks Hauling Junk Franchising LLC ("CHHJ") is a moving and junk removal franchisor which brought suit against its former franchisee, Spaulding Hauling & Moving LLC ("Spaulding Hauling") and Victor Spaulding (together, "Defendants") for breaching a post-termination non-compete agreement and continuing to use CHHJ's trademarks in connection with competing agreements. In support of its motion to dismiss, Defendants argued that they never "used" the marks within the meaning of the Lanham Act because they did not do anything except passively allow their preexisting signs to remain on their building. The court rejected this argument and denied Defendant's motion. The court reasoned that the language of the franchise agreement, which required Defendants to "immediately discontinue the use of . . . Proprietary Marks," naturally demands an affirmative step for the defendants to disassociate themselves from the former franchise. Thus, the court found that Defendants' display of the mark at its office would satisfy "use" under the Lanham Act. The court also found Defendants' argument they did not have control over the marks being posted on third-party websites unpersuasive. The court stated that Defendants could have requested the marks be removed which demonstrates that they had some control over the listings. Notwithstanding its views on the merits, the court granted

Defendants' motion to dismiss CHHJ's claim for preliminary and permanent injunctions and attorney fees, finding that these claims were for remedies, rather than independent claims for relief.

Massimo Motor Sports, LLC v. Shandong Odes Industry Co., Ltd., No. 3:21-CV-2180-X, 2024 WL 476967 (N.D. Tex.Feb. 6, 2024). In this case, Massimo Motor Sports, LLC ("Massimo"), a distributor of ATVs and UTVs in the United States, filed suit against Shandong Odes Industry Co., Ltd. ("Shandong"), a manufacturer of similar vehicles, as well as other defendants. Both parties claim ownership rights, with Massimo purchasing the marks through bankruptcy proceedings and Shandong asserting prior use and registration in China. Massimo alleged (1) Shandong infringed on Massimo's use of the trademarks; (2) Shandong breached the exclusive distribution agreement between the parties by selling products outside their agreement, while Shandong accuses Massimo of using its trademarks post-agreement; (3) Shandong engaged in unfair competition and cybersquatting; and (4) the other defendants misappropriated Massimo's trade secrets and confidential information. The court denied the motions for summary judgment on the unfair trademark use claims, breach of contract claims, unfair competition claims, and cybersquatting and trade secrets claims finding there were substantial disputes of fact regarding the ownership and use of the "Odes Marks."

Amazing Lash Franchise, LLC v. Amazing Lash Studio, Inc., No. CV231224JXNJBC, 2024 WL 658597 (D.N.J. Feb. 15, 2024). The United States District Court for the District of New Jersey denied Defendants Amazing Lash Studio, Inc. and Lash Café LLC's motion to dismiss and allowed Plaintiff Amazing Lash Franchise, LLC to proceed on its trademark infringement and unfair competition claims, finding that the complaint sufficiently alleged each required element.

LeTip World Franchise LLC v. Long Island Soc. Media Grp. LLC, No. CV-24-00165-PHX-SMB, 2024 WL 1285621 (D. Ariz. Mar.

26, 2024). This case against a former franchisee who was violating its non-compete and infringing on the franchisor's trademarks is discussed in Chapter 4, Section II.

Mister Softee, Inc. v. Abdallah, No. 22-CV-829-LJV, 2024 WL 1363677 (W.D.N.Y. Mar. 30, 2024). The United States District Court for the Western District of New York granted, in part, franchisor Mister Softee, Inc.'s motion for default judgment, permanent injunction and attorneys' fees and costs against the defendant. Defendant was a former licensee, alleged to have continued operating ice cream trucks using the Mister Softee marks and trade dress without authorization after Mr. Softee terminated the license agreement and sent a cease and desist demanding the defendant de-identify the trucks and reprogram the music box that played the Mister Softee jingle. The court found that Mister Softee established that the defendant operated her ice cream truck in violation of the Lanham Act's prohibition on trademark infringement finding that: (1) Mister Softee had a valid trademark; (2) there was a likelihood of confusion since the Mister Softee logos, jingle, and truck design are registered and uncontested trademarks, have been used since 1959, and the defendant continued operating as a franchisee in the same vicinity; and (3) equitable considerations weighted in favor of Mister Softee since the violation was willful and deliberate. The court granted the permanent injunction but denied the award of attorney's fees finding that there was not enough to make the case "exceptional" under the Lanham Act to grant attorneys' fees to Mister Softee.

Wheelmaxx Inc. v. Maraaj Singh Mahal, No. 122CV01506KESSKO, 2024 WL 1343128 (E.D. Cal. Mar. 29, 2024). This default judgment case involving a claim for trademark infringement is discussed in Chapter 8, Section XI.

III. Copyright, Patent Infringement

Deere & Co. v. XAPT Corp., No. 419CV04210SLDJEH, 2023 WL 8654362 (C.D. Ill. Dec. 14, 2023). Plaintiff Deere & Company

("Deere"), a manufacturer of heavy equipment, hired defendant XAPT KFT ("KFT") to deliver an integrated computer software with the goal of bringing all of Deere's dealer businesses together into one business system. Deere intended for the business system to be used by Deere and its dealers. During Deere and KFT's relationship, Deere accessed KFT's developed software and progressively gained an understanding of how it was coded. At some point, the parties' relationship started to deteriorate, and Deere sought to terminate their agreement. Despite the termination resulting in Deere losing privileges to its KFT subscription and license to use KFT's developed software, Deere continued to utilize the software. Eventually Deere began adding additional features and capabilities to the program. Shortly after, Deere filed suit for breach of contract, fraudulent inducement, reformation, conversion, and replevin. Consequently, KFT asserted counterclaims for direct copyright infringement, indirect copyright infringement, and unjust enrichment.

Deere filed a motion to dismiss the counterclaims. First, Deere argued that the agreement between the parties assigned intellectual property rights to Deere for all work product created under the agreement. The court rejected this argument and refused to interpret the terms of the agreement and apply them to the issue at that stage in the proceeding. Second, Deere argued that KFT's direct copyright infringement claim failed to identify specific works that were infringed. The court determined that KFT sufficiently alleged that it had ownership of the copyright for the developed software and that the allegations properly alleged that Deere infringed on those rights. Third, Deere argued that KFT failed to sufficiently allege a claim for indirect copyright infringement. Even though the court recognized that KFT was not able to identify all of the third parties involved in the dispute, it found that KFT's allegations were sufficient because it was able to point out some of Deere's technology vendors as some of the third parties. Lastly, the court rejected Deere's arguments pertaining to unjust enrichment because the arguments were unsupported and underdeveloped. In sum, the court denied Deere's motion to dismiss KFT's counterclaims.

Tiare Tech., Inc. v. Dine Brands Global, Inc., No. 222CV00490JRGRSP, 2024 WL 607407 (E.D. Tex. Jan. 4, 2024). This case, involving application of the Patent Act's venue statute, is discussed in Chapter 8, Section III.

IV. Misappropriation of Trade Secrets

Crumbl LLC v. Dirty Dough, LLC, No. 2:22-CV-318-HCN-CMR, 2023 WL 5180370 (D. Utah, Aug. 11, 2023). This case involved a trade secret dispute between two franchisors in the gourmet cookie market. Plaintiff Crumbl started doing business in Utah in 2017, and as of August 2023, had hundreds of franchised stores throughout the United States. One of the prospective franchisees it rejected was Bennett Maxwell, who was notified in late March 2019 that Crumbl would not go forward with his franchise application.

At about that same time, Bennett Maxwell's brother Bradley went to work for Crumbl as a process engineer. He signed a general employee confidentiality and noncompetition agreement, and a more specific recipe confidentiality agreement. By mid-May 2019, both Bennett and Bradley Maxwell had bought interests in a competing gourmet cookie franchisor named Dirty Dough, located in Arizona, and by January 2021 Bennett had bought out all Dirty Dough owners other than Bradley. In July 2019, Crumbl fired Bradley, and during the last week of Bradley's employment there he downloaded sixty-six cookie recipes and other Crumbl information, including sales records, the results of recipe experiments, and guides to building out franchised stores. In September 2021, Bradley uploaded all of the Crumbl documents he had obtained to the Dirty Dough Google Drive. Bradley also shared the Crumbl information with Dirty Dough executives and managers.

Crumbl sued Dirty Dough under the Lanham Act and for common law unfair competition and amended its complaint to add claims for misappropriation of trade secrets after learning that its information had been disclosed to Dirty Dough. The court ordered a forensic examination of Dirty Dough's devices containing electronic data, and after a two-day preliminary injunction hearing Crumbl and Dirty Dough stipulated to an order requiring Dirty Dough and Bradley Maxwell to return all Crumbl information, to give Crumbl any notes or other records that contained the Crumbl information, and to verify under oath that they had returned all Crumbl information and not retained copies in any format.

The stipulated order mooted much of the injunctive relief Crumbl had sought, but Crumbl continued to press its claims for an injunction: (1) ordering Dirty Dough to issue a corrective public statement admitting that it had improperly acquired Crumbl information; and (2) preventing Dirty Dough from opening more franchised stores until the court decided that Dirty Dough would not use any Crumbl information in those efforts. The court denied both requests for injunctive relief.

Although the court had no trouble ruling that Crumbl had shown a likelihood of success on the merits, it rejected Crumbl's arguments that it would suffer irreparable harm, based on its finding that the evidence unequivocally showed that the companies' recipes, baking processes, and business models differed substantially, notwithstanding Dirty Dough's possession of the Crumbl trade secrets. The court also found that the balance of harms weighed heavily in Dirty Dough's favor, because it presented credible evidence that it would go out of business if it were barred from opening new franchised outlets, and Crumbl failed to show any ongoing harm that would justify such a harsh result. Finally, the court noted that even in the context of a defamation case, a court-compelled retraction or correction would be an extraordinary remedy, so Crumbl failed to show any harm that outweighed

Bennett Maxwell's First Amendment rights against compelled speech in the future.

JTH Tax LLC v. Cortorreal, No. 2:23-cv-0355, 2024 WL 897605 (E.D. Va. Mar. 1, 2024). JTH Tax LLC, doing business as Liberty Tax Service ("Liberty"), the franchisor of income tax preparation centers, filed a complaint against defendants ("Franchisee") for various breaches of their franchise agreements, violations of the Defense of Trade Secrets Act of 2016, unjust enrichment, conversion, and tortious interference with franchise agreements and business relationships. Franchisee filed motions to dismiss all counts under Rule 12(b)(6) for failure to state a claim upon which relief can be granted. The United States District Court for the Eastern District of Virginia granted Franchisee's motions to dismiss. Liberty entered into franchise agreements with the defendants licensing the right for Franchisee to operate two franchises in Texas. After the franchise agreements were terminated, the defendants began operating a competing tax preparation business, The Eagles Team, allegedly using Liberty's confidential information to solicit former clients. Liberty claimed this caused irreparable harm to its franchised system and goodwill. The court found that Liberty's allegations of trade secret violations lacked specific details about the nature of the purported trade secrets and their nexus to interstate commerce. Since the court dismissed the federal claim, it opted not to exercise supplemental jurisdiction over the state law claims.

V. Injunctive Relief

Crumbl LLC v. Dirty Dough, LLC, No. 2:22-CV-318-HCN-CMR, 2023 WL 5180370 (D. Utah, Aug. 11, 2023). The district court denied plaintiffs' motion for an injunction compelling the defendant to make statements effectively retracting previous false statements it had made, reasoning that the First Amendment prohibits compelled speech and injunctive relief will not redress past wrongs. The court also denied plaintiff's request for an injunction barring the defendant from opening new franchised gourmet cookie stores until the court had found that the defendant was not using the plaintiff's trade secrets, ruling that the court had already ordered all of plaintiff's information returned to plaintiff and deleted from defendant's devices, and the significantly different business models of the plaintiff and defendant could not support an order that would have effectively put the defendant out of business. This case is discussed in Chapter 5, Section IV.

Get Bak'd OKC, LLC v. Releaf Labs, LLC, No. 119859, 2023 WL 8445825 (Okla. Civ. App. Div. 4 Oct. 26, 2023). Plaintiff Get Bak'd, LLC ("Get Bak'd") filed a motion for a preliminary injunction on a trademark infringement and deceptive trade practices action against Releaf Labs, LLC ("Releaf") and one of Releaf's owners. The district court denied the motion on the basis that Get Bak'd failed to establish the irreparable harm that is necessary for a preliminary injunction.

On appeal, Get Bak'd argued that Releaf's use of "ALTRD Thundersticks" was too similar to its trademarked product, "Thunder Stixx." It claimed that the similarities created confusion among its consumers and harmed its business reputation. In response, Releaf asserted that Get Bak'd was more likely to benefit from the confusion based on the district court's discovery that, during the relevant time, Releaf's product won a prestigious award in Oklahoma. Taking that into account, along with the lack of evidence that Releaf's product was actually inferior, the appellate court found that Get Bak'd failed to advance its argument for irreparable harm. Get Bak'd further argued that it was entitled to a presumption of irreparable harm pursuant to federal law because the common law codified the relevant provision for trademark infringement cases. The court recognized that Get Bak'd was entitled to the presumption but specified that the 2020 Lanham Act explicitly makes the presumption rebuttable. Therefore, while Get Bak'd was entitled to the presumption of irreparable harm, it was not dispositive to the appeal. The court considered the evidence concerning irreparable harm and found that all of the evidence that

Get Bak'd offered was speculative and theoretical. Because Get Bak'd failed to provide actual evidence that Releaf's product was inferior, the court found that the evidence was sufficient to rebut the presumption of irreparable harm.

Lastly, the court considered whether there was an equitable basis to grant a preliminary injunctive relief. The court pointed out that the relief Get Bak'd requested would result in the court ordering a mandatory injunction directing Releaf to stop selling all of its Thunderstick products. In contrast, Get Bak'd still had other viable statutory remedies that would provide adequate relief for any of the damage it incurred for the alleged infringement of its trademark. Overall, the court determined that the equitable principles underlying the preliminary injunction did not favor granting the requested mandatory injunction. Therefore, the court affirmed the district court's decision to deny the preliminary injunction.

VI. Other Trademark Issues

F19 Franchising, LLC v. Endo Fitness LL, LLC, No. 2:23-cv-00185-MEMF-JC, 2024 WL 2979530 (C.D. Cal. June 11, 2024). Defendant, Endo Fitness LL, LLC ("Endo") filed a motion to dismiss plaintiff's, F19 Franchising, LLC ("F19") claims for trade dress infringement. The court denied Endo's motion finding that F19, a fitness franchisor, sufficiently plead the cause of action, although it would need to prove that (1) the trade dress is nonfunctional; (2) the trade dress has acquired secondary meaning; and (3) the infringing trade dress creates a likelihood of confusion as to source, sponsorship, affiliation or connection between plaintiff and defendant's products or services. For motion to dismiss purposes it was sufficient that the plaintiff described listed trade dress such as the signs, exterior appearance, color scheme, air conditioning temperature, music selection, machines and site selection, but it would need to specifically show the elements are non-functional in discovery. Second, the uniformity of an allegedly unique and distinctive décor among its franchisee suggests that the trade dress had attained secondary meaning. Finally, the court found that F19 properly alleged that Endo infringed the identified trade dress.

CHAPTER 6

Other Federal and State Law Issues

I. Introduction

Once again, this Chapter was dominated by sex trafficking claims asserted by plaintiffs under the federal Trafficking Victim Protection Reauthorization Act ("TVPRA"). The landscape of franchisor liability under the TVPRA is continuing to evolve as courts grapple with the implications of holding franchisors accountable for sex trafficking activities occurring at their franchisee-operated properties. Franchisors, with limited control over the day-to-day operations of a property, are often able to avoid liability unless a plaintiff can show the franchisor had significant control over the franchisee's operations. Franchisees, on the other hand, have potential larger exposure under TVPRA for sex trafficking that occurs on their properties.

In most cases, plaintiffs assert claims under a theory of beneficiary liability, which allows a plaintiff to bring a direct civil claim against those who knowingly benefit financially or receive anything of value from their participation. Many of these claims against franchisors were dismissed. Courts often found that plaintiffs failed to sufficiently allege that franchisor had knowledge of or participation in the sex trafficking ventures. For example, Courts have found that a failure to implement protective policies is insufficient to show participation in a sex trafficking venture under beneficiary liability theory.

However, in a series of decisions in the Southern District of Ohio in March 2024, the court demonstrated a significant shift towards recognizing the franchisors' roles in sex trafficking occurring at franchisee-properties. In these decisions, the district court found that a plaintiff's allegations that a franchisor profited from trafficking by renting rooms to the plaintiff's traffickers was sufficient to satisfy the knowingly benefitted element of a TVPRA claim. Moreover, a plaintiff's allegations that a franchisor profited, failed to implement preventative policies, and maintained expansive control over a franchisee's operations met the participation element. Additionally, a plaintiff's specific allegations about hotel staff's knowledge of their individual trafficking, in combination with a franchisor's general knowledge of the prevalence of sex trafficking at their hotels without preventative action is sufficient to meet the "knew or should have known" element.

While these cases have yet to be decided on the merits, this shift indicates a growing judicial willingness to find franchisors liable where there is evidence of their substantial control and economic benefit from the operations that facilitate trafficking.

Plaintiffs have also been successful in defeating motions to dismiss under "joint employer" theories of liability, which have hinged on the degree to which a franchisor participates in the day-to-day employment of hotel staff. Courts have found that it is sufficient, even if a plaintiff does not explicitly use the words "joint employer" to find liability through joint employment when a plaintiff alleges the franchisor has control over key employment-related policies such as training and setting the rates of pay. However, it is insufficient that the franchisor merely sets the company culture and provides training and orientation material.

Plaintiffs have also attempted to show direct liability, which has a much higher burden, with limited success. Plaintiffs generally must show that there was some direct contact that could be imputed to the franchisor. For example, when the managerial staff of a franchisee property have actual knowledge of and direct involvement in the trafficking scheme, it can be imputed to the franchisor defendant.

In cases that have reached the summary judgment stage, plaintiffs have generally been unsuccessful in holding franchisors responsible. For example, the Northern District of Ohio granted summary judgment to franchisor defendants because the TVPRA was not imputable to the franchisor under an actual agency theory because the franchise agreement did not grant the franchisor defendants any control over the franchisee hotels' daily operations. The franchisors similarly were not found liable under apparent agency or joint employer theories. To overcome summary judgment, plaintiffs needed to establish that the franchisor had actual or constructive knowledge of the trafficking activities and knowingly benefitted from the sex trafficking.

There are several facts that may help a plaintiff survive summary judgment. First, courts found sufficient evidence where plaintiffs were able to point to specific instances of a continuous business relationship between hotel staff and traffickers, such as regularly renting rooms despite obvious signs of trafficking occurring or assisting the traffickers by serving as lookouts for law enforcement. Second, arguments that franchisors failed to implement anti-trafficking policies despite known risks were often pivotal to sufficient pleadings. For example, evidence that franchisors maintained extensive control over hotel operations yet did nothing to prevent trafficking were especially persuasive. Third, courts were more likely to find sufficient evidence when plaintiffs provided detailed examples of management level hotel staff witnessing trafficking-related activities or being bribed to ignore them.

The evolving case law on franchisor liability under the TVPRA highlights significant changes in judicial interpretation over the past year. While the majority of cases result in dismissals due to insufficient allegations of franchisors' knowledge or participation in trafficking ventures, recent decisions indicate a shift toward a more nuanced understanding of franchisor liability.

In short, generally, the courts denied a franchisor's motions to dismiss claims for direct and vicarious liability, and granted for joint employer theories of liability, actual agency, beneficiary liability, and perpetrator liability.

II. Antitrust

Winn-Dixie Stores, Inc. v. Eastern Mushroom Marketing Cooperative, Inc., 81 F.4th 323 (3rd Cir. Aug. 28, 2023). The plaintiff grocery store, Winn-Dixie Stores, Inc. ("Winn-Dixie"), filed a lawsuit against Eastern Mushroom Marketing Cooperative, Inc. ("EMMC"), its members, and distributors, alleging that their price-fixing agreement violated Section 1 of the Sherman Act. EMMC was a cooperative of mushroom growers in the Eastern United States that initially controlled over ninety percent of the fresh mushrooms in the market after it was formed in 2001, which later declined to about seventeen percent by 2010. EMMC's goal was to establish a "Minimum Pricing Policy" to standardize minimum prices for its members to charge customers. EMMC had various types of arrangements with its members and distributors. Some members were grower-only entities, while others had specific partnerships with distributors. However, distributors were not part of the cooperative and were not bound by its minimum pricing policy.

The lower court applied the "rule-of-reason" approach, requiring a thorough examination of the anticompetitive effects, rather than the "quick-look" approach that presumes anticompetitive effects. After a jury trial, the district judge entered judgment in favor of EMMC after the jury found that there was an overall conspiracy to increase mushroom prices, but Winn-Dixie failed to meet its burden of showing the conspiracy had anti-competitive effects. Winn-Dixie then appealed the district court's denial of its post-trial motions for a new trial and judgment notwithstanding the verdict.

Winn-Dixie argued a "quick-look" analysis should have been applied in analyzing the alleged anticompetitive effects of the EMMC's pricing policy under the Sherman Act. The court held that the lower court used the appropriate burden of proof because EMMC's price fixing agreement involved a hybrid vertical integration and not a simple horizontal arrangement. Because the hybrid scheme resembles both a horizontal and vertical arrangement, the rule of reason analysis should apply. Further, there was sufficient evidence for the jury to find that EMMC's arrangement did not have the effect of causing competitive harm. Despite EMMC's efforts, EMMC members testified that most did not really follow the minimum pricing schedule and routinely invoked exemptions that swallowed up the minimum pricing rules. Members also testified to facing pricing competition from non-EMMC and foreign growers, and Walmart and Sysco utilizing buyer power to impact pricing. An expert economist testified that mushroom prices were flat. Evidence showed varying compliance with EMMC's pricing policy and competing narratives about its effects on the market.

The court affirmed the district court's ruling, deciding it did not err in applying the rule of reason test and there was more than sufficient evidence for the jury to make its findings.

International Construction Products, LLC v. Ring Power Corp., No. 22-10231, 2023 WL 7127515 (11th Cir. Oct. 30, 2023). The Eleventh Circuit Court of Appeals affirmed the summary judgment entered against plaintiff International Construction Products, LLC ("ICP"), a distributor of heavy construction equipment, in its antitrust suit against defendants Ring Power Corporation, Thompson Tractor Company, and Ziegler Inc. ("Ring Power") for alleged violations of section 1 of the Sherman Act. The district court granted Ring Power's summary judgment motion finding that ICP did not produce sufficient evidence to show that Ring Power conspired against it to harm ICP's relationship with a heavy construction equipment auction site ("IronPlanet"), by boycotting and severing ties with IronPlanet if it did not cut ties with ICP. The Eleventh Circuit affirmed.

ICP and IronPlanet agreed to a deal where ICP would sell its products through a dedicated storefront on the IronPlanet auction site. The structure was a shift in how heavy equipment was sold and garnered a lot of attention in the industry when the business deal was announced. One month later, IronPlanet abruptly terminated its relationship with ICP. IronPlanet testified in depositions that the deal was not as profitable as anticipated and consumed extensive technological resources. ICP then sued Caterpillar, CAS, and various other manufacturers, and then amended the lawsuit to include the Ring Power defendants. The amended complaint raised two claims under Section 1 of the Sherman Anti-Trust Act, 15 U.S.C. § 1, and two claims for tortious interference under state law (Counts 3 and 4). The district court granted Ring Power's motions for summary judgment on all counts and ICP appealed. The court held that ICP's Sherman Act claims failed because ICP did not present sufficient evidence of a conspiracy among the Defendants.

First, ICP failed to present any direct evidence proving that Ring Power conspired to boycott IronPlanet until it terminated its relationship with ICP. ICP had only made the conclusory argument that the alleged conspiracy was economically rational for Ring Power. The tortious interference claims also failed as ICP presented no evidence that a jury could find that Ring Power intentionally and unjustifiably interfered with the business relationship between ICP and IronPlanet or induced IronPlanet to breach its agreement with ICP.

In re: Deere & Company Repair Service Antitrust Litigation, No. 3:22-cv-50188, MDL No. 3030, 2023 WL 8190256 (N.D. Ill. Nov. 27, 2023). The United States District Court for the Northern Division of Illinois denied defendant Deere & Company's (the maker of John Deere tractors), motion to dismiss plaintiffs' claims that the defendant violated antitrust laws by conspiring with its dealerships and deliberately designing purchased equipment to require frequent diagnostics and repairs that cannot be serviced outside the John Deere network. The court found that the plaintiffs, consisting of six classes of farmers, met the burden of pleading that John Deere exercised a monopoly of power in the repair market and rejected John Deere's argument that the farmers lacked Article III standing and antitrust standing.

Tiz, Inc. v. Southern Glazer's Wine & Spirits, LLC, No. 22 CV 1648, 2024 WL 2785142 (N.D. Ill. May 30, 2024). The United States District Court for the Northern District of Illinois denied defendants' motion to dismiss plaintiffs' claims that the defendants violated the Sherman Act and related state laws by entering horizontal and vertical conspiracies, monopolization or attempted monopolization, violations of the Illinois Antitrust Act and the California Unfair Competition Law, and tortious interference with business expectancy. The court found that the plaintiffs plausibly stated their claims and adequately alleged antitrust standing.

U.S. Wholesale Outlet & Distribution, Inc. v. Innovation Ventures, LLC, 89 F.4th 1126 (9th Cir. 2023). The Ninth Circuit Court of Appeals denied wholesalers' request for an injunction under Section 2(d) of the Robinson-Patman Act in response to defendant, Living Essentials, the supplier of 5-Hour Energy caffeinated drinks, selling its products to Costco at a lower price than it charged the independent wholesalers. Several wholesalers filed a complaint alleging that Living Essentials violated the Robinson-Patman Act by giving Costco preferential prices and discounts on its 5-Hour Energy drink product. The wholesalers sought damages under Section 2(a) of the Robinson-Patman Act and an injunction under Section 2(d) of the Act. The Ninth Circuit affirmed the lower court's denial of injunctive relief, reasoning that the jury implicitly found there was no competition between the plaintiff wholesalers and Costco, as required for injunctive relief under Section 2(d). However, the court found the district court erred in denying injunctive relief to the wholesalers on the basis that Costco and the wholesalers operated at different functional levels and competed for different customers.

Deslandes v. McDonald's USA, LLC, 81 F.4th 699 (7th Cir. 2023), cert. denied, No. 23-562, 2024 WL 1143666 (S. Ct. Mar. 18, 2024). The Seventh Circuit Court of Appeals considered whether the district court properly dismissed allegations that anti-poaching clauses in McDonald's franchise agreements–allegedly preventing McDonald's employees from taking higher-paying jobs at other McDonald's locations–violated Section 1 of the Sherman Act. Claims under Section 1 are divided into two categories: naked restraints, which are unlawful per se, and other restraints, which are evaluated under the "Rule of Reason." The Court of Appeals affirmed the district court's decision on a motion to dismiss with respect to the Rule of Reason claim, determining that without an allegation that McDonald's held market power in the market for restaurant worker labor, that the claim was implausible. Although plaintiff argued that an allegation of market power was "too obvious" to require allegations or proof, the Seventh Circuit determined that because workers entering and moving through the labor market may choose where to work, fast food restaurants being one of only many options, and being able to move between fast food restaurants at will, that it would be "impossible" to treat employees at a single chain (McDonalds) as a market.

However, the court vacated as premature the district court's order dismissing plaintiff's "per se" claim under the Sherman Act. Plaintiff's complaint alleged a horizontal restraint among McDonald's franchises, and market power, mandatory to the Rule of Reason analysis, is not an essential consideration in antitrust claims governing naked agreements between competitors. The district court had determined that the anti-poaching clause was not "naked" because it was justified as an ancillary restraint, because it appeared in franchise agreements, which each expanded outputs of food in the market. The Court of Appeals disagreed—holding that this approach treated benefits to consumers as justifying detriments to workers and determining that a restraint is not ancillary simply because it is a part of another agreement that is lawful, or that promotes production. The Seventh Circuit cast doubt on the idea that the anti-poaching clause truly promoted output, instead suggesting that it might simply promote profits by preventing workers from taking their training and skills elsewhere for higher wages. The court raised several questions as to the purpose of the no-poaching clause, including questioning the national scope of the clause, and that the no-poaching clause was linked to the time of employment, rather than the time of training or some other factor that matched traditional economic incentives.

The Court of Appeals ultimately determined that the question of whether a restraint is "ancillary" to be a defense, one the plaintiff should not be required to plead around. The court determined the district court's dismissal to be improper and remanded for further proceedings—including a strong suggestion that the lower court reconsider its earlier decision to deny class certification.

Goforth v. Transform Holdco LLC, No. 6:23-CV-03167-MDH, 2024 WL 3461077 (W.D. Mo. July 18, 2024). Defendants filed a motion to dismiss plaintiffs' claims alleging violations of Section One of the Sherman Antitrust Act in relation to a dealership agreement governing the retail business of selling home appliances to rural markets. The district court denied defendants' motion to dismiss for failure to state a claim because the plaintiffs sufficiently and plausibly pled violations of the antitrust laws, including an impact on interstate commerce, an antitrust injury, and restraint of trade.

International Construction Products, LLC v. Caterpillar Inc., No. 15-108-RGA, 2024 WL 1619836 (D. Del. Apr. 15, 2024). Plaintiff, International Construction Products, LLC ("ICP"), was a seller of Chinese-manufactured heavy construction equipment. Unlike defendant Caterpillar Inc. ("Caterpillar"), ICP did not sell its products through local equipment dealers, and instead sold its equipment through an online platform hosted by IronPlanet. ICP filed a claim against Caterpillar alleging it coerced IronPlanet to terminate its agreement with ICP, effectively stifling ICP's business operations. Caterpillar filed a motion for summary judgment on ICP's claims under the Sherman Act and for tortious interference. The court denied summary judgment. With respect to the antitrust claim, the court found sufficient evidence that could lead a reasonable jury to conclude there was a conspiracy by Caterpillar to exclude ICP from the market. Similarly, the court found enough evidence of anticompetitive actions potentially causing harm to the market and ICP to warrant denial of the motion on the tortious interference claim.

III. Bankruptcy

Matter of Thornhill Brothers Fitness, LLC, 85 F.4th 321 (5th Cir. 2023). In an appeal to the Fifth Circuit Court of Appeals from a Chapter 11 bankruptcy proceeding, the court considered whether a bankruptcy court could approve the partial assignment of a debtor-franchisee's executory contract, in a manner that left franchisor liability on the table by way of assigning only rights the franchisee may have had against the franchisor.

After Anytime Fitness member William Flynn ("Flynn") suffered neuromuscular injuries from malfunctioning gym equipment, he filed a personal injury suit against the owner of an Anytime Fitness franchise, Thornhill Brothers Fitness, LLC ("Thornhill"), and the franchisor, Anytime Fitness, LLC ("Anytime Fitness"). Anytime Fitness was dismissed with prejudice during the pendency of the litigation, leaving Thornhill as the sole defendant. Shortly before a multi-day jury trial was set to ensue on the claim, Thornhill filed Chapter 11 bankruptcy, listing the unknown litigation verdict as its sole significant non-insider liability.

Within 48 hours, Thornhill contacted the bankruptcy court and obtained its approval for a settlement offer that had been arranged between Thornhill and Flynn. That settlement set out that Thornhill's insurer would pay out the maximum on a $1 million dollar policy. Thornhill also signed a separate document titled a "Confession of Judgment," admitting $7 million dollars in total liability to Flynn. Thornhill then assigned to Flynn any rights it had "against Anytime Fitness" (including arising from the Franchise Agreement's indemnity provision). Flynn agreed that Thornhill would remain in the personal injury suit "in name only," for the specific purpose of recovering against Anytime Fitness, and Flynn waived any rights to pursue Thornhill for any portion of the judgment beyond the $1 million dollar payment.

Flynn then filed a new lawsuit against Anytime Fitness, alleging that Thornhill's "confession," the indemnity provisions of the Thornhill's franchise agreement, the assignment of Thornhill's rights to Flynn, and the bankruptcy court's approval of each of these made Anytime Fitness liable to Flynn for the "confessed" amount of $7 million. Anytime Fitness, shocked and previously unaware of the bankruptcy settlement, moved to dismiss the new suit, but was unsuccessful. Anytime Fitness then objected to the settlement agreement in the bankruptcy court, but the court ratified its decision, and the district court affirmed the bankruptcy court's decision.

The Fifth Circuit Court of Appeals reversed, determining that the bankruptcy settlement violated 11 U.S.C. § 365 governing the treatment of executory contracts in bankruptcy. Both parties to the suit agreed that the Franchise Agreement was an executory contract, i.e., a contract "[t]hat neither party has finished performing." The court ultimately determined that the assignment of an executory contract must be an all or nothing premise. Being able to chop up a contract through partial assignment would allow a debtor to change the nature of the contract's obligations. "A debtor cannot use § 365 to create a different deal than the one it had originally." The court deliberately stopped short of declaring Franchise Agreements as executory contracts in every circumstance, but declared that such a characterization "made sense" as a general rule giving the ongoing obligations inherent in typical franchise relationships. Because Thornhill had assigned its franchise agreement's indemnity rights under § 365(f) of the Bankruptcy Code (but not the remainder of the agreement) the Court of Appeals determined the partial assignment, and the settlement, to be invalid.

FUSA Franchisor SPV LLC v. Moda Collision Repair, LLC, No. 23-CV-1559 JLS, 2024 WL 947467 (S.D. Cal. Mar. 5, 2024). Franchisor, FUSA Franchisor SPV LLC ("FUSA"), filed a complaint against franchisee, Moda Collision Repair, LLC ("Moda"), seeking declaratory judgment and claims for breach of a franchise agreement and breach of personal guaranty after the franchise agreement was terminated for non-payment and after FUSA learned that Moda sold its shop without its consent. The sole owner of Moda, and guarantor of the franchise agreement, Andrey Stefanco ("Stefanco"), then filed for Chapter Seven bankruptcy, but he allegedly did not list the personal guaranty in his bankruptcy filing nor did he inform FUSA of the proceedings. FUSA sought a declaratory judgment that Stefanco's bankruptcy discharge did not absolve him of debts under the personal guaranty. Stefanco argued that the discharge injunction from his bankruptcy case barred FUSA's claim. The court found that factual disputes surrounding whether FUSA was properly informed of the bankruptcy proceedings. The court denied Stefanco's motion to dismiss, allowing FUSA's claims to proceed. It concluded that factual disputes regarding the bankruptcy proceedings' notice to FUSA need resolution before determining the applicability of the bankruptcy discharge to Stefanco's debt under the personal guarantee. Stefanco also argued that bankruptcy court was a more suitable forum, and the court disagreed with that argument finding that the bankruptcy proceedings concluded and that district courts have concurrent jurisdiction over dischargeability issues.

In re: Empower Central Michigan, Inc., No. 23-31281-jda, 2024 WL 1848504 (E.D Mich. Bank. Ct. Apr. 26, 2024). On August 4, 2023, Empower Central Michigan, Inc. ("Empower"), an Auto Lab Complete Car Care Center Franchise in Fenton, Michigan, filed for Chapter 11 bankruptcy. Empower was party to a Franchise Agreement and a separate Confidentiality Agreement with Auto Lab Franchising, LLC ("Auto Lab"). Empower decided to reject the Franchise Agreement and related agreements, opting to operate as an independent auto repair shop and filed a motion to reject executory contracts ("motion") with thc bankruptcy court. Empower argued that the Franchise Agreement no longer provided tangible benefits and that the monthly franchise fees were burdensome. Empower began distancing itself from the franchisor by repainting the shop, ceasing sales reporting, notifying customers of the name change to Fenton Car Care Center, and copying customer lists and other confidential information while continuing to use Auto Lab's trademarks. Auto Lab objected to the motion, asserting that while the Franchise Agreement might be executory, the non-compete clause was not and remained enforceable post-rejection and that the Confidentiality Agreement, being fully performed by Auto Lab, was non-executory and thus not subject to rejection. The court acknowledged that under 11 U.S.C. § 365(a), a debtor can assume or reject any executory contract where performance remains due on both sides and the court generally approves such decisions under the business judgment rule. Auto Lab argued it fully performed its obligations under the Franchise Agreement and Confidentiality Agreement by providing confidential business practices, trademarks, and intellectual property to Empower. The court held the Franchise Agreement was executory, allowing for its rejection. However, the non-compete clause within the Franchise Agreement remained enforceable post-rejection because restrictive covenants are typically non-executory and survive rejection, as they do not constitute a right to payment but rather an equitable remedy. The court also held that the Confidentiality Agreement was non-executory because Auto Lab had no material obligations left to perform and could not be rejected and remains enforceable.

In re IYS Ventures, LLC, No. 23 B 6782, 2024 WL 1464455 (Bankr. N.D. Ill. Apr. 4, 2024). This was a dispute in bankruptcy court between a franchisee debtor and franchisor fuel supplier about whether the debtor should continue to perform executory contracts for supply of fuel after a Chapter 11 reorganization. The bankruptcy court authorized the continuation of the contracts because the contracts were beneficial to the debtor and served to advance the debtor's reorganization.

In re the Neely Group, Inc., No. 24 B 3859, 2024 WL 2946219 (Bankr. N.D. Ill. June 11, 2024). A franchisee defaulted under its franchise agreement and the franchisor terminated the relationship. Four days later, the franchisee filed a petition under Chapter 11 of the U.S. Bankruptcy Code. The franchisee then filed a motion in bankruptcy court to enforce the automatic stay against the franchisor. The court denied the motion because the franchise agreement was terminated before the franchisee filed for bankruptcy. As a result, the bankruptcy court determined that the franchisor had not violated the automatic stay imposed when the franchisee filed its petition.

In re Welcome Group 2, LLC, No. 2:23-bk-53043, 2024 WL 3359379 (Bankr. S.D. Ohio July 10, 2024). This bankruptcy case decided whether a debtor can assume under, Section 365 of the Bankruptcy Code, a Hilton Hotel franchise agreement without the consent of Hilton. Hilton asserted that the Franchise Agreement could not be assumed by the Debtor pursuant to 11 U.S.C. § 365(c)(1) because the plain language of the statute requires the Court to apply a "hypothetical test" to determine whether the

Franchise Agreement can be assumed absent consent from Hilton, if applicable law prohibits the assignment of the contract, even if the Debtor has no intention of assigning the Franchise Agreement. Hilton argued that the Franchise Agreement could not be assumed by the Debtor because applicable non-bankruptcy law (i.e., The Lanham Act, 15 U.S.C. §§ 1051-1141n) prohibits the assignability of the Franchise Agreement and Hilton does not consent to the Franchise Agreement being assumed. The Debtor argued that the court should apply the "actual test" in interpreting Section 365(c)(1) as there was no actual assignment but merely assumption under Section 365(f). The court decided as an issue of first impression within its Federal Circuit that the actual test should apply and that consent was not necessary from Hilton to assume the franchise agreement.

IV. Civil Rights

Mason v. 7 Eleven, Inc., No. CV TJS-22-1559, 2024 WL 1346863 (D. Md. Mar. 29, 2024). This case involved the liability of a franchisor for a franchisee's alleged racial profiling at a 7-Eleven in Maryland. This case is discussed in Chapter 7, Section III.

Sampson v. HB Boys, LC, 548 P.3d 538 (Utah Ct. App. 2024). Customer of a Burger King franchise appealed a state trial court ruling that the common law doctrines of respondeat superior and agency did not apply and, therefore, a franchise owner could not be held liable under the Utah Civil Rights Act ("UCRA") for alleged violations of the statute due to racial slurs issued by the franchisee's employee toward the customer. The Utah Court of Appeal reversed the decision, citing unresolved factual disputes that should have precluded granting summary judgment.

Prieto Automotive, Inc. v. Volvo Car USA, LLC, No. 1:21-CV-01085-KES-EPG, 2024 WL 3011170 (E.D. Cal. June 14, 2024). Defendants Haron Motor Sales and Volvo Car USA, LLC each filed a motion to dismiss a complaint directed at their alleged refusal to complete an asset purchase of a Volvo dealership on the account of plaintiff's race, ethnicity, and national origin and based on alleged tortious interference with the underlying asset purchase agreement. The district court granted both motions, finding in relation to the statutory claim for discrimination that plaintiff had failed to allege sufficient facts to plausibly establish discriminatory intent. It granted the motion to dismiss the intentional interference with contract claim because plaintiff failed to state a plausible claim that interference as defined under California law occurred and due to the failure to plausibly allege causation. The court granted the plaintiff leave to amend the complaint.

V. Employment

Hurlow v. Toyota Motor North America, Inc., No. 21 C 4049, 2024 WL 689961 (N.D. Ill. Feb. 20, 2024). The United States District Court for the Northern District of Illinois granted a franchisor's motion for summary judgment on all claims brought under the Family Medical Leave Act ("FMLA") and the Illinois Human Rights Act ("IHRA") for sex discrimination and retaliation. Plaintiff failed to introduce evidence that would lead a reasonable jury to find that there were discriminatory practices or that the defendant retaliated against plaintiff for taking family leave.

Lofton v. EYM Pizza of Illinois, LLC, No. 18-CV-5743, 2024 WL 1283743 (N.D. Ill. Mar. 26, 2024). In a collective action brought by a pizza delivery driver under the Fair Labor Standards Act ("FLSA"), the district court denied a Pizza Hut franchisee's motion for summary judgment because there was a material dispute of fact on whether the reimbursement rate for vehicle expenses was reasonable and should have been reimbursed by the defendant under the FLSA. Because the district court held the reimbursement rate was something to be determined at trial, it denied plaintiff's motion to strike defendants' expert witness without prejudice and reserved the issue for a later determination at trial.

Hooters of America, LLC v. The Superior Court of Riverside County, No. E082896, 2024 WL 2793404 (Cal. Ct. App. May 31, 2024). The California court of appeals denied a franchisor's petition for writ of mandate seeking to compel the trial court to vacate its order denying Hooters' request for summary adjudication on a claim involving the aiding and abetting violations of the Fair Employment and Housing Act ("FEHA"). The court of appeals agreed with the trial court that Hooters failed to satisfy its initial burden as the moving party seeking summary adjudication and returned the matter for further proceedings.

VI. Tax

Sinopoli v. Commissioner of Internal Revenue, Nos. 10838-20, 26360-21, T.C. Memo 2023-105 (T.C. R. Aug. 14, 2023). The Internal Revenue Service (IRS) challenged certain tax deductions, including advertising deductions, claimed by a group of owners of a Planet Fitness franchise. After years of paying advertising providers directly for their services, the owners of the franchise decided to form their own marketing companies. Planet Fitness paid those new affiliated entities for advertising services instead of contracting directly through the previous service providers. The tax court disallowed the deductions for advertising expenses beyond those that could be substantiated. The court found no credible evidence supporting the excess marketing fees claimed by the Planet Fitness franchise.

Hyatt Hotels Corporation & Subsidiaries v. Commissioner, T.C. Memo, 2023-122 (T.C.R. Oct. 2, 2023). In this appeal over the tax treatment of reward program income, the Tax Court concluded that the revenue Hyatt Hotels Corporation and its Subsidiaries (collectively, "Hyatt") received from its loyalty rewards program was includable in Hyatt's gross income.

Hyatt operated a customer loyalty program, branded as the Gold Passport Program (the "Program"). Participating customers

("Members") could earn rewards points ("Points") based on their eligible spending at Hyatt-branded hotels or instead receive miles ("Miles") redeemable from third-party travel partners of Hyatt ("Partners"). The Points could be redeemed for various purposes, such as stays at Hyatt-branded hotels, as well as goods and services offered by Partners. Usage of Miles was governed by the applicable Partner's loyalty program. The manner and rate at which Points were earned and redeemed varied from time to time at Hyatt's discretion.

Hyatt-branded hotels are hotels owned by Hyatt ("Owned Hotels") and hotels owned by third party hotel owners ("TPHO"). TPHOs had a variety of contractual relationships with Hyatt through which they were branded as Hyatt hotels, including management relationships and franchise agreements. During the years at issue in this case, twenty to twenty-five percent of the Hyatt-branded hotels were Owned Hotels, while THPOs owned the balance.

Hyatt maintained a fund called the Gold Passport Fund ("Fund") which it used to operate the Program. The Fund received revenue from four sources all of which was deposited into Hyatt-owned bank accounts: (1) it charged a hotel a percentage of the amounts paid by Members for a stay if the Member elected to have such stay earn Points; (2) it charged a hotel a specific amount if the Member elected to earn Miles instead of Points, which amount had been negotiated between the TPHO and Hyatt; (3) it sold Points for cash to Members at Owned Hotels and TPHOs; and (4) it invested the funds from items 1-3, inclusive in marketable securities.

Hyatt disbursed the Fund in three ways: (1) when a Member redeemed Points such as using it for a free stay or an upgrade, it paid the Owned Hotel or TPHO hotel at which such Points were redeemed; (2) it paid Partners the negotiated amounts for Miles; and (3) it paid the Program's administrative and advertising expenses.

Hyatt filed a consolidated Form 1120, U.S. Corporate Income Return for the years at issue and reported the Fund's assets and liabilities on Schedule L, Balance Sheets per Books to such returns. Hyatt did not report the Fund's total annual revenue or expenses on its Income Tax return in its capacity as an agent for the Owned Hotels and TPHO. Hyatt, however, treated the amounts allocated for disbursement to Owned Hotels in its income and took deductions for its share of expenses in the years with respect to which payments were made to Owned Hotels.

The Internal Revenue Service ("Service") determined that Hyatt's treatment of the Program's income and expenses was improper, and issued a notice of deficiency. Hyatt filed a petition with the Tax Court.

The Tax Court held that Hyatt is required, under I.R.C. Section 61, to include the revenue from the Program in its gross income. Hyatt asserted among other things that it was permitted to treat these funds as money it was holding in "trust" for the Owned Hotels and TPHO hotels, relying on ***Seven-Up Co. v. Commissioner***, 14 T.C. 965 (1950).

In *Seven-Up*, the taxpayer created an advertising fund in which its third-party bottlers could voluntarily contribute. The court in *Seven-Up*, declined to treat these payments as income to the taxpayer because the payments were not for goods or services and the taxpayer did not have any gain from these funds, in part because of contractual restrictions on the taxpayer's use of these funds. The court in *Hyatt*, noted that the trust fund doctrine as expanded from *Seven-Up*, could apply a taxpayer if such taxpayer "(1) receives funds in trust, subject to a legally enforceable restriction that they be spent in their entirety for a specific purpose; and (2) does not profit, gain, or benefit from spending the funds for that purpose." The court noted that Hyatt had complete control over the Program. The court also noted that the TPHOs had no input into how the funds would be invested or the nature and types of promotional and advertising costs incurred. The court also found Hyatt had a direct benefit from the promotional aspects of the Program, and increased its goodwill.

As a result of this, Hyatt was required to include the revenue from the Program in its gross income.

VII. Insurance

S.R. v. Wyndham Hotels & Resorts, Inc., No. 2:23-CV-1731, 2024 WL 2795784 (S.D. Ohio May 31, 2024). A plaintiff alleged she had been trafficked for commercial sex at Wyndham branded hotels in Columbus, Ohio and sued the hotel owners and the franchisor under the Trafficking Victims Protection Reauthorization Act ("TVPRA"). Wyndam's insurance company, Erie Insurance Exchange, brought two motions to intervene seeking a declaratory judgment regarding its obligations, if any, to defend and indemnify Wyndham. The court denied both motions because Erie's interests in the case were contingent on whether Wyndham was liable under the TVPRA.

VIII. Consumer Protection

Pinn v. CycleBar Franchising, LLC, No. 3:23-CV-01540-M, 2023 WL 8374749 (N.D. Tex. Dec. 4, 2023). In this case, the court dismissed a plaintiff's individual and putative class claims made against CycleBar Franchising, LLC, ("CycleBar") for violations of the Texas statute incorporating the TCPA, on the grounds that plaintiff (with a number on the National Do-Not-Call Registry) failed to allege that they had received more than one communication from CycleBar.

Soliman v. Subway Franchisee Advertising Fund Trust, Ltd., 101 F.4th 176 (2d Cir. 2024). Plaintiff appealed a district court's decision to dismiss her putative class action against the Subway Franchisee Advertising Fund Trust, Ltd. that alleged that repeated automated marketing text messages from Subway over a free bag of potato chips violated the Telephone Consumer Protection Act

("TCPA"). The Second Circuit Court of Appeals affirmed the district court's decision to dismiss because the text messages did not violate the TCPA. The court reasoned that the TCPA does not prohibit the use of a stored list of pre-existing telephone numbers where the text messages did not use an artificial or prerecorded voice. In reaching its decision, the Second Circuit adopted the district court's reliance on the Supreme Court's decision in *Facebook, Inc. v. Duguid*, 592 U.S. 395 (2021) where the Court determined that the TCPA is designed to protect against the generation of random or sequential telephone numbers, not a system that calls random or sequential telephone numbers from pre-existing telephone numbers generated in other ways.

IX. Constitutional

Northern Virginia Hemp & Agriculture LLC v. Virginia, No. 123CV1177LMBIDD, 2023 WL 7130853 (E.D. Va. Oct. 30, 2023). The district court denied hemp producers, sellers, and an individual's motion for a preliminary injunction seeking an order prohibiting defendants from enforcing a provision in a recently-passed Virginia law which imposes a limit on substances containing a certain amount of tetrahydrocannabinol ("THC"). The Virginia law is more restrictive than the limit defined in the federal Agricultural Improvement Act of 2018 (the "Farm Act"). The court reasoned that the plaintiffs did not have standing to pursue the claim and noted that the Farm Act explicitly permits states to impose their own regulations, even if they are more stringent than federal law.

Doe (K.B.) v. G6 Hospitality, LLC, No. 1:23-CV-2597-TWT, 2023 WL 8650785 (N.D. Ga. Dec. 14, 2023). The court found that none of the provisions in the Trafficking Victims Protection Reauthorization Act ("TVPRA") are unconstitutionally vague and rejected defendant franchisee's argument that its due process rights would be violated if the court enforced the relevant TVPRA provisions. This case is discussed in Chapter 6, Section X.

X. Trafficking Victims Protection Reauthorization Act

A.D. v. Best Western International, Inc., No. 2:22-CV-651-JES-NPM, 2023 WL 5510064 (M.D. Fla. Aug. 25, 2023). Plaintiff, who alleged she was trafficked for commercial sex at a branded hotel in Fort Myers, Florida, sued the hotel owners and the franchisor under the Trafficking Victims Protection Reauthorization Act ("TVPRA"). The district court granted the franchisor's motion to dismiss. The court reasoned that while the franchisor did knowingly benefit from the sex trafficker, the plaintiff failed to plausibly allege that the franchisor participated in a common sex trafficking venture, as required by the TVPRA. The plaintiff failed to sufficiently plead that the franchisor's participation in shared revenue went beyond its normal role in the franchise relationship. Conversely, the district court denied the franchisee's motion to dismiss, reasoning that the plaintiff alleged sufficient facts to satisfy the statutory requirements for a TVPRA beneficiary claim. Unlike the claim against the franchisor, the plaintiff alleged that the franchisee's employees had continuous business relationships with the traffickers, i.e., consistently renting rooms to the traffickers despite witnessing suspicious activity. The court found that this was sufficient to at least plausibly allege that the franchisees were participating in a sex trafficking venture.

A.D. v. Choice Hotels International, Inc., No. 2:22-CV-646-JES-NPM, 2023 WL 5510090 (M.D. Fla. Aug. 25, 2023). Plaintiff, who was allegedly trafficked for commercial sex at a branded hotel in Florida, sued the hotel owner and franchisor under the Trafficking Victims Protection Reauthorization Act ("TVPRA"). The district court granted the franchisor's motion to dismiss. It reasoned that while the franchisor did knowingly benefit from the sex trafficking, the plaintiff failed to plausibly allege that the franchisor participated in a common sex trafficking venture, as required by the TVPRA. Conversely, the district court denied the franchisee's motion to dismiss, reasoning that the plaintiff alleged sufficient facts to satisfy the statutory requirements for a TVPRA beneficiary claim. Unlike the franchisor, the plaintiff alleged that the franchisee's employees had continuous business relationships with the traffickers, i.e., assisting the sex traffickers by serving as lookouts for law enforcement. The court also found that personal relationships the trafficker had with the franchisee's staff supported an inference of the franchisee participating in a sex trafficking venture under the statute. For example, the plaintiff had alleged an instance where the trafficker gave a housekeeper cash to keep quiet after finding drugs, and an excessive amount of cash while cleaning a room. These facts were sufficient to avoid a motion to dismiss.

A.D. v. Marriott International, Inc., No. 2:22-CV-645-JES-NPM, 2023 WL 5510268 (M.D. Fla. Aug. 25, 2023). Plaintiff brought suit pursuant to the Trafficking Victims Protection Reauthorization Act ("TVPRA") against franchisor Marriott International, Inc. ("Marriott") and its franchisee, CHM Naples Partners, LLC ("CHM Naples"). The district court granted defendants' motion to dismiss with leave to file an amended complaint. Plaintiff proceeded to file a consolidated amended complaint against both defendants alleging that they knowingly participated in sex trafficking and prostitution operations while reaping various benefits such as the profits from room rentals, third party fees, and an enhanced reputation of the Marriott brand. Defendants renewed their motions to dismiss for failure to state a claim.

Plaintiff alleged that they were trafficked for commercial sex at SpringHill Suites ("SpringHill") by Marriott in Naples, Florida. Pursuant to the franchise agreement, CHM Naples owns and supervises SpringHill and Marriott is in charge of making decisions that directly impacts SpringHill. Further, Plaintiff alleged that there was an agency relationship between the defendants that authorized Marriott to maintain an "ongoing systemic right of control over SpringHill hotel." The TVPRA requires that a plaintiff filing a claim for beneficiary liability show that the defendant (1) knowingly benefitted; (2) from participating in a venture; (3) that the venture violated the TVPRA; and (4) the defendants knew or should have known that the venture violated the TVPRA.

The district court noted that a plaintiff can satisfy the first element by alleging that there was a "continuous business relationship." The allegation that Marriott and CHM Naples both financially benefited from the venture sufficed to show a "continuous business relationship." Thus, the court found that Plaintiff sufficiently alleged the first prong of the test.

The court then analyzed the second element regarding Marriott's participation in the venture. Plaintiff alleged that Marriott had actual or constructive knowledge of the sex trafficking and failed to implement or impose any policies that could have protected the plaintiff and other victims. As such, plaintiff asserted that Marriott's "participation" was its failure to impose effective preventative procedures. The district court disagreed with plaintiff's assertion and granted Marriott's motion to dismiss. It found that the franchisor's alleged failure to implement protective policies was insufficient to establish that it participated in the sex trafficking venture.

The court then addressed the allegations against CHM Naples in regard to the second element of the statute. Plaintiff alleged that CHM Naples knew or should have known that Plaintiff was being trafficked because of several alarming encounters with hotel staff and the traffickers. Some of these encounters included excessive requests for sheets, a personal relationship between staff and the traffickers, and Plaintiff constantly checking in and paying for one night. Plaintiff also recounted an incident where the trafficker hosted a loud party with visibly underage attendees and the hotel staff did not break it up, despite the complaints received by the franchisee. The court recognized that a plaintiff is not required to show that a defendant had actual knowledge to satisfy the participation element under the statute. Instead, a plaintiff can allege facts that a court could reasonably infer a tacit relationship between the hotel and the trafficker. The court found that Plaintiff had pleaded sufficient facts to establish a plausible inference that CHM Naples's employees were participating in the venture.

Lastly, the court found that Plaintiff had plausibly alleged the remaining elements of a TVPRA violation against CHM Naples, including a violation of the TVPRA and that CHM Naples knew or should have known that the venture violated the TVPRA. Accordingly, the court denied CHM Naples' motion to dismiss.

Doe K.R. v. Choice Hotels International, Inc., No. 6:23-CV-1012-JSS-LHP, 2024 WL 2955728 (M.D. Fla. June 12, 2024). A plaintiff alleged she had been trafficked for commercial sex at a Choice Hotels branded franchise in Orlando, Florida and sued the hotel owners and the franchisor under the Trafficking Victims Protection Reauthorization Act ("TVPRA"). The franchisor defendants moved to dismiss, arguing that the claims were time-barred under the TVPRA's ten-year statute of limitations and for failure to state a claim, and, alternatively, to strike plaintiff's allegations. The district court denied the franchisor's motions. The court held that under the continuing tort doctrine or through equitable tolling, the claims were not time barred and the plaintiff sufficiently alleged facts to survive dismissal at the pleading stage. The court also held that plaintiff sufficiently alleged her perpetrator, beneficiary, and vicarious liability claims under the TVPRA. First, drawing all reasonable inferences in favor of plaintiff, the district court held that plaintiff sufficiently plead that defendants knowingly harbored plaintiff with actual knowledge or reckless disregard of the fact that force, threats of force, or coercion were used to force plaintiff into commercial sex acts. Second, plaintiff's allegations that the franchisor profited from the trafficking by renting rooms to plaintiff's traffickers was sufficient to satisfy that the franchisor knowingly benefitted from the scheme. And third, in Florida, franchisors may enter into an agency relationship with a franchisee, and therefore, the plaintiff sufficiently plead vicarious liability under the TVPRA. The district court also denied defendants' motion to strike certain paragraphs of the complaint because it did not find the allegations to be immaterial or impertinent as required by the rule.

T.E. v. Wyndham Hotels & Resorts, Inc., No. 2:22-cv-3185, 2023 WL 5531441 (S.D. Ohio, Aug. 28, 2023). A sex trafficking victim filed an action under the Trafficking Victims Protection Reauthorization Act ("TVPRA") against Wyndham Hotels & Resorts, Inc., Red Roof Inns, Inc., and Red Roof Franchising, LLC (together, "Red Roof") alleging that Red Roof facilitated violations of the TVPRA. Red Roof filed a motion to dismiss. The court denied the motion to dismiss the claims based on the theories of direct and vicarious liability against Red Roof and granted the motion to dismiss the claim based on a joint employer theory.

Under the TVPRA, a victim of sex trafficking can assert a civil claim against any party that "knowingly benefits, financially or by receiving anything of value from participation in a venture which that person knew or should have known has engaged in an act in violation of [the TVPRA]." Red Roof alleged that it could not be held liable for the misuse of its property, especially when there is no evidence that Red Roof knew of the trafficking. As a franchisor, Red Roof argued it was an owner, operator or employer of the hotel or staff and was too far removed to have participated or benefited from the trafficking. However, the plaintiff argued that Red Roof could not simply bury its head in the sand. According to the plaintiff, Red Roof controlled every aspect of the hotel's day-to-day operations and had access to incident reports, suspicious criminal activity, police reports from its hotels, customer reviews, and online data, but failed to implement policies to prevent trafficking.

The court examined previous cases and concluded that failure to implement policies to combat known problems could meet the standard of willful blindness or negligence. The court also found that failing to implement these policies while maintaining control over the hotel operations and benefiting from the renting of the rooms could meet the TVPRA's element of "participation in a venture." The court decided the plaintiff sufficiently state a claim that Red Roof is liable under the TVPRA based on a direct liability theory. The court also found the plaintiff's allegations that Red Roof exercised control over the franchisee hotels sufficient to meet the federal pleadings standards for purposes of asserting a vicarious liability claim under the TVPRA. The court denied the motion to dismiss under the direct and vicarious liability theories.

The court granted Red Roof's motion to dismiss as to plaintiff's joint employer theory of liability. Although the analysis under a vicarious liability claim and joint employer claim are similar, with a joint employer claim, the court examines the control exercised by the franchisor specific to employment policies when determining whether plaintiff has satisfied its burden. The fact that Red Roof posted open personnel positions on its website and set core values and culture for all hotel employees was insufficient to survive a motion to dismiss where Red Roof did not have any other control over hiring, training, and other employment specific policies.

B.D.G. v. Choice Hotels International, Inc., 2:22-cv-3202, 2023 WL 5935646 (S.D. Ohio Sept. 12, 2023). This is another case out of the Southern District of Ohio where a sex trafficking victim filed an action under the Trafficking Victims Protection Reauthorization Act ("TVPRA") against a hotel franchisor. In this case, plaintiff alleged that Choice Hotels International, Inc. ("Choice") facilitated violations of the TVPRA under a direct liability theory, vicarious liability theory, and joint employment liability theory. Choice filed a motion to dismiss. The court denied the motion to Dismiss the direct and vicarious liability claims and granted the motion to dismiss the joint employer claim.

Under the TVPRA, a victim of sex trafficking can assert a civil claim against any party that "knowingly benefits, financially or by receiving anything of value from participation in a venture which that person knew or should have known has engaged in an act in violation of [the TVPRA]." As in *T.E. v. Wyndham Hotels &*

Resorts, Inc. the court decided the plaintiff sufficiently stated a claim that Choice is directly civilly liable under the TVPRA. The court found that knowledge of the issue of sex trafficking generally, along with signs that should have alerted the defendants to sex trafficking issues, and the failure to take adequate steps to train staff to prevent sex trafficking, was sufficient to meet the constructive knowledge requirement under the TVPRA. The court also found the plaintiff's allegations that Choice exercised control over the franchisee hotels sufficient to meet the federal pleadings standards for purposes of asserting an actual agency claim under the TVPRA capable of surviving a motion to dismiss. The court denied the motion to dismiss under the direct and vicarious liability theories.

B.J. v. G6 Hospitality, LLC, 22-cv-03765-MMC, 2023 WL 6120682 (N.D. Cal. Sept. 18, 2023). A sex trafficking victim filed an action under the Trafficking Victims Protection Reauthorization Act ("TVPRA") against five different franchisors of hotel franchise brands where the plaintiff was allegedly trafficked and sexually exploited over the course of several years. The franchisors of the five California hotels filed Motions to Dismiss plaintiff's claims. The plaintiff alleged direct beneficiary claims under the TVPRA as well as vicarious beneficiary liability claims.

To succeed under a direct beneficiary TVPRA claim, the plaintiff must show the defendants (1) knowingly benefited from the alleged trafficking; (2) participated in the venture; and (3) knew or should have known the person had engaged in trafficking. The court analyzed the evidence provided against each of the hotel brand defendants. The court found that the plaintiff failed to establish prong two and three against the Marriott, Choice, and Hilton hotel brands. In these claims the plaintiff did not show that any employee was in a position to witness the trafficking instances she used as evidence. However, in the case against Studio 6 Concord, and G6, the plaintiff did provide allegations supporting element two and three. In the Studio 6 Concord case, plaintiff alleged the manager of the hotel trained the traffickers on being discrete, exchanged room discounts for sexual favors and assisted the traffickers in avoiding police detection. In the G6 case, plaintiff alleged the manager knew of the trafficking, attempted to keep the trafficking hidden, and had employees supervise children of the victims while the mothers were sold for sex. The plaintiff also alleged that the employees saw obvious signs of abuse, like visible bruising, malnourishment and inappropriate clothing for the weather. The court dismissed the direct beneficiary claims against Marriott, Choice and Hilton, but not Studio 6 Concord and G6.

Because no direct claim was established against Marriott, Choice, and Hilton, the court dismissed the vicarious liability claims against the three brands. The court also dismissed the vicarious liability claim against G6 predicated on an actual agency theory, because the plaintiff was unable to show the franchisor brand had control over the instrumentality of plaintiff's harm, which was the hiring, firing, and compensation of individual employees who participated in the venture. The claim under the apparent agency theory was also dismissed because there was no allegation that the plaintiff relied on any representation made by the defendants. The vicarious liability claims were dismissed.

Finally, the plaintiff attempted to hold the franchisors liable as direct perpetrators of the trafficking. The court found that the facts in the claim against Concord Inn could support a claim because plaintiff alleged facts demonstrating that the manager of the hotel had actual knowledge and direct involvement in the trafficking scheme which could be imputed on the defendant. The remaining claims were dismissed.

S.R. v. Wyndham Hotels & Resorts, Inc., No. 2:23-CV-1731, 2024 WL 3226126 (S.D. Ohio June 28, 2024). A plaintiff alleged she was trafficked for commercial sex at a Wyndham Hotels & Resorts, Inc. ("Wyndham") franchises in the Columbus, Ohio area, including the Crowne Plaza by IHG. Plaintiff sued the hotel owners and the franchisor under the Trafficking Victims Protection Reauthorization

Act ("TVPRA"). Six Continents Hotels, Inc. and Holiday Hospitality Franchising, LLC (the "IHG Defendants") moved to dismiss the claim that they were liable as beneficiaries of their participation in a commercial venture that they knew, or should have known, violated the TVPRA. The district court denied in part and granted in part IHG Defendants' motion. The court denied the IHG Defendants' motion except for that portion of plaintiff's beneficiary theory claims for conduct prior to December 23, 2008, which claims were dismissed with prejudice on statute of limitations grounds. As to the actionable claims after that date, the district court held that plaintiff plausibly stated a claim to hold the IHG Defendants liable as a beneficiary under the TVPRA. First, plaintiff's allegations that the IHG Defendants profited from the trafficking by renting rooms to plaintiff's traffickers was sufficient to satisfy that the franchisor knowingly benefitted from the scheme. Second, the court found that plaintiff's allegations that the IHG Defendants profited, failed to implement policies, and maintained expansive control over the hotel's operations, met the standards of the TVPRA for participation in the venture.

S.R. v. Wyndham Hotels & Resorts, Inc., No. 2:23-CV-1731, 2024 WL 3227029 (S.D. Ohio June 28, 2024). A plaintiff alleged she was trafficked for commercial sex at a Wyndham Hotels & Resorts, Inc. ("Wyndham") franchise in the Columbus, Ohio area and sued the hotel owners and the franchisor under the Trafficking Victims Protection Reauthorization Act ("TVPRA"). The franchisor, Wyndham, moved to dismiss the claim. The district court denied the franchisor's motion, holding that the plaintiff sufficiently stated a claim to hold the franchisor liable as a beneficiary under the TVPRA. First, plaintiff's allegations that the franchisor profited from the trafficking by renting rooms to plaintiff's traffickers was sufficient to satisfy that the franchisor knowingly benefitted from the scheme. Second, the court found that plaintiff's allegations that the franchisor profited, failed to implement policies, and maintained expansive control over the hotel's operations, met the standards of the TVPRA for participation in the venture. This case is discussed above.

J.K. v. Ramada Worldwide, Inc., No. 23-00108, 2023 WL 5621913, (N.D. Ga. Aug. 30, 2023). Ramada Worldwide, Inc. ("Ramada") was able to secure dismissal of a Trafficking Victims Protection Reauthorization Act ("TVPRA") claim based on vicarious liability. Plaintiff J.K. was an alleged victim of sex trafficking at a franchisee owned Ramada Limited Suites hotel in Georgia. Ramada moved for dismissal arguing (1) the TVPRA does not provide for indirect liability based on agency theories; and (2) the franchise agreement did not provide a basis to impute liability to Ramada.

J.K. alleged four separate theories of vicarious liability: actual agency, apparent agency, aiding and abetting, and joint venture. The court immediately rejected the aiding and abetting theory for the imputed liability claims under ***Central Bank of Denver v. First Interstate Bank of Denver***, 511 U.S. 164, 177 (1994) (holding no aiding and abetting liability unless the actor caused the harm).

The court dismissed the actual agency arguments because the allegations did not plausibly allege that Ramada exercised such complete control over the day-to-day operations of the franchisee's business that its purported independence "may be fairly dismissed as a fiction." The court found that plaintiff's claim that "Ramada controlled the daily actions . . . because it determined the 'ultimate daily decision making for the [hotel's] operation" failed to allege any facts supporting actual agency. The court distinguished contrary holdings based on factual differences. Liability on the joint venture claim was similarly dismissed for lack of facts supporting mutual control of the hotel.

The court also dismissed the apparent authority claims concluding that plaintiff failed to prove any of the three elements. The first element requires a representation to the plaintiff, and the court concluded that general advertising of the Ramada brand is not sufficient to prove that Ramada caused plaintiff to have a belief about the authority of the franchisee to act on behalf of Ramada. The second element requires a representation that would have caused plaintiff to believe that franchisee was authorized to act for Ramada's benefit. The third element requires a showing that plaintiff relied to its detriment on such representations, but none of the representations addressed the authority of the franchisee and was only general branding representing that the Ramada brand was law abiding. The court dismissed all claims against Ramada.

A.M.L. v. Wyndham Hotels and Resorts, No. 823CV01554JVSJDEX, 2023 WL 8888836 (C.D. Cal. Nov. 13, 2023). The district court granted in part and denied in part defendant Wyndham Hotels and Resorts' ("Wyndham") motion to dismiss Plaintiff's complaint brought pursuant to the Trafficking Victim Protection Reauthorization Act ("TVPRA"). In the complaint, Plaintiff alleged that she was sex trafficked at the Days Inn by Wyndham Anaheim West located in Anaheim, California. Although the hotel staff received various complaints about loud noises and observed apparent signs of trafficking, Plaintiff alleged that they failed to respond. Plaintiff further alleged that hotel guests and staff witnessed specific incidents of physical abuse. Some of the business decisions included which types of payments were permitted, employee wages, and training programs.

The court first addressed Wyndham's motion to dismiss the TVPRA claim under beneficiary liability. Wyndham argued that the Plaintiff failed to sufficiently allege that Wyndham participated in the trafficking venture or that Wyndham knew or should have known about the trafficking. The court agreed with this argument, finding that Plaintiff alleged insufficient facts to support the assertion that Wyndham participated in the venture or that it had either actual or constructive knowledge of Plaintiff's particular trafficking, as required by the TVPRA. For similar reasons, the court dismissed the TVPRA claim under the theory of perpetrator liability.

Next, the court addressed Wyndham's motion to dismiss the TVPRA claim under vicarious liability for the establishment's owner and operator's actions. Wyndham argued that Plaintiff failed to assert that they exercised control over their franchisee hotels to support an agency relationship. The court disagreed, and instead, found that the complaint plausibly alleged a principal-agent relationship between Wyndham and the owner and operator of the Days Inn. Thus, the court denied the portion of Wyndham's motion to dismiss the TVPRA claim for vicarious liability.

In re Hotel TVPRA Litigation, No. 22-3845, 2023 WL 8230011 (S.D. Ohio, Nov. 28, 2023). In this procedural decision, the United States District Court for the Southern District of Ohio evaluated whether Red Roof Inn's insurer, Liberty Mutual, had a right to intervene in twenty-six consolidated cases in which the individual Plaintiffs all alleged, in separate actions, that Red Roof Inn Inc. (corporate parent) and Red Roof Franchising, LLC) (franchisor) (collectively, "Red Roof") had violated the Trafficking Victims Protection Reauthorization Act ("TVPRA") for ignoring and facilitating commercial sex trafficking at their properties, while enjoying the profits of the rooms used by victims. Red Roof (the franchisor) sought insurance coverage for all of these claims from Liberty Mutual under a series of policies. Liberty Mutual agreed to defend Red Roof under a reservation of rights, and sought to intervene for the purpose of obtaining a declaratory judgment in each of the twenty-six cases that it was not obligated to further defend or indemnify Red Roof for the trafficking claims. Liberty Mutual asserted that it was entitled to intervention as a matter of right under Fed. R. Civ. P. 24(a), or alternatively, was entitled to permissive intervention under Fed. R. Civ. P. 24(b)(1). Plaintiffs and Red Roof opposed the motions.

The district court first analyzed Liberty Mutual's request for intervention as of right. It found that in the Sixth Circuit, an intervention of right can only be granted if the entity seeking to intervene has a "substantial and direct interest in a proceeding, not a contingent one." The district court denied the motion for intervention as of right, holding that Liberty Mutual's interest was contingent, not direct, because it was an open question on two issues: (1) whether the TVPRA applied to Red Roof; and (2) whether Liberty Mutual would ultimately owe Red Roof a duty to defend and indemnify under the insurance contract. Importantly, the district court noted that allowing Liberty Mutual to intervene would likely permit it to interfere and essentially control the defense when the insurer and the insured's interests were not fully aligned.

The district court also denied Liberty Mutual's motion for permissive intervention. It held that while Liberty Mutual was interested in the question of liability in the underlying cases, its interest was limited to whether it would have any coverage obligations, not the ultimate outcome. It further noted that permitting intervention would risk delay and prejudice to the other parties, particularly the plaintiff, who had no direct interest in the coverage dispute.

Doe v. Scottsdale Inns LLC, No. CV-23-00759-PHX-JJT, 2024 WL 3494375 (D. Ariz. July 22, 2024). A plaintiff alleged she had been trafficked for sex at a Howard Johnson hotel in Scottsdale, Arizona and sued the hotel owners and the franchisor under the Trafficking Victims Protection Reauthorization Act ("TVPRA"). The franchisor, Wyndham Hotels & Resorts, moved to dismiss for failure to state a claim. The court granted in part Wyndham's motion regarding the direct liability claim because plaintiff failed to plausibly allege that Wyndham participated in a venture with plaintiff's sex traffickers and because plaintiff failed to allege facts supporting either Wyndham's actual or constructive knowledge of the trafficking. However, regarding plaintiff's vicarious liability claim, the court denied Wyndham's motion because plaintiff's allegations were sufficient for the district court to plausibly infer an agency relationship between Wyndham and Scottsdale Inn, its franchisee.

K.B. v. G6 Hospitality, LLC, No. 1:23-CV-2597-TWT, 2023 WL 8650785 (N.D. Ga. Dec. 14, 2023). The district court granted defendants G6 Hospitality, LLC, G6 Hospitality Franchising, LLC, G6 Hospitality IP, LLC, G6 Hospitality Property, LLC, G6 Hospitality Purchasing, LLC, and Motel 6 Operating, LP's (collectively, "G6") motion to dismiss Plaintiff's complaint brought pursuant to the Trafficking Victims Protection Reauthorization Act ("TVPRA") and O.C.G.A Section 51-1-56. The court also granted in part and denied in part, defendant Hare Krishna Savannah Hotel, LLC's ("Hare Krishna") motion to dismiss and denied its motion for private disclosure of Plaintiff's identity.

In the complaint, Plaintiff alleged that she was trafficked for commercial sex at a Motel 6 in Savannah, Georgia. Plaintiff further alleged that Hare Krishna owned the franchise and jointly operated and managed the motel with G6. Plaintiff claimed that Hare Krishna and G6 knowingly benefitted from, participated in and had actual or constructive knowledge that the sex trafficking venture violated the TVPRA.

The court granted G6's motion to dismiss finding that Plaintiff failed to sufficiently plead the required elements of a TVPRA claim. Specifically, Plaintiff did not sufficiently plead that G6 participated in the sex trafficking venture, nor did she sufficiently plead that G6 had actual or constructive knowledge. The court also found the assertion that there was an agency relationship between the defendants that authorized G6 to maintain systemic control of Motel 6 insufficient to plausibly state a claim against G6.

Next, the court addressed Hare Krishna's motions. Hare Krishna argued that Plaintiff failed to sufficiently allege that it had notice of or participated in the alleged trafficking because Plaintiff never accused hotel staff of witnessing someone using force against Plaintiff, nor did the complaint adequately allege that Hare Krishna actively participated in the venture. The court rejected the argument noting that the TVPRA does not require actual knowledge, rather, it explicitly permits claims where a party should have known about the trafficking. A court determines whether such an allegation is plausible based on the surrounding circumstances set forth in a complaint. The court acknowledged that the complaint established that Hare Krishna should have known about the trafficking based on various factors. Thus, the district court denied Hare Krishna's motion to dismiss Plaintiff's TVPRA claim. The court also denied Hare Krishna's motion for private disclosure of Plaintiff's identity. However, the court advised Plaintiff to seek leave to proceed anonymously or disclose her identity within fourteen days. Lastly, the court granted Hare Krishna's motion to dismiss Plaintiff's state claim under O.C.G.A Section 51-1-56 because there is a presumption against retroactivity in Georgia which applied to the timeline in this case.

Doe (K.B.) v. Hare Krishna Savannah Hotel, LLC, 346 F.R.D. 150 (N.D. Ga. Mar. 25, 2024). Plaintiff, who alleged she was trafficked for commercial sex at a Motel 6 in Savannah, Georgia, sued the hotel franchisor and its franchisee under the Trafficking Victims Protection Reauthorization Act ("TVPRA"). After the district court granted the franchisor and franchisee's motion to dismiss, plaintiff filed a motion to proceed under a pseudonym, for protective order, and for leave to amend the complaint. The court granted all of plaintiff's motions because defendants did not oppose proceeding under a pseudonym for pretrial proceedings and protective orders are warranted to protect TVPRA plaintiff identities. The court granted plaintiff's motion to amend because although the court previously granted defendants' motion to dismiss, the court did not enter a final judgment, so plaintiff was allowed to amend the pleading and try again to state a claim.

P.B. v. Wyndham Hotels & Resorts, Inc., No. CV231493ZNQRLS, 2023 WL 8890229 (D.N.J. Dec. 26, 2023). The district court denied defendant Dorca Co. Inc.'s ("Dorca") motion to dismiss Plaintiff's complaint brought pursuant to the Trafficking Victim Protection Reauthorization Act ("TVPRA"). The court also granted in part and denied in part defendants Wyndham Hotels & Resorts, Inc. and Ramada Worldwide Inc.'s (together, "Franchisors") motion to dismiss.

Plaintiff alleged that she was a victim of sex trafficking at a Ramada Inn in Toms River, New Jersey. Although Plaintiff was unable to recall all of the specific dates she visited the hotel, she was able to recall two specific dates and provide a generalized extended period of time. Plaintiff further alleged that the Franchisors maintained consistent standards for its franchisees and periodically conducted on-site inspections to inform them when making business decisions. Some of the business decisions included which types of payments were permitted, employee wages, and training programs.

The court first addressed Dorca's motion to dismiss. Dorca argued that the court should reject the allegation against it because Plaintiff cannot plausibly make general allegations about the time frame. The court rejected this argument, reasoning that Plaintiffs allegations were plausible. Specifically, the court noted that Plaintiff's inability to recall more than two specific dates did not preclude her from pleading plausible allegations as to the defined and extended period.

Next, the court addressed the franchisor's motion to dismiss. The Franchisors argued that Plaintiff failed to sufficiently allege that Franchisors knew or should have known of the circumstances surrounding Plaintiff's trafficking. The court agreed with this argument, finding that Plaintiff had insufficient facts to support the assertion that Franchisors had either actual or constructive knowledge of Plaintiff's particular trafficking, as required by the TVPRA. Therefore, the court granted in part Franchisors' motion to dismiss. However, the court went on to consider Plaintiff's claim against Franchisors for vicarious liability relating to Dorca's conduct. Franchisors argued that Plaintiff failed to assert that they exercised control over their franchisee hotels to support an agency relationship. The court disagreed, and instead, found that the complaint plausibly alleges a principal-agent relationship between

Dorca and Franchisors. Thus, the court denied the portion of Franchisors' motion to dismiss the claim for vicarious liability.

J.M. v. Red Roof Inns, Inc., No. 2:22-cv-00672-KJM-JDP 2024 WL 532336 (E.D. Cal. Jan. 24, 2024). The United States District Court for the Eastern District of California denied plaintiff's motion to stay a sex-trafficking case pending a pending a decision from the Judicial Panel on Multidistrict Litigation ("JPML") on whether the case would be transferred to a different court for a multidistrict litigation proceeding (MDL). In 2020, the JPML denied a motion to centralize approximately three dozen cases brought by sex trafficking survivors against hotel brand franchisors, franchisees, and related entities, alleging violations under the Trafficking Victims Protection Reauthorization Act ("TVPRA"). The JPML denied the motion based on the "unique issues concerning" the allegations in each of these actions and pending before the JPML was a motion seeking reconsideration. The court found that given the very late date of plaintiff's motion to stay, filed so close to the fact discovery cutoff and start of expert discovery, a stay of proceedings at this stage would prejudice the defendant and plaintiff had not shown it would suffer hardship or inequity.

Doe v. Wyndham Hotels & Resorts, No. 8:23-CV-01554-JVS (JDEX), 2024 WL 2104596 (C.D. Cal. Feb. 28, 2024). A plaintiff alleged she had been trafficked for commercial sex at a Days Inn, a Wyndham branded hotel, in Anaheim, California. She sued the hotel owners and the franchisor under beneficial liability of the Trafficking Victims Protection Reauthorization Act ("TVPRA"). The franchisor moved to dismiss the claim. The court granted the franchisor's motion, holding that the plaintiff failed to sufficiently state elements of the claim, but granted plaintiff leave to amend her complaint.

T.E. v. Wyndham Hotels & Resorts, Inc., No. 2:22-cv-3185, 2024 WL 474400 (S.D. Ohio Feb. 7, 2024). A sex trafficking victim filed an action under the Trafficking Victims Protection Reauthorization Act ("TVPRA") against Wyndham Hotels & Resorts, Inc., Red Roof Inns, Inc. and Red Roof Franchising, LLC (together, "Red Roof") alleging that Red Roof facilitated violations of the TVPRA. Red Roof filed a motion to dismiss. The court denied the motion to dismiss the claims based on the theories of direct and vicarious liability against Red Roof and granted the motion to dismiss the claim based on a joint employer theory. This decision is substantially the same as the earlier August 2023 decision and issued only to correct typographical errors.

S.C. v. Wyndham Hotels & Resorts, Inc., No. 1:23-cv-00871, 2024 WL 584996 (N.D. Ohio Feb. 13, 2024). The United States District Court for the Northern District of Ohio denied defendant Choice Hotel's motion for reconsideration of the court's order denying its motion to seal a hotel franchise agreement, hotel brand standards, and quality assurance reports, in a sex trafficking case. The court did permit Choice to redact fee and royalty terms from the franchise agreement. Choice argued that the failure to seal this information was clear error and manifest injustice. The court disagreed holding that Choice did not meet the high "compelling reasons" bar for sealing in the first instance, let alone establish clear error or manifest injustice. The court found that Choice's brand standards and quality assurance reports appear to be at the crux of plaintiff's argument that the franchisee hotel where plaintiff was trafficked was Choice's agent, were potentially important to how much control Choice exercised over its franchisee hotel, and that the brand standards and quality assurance reports may contain important evidence regarding Choice's relation to the franchised hotel where the trafficking allegedly occurred.

Jane Doe (L.M.) v. 42 Hotel Raleigh, LLC, No. 5:23-CV-235-FL, 2024 WL 631482 (E.D.N.C. Feb. 13, 2024). The United States District Court for the Eastern District of North Carolina granted defendants' motion to dismiss the plaintiff's complaint alleging that the defendant franchisor, Hilton, and one of its hotel franchisees violated the Trafficking Victims Protection Reauthorization Act ("TVPRA"). The court dismissed the complaint after finding that plaintiff failed to establish they were a victim of sex trafficking within the meaning of the TVPRA, that the defendant franchisor and franchisee did not participate in a sex trafficking enterprise as defined by the TVPRA, and that defendants' lacked actual or constructive knowledge of plaintiff's trafficking.

Doe (S.C.) v. Sheraton, LLC, No. 23CV00451 KG/JMR, 2024 WL 1329422 (D.N.M. Mar. 28, 2024). Court denied motion to dismiss over Trafficking Victims Protection Reauthorization Act ("TVPRA") claims against hotel franchisee, granted motion to dismiss vicarious liability TVPRA claims against franchisor and affiliated corporations, and denied motion to dismiss successor liability claim against hotel franchisor that acquired subsidiary of original franchising company.

R.C. v. Choice Hotels International Inc., No. 5:23-cv-00872, 2024 WL 713036 (N.D. Ohio Feb. 21, 2024). The United States District Court for the Northern District of Ohio denied in part, defendant, Choice Hotels International Inc. ("Choice") motion to seal franchise related information, including its franchise agreement, rules and regulations, quality reports, and similar information ruling that the documents contained important information going to the question of how much control Choice had over the franchisee hotel in a Trafficking Victims Protection Reauthorization Act case.

K.F. v. Choice Hotels International, Inc., No. 2:22-cv-3839, 2023 WL 1256052 (S.D. Ohio Mar. 25, 2024). The United States District Court for the Southern District of Ohio denied Choice Hotel International's ("Choice") motion to dismiss, transfer, or sever the plaintiff's complaint. The court found that the plaintiff, an alleged child victim of sex trafficking, stated a cause of action under the Child Abuse Victim's Rights Act ("CAVRA") that she was trafficked as a minor. Because plaintiffs properly asserting claims under CAVRA may bring a lawsuit in any appropriate district court, the court denied the motion. The court rejected Choice's argument that CAVRA required actual knowledge, instead of constructive knowledge, under the civil portion of the statute. The court also rejected Choice's argument that the statute only permitted lawsuits against the actual offenders or perpetrators of the crimes. Finally, the court found plaintiff's allegations against Choice for violations of the Trafficking Victims Protection Reauthorization Act ("TVPRA") were sufficient to pass the plausibility standard under a 12(b)(6) motion to dismiss where defendant was alleged to have profited, failed to implement policies, and maintained expansive control over the hotel operation standards, thereby meeting the TVPRA's definition of "participation in a venture." Here, Choice was alleged to be involved in a business venture with the franchisee hotels, and both groups benefited by renting rooms to traffickers despite having at least constructive knowledge of ongoing trafficking based on the totality of the circumstances.

T.D.P. v. Choice Hotels International, Inc., No. 2:22-cv-3837, 2023 WL 1256053 (S.D. Ohio March 25, 2024). The United States District Court for the Southern District of Ohio denied Choice Hotel International's motion to dismiss, transfer, or sever the plaintiff's claims under the same analysis set forth in the case of *K.F. v. Choice Hotels International, Inc.*, No. 2:22-cv-3839, 2023 WL 1256052 (D. Ohio March 25, 2024) detailed above.

G.M. v. Choice Hotels International, Inc., No. 2:22-cv-3788, 2023 WL 1256051 (S.D. Ohio Mar. 25, 2024). The United States District Court for the Southern District of Ohio denied Choice Hotel International's motion to dismiss, transfer, or sever the plaintiff's claims under the same analysis set forth in the case of *K.F. v. Choice Hotels International, Inc.*, No. 2:22-cv-3839, 2023 WL 1256052 (S.D. Ohio Mar. 25, 2024) detailed above.

A.Y. v. Red Roof Inns, Inc., No. 2:22-CV-3768, 2024 WL 1332237 (S.D. Ohio Mar. 28, 2024). Plaintiff alleged she had been trafficked for commercial sex at Red Roof Inn franchise located in Tucson,

Arizona, and sued the hotel owners and franchisor under the Trafficking Victims Protection Reauthorization Act ("TVPRA"). The franchisor moved to dismiss the claim. The court denied the franchisor's motion, holding that the plaintiff sufficiently stated a claim to hold the franchisor liable as a beneficiary under the TVPRA. In so deciding, the Court determined that plaintiff's allegations that the franchisor profited from the trafficking by renting rooms to plaintiff's traffickers was sufficient to satisfy that the franchisor knowingly benefitted from the scheme. However, the court rejected plaintiff's alternative contention that the franchisor knowingly benefited by collecting the trafficker's personal data through the hotel's WIFI. Second, the court found that plaintiff's allegations that the franchisor profited, failed to implement policies, and maintained expansive control over the hotel's operations met the standards of the TVPRA for participation in the venture.

A.Y.S. v. Red Roof Inns, Inc., No. 2:22-CV-3767, 2024 WL 1332223 (S.D. Ohio Mar. 28, 2024). Plaintiff alleged to have been trafficked for commercial sex at Red Roof Inn franchise located in Naperville, Illinois. She sued the hotel owners and the franchisor under the Trafficking Victims Protection Reauthorization Act ("TVPRA"). Thereafter, the franchisor moved to dismiss the claim. The court denied the franchisor's motion, holding that the plaintiff sufficiently stated a claim to hold the franchisor liable as a beneficiary under the TVPRA. First, plaintiff's allegations that the franchisor profited from the trafficking by renting rooms to plaintiff's traffickers was sufficient to satisfy that the franchisor knowingly benefitted from the scheme. However, the court rejected plaintiff's alternative contention that the franchisor knowingly benefited by collecting the trafficker's personal data through the hotel's WIFI. Second, the court found that Plaintiff's allegations that the franchisor profited, failed to implement policies, and maintained expansive control over the hotel's operations met the standards of the TVPRA for participation in the venture.

C.B. v. Red Roof Inns, Inc., No. 2:22-CV-3772, 2024 WL 1332228 (S.D. Ohio Mar. 28, 2024). Plaintiff alleged she had been trafficked for commercial sex at several Red Roof properties throughout multiple states, and sued the hotel owners and the franchisors under the Trafficking Victims Protection Reauthorization Act ("TVPRA"). Thereafter, the franchisor moved to dismiss the claim. The court denied the motion, holding that the plaintiff sufficiently stated a claim to hold the franchisor liable as a beneficiary under the TVPRA. First, plaintiff's allegations that the franchisor profited from the trafficking by renting rooms to her traffickers was sufficient to satisfy that the franchisor knowingly benefitted from the scheme. However, the court rejected plaintiff's alternative contention that the franchisor knowingly benefited by collecting the trafficker's personal data through the hotel's WIFI. Second, the court found that plaintiff's allegations that the franchisor profited, failed to implement policies, and maintained expansive control over the hotel's operations met the standards of the TVPRA for participation in the venture.

D.K. v. Red Roof Inns, Inc., No. 2:22-CV-3786, 2024 WL 1332195 (S.D. Ohio Mar. 28, 2024). A plaintiff alleged she was trafficked for commercial sex at a Red Roof franchise located in Seattle, Washington, and sued the hotel owners and the franchisor under the Trafficking Victims Protection Reauthorization Act ("TVPRA"). The franchisor moved to dismiss the claim. The court denied the franchisor's motion, holding that the plaintiff sufficiently stated a claim to hold the franchisor liable as a beneficiary under the TVPRA. In so doing, the court determined that plaintiff's allegation that the franchisor profited from the trafficking by renting rooms to the traffickers was sufficient to satisfy that the franchisor knowingly benefitted from the scheme. However, the court rejected plaintiff's alternative contention that the franchisor knowingly benefited by collecting the trafficker's personal data through the hotel's WIFI. The court further found that plaintiff's allegations that the franchisor profited, failed to implement policies, and maintained expansive control over the hotel's operations met the standards of the TVPRA for participation in the venture.

D.T. v. Red Roof Inns, Inc., No. 2:22-CV-3844, 2024 WL 1332193 (S.D. Ohio Mar. 28, 2024). A plaintiff alleged she had been trafficked for commercial sex at Red Roof Inn franchise located in Dayton, Ohio, and sued the hotel owners and the franchisor under the Trafficking Victims Protection Reauthorization Act ("TVPRA"). The franchisor moved to dismiss the claim. The court denied the franchisor's motion, holding that the plaintiff sufficiently stated a claim to hold the franchisor liable as a beneficiary under the TVPRA. In deciding the motion, the trial court determined that the allegation that the franchisor profited from the trafficking by renting rooms to plaintiff's traffickers was sufficient to satisfy that the franchisor knowingly benefitted from the scheme. However, the court rejected plaintiff's alternative contention that the franchisor knowingly benefited by collecting the trafficker's personal data through the hotel's WIFI. Second, the court found that plaintiff's allegations that the franchisor profited, failed to implement policies, and maintained expansive control over the hotel's operations met the standards of the TVPRA for participation in the venture.

J.B. v. Red Roof Inns, Inc., No. 2:22-CV-3776, 2024 WL 1332255 (S.D. Ohio Mar. 28, 2024). A plaintiff alleged she had been trafficked for commercial sex at a Red Roof property located in Chattanooga, Tennessee, and sued the hotel owners and the franchisor under the Trafficking Victims Protection Reauthorization Act ("TVPRA"). The franchisor moved to dismiss the claim. The court dismissed the franchisor's motion, holding that the plaintiff sufficiently stated a claim to hold the franchisor liable as a beneficiary under the TVPRA. First, plaintiff's allegations that the franchisor profited from the trafficking by renting rooms to plaintiff's traffickers was sufficient to satisfy that the franchisor knowingly benefitted from the scheme. However, the court rejected plaintiff's alternative contention that the franchisor knowingly benefited by collecting the trafficker's personal data through the hotel's WIFI. Second, the court found that plaintiff's allegations that the franchisor profited, failed to implement policies, and maintained expansive control over the hotel's operations met the standards of the TVPRA for participation in the venture.

K.D. v. Red Roof Inns, Inc., No. 2:22-CV-3787, 2024 WL 1332232 (S.D. Ohio Mar. 28, 2024). Plaintiff alleged she was trafficked for commercial sex at a Red Roof franchise located in Houston, Texas. She sued the hotel owners and the franchisor under the Trafficking Victims Protection Reauthorization Act ("TVPRA"). The franchisor moved to dismiss the claim. The court denied the franchisor's motion, holding that the plaintiff sufficiently stated a claim to hold the franchisor liable as a beneficiary under the TVPRA. First, plaintiff's allegations that the franchisor profited from the trafficking by renting rooms to the traffickers was sufficient to satisfy that the franchisor knowingly benefitted from the scheme. However, the court rejected plaintiff's alternative contention that the franchisor knowingly benefited by collecting the trafficker's personal data through the hotel's WIFI. Second, the court found that Plaintiff's allegations that the franchisor profited, failed to implement policies, and maintained expansive control over the hotel's operations met the standards of the TVPRA for participation in the venture.

K.L. v. Red Roof Inns, Inc., No. 2:22-CV-3769, 2024 WL 1332225 (S.D. Ohio Mar. 28, 2024). A plaintiff alleged she had been trafficked for commercial sex at a Red Roof property located in Laurel, Maryland. She sued the hotel owners and the franchisor under the Trafficking Victims Protection Reauthorization Act ("TVPRA"). The franchisor moved to dismiss the claim. The court denied the franchisor's motion, holding that the plaintiff sufficiently stated a claim to hold the franchisor liable as a beneficiary under the TVPRA. First, plaintiff's allegations that the franchisor profited from the trafficking by renting rooms to the traffickers was sufficient to satisfy that the franchisor knowingly benefitted from the scheme. However, the court rejected plaintiff's alternative theory that the franchisor knowingly benefited by collecting the trafficker's personal data through the hotel's WIFI. Second, the court found that plaintiff's allegations that the franchisor profited, failed to implement policies, and maintained expansive control over the hotel's operations met the standards of the TVPRA for participation in the venture.

K.R.L. v. Red Roof Inns, Inc., No. 2:22-CV-3773, 2024 WL 1332199 (S.D. Ohio Mar. 28, 2024). Plaintiff alleged she had been trafficked for commercial sex at a Red Roof property located in Jacksonville, Florida, and sued the hotel owners and the franchisors under the Trafficking Victims Protection Reauthorization Act ("TVPRA"). The franchisor moved to dismiss the claim. The court denied the franchisor's motion and held that the plaintiff sufficiently stated a claim to hold the franchisor liable as a beneficiary under the TVPRA. First, plaintiff's allegations that the franchisor profited from the trafficking by renting rooms to plaintiff's traffickers was sufficient to satisfy that the franchisor knowingly benefitted from the scheme. However, the court rejected plaintiff's alternative contention that the franchisor knowingly benefited by collecting the trafficker's personal data through the hotel's WIFI. Second, the court found that plaintiff's allegations that the franchisor profited, failed to implement policies, and maintained expansive control over the hotel's operations met the standards of the TVPRA for participation in the venture.

K.W. v. Red Roof Inns, Inc., No. 2:22-CV-3845, 2024 WL 1332231 (S.D. Ohio Mar. 28, 2024). A plaintiff alleged she had been trafficked for commercial sex at a Red Roof property located in Kalamazoo, Michigan. The plaintiff sued the hotel owners and the franchisor under the Trafficking Victims Protection Reauthorization Act ("TVPRA"). Thereafter, the franchisor moved to dismiss the claim. The court denied the franchisor's motion, finding that the plaintiff sufficiently stated a claim to hold the franchisor liable as a beneficiary under the TVPRA. First, plaintiff's allegations that the franchisor profited from the trafficking by renting rooms to the traffickers was sufficient to satisfy that the franchisor knowingly benefitted from the scheme. However, the court rejected plaintiff's alternative contention that the franchisor knowingly benefited by collecting the trafficker's personal data through the hotel's WIFI Second, the court found that Plaintiff's allegations that the franchisor profited, failed to implement policies, and maintained expansive control over the hotel's operations met the standards of the TVPRA for participation in the venture.

N.B. v. Red Roof Inns, Inc., No. 2:22-CV-3771, 2024 WL 1332386 (S.D. Ohio Mar. 28, 2024). A plaintiff alleged she had been trafficked for commercial sex at a Red Roof property located in Terre Haute, Indiana, and sued the hotel owners and the franchisor under the Trafficking Victims Protection Reauthorization Act ("TVPRA"). The franchisor moved to dismiss the claim. The court denied the franchisor's motion and held that the plaintiff sufficiently stated a claim to hold the franchisor liable as a beneficiary under the TVPRA. First, plaintiff's allegations that the franchisor profited from the trafficking by renting rooms to plaintiff's traffickers was sufficient to satisfy that the franchisor knowingly benefitted from the scheme. However, the court rejected plaintiff's alternative contention that the franchisor knowingly benefited by collecting the trafficker's personal data through the hotel's WIFI. Second, the court found that plaintiff's allegations that the franchisor profited, failed to implement policies, and maintained expansive control over the hotel's operations met the standards of the TVPRA for participation in the venture.

R.C.C. v. Red Roof Inns, Inc., No. 2:22-CV-3770, 2024 WL 1332238 (S.D. Ohio Mar. 28, 2024). Plaintiff alleged she was trafficked for commercial sex at a Red Roof Inn franchise located in Phoenix, Arizona, and sued the hotel owners and the franchisor under the Trafficking Victims Protection Reauthorization Act ("TVPRA"). Thereafter, the franchisor moved to dismiss the claim. The court denied the franchisor's motion, holding that the plaintiff sufficiently stated a claim to hold the franchisor liable as a beneficiary under the TVPRA. First, plaintiff's allegations that the franchisor profited from the trafficking by renting rooms to Plaintiff's traffickers was sufficient to satisfy that the franchisor knowingly benefitted from the scheme. However, the court rejected plaintiff's alternative contention that the franchisor knowingly benefited by collecting the trafficker's personal data through the hotel's WIFI. Second, the court found that plaintiff's allegations that the franchisor profited, failed to implement policies, and maintained expansive control over the hotel's operations met the standards of the TVPRA for participation in the venture.

R.K. v. Red Roof Inns, Inc., No. 2:22-CV-3782, 2024 WL 1332152 (S.D. Ohio Mar. 28, 2024). A plaintiff alleged she had been trafficked for commercial sex at Red Roof Inn franchise located in Plymouth, Minnesota, and sued the hotel owners and the franchisor under the Trafficking Victims Protection Reauthorization Act ("TVPRA"). The franchisor moved to dismiss the claim. In denying the motion, the court held that the plaintiff sufficiently stated a claim to hold the franchisor liable as a beneficiary under the TVPRA. First, plaintiff's allegations that the franchisor profited from the trafficking by renting rooms to plaintiff's traffickers was sufficient to satisfy that the franchisor knowingly benefitted from the scheme. Notwithstanding this conclusion, the court rejected plaintiff's alternative contention that the franchisor knowingly benefited by collecting the trafficker's personal data through the hotel's WIFI. Second, the court found that plaintiff's allegations that the franchisor profited, failed to implement policies, and maintained expansive control over the hotel's operations met the standards of the TVPRA for participation in the venture.

R.H. v. Red Roof Inns, Inc., No. 2:22-CV-3774, 2024 WL 1332226 (S.D. Ohio Mar. 28, 2024). A plaintiff alleged she had been trafficked for commercial sex at a Red Roof property located in Rockville, Maryland, and sued the hotel owners and the franchisor under the Trafficking Victims Protection Reauthorization Act ("TVPRA"). The franchisor moved to dismiss the claim. The court dismissed the franchisor's motion, holding that the plaintiff sufficiently stated a claim to hold the franchisor liable as a beneficiary under the TVPRA. First, plaintiff's allegations that the franchisor profited from the trafficking by renting rooms to plaintiff's traffickers was sufficient to satisfy that the franchisor knowingly benefitted from the scheme. However, the court rejected plaintiff's alternative contention that the franchisor knowingly benefited by collecting the trafficker's personal data through the hotel's WIFI. Second, the court found that plaintiff's allegations that the franchisor profited, failed to implement policies, and maintained expansive control over the hotel's operations met the standards of the TVPRA for participation in the venture.

R.Z. v. Red Roof Inns, Inc., No. 2:22-CV-3784, 2024 WL 1332229 (S.D. Ohio Mar. 28, 2024). A plaintiff alleged she had been trafficked for commercial sex at multiple Red Roof properties located in Illinois and sued the hotel owners and the franchisor under the Trafficking Victims Protection Reauthorization Act ("TVPRA"). Thereafter, the franchisor moved to dismiss the claim. The court denied the franchisor's motion, holding that the plaintiff sufficiently stated a claim to hold the franchisor liable as a beneficiary under the TVPRA. In so doing, the court determined that plaintiff's allegation that the franchisor profited from the trafficking by renting rooms to plaintiff's traffickers was sufficient to satisfy that the franchisor knowingly benefitted from the scheme. The court nevertheless rejected plaintiff's alternative contention that the franchisor knowingly benefited by collecting the trafficker's personal data through the hotel's WIFI. Second, the court found that Plaintiff's allegations that the franchisor profited, failed to implement policies, and maintained expansive control over the hotel's operations met the standards of the TVPRA for participation in the venture.

R.C. v. Choice Hotels International, Inc., No. 5:23-cv-00872, 2024 WL 1443412 (N.D. Ohio Apr. 2, 2024). The United States District Court for the Northern District of Ohio granted defendants' motions for summary judgment against an alleged sex trafficking victim because the record showed no evidence that the defendant hotels knew of her trafficking or that the plaintiff or her traffickers kept her isolated or imprisoned at the hotels during the time. The plaintiff acknowledged significant outside contact during her trafficking period, including visits to a hospital to give birth at least twice during her trafficking period, contact with adoption agencies and children's adoptive parents who paid for her housing, contact with her parents during the trafficking period who bought her a phone and interactions with police "[m]ultiple times" during her trafficking, and a trip to Florida away from her traffickers.

K.O. v. G6 Hospitality, LLC, No. 22-11450, 2024 WL 1396269 (E.D. Mich. Mar. 31, 2024). Plaintiff filed a lawsuit against hotel chains located in the southeast Michigan region, alleging that she was trafficked at twelve different hotels and the defendants were either directly, indirectly, or vicariously liable for her sex trafficking in violation of the Trafficking Victims Protection Reauthorization Act ("TVPRA"). The defendants moved to dismiss on the basis that: (1) because the TVPRA cannot apply retroactively, plaintiff may only bring claims under the civil remedy provision of the TVPRA that occurred after December 23, 2008; (2) plaintiff's claims were barred by the TVPRA's ten-year statute of limitations; (3) plaintiff engaged in impermissible shotgun pleading; (4) plaintiff failed to allege that Defendants participated in a sex trafficking "venture" under the TVPRA; and (5) plaintiff failed to sufficiently allege vicarious liability and an agency relationship on behalf of the hotel chains. The court dismissed the time-barred claims. The court denied dismissal under the shotgun pleading argument, finding that the inclusion of these broad allegations, when combined with other more specific facts about each location, did not alone merit the dismissal of the case. The court then analyzed the TVPRA claims utilizing a three-part test, which asks whether the defendants: (1) knowingly benefitted, (2) from participation in a venture, (3) which the defendant knew or should have known has engaged in sex trafficking. The court found that the plaintiff alleged sufficient facts against only one of the defendant's, Farmington Hospitality, to state a direct liability claim under the TVPRA. In that case, defendant alleged she was brought so frequently to the hotel that the hotel reserved a room for the trafficker, and she begged hotel staff to provide her a telephone to call a family member after she was beaten and she attempted suicide in the parking lot by purposely walking in front of vehicles. The claims against the rest of the defendants were dismissed.

S.C. V. Wyndham Hotels and Resorts, Inc., No. 1:23-cv-00871, 2024 WL 1429114 (N.D. Ohio Apr. 2, 2024). The United States District Court for the Northern District of Ohio granted summary judgment to Wyndham Hotel in a case brought under the Trafficking Victims Protection Reauthorization Act ("TVPRA"). The court held that the franchisor (as compared to the franchisee) was not liable to the plaintiff under the TVPRA because the TVPRA was not imputable to the franchisor under an actual or apparent agency theory.

I.R. v. Khodiyar, No. 1:22-CV-00844-SEG, 2024 WL 1928755 (N.D. Ga. Mar. 18, 2024). The United States District Court for the Northern District of Georgia found that the plaintiff provided sufficient evidence for a jury to conclude that plaintiff was sex trafficked, and that the defendant, America's Best Value Inn, knowingly benefited from participating in a venture with her traffickers, and denied the defendant's motion for summary judgment.

S.C. v. Wyndham Hotels & Resorts, Inc., No. 1:23-cv-00871, 2024 WL 2186173 (N.D. Ohio May 15, 2024). The United States District Court for the Northern District of Ohio denied plaintiff's motion to reconsider a summary judgment ruling in favor of Wyndham Hotels, where the plaintiff, a sex trafficking victim, filed a lawsuit against the franchisor and not the hotel operators. Plaintiff was unable to show that the franchisor had the requisite participation and knowledge required under a Trafficking Victims Protection

Reauthorization Act claim to overcome a summary judgment motion. The case upon which the original ruling is based is discussed above.

G.P. v. Wyndham Hotels & Resorts, Inc., No. 2:22-CV-2682, 2024 WL 1347407 (S.D. Ohio Mar. 29, 2024). A plaintiff alleged she had been trafficked for commercial sex at a Wyndham branded hotel in Cincinnati, Ohio, and sued the hotel owners and the franchisor under the Trafficking Victims Protection Reauthorization Act ("TVPRA"). The franchisor moved to dismiss the claim. The court denied the franchisor's motion, holding that the plaintiff sufficiently stated a claim to hold the franchisor liable as a beneficiary under the TVPRA. First, plaintiff's allegations that the franchisor profited from the trafficking by renting rooms to plaintiff's traffickers was sufficient to satisfy that the franchisor knowingly benefitted from the scheme. However, the court rejected plaintiff's alternative contention that the franchisor knowingly benefited by collecting the trafficker's personal data through the hotel's WIFI. Second, the court found that plaintiff's allegations that the franchisor profited, failed to implement policies, and maintained expansive control over the hotel's operations, met the standards of the TVPRA for participation in the venture. A critical distinction that impacted the court's analysis regarding the franchisor-franchisee relationship between defendants and the hotel operators was that plaintiff alleged that defendants were engaged in commercial business ventures at the property where plaintiff was trafficked, not that the defendants participated in the sex trafficking themselves.

H.S. v. Red Roof Inns, Inc., No. 2:22-CV-3778, 2024 WL 1347393 (S.D. Ohio Mar. 29, 2024). A plaintiff alleged she had been trafficked for commercial sex at a Red Roof Inn franchise in Memphis, Tennessee, and sued the hotel owners and the franchisor under the Trafficking Victims Protection Reauthorization Act ("TVPRA"). The franchisor moved to dismiss the claim. The court denied the franchisor's motion, holding that the plaintiff sufficiently stated a claim to hold the franchisor liable as a beneficiary under the

TVPRA. First, plaintiff's allegations that the franchisor profited from the trafficking by renting rooms to plaintiff's traffickers was sufficient to satisfy that the franchisor knowingly benefitted from the scheme. However, the court rejected plaintiff's alternative contention that the franchisor knowingly benefited by collecting the trafficker's personal data through the hotel's WIFI. Second, the court found that plaintiff's allegations that the franchisor profited, failed to implement policies, and maintained expansive control over the hotel's operations, met the standards of the TVPRA for participation in the venture. A critical distinction that impacted the court's analysis regarding the franchisor-franchisee relationship between the defendants and the hotel operators was that the plaintiff alleged that the defendants were engaged in commercial business ventures at the property where plaintiff was trafficked, not that the defendants participated in the sex trafficking themselves.

A.S. v. Red Roof Inns, Inc., No. 2:22-CV-3846, 2024 WL 1347403 (S.D. Ohio Mar. 29, 2024). A plaintiff alleged she had been trafficked for commercial sex at Red Roof Inn franchises in Seattle, Washington, and Portland, Oregon, and sued the hotel owners and the franchisor under the Trafficking Victims Protection Reauthorization Act ("TVPRA"). The franchisor moved to dismiss the claim. The court denied the franchisor's motion, holding that the plaintiff sufficiently stated a claim to hold the franchisor liable as a beneficiary under the TVPRA. First, plaintiff's allegations that the franchisor profited from the trafficking by renting rooms to plaintiff's traffickers was sufficient to satisfy that the franchisor knowingly benefitted from the scheme. However, the court rejected plaintiff's alternative contention that the franchisor knowingly benefited by collecting the trafficker's personal data through the hotel's WIFI. Second, the court found that plaintiff's allegations that the franchisor profited, failed to implement policies, and maintained expansive control over the hotel's operations, met the standards of the TVPRA for participation in the venture. A critical distinction that impacted the court's analysis regarding the franchisor-franchisee relationship between the defendants and the hotel operators was that the plaintiff alleged that the defendants were engaged in commercial business ventures at the property where plaintiff was trafficked, not that the defendants participated in the sex trafficking themselves.

G.M. v. Red Roof Inns, Inc., No. 2:22-CV-3788, 2024 WL 1347737 (S.D. Ohio Mar. 29, 2024). Plaintiff alleged to have been trafficked for commercial sex at a Red Roof Inn franchise located in Indianapolis, Indiana. She sued the hotel owners and the franchisor under the Trafficking Victims Protection Reauthorization Act ("TVPRA") and the Child Abuse Victim's Rights Act ("CAVRA"). The franchisor moved to dismiss the claims. The court denied the franchisor's motion, holding that the plaintiff sufficiently stated a claim to hold the franchisor liable as a beneficiary under the TVPRA. First, plaintiff's allegations that the franchisor profited from the trafficking by renting rooms to plaintiff's traffickers was sufficient to satisfy that the franchisor knowingly benefitted from the scheme. However, the court rejected plaintiff's alternative contention that the franchisor knowingly benefited by collecting the trafficker's personal data through the hotel's WIFI. Second, the court found that Plaintiff's allegations that the franchisor profited, failed to implement policies, and maintained expansive control over the hotel's operations, met the standards of the TVPRA for participation in the venture. The court denied the motion to dismiss the CAVRA claim because plaintiff sufficiently pleaded a cause of action under CAVRA that she was trafficked as a minor. Unlike many of the TVPRA cases in this book, the inclusion of the CAVRA claim made this case factually distinct.

K.F. v. Red Roof Inns, Inc., No. 2:22-CV-3839, 2024 WL 1347729 (S.D. Ohio Mar. 29, 2024). Plaintiff alleged she had been trafficked for commercial sex at a Red Roof Inn franchise located in North Canton, Ohio. She sued the hotel owners and the franchisor under the Trafficking Victims Protection Reauthorization Act ("TVPRA") and the Child Abuse Victim's Rights Act ("CAVRA"). The franchisor moved to dismiss the claims. The court denied the franchisor's motion, holding that the plaintiff sufficiently stated a claim to hold the franchisor liable as a beneficiary under the TVPRA. First, plaintiff's allegations that the franchisor profited from the trafficking by renting rooms to plaintiff's traffickers was sufficient to satisfy that the franchisor knowingly benefitted from the scheme. However, the court rejected plaintiff's alternative contention that the franchisor knowingly benefited by collecting the trafficker's personal data through the hotel's WIFI. Second, the court found that Plaintiff's allegations that the franchisor profited, failed to implement policies, and maintained expansive control over the hotel's operations, met the standards of the TVPRA for participation in the venture. The court also denied the CAVRA claim because plaintiff sufficiently pleaded a claim for relief under CAVRA that she was trafficked as a minor. Unlike many of the TVPRA cases summarized in this book, the inclusion of the CAVRA claim makes it distinct.

A.M. v. Red Roof Inns, Inc., No. 2:22-CV-3797, 2024 WL 1347744 (S.D. Ohio Mar. 29, 2024). Plaintiff alleged to have been trafficked for commercial sex at a Red Roof Inn franchise located in Linthicum Heights, Maryland. She sued the hotel owners and the franchisor under the Trafficking Victims Protection Reauthorization Act ("TVPRA") and the Child Abuse Victim's Rights Act ("CAVRA"). The franchisor moved to dismiss the claims and the court denied and granted the motion in part. The court denied the franchisor's motion to dismiss the TVPRA claim, holding that the plaintiff sufficiently stated a claim to hold the franchisor liable as a beneficiary under the TVPRA. First, plaintiff's allegations that the franchisor profited from the trafficking by renting rooms to plaintiff's traffickers was sufficient to satisfy that the franchisor knowingly benefitted from the scheme. However, the court rejected plaintiff's alternative contention that the franchisor knowingly benefited by collecting the trafficker's personal data through the hotel's WIFI. Second, the court found that Plaintiff's allegations that the franchisor profited, failed to implement policies, and maintained expansive control over the hotel's operations, met the standards of the TVPRA for participation in the venture. The court granted the motion to dismiss the CAVRA claim because the plaintiff was not a minor at the time she was trafficked at the Maryland Red Roof location.

A.M. v. Wyndham Hotels & Resorts, Inc., No. 2:22-CV-3797, 2024 WL 1347301 (S.D. Ohio Mar. 29, 2024). A plaintiff alleged she had been trafficked for commercial sex at five Wyndham branded hotels in Southern California and sued the hotel owners and the franchisor under the Trafficking Victims Protection Reauthorization Act ("TVPRA") and the Child Abuse Victim's Rights Act ("CAVRA"). The franchisor moved to dismiss the claims. The court denied the franchisor's motion, holding that the plaintiff sufficiently stated a claim to hold the franchisor liable as a beneficiary under the TVPRA. First, plaintiff's allegations that the franchisor profited from the trafficking by renting rooms to plaintiff's traffickers was sufficient to satisfy that the franchisor knowingly benefitted from the scheme. However, the court rejected plaintiff's alternative contention that the franchisor knowingly benefited by collecting the trafficker's personal data through the hotel's WIFI. Second, the court found that plaintiff's allegations that the franchisor profited, failed to implement policies, and maintained expansive control over the hotel's operations, met the standards of the TVPRA for participation in the venture. A critical distinction that impacted the court's analysis regarding the franchisor-franchisee relationship between defendants and the hotel operators was that plaintiff alleged that defendants were engaged in commercial business ventures at the property where plaintiff was trafficked, not that the defendants participated in the sex trafficking themselves. The court denied the motion to dismiss the CAVRA claim because plaintiff sufficiently pleaded a cause of action under CAVRA that she was trafficked as a minor.

G.M. v. Choice Hotels International, Inc., No. 2:22-CV-3788, 2024 WL 1347722 (S.D. Ohio Mar. 29, 2024). A plaintiff alleged she had been trafficked for commercial sex at four Choice branded hotels in Indianapolis, Indianna and sued the hotel owners and the franchisor under the Trafficking Victims Protection Reauthorization Act ("TVPRA") and the Child Abuse Victim's Rights Act ("CAVRA"). The franchisor moved to dismiss the claims. The court denied the franchisor's motion, holding that the plaintiff sufficiently stated a claim to hold the franchisor liable as a beneficiary under the TVPRA. First, plaintiff's allegations that the franchisor profited from the trafficking by renting rooms to plaintiff's traffickers was sufficient to satisfy that the franchisor knowingly benefitted from the scheme. However, the court rejected plaintiff's alternative contention that the franchisor knowingly benefited by collecting the trafficker's personal data through the hotel's WIFI. Second, the court found that plaintiff's allegations that the franchisor profited, failed to implement policies, and maintained expansive control over the hotel's operations, met the standards of the TVPRA for participation in the venture. A critical distinction that impacted the court's analysis regarding the franchisor-franchisee relationship between defendants and the hotel operators was that plaintiff alleged that defendants were engaged in commercial business ventures at the property where plaintiff was trafficked, not that the defendants participated in the sex trafficking themselves. The court denied the motion to dismiss the CAVRA claim because plaintiff sufficiently pleaded that she was trafficked as a minor.

C.C. v. Wyndham Hotels & Resorts, Inc., No. 2:22-CV-3799, 2024 WL 1347303 (S.D. Ohio Mar. 29, 2024). A plaintiff alleged she had been trafficked for commercial sex at Wyndham branded hotel in Houston, Texas and sued the hotel owners and the franchisor under the Trafficking Victims Protection Reauthorization Act ("TVPRA") and the Child Abuse Victim's Rights Act ("CAVRA"). The franchisor moved to dismiss the claims. The court denied the franchisor's motion, holding that the plaintiff sufficiently stated a claim to hold the franchisor liable as a beneficiary under the TVPRA. First, plaintiff's allegations that the franchisor profited from the trafficking by renting rooms to plaintiff's traffickers was sufficient to satisfy that the franchisor knowingly benefitted from the scheme. However, the court rejected plaintiff's alternative contention that the franchisor knowingly benefited by collecting the trafficker's personal data through the hotel's WIFI. Second, the court found that plaintiff's allegations that the franchisor profited, failed to implement policies, and maintained expansive control over the hotel's operations, met the standards of the TVPRA for participation in the venture. A critical distinction that impacted the court's analysis regarding the franchisor-franchisee relationship between defendants and the hotel operators was that plaintiff alleged that defendants were engaged in commercial business ventures at the property where plaintiff was trafficked, not that the defendants participated in the sex trafficking themselves. The court denied the motion to dismiss the CAVRA claim because plaintiff sufficiently pleaded that she was trafficked as a minor.

G.G. v. Red Roof Inns, Inc., No. 2:22-CV-3766, 2024 WL 1347401 (S.D. Ohio Mar. 29, 2024). A plaintiff alleged she had been trafficked for commercial sex at a Red Roof Inn franchise in Council Bluffs, Iowa and sued the hotel owners and the franchisor under the Trafficking Victims Protection Reauthorization Act ("TVPRA"). The franchisor moved to dismiss the claim. The court denied the franchisor's motion, holding that the plaintiff sufficiently stated a claim to hold the franchisor liable as a beneficiary under the TVPRA. First, plaintiff's allegations that the franchisor profited from the trafficking by renting rooms to plaintiff's traffickers was sufficient to satisfy that the franchisor knowingly benefitted from the scheme. However, the court rejected plaintiff's alternative contention that the franchisor knowingly benefited by collecting the trafficker's personal data through the hotel's WIFI. Second, the court found that plaintiff's allegations that the franchisor profited, failed to implement policies, and maintained expansive control over the hotel's operations, met the standards of the TVPRA for participation in the venture. A critical distinction that impacted the court's analysis regarding the franchisor-franchisee relationship between defendants and the hotel operators was that plaintiff alleged that defendants were engaged in commercial business ventures at the property where plaintiff was trafficked, not that the defendants participated in the sex trafficking themselves.

A.W. v. Best Western International, Inc., No. 2:21-CV-4934, 2024 WL 1340264 (S.D. Ohio Mar. 29, 2024). A plaintiff alleged she had been trafficked for commercial sex at Best Western branded hotels and sued the hotel owners and the franchisor under the Trafficking Victims Protection Reauthorization Act ("TVPRA"). Franchisor Best Western requested, and was permitted, to file a proposed third-party complaint against its franchisee, Columbus Hotel Inc. ("Franchisee"). Best Western pled that if Best Western is held liable to Plaintiff in violation of TVPRA, the Franchisee is at least partially responsible, and is therefore liable to Best Western for all or some of the damages. Plaintiff moved to strike for failure to state a claim or to sever and stay Best Western's third-party complaint against the franchisee. The court analyzed plaintiff's claims regarding federal indemnification and state-law contract-based indemnification. The court struck Best Western's TVPRA contribution claim because it was not based in common law or contractual rights. The court also struck Best Western's common law claim of "Common Law/Implied/Equitable Indemnification/Negligence" because common law indemnification claims amount to claims for contribution. Best Western sought to bring Arizona state law claims against the franchisee for contractual indemnification and breach of contract of the franchise agreement. While no Arizona law was found on point on the issue of the assertion of contract-based indemnification, the court relied on a Pennsylvania case where that court granted a motion to file a third-party complaint like the proposed third-party complaint from Best Western. The court denied plaintiff's motion to strike Best Western's third-party complaint for its contractual claims because Best Western's contract with its franchisee included an express right to indemnification. The court denied without prejudice plaintiff's motion to sever and stay the third-party suit because the facts, parties, and evidence of the main case and the third-party action overlap.

T.P. v. Best Western International, Inc., No. 2:21-CV-4933, 2024 WL 1347451 (S.D. Ohio Mar. 29, 2024). The United States District Court for the Southern District of Ohio granted in part and denied in part plaintiff's motion to strike and denied without prejudice plaintiff's motion to sever and stay the plaintiff's claims under the same analysis set forth in the case of *A.W. v. Best W. Int'l, Inc.*, No. 2:21-CV-4934, 2024 WL 1340264 (S.D. Ohio Mar. 29, 2024), detailed above. The district court did grant Best Western the right to file a third-party complaint seeking to hold its franchisee accountable for the alleged TVPRA violations alleged by plaintiff.

In re Hotel Industry Sex Trafficking Litigation (No. II), No. MDL 3104, 2024 WL 1596932 (U.S. Jud. Pan. Mult. Litig. Apr. 11, 2024). The U.S. Judicial Panel on Multidistrict Litigation denied plaintiffs' motion to centralize litigation of thirty-three actions pending in five districts in the Southern District of Ohio. Plaintiffs all alleged that they were victims of sex trafficking at hotel properties located across the country and that the hotel defendants were liable for damages under the Trafficking Victims Protection Reauthorization Act ("TVPRA") and, in some instances, state law. This litigation was previously before the court in January 2020 where the court also denied the motion for centralizing twenty-one cases. In both circumstances, the court relied on the same reasoning: that centralization is not necessary for the convenience of the parties and witnesses to further efficient litigation and that the actions do not share sufficient common factual questions to justify centralization. The court further reasoned that the case-specific facts relating to the alleged parties involved (there were over 200 differently named defendants), the relevant time periods, and each plaintiff's experience are too varied. Placing all these cases in front of a single judge would, in the eyes of the court, prove inefficient.

G.W. v. Northbrook Industries, Inc., No. 1:20-cv-05232-JPB, 2024 WL 3166083 (N.D. Ga. June 14, 2024). A sex trafficking victim filed an action under the Trafficking Victims Protection Reauthorization Act ("TVPRA") against a hotel alleging negligence and a beneficiary claim. Plaintiff alleged she was trafficked for sex more than thirty times during the year 2017. The court found that 2012 to 2016, local police visited defendant at least seven times in connection with commercial sex crimes. The property was known as a "problem hotel" for drugs and prostitution. Defendant's manager claimed to be aware of between five and six instances of prostitution at the hotel during the relevant period and called the police many times. Defendant also discussed with the police ways to reduce prostitution at the hotel. The majority owner of the defendant lived onsite most of the year and asked staff to watch for crimes, such as commercial sex activities. Based on these facts, the plaintiff was unable to establish that the hotel defendant acted pursuant to the common goal of the trafficking venture or took steps with the traffickers to facilitate the illicit activities. Instead, the record presented here showed that the defendant took actions that would be expected to further the interest of a hotel enterprise. For liability to attach, the plaintiff must have shown more than knowledge on the defendant's part. Accordingly, the court granted the hotel's motion for summary judgment holding that the hotel did not participate in common venture with traffickers, precluding plaintiff's beneficiary claim under TVPRA. In addition, under Georgia law, the victim was characterized as a licensee of defendant, and plaintiff's failure to argue that the hotel willfully or wantonly caused her injury precluded the victim's negligence claim.

Jane Doe v. Wyndham Hotels and Resorts, No. 2:23-cv-01676-DAD-CSK, 2024 WL 3088722 (E.D. Cal. June 20, 2024). The United States District Court for the Eastern District of California granted defendants Wyndham Hotel Group, LLC's and Vitarag Hospitality, Inc.'s motion to dismiss claims filed by an alleged sex trafficking victim under the Trafficking Victims Protection Reauthorization Act. However, the court did not dismiss the claim against defendant Marriott International, Inc. under a agency liability theory finding that plaintiff alleged sufficient facts to establish a plausible claim of an agency relationship between defendant Marriott and defendant franchisee. Plaintiff plausibly alleged that Marriott exercised systemic control over the franchisee with respect to operation of the hotel, through policies and procedures regarding hotel security, identification requirements, payment method requirements, response to signs of human trafficking, and requirements for hotel staff to report suspicions of criminal activity. Plaintiff further alleged that defendant Marriott restricted the ability of the franchisee to refuse or cancel a reservation, controlled the price of rooms, and controlled all details of the customer loyalty. The court concluded that the allegations provided a sufficient basis upon which to assert that a franchisor exercised substantial control for the purposes of an agency relationship.

Mitchell v. Grand Hotel, Inc., No. 23-cv-605-wmc, 2024 WL 3378035 (W.D. Wis. July 11, 2024). The plaintiff, Lisa Mitchell ("Mitchell"), filed a lawsuit under the Trafficking Victims Protection Reauthorization Act ("TVPRA") and Title II of the Civil Rights Act of 1964 and state law, claiming that defendants knowingly participated in a criminal venture that subjected her to human trafficking, sexual assault, battery, and severe mental and physical abuse. More specifically, Mitchell alleges that a male owner of Rodeway Inn and Suites took advantage of her inability to afford housing to sexually assault her and threatened to kick her out of the hotel if she rejected sexual contact. The court denied a motion to dismiss filed by defendant Choice Hotels International Inc. ("Choice") finding that Mitchell plausibly alleged all four elements of participant liability under the TVPRA. Mitchell's allegations that Choice was told on more than one occasion that the owner of one of its franchised hotels was engaging in a specific pattern of trafficking exploited guests. This was distinguishable from other cases where plaintiffs argued that the hotel brand should have seen signs of trafficking or received negative customer reviews mentioning trafficking. The court found these specific allegations were enough to proceed to discovery.

CHAPTER 7

Control-Related Liability of Franchisors

I. Introduction

Annual developments in control related liability of franchisors were dominated by the Trafficking Victims Protection Reauthorization Act summarized in the previous chapter. However, there were several notable cases during the reporting period unrelated to hotel sex trafficking claims. The Texas Court of Appeals affirmed a trial court's judgment holding Massage Heights Franchising 15% liable for harm due to its negligent practices resulting in the sexual assault of a franchisee customer finding the franchisor "controlled the minutiae of its franchise locations and the work performed by the masseuses." (*Massage Heights Franchising, LLC v. Hagman*). The North Carolina Court of Appeals denied hotel franchisor Extended Stay America's motion to dismiss claims made by a guest of a franchised hotel arising from the franchise system's reservation management system and use of a "Do Not Rent" list used by its franchisees. The court found these facts were sufficient to allow the court to infer that the franchisor was liable for the actions of the hotel franchisees under an actual agency theory. Domino's avoided vicarious liability when the Pennsylvania Superior Court reversed a jury's findings that it was liable for the negligence of a franchisee's delivery driver holding that it did not exercise such control over the franchisee that it created a master-servant relationship, which would establish grounds for vicarious liability under Pennsylvania law. *(Coryell v. Morris).* On the issue of employee misclassification, a Texas district court denied a summary judgment motion in a class action case filed by its truck delivery drivers that they were misclassified as independent contractors and the defendant failed to pay the distributor drivers overtime pay in violation of the Fair Labor Standards Act concluding that, as a matter of economic reality, the drivers were dependent on defendant, rather than being in business themselves. (*Lagunas v. La Ranchera, Inc.).*

II. Franchisor-Franchisee Liability to Franchisee's Employees

Moody v. Empire Hotel Development, Inc., No. 20-CV-02203 (PMH), 2023 WL 5480729 (S.D.N.Y. Aug. 24, 2023). In this case, the United States District Court for the Southern District of New York granted summary judgment to Hyatt Corporation, Hyatt Place Franchising, LLC, and Hyatt Hotels Corporation (the "Hyatt Defendants"), dismissing claims against them for discrimination, hostile work environment, retaliatory constructive discharge under Title VII of the Civil Rights Act of 1964, the NY State Human Rights Law, and 42 U.S.C. Section 1981. The plaintiffs, who claimed workplace violations, were employees of Empire, a franchisee of the Hyatt brand. The Hyatt Defendants argued that no joint employer liability, or any other liability theory, applied to hold the Hyatt Defendants liable for the alleged causes of action. Following Second Circuit law, the Court determined that "to establish a joint employment relationship with an entity other than a direct employer, the plaintiff must show that the purported joint employer exercised 'significant control' over the terms and conditions of the employee's employment," and not "just operational or supervision over the plaintiff's formal employer . . . [C]ourts have generally concluded that franchisors are not employers." The court interpreted the franchise agreement to exclude control over the franchisee's employees and no facts established any actual involvement by the Hyatt Defendants. The court dismissed the Hyatt Defendants. The case is currently on appeal to the Second Circuit.

Chateau La Coste v. Fox Beverages USA Inc, No. 223CV02053WLHRAOX, 2023 WL 8522987 (C.D. Cal. Oct. 10, 2023). The district court granted Patrick Fox ("Fox") and American Spirits Exchange Ltd.'s ("ASE") motions to dismiss, finding that plaintiff Château La Coste ("CLC") failed to adequately allege sufficient facts to state a claim. The district court gave the plaintiff the right to re-plead.

Fox owns Fox Beverages USA, Inc. ("Fox Beverages") which imports and distributes CLC's wine throughout the United States. At the time, Fox Beverages used ASE for its accounting, billing, and distribution services. Despite CLC's numerous requests, CLC never received payment in return for it fulfilling all the purchase orders submitted by Fox Beverages and ASE. CLC filed suit against Fox, Fox Beverages, and ASE alleging eight claims for relief: (1) breach of written contract; (2) unjust enrichment; (3) unfair competition pursuant to California law; (4) claim and delivery; (5) breach of implied covenant of good faith and fair dealing; (6) open book account; (7) account stated; (8) declaratory relief. In response, Fox and ASE separately filed motions to dismiss the complaint. Fox alternatively requested that the court order CLC to provide a more definite statement.

First, Fox argued that the complaint failed to sufficiently allege a claim for vicarious liability under the theory of alter ego, agency, or ratification. The court agreed, explaining that CLC submitted only conclusory statements about its suspicions that Fox was using Fox Beverages' company funds for his own personal use. CLC argued in its opposition brief that Fox was Fox Beverages' principal officer and president, negotiated all of its contracts with CLC, and shared the same address as the company. The court acknowledged that it could only consider allegations contained in the complaint or matters subject to judicial notice, and therefore, it could not take the new evidence into consideration. Thus, the court found CLC's allegations against Fox insufficient to support a claim for vicarious liability and granted Fox's motion to dismiss. Second, ASE argued that it was acting as an agent of Fox Beverages, and as an agent, it could not be held liable for the claims that stemmed from contracts between CLC and ASE's principal. The court agreed, reasoning that the complaint alleged an apparent agency relationship between Fox Beverages and ASE, and CLC never alleged that ASE acted beyond the scope of its authority. Accordingly, the court granted ASE's motion to dismiss in its entirety.

Modlin v. Piazza Management Co., No. 23-279, 2023 WL 7386682 (E.D. Pa., Nov. 7, 2023). This case denied a franchisor's motion to dismiss Title VII sexual harassment claim by franchisee's employee against franchisee and franchisor because plaintiff's allegations narrowly satisfied the plausibility standard for alleging joint employer liability.

Ayala v. Nissan North America, Inc., No. 23-11027, 2024 WL 489723 (11th Cir. Feb. 8, 2024). The Eleventh Circuit affirmed a district court's denial of two automotive technicians' ("Technicians") motions for class certification in their Fair Labor Standards Act ("FLSA") action, and its grant of Nissan North America's ("Nissan") motion for summary judgment. The Technicians were employed at a Florida Nissan dealership, where they repaired and serviced Nissan vehicles. In their complaint, the Technicians alleged that they were not compensated for the work they performed. Because Nissan provided an Assurance Products Resource Manual ("APRM") and had dealership agreements that outlined how much Nissan would pay the dealerships for any warranty work performed, the Technicians argued that Nissan was responsible for compensating them. The court disagreed and found that the trial court properly concluded that Nissan was not a joint employer, and therefore, could not be held liable for the dispute. The court applied the eight factors from ***Layton v. DHL Express (USA), Inc.***, 686 F.3d 1172 (11th Cir. 2012) to determine whether Nissan could be held liable as a joint employer and found that none of the factors weighed in favor of the Technicians.

Daniel v. Musleh Fitness Inc., No. 2:23CV170-PPS/JEM, 2024 WL 983751 (N.D. Ind. Mar. 7, 2024). Plaintiff, Diane Daniel ("Daniel"), filed a lawsuit alleging sex discrimination against her former employer, Musleh Fitness Inc., an Anytime Fitness franchisee ("Franchisee"), the Franchisee's owners, and the franchisor, Anytime Fitness Franchisor, LLC ("Franchisor"). Daniel claimed that she was propositioned for sexual favors by Ammr Musleh, an individual associated with the Franchisee, in exchange for employment at a new location in Winfield, Indiana. After rejecting the advances, she alleges she was denied employment, and that Defendants also interfered with her opportunities at another employer. Daniel also claimed she filed a sexual harassment complaint with the Franchisor, which was acknowledged, but not investigated. Franchisor filed a motion to partially dismiss the complaint, arguing that Daniel failed to exhaust administrative remedies regarding her Title VII claims against it since Franchisor was not properly named or served in the EEOC Charge of Discrimination filed by Daniel. The court denied the Franchisor's motion to dismiss, concluding that Daniel made a sufficient attempt to include the Franchisor in her EEOC charge, satisfying the exhaustion requirement for her Title VII claims. The court emphasized that a strict application of the identification requirement in the administrative stage is disfavored, especially when there is an attempt to identify the employer, even if not perfectly executed. The court also pointed out that the Franchisor failed to provide evidence challenging the adequacy of notice regarding the EEOC proceedings. The court allowed Daniel's Title VII claims against the Franchisor to proceed.

III. Franchisor-Franchisee Liability to Third Parties

T.E. v. Wyndham Hotels & Resorts, Inc., No. 2:22-cv-3185, 2023 WL 5531441 (S.D. Ohio, August 28, 2023). A sex trafficking victim filed an action under the Trafficking Victims Protection Reauthorization Act ("TVPRA") against Wyndham Hotels & Resorts, Inc., Red Roof Inns, Inc. and Red Roof Franchising, LLC (together, "Red Roof") alleging that Red Roof facilitated violations of the TVPRA. The also found the plaintiff's allegations that Red Roof exercised control over the franchisee hotels sufficient to meet the federal pleadings standards for purposes of asserting a vicarious liability claim under the TVPRA but granted Red Roof's motion to dismiss the claim under a joint employer theory of liability. This case is discussed in Chapter 6, Section X.

K.M. v. CPA Hotels of Atlanta, LLC, No. 1:23-CV-190-TWT, 2023 WL 5747490 (N.D. Ga. Aug. 30, 2023). A sex trafficking victim filed an action under the Trafficking Victims Protection Reauthorization Act against both a Red Roof Inn franchisee located in Georgia, and the franchisor, Red Roof Franchising, LLC ("Red Roof"). The plaintiff alleged she was repeatedly trafficked at the Red Roof Inn location for a six-month period in 2015. The plaintiff brought the claim against the franchisor defendant under (1) actual agency; (2) apparent agency; and (3) joint venture theories of vicarious liability. The trial court found that the plaintiff's theories failed as a matter of law and granted Red Roof's motion to dismiss. The court concluded that the facts in the record showed that Red Roof limited its involvement with its franchisees to ensuring uniformity and standardization of the brand. The plaintiff failed to show Red Roof exercised control over the franchisee's day-to-day operations. As such, the factual circumstances in this particular case did not give rise to an actual agency claim.

To succeed on an apparent agency claim, a plaintiff must establish (i) a representation by the principal (Red Roof) to the plaintiff; (ii) which causes the plaintiff to reasonably believe that the alleged agent is authorized to act for the principal's benefit; and (iii) that induces the plaintiff's detrimental, justifiable reliance upon the appearance of agency. Under an apparent agency theory, the plaintiff alleged that Red Roof's years of advertising communicated to the plaintiff that any hotel operated under the Red Roof marks would be reputable and law abiding. The apparent agency theory failed because there was no allegation that Red Roof made an actual representation, and plaintiff's impressions and conclusions were not sufficient to meet the apparent agency elements. Finally, the joint venture theory of vicarious liability failed because the plaintiff failed to allege plausibly that the franchisor and franchisee exercised mutual rights of control over the hotel location. Red Roof's motion to dismiss was therefore granted.

B.D.G. v. Choice Hotels International, Inc., 2:22-cv-3202, 2023 WL 5935646 (S.D. Ohio September 12, 2023). A sex trafficking victim filed an action under the Trafficking Victims Protection Reauthorization Act ("TVPRA") against Choice Hotel. The court denied the motion to dismiss under an actual agency theory of vicarious liability finding the plaintiff's allegations that Choice exercised control over the franchisee hotels sufficient to meet the federal pleadings standards, but granted Choice's motion to dismiss plaintiff's claim under a joint employer theory of liability because there was no evidence that the franchisor controlled specific employment policies. This case is discussed in Chapter 6, Section X.

B.J. v. G6 Hospitality, 22-cv-03765-MMC, 2023 WL 6120682, (N.D. Cal. September 18, 2023). A sex trafficking victim filed an action under the Trafficking Victims Protection Reauthorization Act against five hotel franchisors. The claims under a vicarious liability theory were dismissed under both an actual agency theory, because the plaintiff was unable to show the franchisor brand had control over the hiring, firing and compensation of individual employees who participated in the venture and an apparent agency theory because there was no allegation that the plaintiff relied on any representation made by the defendants. This case is discussed in Chapter 6, Section X.

Massage Heights Franchising, LLC v. Hagman, No. 12-22-00160-CV, 2023 WL 7029384 (Tex. Ct. App. 14th Dist. Oct. 26, 2023). Danette Hagman ("Hagman"), a customer, was sexually assaulted by a masseuse ("Rubio") at a Massage Heights franchise location. Hagman sued Rubio, the franchisee and its affiliates, and the franchisor Massage Heights Franchising, LLC ("MH Franchising"), alleging negligence, premises liability, vicarious liability, and gross negligence. The jury trial found all defendants negligent, with MH Franchising bearing fifteen percent responsibility, and awarded Hagman $1.5 million in damages and $1.8 million in exemplary damages. MH Franchising appealed.

MH Franchising contended that it was not liable under a negligence theory, arguing it had no control over the franchisee's employment practices and was unaware of complaints about Rubio. The Texas Court of Appeals nevertheless found that under the franchise agreement and operations manual, MH Franchising "controlled the minutiae of its franchise locations and the work performed by the masseuses." This control included how to train masseuses, how masseuses could earn customer trust, how to interact with customers, the types of massages, how to drape customers, and how to handle appointments. The court was not persuaded by MH Franchising's argument that the franchisee retained control over hiring, firing, and training. The franchisee retaining hiring, firing, and training control over employees did not excuse the franchisor from its duty to act reasonably regarding the details it did retain control—namely, providing massages to customers.

The court of appeals also examined whether MH Franchising breached its duty to use reasonable care with respect to the customer. Evidence showed that MH Franchising did not provide disqualifying criteria for masseuses' employment, allowing franchisees to hire staff despite criminal backgrounds. While MH Franchising disputed evidence of proximate causation, the court noted that the franchisee's ability to hire Rubio despite his criminal history was enabled by MH Franchising's policies. The court thus concluded the customer's harm was foreseeable given Rubio's violent history and the nature of massage services. MH Franchising argued that Rubio's criminal act was a new and independent cause of Hagman's injury, absolving it from liability. The Court of Appeals disagreed, stating that the franchisor's negligence and the criminal act were concurrent causes of the injury.

The court of appeals ultimately affirmed the trial court's judgment regarding MH Franchising's negligence and the damages awarded, but reversed the part awarding punitive damages against MH Franchising. It held that while MH Franchising was partially liable for the harm due to its negligent practices, it could not be penalized with exemplary damages because the injury also resulted from Rubio's criminal act.

Mason v. 7 Eleven, Inc., No. CV TJS-22-1559, 2024 WL 1346863 (D. Md. Mar. 29, 2024). In a case brought by a customer of a 7-Eleven franchise who asserted that he had been racially profiled by a store employee in violation of 42 U.S.C. § 1981, the district court granted 7-Eleven's unopposed summary judgment motion because there was no principal-agent relationship between 7-Eleven and its franchisee, HEMASAFA, Inc. To the contrary, HEMASAFA was an independent contractor and 7-Eleven had no authority to control the actions of HEMASAFA or its employees.

Coryell v. Morris, 1977 EDA 202, 2023 WL 7381479 (Pa. Super. Ct. Nov. 8, 2023). This case came on appeal from the Court of Common Pleas of Philadelphia County where a jury found franchisor, Domino's Pizza LLC ("Domino's"), vicariously liable for the negligence of one of its franchisee's delivery drivers ("Morris"). On appeal, the Superior Court of Pennsylvania decided that Domino's did not exercise such control over the franchisee ("Robizza") that it created a master-servant relationship, which would establish grounds for vicarious liability under Pennsylvania law. The Court affirmed that vicarious liability only attaches in a business relationship where the master "controls not only the result of the work but also has the right to direct the manner in which the work shall be accomplished."

Robizza operated a Domino's location under the Standard Franchise Agreement. Defendant Morris was working as a delivery driver and driving a car leased by Robizza's owner. While returning from a delivery, Morris collided with a motorcycle driven by plaintiff Coryell. Coryell and Domino's filed cross-motions for summary judgment on the vicarious liability claim, which were denied by the trial court, stating that there were genuine issues of material fact as to the extent of control asserted by Domino's.

The witnesses at trial testified about the nature of the franchise relationship based on paragraphs of the franchise documents. A former Domino's executive testified that franchisees were required to follow set hours; adhere to specifications regarding equipment, fixtures, furniture and signage; comply with quality of ingredients; confirm to lease standards; maintain financial records in a manner set by Dominos; allow inspections of the premises at any time; and even follow specifications on how employees acted and presented themselves. The operations manual even had requirements regarding the permitted length of employees' fingernails and facial hair, and amount of jewelry an employee could wear on shift. However, the same witness also testified that standards to ensure a consistent customer experience are inherent in any franchise relationship to protect the value of the brand and its reputation. No one at Dominos instructed the franchisee or its employees how to meet the standards on a daily basis and Robizza owners alone supervised employees.

As to the delivery operation, Domino's witnesses testified that it required Robizza to ensure that its employees make all deliveries in compliance with all applicable laws, rules of the road and with due care and caution. Domino's never inspected, drove, or maintained the vehicle, nor did it train or test any of Robizza's drivers.

The appellate court noted that at both the summary judgment stage and during trial, the parties agreed that the franchise agreement was unambiguous and controlled the franchisor-franchisee relationship. The appellate court concluded that the parties merely disagreed over the construction of the franchise agreement and whether it created a master-servant relationship. Because no factual issues existed over the interpretation of the contract, the appellate court held that vicarious liability was a legal issue that should have been decided by the trial court. On appeal, the appellate court was entitled to decide this issue of law, regardless of whether their review was from a denied summary judgment motion or a judgment notwithstanding the verdict.

At the summary judgment stage, no facts were at issue and the trial court could have dismissed the vicarious liability claims based on the language of the franchise agreement. Because the trial court held that there were factual issues, although none had been raised regarding the scope of control by Domino's, the case proceeded with vicarious liability as an issue. Plaintiffs had the ability at trial to establish a master-servant relationship based not only on the nature and extent of control as defined in the franchise agreement, but also based "on the actual practice of the parties." The Superior Court reviewed the trial record and concluded that none of the witnesses testified that the "actual practice of the parties" was different from the franchise documents.

The Superior Court then analyzed the elements necessary to prove vicarious liability and reviewed applicable precedent in the franchise space, citing that "the mere existence of a franchise relationship" does not necessarily trigger a master-servant relationship, nor does it automatically insulate the parties from such a relationship. Under Pennsylvania law, a franchisor can only be held vicariously liable for the negligence of a franchisee's employee if it exercises the control of a master-servant relationship. Based on the record before the court, it concluded that no master-servant relationship was established by the testimony or the contracts, and that no vicarious liability should have been imposed.

The Superior Court reversed and remanded with instructions that Domino's was not vicariously liable.

Bellard v. ABC Insurance Co., No. 24-38, 2024 WL 3167456 (La. Ct. App. June 26, 2024). Plaintiff filed a personal injury suit for negligence against a trampoline park franchisor, its franchisee, and the insurers of both. Defendants filed a motion for summary judgment on their alleged liability for the injuries sustained by the plaintiff, which the trial court granted on the basis that there was no genuine issue of disputed fact on the claimed negligence. Defendants also filed a peremptory exception of prescription (a procedure specific to Louisiana Civil Code where certain defenses are raised) directed at the lack of remedy for the harm alleged, which the trial court also sustained. Plaintiff appealed both decisions. The Louisiana Court of Appeals determined that plaintiff failed to address the trial court's judgment on sustaining the exception of prescription and deemed the issue abandoned on appeal. The appellate court then affirmed the trial court's decision because plaintiff failed to produce factual support sufficient to establish a genuine issue of material fact necessary to plead the premises liability and negligence claims.

Mary Doe v. Massage Envy Franchising, LLC,, No. S20C-05-005 RHR, 2024 WL 3220281 (Del. Super. Ct. June 28, 2024). Plaintiff sued franchisor, Massage Envy, its franchisee, and the store's operator after allegedly being sexually assaulted by a staff masseuse at a Massage Envy location in Delaware. Defendants moved to dismiss all ten claims. The court granted defendants' motion to dismiss the fraudulent concealment, negligence per se (related to an alleged criminal code violation), and negligent infliction of emotional distress claims because plaintiff failed to sufficiently plead all elements of those claims. But it denied defendants' motions on the remaining claims for vicarious liability, negligence, negligent performance of undertaking to render services, negligent misrepresentation, Delaware Consumer Fraud Act ("DCFPA"), negligence per se (related to an alleged violation of certain retail regulations), and conspiracy because the facts were sufficiently pleaded to survive a motion to dismiss.

Lund v. Calhoun Orange, Inc., No. A23-0149, 2023 WL 8368507 (Minn. Ct. App. Dec. 4, 2023). After a customer suffered a cardiac arrest and permanent brain injury during an exercise class at an Orangetheory franchise, the customer's representative sued the franchisee under traditional negligence theories. The lawsuit also asserted claims against the franchisor based on allegations of apparent authority, respondeat superior, and joint enterprise due to (1) franchisor requirements that franchisees maintain an automatic external defibrillator (AED), fire extinguisher, and first aid kit on premises; (2) franchisor control over marketing plan, retail vendors, hours of operation, and location; and (3) franchisee's emergency response policy that admittedly borrowed language from franchisor's training documents. The trial court dismissed the claims against the franchisor on summary judgment and the Minnesota Court of Appeals affirmed on appeal because the franchisor did not exercise control over the franchisee's actions that allegedly led to the harm.

Blackstock v. Accede Inc., No. 1182, 2023 WL 8598640 (N.Y. App. Div. 1st Dept. Dec. 12, 2023). Plaintiff was a pedestrian who tripped and fell at a gas station and brought a claim for negligence against the franchisor. The court affirmed its decision to grant summary judgment in favor of the defendant, finding that a dealer supply agreement between a franchisor and franchisee does not create vicarious liability on the franchisor's part for such an incident.

Fant v. Beamteam, Inc., No. 2023-CA-0280-MR, 2024 WL 387729 (Ky. Ct. App. Feb. 2, 2024). The Kentucky Court of Appeals affirmed a trial court decision granting the defendant franchisor's motion for summary judgment on plaintiff's negligence claims. The court rejected plaintiff's argument that the franchisor should be vicariously liable for a car accident that its franchisee's employee caused during the scope of its employment which resulted in bodily injury. In its analysis, the court applied a restrictive rule for determining agency, which required the franchisor's level of control to signal that the franchisee was nothing more than an alter ego to the franchisor. The court found that the provisions in the franchise agreement between the parties did not afford the franchisor the level of control required to establish an agency relationship between the franchisor and the driver. Therefore, the franchisor could not be held vicariously liable.

Kelly v. Prohaska, No. CA 23-00529, 2024 WL 394410 (Sup. Ct. N.Y. Feb. 2, 2024). In this case, the Supreme Court of New York modified a lower court grant of franchisor, Snap-on Credit LLC's ("Franchisor") motion for summary judgment against a third-party claim of vicarious liability for the negligence allegedly caused by a Snap-On franchisee. Plaintiff filed a personal injury action arising from a motor vehicle accident where a van operated by defendant franchisee struck plaintiff. The Snap-on van was owned by the Franchisor and was leased to the franchisee. The lower court granted the Franchisor's motion for summary judgment on the basis that the "Graves Amendment" (49 U.S.C. § 30106) which provides that provides that the owner of a leased or rented motor vehicle cannot be held liable for personal injuries resulting from the use of such vehicle by reason of being the owner of the vehicle for harm to persons or property that results or arises out of the use, operation, or possession of the vehicle during the period of the rental or lease if: (1) the owner is engaged in the trade or business of renting or leasing motor vehicles; and (2) there is no negligence or criminal wrongdoing on the part of the owner (or an affiliate of the owner), and plaintiff appealed. The court agreed with the lower court analysis that found the Franchisor established on its motion that it was free of direct negligence because it was not responsible for hiring or supervising the driver, who was not a Snap-on Credit employee. However, the court found that the Franchisor failed to establish that it was "engaged in the trade or business of renting or leasing motor vehicles" within the meaning and intent of the Graves Amendment. The facts showed that the Franchisor only leased vans to franchisees, not the general public and the record did not indicate how many franchisees actually leased the vehicles. Under those facts, the court concluded that the Franchisor failed to meet its initial burden on its motion of establishing that the Graves Amendment protects it from liability, and that the court erred in granting motion insofar as it sought summary judgment dismissing plaintiffs' vicarious liability claims.

Durham v. Domino's Pizza, LLC, No. 2022-CA-1155-MR, 2024 WL 1122350 (Ky. Ct. App. Mar. 15, 2024). The Kentucky Court of Appeals affirmed the lower court's grant of summary judgment to defendant, Domino's Pizza, LLC ("Dominos") in a negligence action against Domino's, its franchisee, and a franchisee delivery driver. Domino's asserted in its motion for summary judgment that it was not vicariously liable for the actions of its franchisee or franchisee's employee as a matter of law after the franchisee's delivery driver hit and injured a pedestrian hit with its vehicle during a delivery. The lower court agreed and granted Domino's motion. On appeal, plaintiff argued that the trial court committed reversible error by denying a motion for additional time to complete discovery. The court found no abuse of discretion by the trial court, finding all parties were dilatory in responses to each other. The court also found that plaintiff failed to establish that Domino's was vicariously liable. The operating contract provisions in the franchise agreement requiring minimum standards for drivers, compliance reviews conducted by Domino's, the driving safety posters, the driver's statements naming Domino's as her employer were insufficient evidence of the requisite control over the daily delivery operations of the franchisee's employee. The court also found that the requirement that drivers use Domino's branded app which, after a driver selects a delivery assignment, provides turn-by-turn directions, shows a satellite view of the delivery address, and affords the customer the ability to track the delivery, did not establish vicarious liability. The court rejected plaintiff's argument that use of the app is equivalent of supervisory control and management over franchisee employees. The mere requirement that franchisee employees use a tool that mechanically aids deliveries does not meet the legal standard of directly supervising the daily activities of the franchisee or having the right to do so.

Brittian v. Extended Stay America, No. 3:22-cv-663-MOC, 2024 WL 1841600 (W.D. N.C. April 26, 2024). Plaintiff, a guest at various Extended Stay America franchised hotels, filed a breach of contract claim against the franchisor ("ESA"), for breach of contract over their reservation management system and use of a "Do Not Rent" list. Plaintiff alleged that franchisor's "Do Not Rent" policy amounted to a nationwide practice to refuse rooms to guests while retaining prepaid non-refundable deposits and filed a lawsuit against the franchisor under an actual agency and apparent agency. Plaintiff's complaint alleged that in North Carolina, "[a] franchisor is vicariously liable for the tortious acts of its franchisee when an agency relationship exists, and the acts are committed within the scope of the agent's authority." ESA filed a motion to dismiss. The court denied the motion holding that Plaintiff's complaint contained facts from which the Court could reasonably infer an agency relationship existed in that ESA (1) maintained a nationwide "Do Not Rent" list through the ESA reservation and property management systems; (2) maintained a nationwide policy and practice of using the list to refuse accommodation to guests; and (3) permitted hotel staff to place on the list guests who complain about poor conditions or unfair business practices. Plaintiff's complaint further alleged that ESA hotels' use of the Do Not Rent list constituted a "nationwide, top-down policy and practice" and ESA controlled employees by directing staff to place guests on the DNR list and subsequently to deny them accommodation. The court found these facts were sufficient to allow the court to infer that ESA was liable for the actions of the hotel franchisees under an actual agency theory.

Allied Services, LLC v. Smash my Trash, LLC, No. 21-cv-00249-SRB, 2024 WL 2842633 (W.D. Mo. May 16, 2024). The United States District Court for the Western District of Missouri granted summary judgment in favor of defendant franchisor, Smash my Trash, LLC ("Smash") after plaintiff, a waste and recycling service business ("Allied") filed a lawsuit alleging that Smash's methods of compressing its customer's trash caused permanent damage to its trash cans. In its finding of facts and conclusions of law, the court found that, as the franchisor, Smash does not operate any of the smash machines or smash trucks purported to cause the damage, and all activity is conducted through franchisees.

IV. Other Franchisor Liability

Shavers v. UPS Store, Inc., 2023 IL App (1st) 221407-U, 2023 WL 5015975 (Ill. Ct. App., Aug. 7, 2023). Unpublished, nonprecedential appellate decision affirming dismissal of three consumer claims against franchisor based on illegally excessive charges for notary services, but reversing dismissal of conspiracy claim against franchisor, holding that complaint adequately alleged franchisor's approval of prices for notary services and its direction to, and encouragement of, franchisees' charging statutorily excessive fees.

Patel v. 7-Eleven, Inc., 81 F.4th 73 (1st Cir. 2023). A putative class of franchisees sought to be deemed employees under Massachusetts law. The First Circuit Court of Appeals certified to the Massachusetts Supreme Judicial Court, as a question of first impression, whether franchisees were "performing any service" within the meaning of the Massachusetts Independent Contractor Law.

V. Employee Misclassification

Provencher v. Bimbo Bakeries USA, Inc., No. 2:22-cv-198, 2023 WL 8436279 (D. Vt. Dec. 5, 2023). The United States District Court for the District of Vermont denied defendants, a wholesale bakery and snack manufacturer and its affiliate ("Bimbo"), motion for judgment on the pleadings and granted the plaintiffs', a class of Bimbo distributors (the "Distributors"), motion to dismiss Bimbo's counterclaim for unjust enrichment.

The plaintiff Distributors delivered Bimbo products to grocery stores and other retailers on behalf of Bimbo and brought putative class asserting claims under the Fair Labor Standards Act ("FLSA") and the Vermont Fair Employment Practices Act ("VFEPA") based on allegations that defendants misclassified distributors as independent contractors instead of employees. Defendants asserted a contingent counterclaim under Vermont law for unjust enrichment, alleging that if distributors were found to be employees, were entitled to restitution for benefits conferred on distributors by virtue of their nominal status as independent contractors. The United States Department of Labor ("DOL") intervened as a plaintiff to oppose the counterclaim.

The court found that the Distributors asserted facts to plausibly support a claim that they: (1) were employees; and (2) were paid wages for services rendered as required to establish a claim for improper wage deductions under Vermont law. In dismissing Bimbo's counterclaims, the court found that the FLSA preempted defendants' unjust-enrichment counterclaim; and VFEPA also barred Bimbo's unjust-enrichment counterclaim.

Lagunas v. La Ranchera, Inc., No. H-22-17, 2024 WL 1258671 (S.D. Tex. Mar. 25, 2024). The United States District Court for the Southern District of Texas denied an employer's motion for summary judgment in a class action case filed by its truck delivery drivers that they were misclassified as independent contractors and defendant failed to pay the distributor drivers overtime pay in violation of the Fair Labor Standards Act ("FLSA"). Each of the drivers entered into a distributor agreement which required the driver to supply its own vehicle, allowed the drivers to employ their own personnel, and required drivers to determine their own delivery schedule. However, in analyzing the relationship, the court concluded that the evidence did not show that the plaintiff exerted such a control over a meaningful part of the business that the driver stands as a "separate economic entity" from the employer. Defendant (1) controlled aspects of how the drivers did their work; (2) determined territories and routes; (3) provided incentives to solicit new customers and terminated those drivers that failed to recruit new customers; (4) disciplined drivers for mistakes or poor performance by docking their pay; (5) prohibited drivers from transporting or selling competing products; and (6) allowed defendant to terminate without advance notice for any reason. Based on these terms, the court concluded that, as a matter of economic reality, the drivers were dependent on the defendant, rather than being in business themselves.

CHAPTER 8

Issues Specific to Litigation and Arbitration

I. Introduction

While this entire book is a tool to assist lawyers embroiled in disputes in franchise, distribution, and dealership relationships, Chapter 8 speaks specifically to issues in litigation and arbitration published in this reporting year (2023-2024).

There have been no major shifts in the law in any one of the areas discussed in this chapter. To be sure, the drumbeat promoting and supporting arbitration rights, long favored by the United States Supreme Court, finds its voice in Section VI (Arbitration) below. Often the contests over arbitration bear on the enforceability of the arbitration clause and (more often) who decides the issue of arbitrability. But there are also interesting case highlights in Section VI-B over binding non-signatories to arbitration provisions, which remains a hot topic in franchising. The value of those cases is obviously in the eye of the beholder as various non-parties this year found themselves both "in" and "out" of arbitration at their desire and at times peril.

The federal courts continue to vigilantly guard their jurisdiction and there are a number of decisions below in Section II (Substantive and

Personal Jurisdiction), Section III (Venue and Choice of Forum), and Section IV (Choice of Law) that reflect this attitude. For certain, state and federal courts are loath to avoid enabling disputes before them where the parties have already agreed to venue in other forums (be it in another court of competent jurisdiction or in arbitration). The lesson appears to be: don't hit your head against the wall. If your client agreed to a dispute resolution mechanism, then use it.

The rest of Chapter 8 deals with nuanced issues encompassed by litigation practice including such things as the amendment of pleadings. The pattern under Fed. R. Civ. P. 15 and its state equivalents is clear: amendments will be freely allowed so long as you don't unduly delay or unfairly prejudice the opposing party when pursuing a new pleading. The too little reported issue of how courts resolve disputes over our discovery rules bears some mention this year in Section X. But what you otherwise see below appears to be a collection of ordinary and useful decisions for use in your trial practice.

II. Substantive and Personal Jurisdiction

Roe v. Wyndham Worldwide, Inc., No. CV 18-1525-RGA-SRF, 2023 WL 5348862 (D. Del. Aug. 21, 2023). A United States diplomat brought a personal injury suit against various Wyndham entities in the United States and overseas related to a sexual assault allegedly committed by a hotel masseuse in Istanbul. The district court denied plaintiff's motion to amend seeking to establish personal jurisdiction. In so doing, the district court determined that it was insufficient to establish personal jurisdiction against the foreign Wyndham defendants merely because the company (1) marketing the hotel through a website accessible in the United States, where the ultimate hotel booking was made by phone; and (2) had a franchise relationship with Wyndham defendants incorporated in Delaware (without evidence that the overseas entities regularly conducted business in Delaware).

Dance Fitness Michigan, LLC v. AKT Franchise, LLC, No. 8:23-CV-01643-JVS(JDEX), 2023 WL 7549894 (C.D. Cal. Nov. 13, 2023). Court denied plaintiff's motion to remand the action back to California state court for lack of diversity jurisdiction, holding that the more appropriate remedy was to require the defendant to file an amended Rule 7.1 disclosure statement to assist the court in determining the completeness of its organizational structure.

Brown v. MUY Pizza-Tejas, LLC, No. 23-1816, 2024 WL 3489201 (N.D. Ga. July 18, 2024). Defendant Bodenstedt, the founder and Chief Executive Officer of defendant MUY Pizza-Tejas, LLC, sought to avoid personal jurisdiction in this wage and hour collective action under the Fair Labor Standards Act ("FLSA"). Until selling the 352 Pizza Hut restaurants in 2021, Bodenstedt operated the business and oversaw its operations. Bodenstedt argued that the district court lacked personal jurisdiction over him for collective claims by out-of-state opt-in plaintiffs pursuing their rights under the statute. The district court rejected Bodenstedt's jurisdictional argument, concluding that out-of-state opt-in plaintiffs in an FLSA collective action could establish personal jurisdiction over Bodenstedt because the claims arose out of or related to Bodenstedt's contacts with the United States, his conduct during the time alleged in the complaint satisfied the purposeful availment requirements to establish jurisdiction, and that he could have reasonably anticipated being hauled into court in the United States.

Burke v. Hyatt Corp., No. FST-CV-23-6061497-S, 2024 WL 3271549 (Conn. Super. Ct. June 26, 2024). Franchisor Hyatt moved to dismiss a slip and fall action related to an accident that occurred at a Dominican Republic hotel for lack of personal jurisdiction. The trial court granted the motion because plaintiff failed to meet the requirements of Connecticut's long arm statute, failed to establish the minimum contacts requirement, and failed to comport with the constitutional due process requirements. Plaintiff also failed to establish in the pleading that the defendant owned or operated the premises.

Mendoza v. Midea Microwave & Electrical Appliances Manufacturing Co., No. 1:20-CV-1133-TLN-CKD, 2023 WL 8527725 (E.D. Cal. Dec. 7, 2023). The court granted Midea Microwave and Electrical Appliances Manufacturing Co., Ltd.'s and Midea America Corp.'s motion to dismiss for lack of personal jurisdiction. Dismissal was proper where defendants did not purposefully target the forum state, California, nor did either of the defendants have control over the distribution of the microwave products once they were sold to a distributor in China.

Smart Shoppers NY LLC v. Tylers Coffee LLC, No. 22 CIV. 4969 (NSR), 2024 WL 113731 (S.D.N.Y. Jan. 10, 2024). The court denied defendant distributor's motion to dismiss for lack of personal jurisdiction. The court recognized that the contacts could be considered minor in isolation; however, it found that the defendant's contacts still constituted an ongoing business relationship because defendant solicited the plaintiff's services. The court also found that exercising jurisdiction was consistent with Due Process because it would not be unreasonable for defendants to anticipate being brought to the state if they failed to perform their obligation under the relevant agreements. This case is discussed in Chapter 4, Section I, Subsection A.

Advantaclean Systems LLC v. JDG Environmental LLC, No. 3:23-CV-1655-X, 2024 WL 202099 (N.D. Tex. Jan. 17, 2024). The United States District Court for the Northern District of Texas granted defendant franchisee's motion to transfer a complaint to the Western District of North Carolina. The court held that, although the franchisor plaintiff, Advantaclean Systems, LLC was now headquartered in Texas, and the franchise was operated in Oklahoma, there is an interest North Carolina has in deciding a case about a franchise agreement governed by North Carolina law, with an express North Carolina forum-selection clause. The court also gave weight to Advantaclean Systems, LLC selection of venue in North Carolina.

Nieto v. CCG MSJC, LLC, No. CV 24-818, 2024 WL 2207509 (E.D. La. May 16, 2024). Plaintiffs Thomas Nieto, Julie Canseco, and Squeeze Holdings, LLC ("Squeeze Holdings") founded a successful franchising business. Defendants, along with their company CCG MSJC, LLC ("CCG"), sought to consult with Plaintiffs to help grow their franchise operation. Plaintiffs and CCG created a new limited liability company and became the co-owners of Main Squeeze Juice Holdings, LLC ("Main Squeeze"). Main Squeeze's operating agreement called for five board members, but the parties failed to choose a fifth board member before disputes arose between them. When issues arose, Plaintiffs filed an action in state court alleging various torts and breach of contract. Defendants removed the case to federal court asserting diversity jurisdiction. Plaintiffs moved to remand the matter to state court. The United States District Court for the Eastern District of Louisiana granted Plaintiffs' motion to remand because Plaintiffs stated a plausible derivative claim to which Main Squeeze was an indispensable party and properly part of the case. Because Plaintiffs and Main Squeeze were both Louisiana citizens, complete diversity was lacking, and the district court did not have subject-matter jurisdiction. Therefore, the case was remanded back to state court for further proceedings.

Motto Franchising, LLC v. UMortgage LLC, No. 1:23-CV-00609-RM-SBP, 2024 WL 1509178 (D. Colo. Feb. 16, 2024). In this case, a magistrate judge recommended granting the defendant's motion to dismiss for lack of personal jurisdiction because the plaintiff failed to show that UMortgage's conduct was expressly aimed at the state of Colorado. The court also requested that UMortgage supplement its Rule 7.1 disclosure statement to assist the court in resolving all potential jurisdictional issues. The district court adopted this recommendation on March 6, 2024 in *Motto Franchising, LLC v. UMortgage, LLC*, No. 23-CV-00609-RM-SBP, 2024 WL 1508824 (D. Colo. Mar. 6, 2024).

Ningbo Daye Garden Mach. Co. v. International Global Resources Corp., No. 4D2023-0803, 2024 WL 591722 (Fla. Dist. Ct. App. Feb. 14, 2024). A merchandise supplier, International Global Resources ("GRS"), sued Ningbo Daye Garden Machinery ("Daye"), a foreign company authorized to do business in China, for breach of contract and tortious interference with business relations after Daye prematurely terminated a Vendor Agreement and failed to pay GRS. The district court denied Daye's motion to dismiss for lack of personal jurisdiction. On appeal, Daye argued that its motion should be granted because GRS failed to introduce sufficient evidence to satisfy the requirements for the minimum contacts test for personal jurisdiction. Further, Daye argued that the agreement did not include a forum-selection clause. The Fourth Circuit Court of Appeals agreed with Daye and reversed the district court's decision.

BGSD, Inc. v. SPAZEUP, LLC, No. 5:23-CV-4855, 2024 WL 688665 (E.D. Pa., Feb. 20, 2024). The United States District Court for the Eastern District of Pennsylvania denied plaintiff BGSD's motion for default judgment on claims against SPAZEUP for using BGSD's copyrighted images online to sell products. The court found that BGSD's assertions that SPAZEUP visited its website and took its photographs was insufficient to confer personal jurisdiction because it was impossible to conclude that the conduct occurred in the relevant state.

Sewalk v. Valpak Direct Marketing Systems, LLC, No. 22-13819, 2024 WL 767619 (11th Cir. Feb. 26, 2024). This dispute arose out of an agreement between Valpak Direct Marketing Systems, LLC ("Valpak") and SMS Business Entities, Inc. ("SMS") whereby Valpak granted SMS an exclusive franchise to operate and sell advertising under Valpak's name in a particular region. Shortly after entering into the agreement, SMS filed for Chapter 11 bankruptcy reorganization without identifying the agreement or naming Valpak as a creditor. Valpak terminated the agreement after learning about the bankruptcy petition. As a result, SMS sued Valpak for breaching the agreement by terminating it without cause. In proceedings below, a magistrate judge directed the parties to attend mediation, which resulted in a confidential settlement agreement. Once the district court received the settlement agreement, it dismissed the case without prejudice subject to the parties' right to address any remaining issues within sixty-days from the date of the order.

After that, SMS filed a motion to reopen the case, arguing that it was criminally extorted and threatened by Valpak. Specifically, SMS alleged that Valpak threatened to expose SMS's alleged bankruptcy fraud to authorities. The district court denied SMS's motion, reasoning that the attached affidavit in support of the motion included confidential information obtained during the mediation.

On appeal, SMS argued that Florida law permits voiding the settlement agreement when extortion is involved during settlement negotiations, and because it alleged a prima facie case of extortion by Valpak during the mediation, the district court should have held an evidentiary hearing on the motion. Valpak responded by arguing that the appellate court did not have jurisdiction over the district court's order because SMS failed to file within the thirty-day period, required by Federal Rule of Appellate Procedure 4(a). The Eleventh Circuit rejected Valpak's argument, finding that Federal Rule of Appellate Procedure 59, and therefore, the motion could be tolled to align with the required thirty-day window. Lastly, the court turned to the merits of the district court's order denying SMS's motion to reopen. The court affirmed the district court's denial and held that Florida case law demonstrated that a threat of lawful criminal prosecution a threat of lawful criminal prosecution does not constitute duress.

Riviezzo v. Hilton Worldwide Holdings, Inc., No. 22-CV-5697 (JS)(LGD), 2024 WL 964819 (E.D.N.Y. Mar. 6, 2024). Plaintiff fractured her ankle when she slipped on algae or some other slippery substance in a hotel parking lot and sued various corporations affiliated with the franchisor and the franchisee. The court granted the defendants' motion to dismiss because the complaint failed to plead the citizenship of several parties and because the injury occurred in New Jersey and was therefore not covered under New York's long-arm statute.

S.C. v. Wyndham Hotels & Resorts, Inc., No. 1:23-CV-00871, 2024 WL 917589 (N.D. Ohio Mar. 4, 2024). The court granted defendant Crowne Plaza, LLC's motion to dismiss for lack of personal jurisdiction because it existed solely to hold stock and receive dividends and did not franchise the hotel where plaintiff was trafficked.

Garland v. Dunkin Donuts LLC, No. 23-cv-06621-SI, 2024 WL 2808653 (N.D. Cal. May 31, 2024). The United States District Court for the Northern District of California granted Dunkin Donut LLC's ("Dunkin") motion to dismiss a lawsuit filed by ten lactose intolerant customers of franchised Dunkin Donuts locations in California alleging that the extra fee charged for substitution of non-dairy alternatives in place of cow's milk in beverages constituted disability discrimination. The court held there was no personal jurisdiction noting that the plaintiffs' few sparse allegations that Dunkin operated a place of public accommodation within the meaning of the American with Disabilities Act ("ADA") did not meet the burden required to establish personal jurisdiction in California over the defendant. However, the court granted the motion with leave to amend to allow Plaintiffs to undertake jurisdictional discovery regarding who owns, operates, or leases the relevant stores, and whether Dunkin requires franchisees to impose a surcharge for non-dairy alternatives. The court also denied Dunkin's request to take judicial notice of the disclosures from its 2023 Franchise Disclosure Document filed with the Wisconsin Department of Financial Institutions which Dunkin argued provided that (1) all the locations operated in plaintiffs' state of residences were franchised (not company owned), no-company owned locations were projected in 2023, under the franchise agreement the franchisee retain authority to set prices for the products sold, including non-dairy alternatives, and that the FDD required franchisees to comply with the ADA and placed the burden for such compliance on the franchisee.

goGLOW Enterprises, LLC v. GP MBM, LLC, No. 23-2698, 2024 WL 3443883 (D. Minn. July 15, 2024). The United States District Court for the District of Minnesota granted GP MBM's ("MBM") motion to dismiss a complaint filed by goGlow, a Minnesota company offering health and beauty goods ("Glow"). Glow alleged trademark infringement and sought damages and an injunction against MBM, an affiliate of WellBiz Brands, Inc., the franchisor of Drybar, Elements Massage, Radiant Waxing, and Amazing Lash Studio. MBM moved to dismiss Glow's complaint for lack of personal jurisdiction. Glow alleged that MBM was subject to jurisdiction because its alter-ego WellBiz exerted control over its twelve franchises in Minnesota. The court turned to previous case precedent that held a franchisor's affiliation with Minnesota through its franchisees is not one of the "exceptional circumstances" sufficient to confer general jurisdiction over WellBiz.

III. Venue and Choice of Forum

Choice Hotels International, Inc. v. Jai Sai Baba, LLC, No. GLS 23-146, 2023 WL 5509211 (D. Md., Aug. 25, 2023). In this case, a district court in Pennsylvania stayed the action and ordered arbitration. After the franchisor prevailed in arbitration, the United States District Court for the District of Maryland denied franchisor's motion to confirm the arbitration award and granted franchisee's motion to transfer venue of the confirmation action to original district court in Pennsylvania.

Doe (K.B.) v. G6 Hospitality, LLC, No. 1:23-CV-2597-TWT, 2023 WL 8650785 (N.D. Ga. Dec. 14, 2023). The district court denied franchisee's motion to dismiss for improper venue in an action brought by a sex trafficking victim against the franchisee and an out-of-state franchisor, alleging violations of state law and the

Trafficking Victims Protection Reauthorization Act. The court concluded that the franchisor waived any objections to personal jurisdiction, and therefore is subject to the court's personal jurisdiction to determine residency for venue purposes. This case is discussed in Chapter 6, Section X.

Hangey v. Husqvarna Professional Products, Inc., 304 A.3d 1120, 1139 (Pa. 2023). The Supreme Court of Pennsylvania concluded that a trial court had improperly determined that venue in a Pennsylvania county was improper based solely on the fact that only .005% of Husqvarna Professional Products' ("HPP") nationwide business was conducted there through an HPP authorized dealer. The supreme court held that the percentage of a company's total revenue derived from the forum county cannot establish, alone, that the company does not regularly conduct business within that county, and that the trial court should have conducted an analysis into whether the business activity at issue was habitual, continuous, and regularly conducted. The court ultimately determined that sales made through HPP's authorized dealer were sufficient to establish proper venue in the Pennsylvania county because they were continuous and regular, even though the quantity was not large in comparison to total sales.

Martin v. Holiday Inn Hotel & Suites, No. 3:24-CV-834, 2024 WL 3071259 (N.D. Ohio June 20, 2024). Plaintiff filed an action asserting diversity jurisdiction over the matter pursuant to 28 U.S.C. § 1332 but only identified the citizenship of two of the six defendants. The district court was unable to determine on the face of the pleadings the citizenship of Holiday Inn Hotel & Suites. To avoid dismissal, the district court ordered the plaintiff to supplement its complaint by filing an affidavit of jurisdiction that incorporated enough information to determine the citizenship of all parties, including the domicile of individuals and each member of any limited liability company, the place of incorporation, and principal place of business of each corporation.

Real Property Management SPV LLC v. Truitt, No. 2:24-CV-00184-DAK, 2024 WL 3358654 (D. Utah July 9, 2024). Plaintiff franchisor filed a motion for preliminary injunction to prohibit the defendant from opening a competitive business. Defendant filed a motion to transfer venue to California, where defendant was operating the competing business. The district court denied the defendant's motion because the forum selection clause in the franchise agreement was valid and mandatory.

Honest Abe Roofing Franchise, Inc. v. Lesjon Holdings, LLC, No. 223CV00395JMSMJD, 2023 WL 8452415 (S.D. Ind. Dec. 6, 2023). Where a franchise agreement contained a mandatory forum selection clause designating the forum for disputes in Illinois, but the accompanying personal guaranty required Indiana as the forum, the court examined the conflicting terms and held that the terms of the franchise agreement were primary and controlling and that the guaranty was secondary because the parties tied it to the obligations under the franchise agreement. The court also examined the venue issue and determined that, although the franchise agreement was executed in Indiana and training occurred there, a transfer to Illinois was appropriate because the franchisee's business was conducted in Illinois, and the claims in the case related to the franchisee's nonperformance in Illinois. The court concluded that for those reasons, under 28 U.S.C. § 1391(b), a ".

Minnebo v. Metal Supermarkets Franchising Am. Inc., No. CV 22-05999, 2024 WL 1928458 (D.N.J. Apr. 30, 2024) KMW-AMD, 2024 WL 1928458 (D.N.J. Apr. 30, 2024). The district court denied plaintiff's motion for reconsideration and alternative motion for leave to file an interlocutory appeal because plaintiff failed to present "new evidence" to alter the court's previous decision to transfer this previously removed case brought under the New Jersey Franchise Practices Act ("NJFPA") to the United States District Court for the Western District of New York pursuant to a forum selection clause in the franchise agreement. The court also rejected plaintiff's assertion that the NJFPA prohibited such transfer. In resolving the motion for reconsideration, the district court rejected plaintiff's reliance on older case law suggesting that transfer was inappropriate because it did not meet the reconsideration requirements of a change in controlling law or newly discovered evidence.

Alamo Intermediate II Holdings, LLC v. Birmingham Alamo Movies, LLC, No. SA-23-CV-01531-JKP, 2024 WL 1813449 (W.D. Tex. Apr. 25, 2024). The co-owner of a franchisee defendant moved to dismiss this case for lack of personal jurisdiction, arguing he was not a signatory to the franchise agreement and personal guaranty in his individual capacity but only as an authorized agent of the franchisee. This was accurate, but the court nevertheless denied the motion applying Texas law because parties who are not signatories to a contract in their individual capacity may nevertheless be bound by the terms of an agreement if their consent to be bound is evinced through the "four corners" of the contract. The fact that the co-owner was named as the "Operating and Controlling Principal" of the business was dispositive to the court's decision. Further, in its application of the "closely related" doctrine, the district court determined that it was foreseeable that the forum selection clause would bind the owner of the franchised business because he was a co-owner of the franchise, named as the operating and controlling principal of the business, was an intended beneficiary of the agreement, had agreed to take individual responsibility related to the development of the location of the franchise, and was aware of the terms of the agreement.

Firexo, Inc. v. Firexo Group Ltd., 99 F.4th 304 (6th Cir. 2024). Defendant Firexo Group Limited ("FGL") is a British company that partnered with Ohio citizen, Scott Smith, to sell FGL fire extinguishers in the United States via a joint distribution agreement. The agreement gave Smith control of one of FGL's subsidiaries, Plaintiff Firexo, Inc. ("Firexo"), and designated Firexo as the entity through which Smith could oversee FGL's American distribution operation. It also contained choice-of-law and forum-selection clauses designating England or Wales as the exclusive jurisdiction to settle any dispute or claim arising out of or in connection with the agreement, its subject matter, or its formation.

Firexo experienced ongoing and worsening problems with the fire extinguishers and sued FGL in an Ohio state court for breach of contract and breach of a separately alleged oral distribution agreement. FGL removed the case to federal court on diversity grounds and then moved to dismiss on the agreement's forum selection clause designating England or Wales as the exclusive jurisdiction. Firexo opposed FGL's motion to dismiss because Firexo was a non-signatory and was not bound by the agreement's forum selection clause. The district court granted FGL's motion, enforced the forum-selection clause, and dismissed the case for lack of jurisdiction. The court held that Firexo was bound by the terms of the distribution agreement even though it was not a party to it. Applying the closely related doctrine, the district court reasoned that Firexo was bound by the clause because Firexo was so closely related to the agreement that it was foreseeable that the clause would be applied to it.

Firexo appealed, arguing that the district court applied the wrong law, and the wrong analytical approach, to determine which law applied to the contract's applicability. At the time, there was a circuit split on this issue. Some federal circuits applied the federal common law and the closely related doctrine to whether forum selection clauses apply. These cases see forum selection as a purely procedural issue, which is governed by federal common law. On the other side of the split are cases that apply the *Erie* doctrine to the forum selection clause.

In the Sixth Circuit's decision, the court of appeals concluded that a forum selection clause's applicability is distinct from, and antecedent to, its enforcement, so the district court erred in not applying traditional *Erie* analysis. The court held that district courts must apply a two-step process when deciding whether to enforce a forum selection clause. First, a court must conduct a choice-of-law analysis under *Erie* to identify the applicable law and use that law to determine the applicability of the forum selection clause. Second, if the clause applies to the dispute, the court must determine whether the clause is enforceable under federal common law.

After concluding that this issue was not governed by federal common law, the majority held that Firexo's rights and obligations with respect to this forum selection clause should be determined under English law. Under that law, Firexo was not bound by the clause as a non-signatory to the contract. Accordingly, the majority held that the district court erred in granting the defendant's motion to dismiss based on the venue provision, reversed the district court's decision, and remanded the case for further proceedings. The Sixth Circuit joined the Second, Third, Fifth, and Tenth Circuit Courts to adopt the *Erie* doctrine approach: that courts should apply state law principles to interpret contracts and to determine the applicability of forum selection clauses before deciding whether the clause is enforceable under federal common law.

Ice Rover, Inc. v. Brumate, Inc., 6:22-CV-00794-ADA-DTG, 2023 WL 5652533 (W.D. Tex. August 28, 2023). The plaintiff, Ice Rover, Inc. ("Ice Rover") filed a patent infringement case against Brumate, Inc. ("Brumate"). Ice Rover asserted venue in the Western District of Texas was proper, claiming Brumate had regular and established places of business in Austin and San Antonio. Brumate filed a 12(b)(3) motion to dismiss for improper venue or transfer to the District of Colorado and argued it had no place of business in Texas. To determine if venue was proper, the court determined whether Brumate had a "regular and established place of business" in the Western District of Texas. Brumate was initially an Indiana LLC, then incorporated in Colorado, and eventually converted into a Delaware corporation. Its headquarters and primary business operations were in Denver, Colorado. Brumate operated primarily online and through third-party retailers, without physical retail locations or employees in Texas. Brumate did sell goods through approximately 150 authorized dealers located in the district and listed the authorized dealers on its website. However, the court found that the relationship between Brumate and its authorized third-party retailers in Texas did not rise to the level of control necessary to make them agents of Brumate. Therefore, the authorized dealer locations could not be considered the defendant's regular and established place of business. The court recommended denying Brumate's motion to dismiss, but agreed that venue in the Western District of Texas was improper, and recommended that the District Judge grant the alternative request to transfer the case to the District of Colorado.

La Michoacana Plus Ice Cream Parlor Corp. v. Windy City Paletas, Inc., No. 2:23-cv-00279, 2024 WL 1376987 (D. Nev. Mar. 31, 2024). The United States District Court for the District of Nevada granted defendants' motion to transfer to the Southern District of California in an intellectual property infringement action filed against defendants. The defendants entered into an agreement with plaintiff, La Michoacana Plus Ice Cream Parlor Corp. ("La Michoacana") to operate storefronts offering La Michoacana frozen dessert products under its trademarks. The defendants opened up eight locations, five in California and three in Nevada, and never paid royalties. The court granted the motion to transfer because the action could have been brought in the Southern District of California, the convenience of the witnesses and the parties favored transfer, and the license agreements were between La Michoacana and California franchisees.

Tiare Tech., Inc. v. Dine Brands Global, Inc., No. 222CV00490JRGRSP, 2024 WL 607407 (E.D. Tex. Jan. 4, 2024). Plaintiff Tiare Technology, Inc. ("Tiare") sued Applebee's Restaurants LLC and Dine Brands Global Inc. (together, "Defendants") alleging that their application for mobile ordering infringed several patents. Defendants filed a motion to dismiss under Rule 12(b)(3) for improper venue.

To establish the proper venue, a plaintiff must show that the defendants had a regular and established place of business. The patent venue statute considers that there was a "regular and established place of business" if there was (1) a physical place in the district; (2) that was regular and established; and (3) it was the place of the defendant. The magistrate judge found that the first requirement was satisfied because neither of the parties disputed whether the establishments were physical places in the district. Therefore, the court turned its analysis to the second requirement.

The magistrate judge rejected the Defendants' argument that Tiara failed to present sufficient evidence to establish that an agency relationship existed to satisfy the second requirement. The premise of Defendants' argument was that they were in the business of providing services to the franchisees of Applebee's and IHOP brands and not the business of operating restaurants. The magistrate judge also rejected the Defendants' argument that they should not be considered franchisors for the second requirement of the venue analysis because of an explicit provision in the franchise agreement. The court reasoned that the Defendants had a sufficient amount of control over the franchisor to demonstrate an agency relationship, which was anything but ancillary to the business. Therefore, the second requirement was met.

Lastly, the magistrate found that there was sufficient evidence to satisfy the third requirement. The magistrate judge relied on the Defendants' marketing, advertisements of the restaurant locations on their website, and its control over the performance of maintenance of the restaurant facilities pursuant to the System Manual. Thus, the magistrate found the venue proper and recommended that the district court deny Defendants' motion to dismiss based on the allegedly improper forum.

Old Chicago II Franchising, LLC v. WD Ventures, LLC, No. 23-cv-02596-NYW-STV, 2024 WL 1911221 (D. Colo. May 1, 2024). The United States District Court for the District of Colorado denied defendant's motion to dismiss based on forum non conveniens. Defendant franchisee argued that the case should be heard in Colorado state court only due to a forum selection clause in the Franchise Agreement that stated any case must be heard exclusively in state courts located in Broomfield, Colorado. The court found that the court's decision to transfer the case to the District of Colorado interpreted the forum selection clause as allowing federal jurisdiction in Colorado. This Court found no clear error or manifest injustice in the ruling and denied the motion.

Meta Med, LLC v. Insulet Corp., No. CV 23-1546 (CVR), 2024 WL 1763610 (D.P.R. Apr. 23, 2024). The trial court granted a manufacturer's motion to dismiss because plaintiff failed to overcome the presumption that the forum selection and choice of law clause in a distributor agreement was invalid, overreaching, unreasonable, or unjust. This case is discussed in Chapter 3, Section V.

World Inspection Network International LLC v. J. Strout Holdings, LLC, No. 1:24cv146, 2024 WL 3566172 (M.D.N.C. July 29, 2024). Plaintiff, a home inspection franchise system ("Franchisor") filed a lawsuit against defendants alleging each was acting in concert to violate the post-termination non-compete under their franchise agreement. Franchisor brought a claim for breach of contract, trade secret misappropriation, and trademark infringement and moved for a preliminary injunction against defendants. The court granted defendants' motion to transfer the case to the United States District Court for the Northern District of Alabama finding that the franchise agreement clause contained a mandatory forum-selection clause and not a permissive forum-selection clause.

Holt Texas, Ltd v. Vita Inclinata Technologies, Inc., No. SA-23-CV-01130-JKP, 2023 WL 8040766 (W.D. Tex. Nov. 20, 2023). This case involved an exclusive distribution relationship for load stability systems manufactured by defendant Vita Inclinata. Vita terminated Holt as its distributor under a written distribution agreement for a myriad of reasons. Holt sued. In a proverbial race to the courthouse, the parties had parallel litigation in both Texas (this case) and in Colorado (a case pursued by Vita). The district court granted Vita's motion to dismiss in this action based on forum non conveniens because Holt failed to satisfy its burden of overcoming the agreement's forum selection clause's presumptive validity (which called for litigation in Colorado state courts) and because plaintiff failed to satisfy its burden of addressing how public-interest factors should weigh in determining whether dismissal was appropriate.

IV. Choice of Law

JTH Tax, LLC v. Yong, No. 4:22-CV-01008-O, 2023 WL 5216496 (N.D. Tex. Aug. 11, 2023). In this case, the United States District Court for the Northern District of Texas granted defendant's 18 U.S.C. § 1404(a) transfer request to the Northern District of California where the Franchise Agreement's forum selection clause designating a Texas court was permissive instead of mandatory. The court also noted that the conduct underlying Plaintiff's claims occurred in California, and reasoned that a "California Addendum" to the Franchise Agreement might require experience with California law.

Wirtgen America, Inc. v Hayden-Murphy Equipment Co., No. 3:22-cv-00308, 2023 WL 591704 (M.D. Tenn. Sept. 11, 2023). A Minnesota dealer filed a counterclaim against a Tennessee-based supplier alleging violations of both Minnesota and Tennessee relationship laws, despite an express choice-of-law provision in the parties' distribution agreement. The trial court denied a motion to dismiss on grounds that pleading in the alternative was appropriate for complaint but cautioned that the dealer must eventually "identify discrete, substantive differences between Minnesota law and Tennessee law, tied to identifiable contested issues raised by this case, which the court can either accept or reject as grounds for applying one state's laws over another's." This case is discussed in Chapter 4, Section III.

Functional Hit Fitness, LLC v. F45 Training Inc., No. 22-10168, 2023 WL 6367691 (E.D. Mich. Sept. 23, 2023). The district court modified a report and recommendation of a magistrate ("R&R"), which resulted in applying Michigan law, rather than the contractual choice of Delaware law. The result was retention of Michigan state law claims and dismissal of Delaware and California statutory claims.

F45 Training operated fitness training studios in Michigan, which it franchised to others, including the plaintiff Functional HIIT Fitness. The plaintiff in 2019 entered into the defendant's franchise agreement for training studios in three locations in Michigan. Later, after signing the franchise agreement, the plaintiff disputed selected provisions of the franchise agreement, including failure to provide timely information related to the agreement and higher costs than were previously disclosed. On failure to reach agreement on these issues, the plaintiff franchisee sued F45, its CEO Adam Gilchrist, and named individuals that played a part in negotiating the franchise agreement: Robert Deutsch, Marc Maranto, Luke Armstrong, and Nick Abrahms.

Functional HIIT Fitness alleged that the defendants, including F45, violated the FTC's Franchise rule, as well as various other state laws, by fraudulently inducing the plaintiff to enter franchise agreements for three F45 Training studios. Specifically, the plaintiff's complaint raised ten claims: breach of contract (Count I); breach of the implied covenant of good faith and fair dealing (Count II); fraud and misrepresentation (Count III); negligent misrepresentation (Count IV); unjust enrichment (Count V); violations of the Michigan Franchise Investment Law ("MFIL") (Counts VI-VIII); violations of the California Franchise Investment Law (CFIL) (Count IX); and violations of the Delaware Deceptive Trade Practices Act (Count X). Defendants moved to dismiss these claims.

The R&R recommended that the defendants' motions to dismiss be granted in part and denied in part, including the dismissal of defendants Gilchrist, Deutsch, Armstrong, and Adams for lack of personal jurisdiction, and the dismissal of Counts II, VI-VII, IX, and X.

The court upheld the R&R recommendation to dismiss the complaint against defendants Gilchrist, Deutsch, Armstrong, and Adams for lack of personal jurisdiction because none of these defendants were held to have sufficient contact with Michigan to warrant asserting personal jurisdiction over them.

Rejecting the R&R finding as to choice of law, the district court concluded that applying Delaware law would be "contrary to a fundamental public policy" of Michigan, and Michigan law should govern in this dispute. The court stated that the MFIL, unlike Delaware law, provided for protecting franchisees from the "superior bargaining power" of franchisors. Specifically, unlike the MFIL, Delaware law does not require pre-contract notice or disclosure. Accordingly, the court stated that Counts VI, VII and VIII would be governed by the MFIL, that the state law claims would be analyzed under Michigan law, and the Delaware and California statutory claims would be dismissed.

Raab v. Nu Skin Enterprises, Inc., No. 38842-5-III, 28 Wash. App. 2d, 536 P.3d 695 (2023). In this case, the Washington Court of Appeals provided an in depth choice of law analysis involving distributors who filed an action seeking relief under Washington's Consumer Protection Act ("WCPA") and its Anti-pyramid Promotional Scheme Act ("WAPSA") despite the fact that their agreement with suppliers required mandatory arbitration of all disputes in Salt Lake County, Utah, and the application of Utah law. This case is discussed in Chapter 8, Section VI, Subsection A.

V. Amendment of Pleadings and Joinder of Claims and Parties

LG2, LLC v. American Dairy Queen Corp., No. 22-cv-1044 (WMW/JFD), 2023 WL 5950714 (D. Minn., Sept. 13, 2023). In this case, the United States District Court for the District of Minnesota rejected an attempt to characterize a motion for leave to amend as an improper motion for reconsideration. In its decision, the court denied the motion for leave to amend as futile because the new proposed allegations, incorporating terms of franchisor's operating manual, did not change the court's prior ruling, which held that requiring consent to the transfer of franchise was not an "offer to sell" in Minnesota that brought the transaction within the ambit of the Minnesota Franchise Act.

Bernard-Moses v. Chick-Fil-A, Inc., 2024 N.Y. Slip. Op. 50123(U), 2024 WL 464370 (Sup. Ct. N.Y. Feb. 6, 2024). The Supreme Court of New York denied a plaintiff's motion to amend a complaint to add a sublessee of a Chick-Fil-A restaurant following the expiration of the statute of limitations based on the "Relation Back Doctrine." The court held that the plaintiff failed to establish that Chick-Fil-A and the prospective defendant sublessee and franchisee were "united in interest" for purposes of the second prong of the relation back doctrine. The only relationship that the prospective plaintiff claimed to exist between Chick-Fil-A and the prospective franchisee was that of franchisor and franchisee. The court held that it was settled law that the franchisor-franchisee relationship does not suffice to establish that two entities are united in interest in the context of the relation back doctrine, and such entities do not share the same defenses.

Willis v. 8UP Elevated Drinkery & Kitchen, No. 3:23-CV-00295-GNS, 2024 WL 1182881 (W.D. Ky. Mar. 18, 2024). A plaintiff sued a franchisee of the Hilton Hotel brand for racial discrimination based on being evicted from the hotel property run by the franchisee. The district court denied plaintiff's motion to amend her complaint because it did not cure defects in the original complaint, did not introduce any new claims or factual allegations, and was deemed futile. The court also granted the defendant's motion to dismiss because plaintiff's statutory civil rights claims under state and federal law were time barred.

Nieto v. Dodd, No. 2024-C-0293, 2024 WL 2269206 (La. Ct. App. May 20, 2024). Plaintiff, the former CEO of Main Squeeze Juice Holdings, LLC ("Main Squeeze"), filed a petition for a writ of quo warranto, against newly named CEO, Jennifer Dodd, seeking a declaration that Main Squeeze's successor CEO had no legal right to hold the office of CEO, that Main Squeeze exceeded its powers in employing Dodd, and to prohibit Main Squeeze from continuing wrongful and ultra vires activities. Defendants responded by filing an exception of lis pendens arguing that this action was an attempt to raise the same issues in a related proceeding, Nieto v. CCG MSJC, LLC, No. CV 24-818, 2024 WL 2207509 (E.D. La. May 16, 2024). The trial court denied the exception of lis pendens. Defendants sought emergency relief from the trial court's ruling. The Louisiana Court of Appeals granted Nieto's writ of quo warranto, reversed the trial court's ruling denying the exception of lis pendens, and lifted the stay of this second action. In so doing, it held that the Defendants met the three elements for a lis pendens exceptions: (1) two or more suits pending; (2) the pending suits involved the same transaction or occurrence; and (3) the pending suits involved the same parties in the same capacities. Although the captions of the two cases were not the same, the court applied the federal rule on identity of parties and considered the underlying issues in both cases. Because the court of appeals found the plaintiffs to be identical in both cases and the facts intertwined, the court determined that the third element for obtaining a lis pendens exception to the suit had been satisfied. The first case is discussed in Chapter 8, Section II.

Coniglio v. Cucuzza, No. 23-CV-2987, 2024 WL 544420 (E.D.N.Y. Feb. 10, 2024). District court granted the plaintiff distributor's motion for leave to amend the complaint for its Lanham Act claim, finding that the defendant failed to meet their burden to demonstrate that leave to amend would be futile.

M.A. Silva Corks USA, LLC v. M.A. Silva Holdings, Inc., No. 22-CV-04345-AMO, 2024 WL 1180999 (N.D. Cal. Mar. 18, 2024). In this case, the United States District Court for the Northern District of California refused to grant leave for defendants to amend their pleadings and add counterclaims against the plaintiff in a dispute over an exclusive distribution agreement involving the sale of Portuguese corks used in the wine industry. The district court found that it would be unduly prejudicial to the plaintiffs and that the defendants had engaged in undue delay. This case is discussed in Chapter 4, Section I, Subsection A.

VI. Arbitration

A. ENFORCEABILITY

Okolish v. Town Money Saver, Inc., CV-2020-07-1883, 2023 WL 5274046 (Ohio Ct. App. Aug. 16, 2023). A coupon clipper magazine franchise, Town Money Saver, Inc. and TMS Franchising, Inc. ("TMS") appealed a decision of the lower court denying their motion to compel arbitration. The franchisee, Kim Okolish ("Okolish"), started mailing clipper coupons in 1996. A year later she partnered with William Zirzwow to operate under the "Town Money Saver" brand. In 2005, Zirzwow decided to franchise the concept and Okolish alleged that she was required to enter into a form of franchise agreement if she wanted to continue operating under the name. A dispute arose regarding an encroaching franchisee and Okolish filed suit against TMS for damages. TMS filed a motion to compel arbitration under the franchise agreement. The trial court denied the motion concluding that the arbitration provision in the franchise agreement was procedurally and substantively unconscionable. The court of appeals disagreed. The court found that Okolish was never required to enter into a franchise agreement to continue operating her territory, only if she desired to expand her region or acquire other markets. Okolish testified to the fact that she wanted to grow her business. The evidence also showed that at least three other similarly situated Town Money saver operators decided not to sign the franchise agreements and continued operating their businesses maintaining the status quo. Further, Okolish was neither rushed to sign a franchise agreement nor prohibited from starting her own business not under the Town Money Saver name. Reviewing this record, the court concluded that the trial court incorrectly determined the arbitration requirement was procedurally unconscionable. Accordingly, the court reversed and remanded the case, requiring the trial court to further consider whether the provision was substantively unconscionable.

Munoz v. Earthgrains Distribution, LLC, No. 22-CV-1269-AJB-AHG, 2023 WL 5986129 (S.D. Cal. Sept. 13, 2023). Three independent distributors of baked goods brought a putative class action against Earthgrains Distribution, LLC ("Earthgrains") and Bimbo Bakeries ("Bimbo") alleging various labor and employment violations. The defendants moved to compel arbitration pursuant to a dispute resolution provision in the Distribution Agreement. The district court denied the motion, agreeing with the plaintiffs that the Distribution Agreement was unenforceable on the grounds that it lacked mutual assent and was unconscionable.

First, the court found that there was no mutual assent because the language in the Distribution Agreement contradicted an addendum that was presented to the plaintiffs when they entered into the agreement. In the district court's view, this evinced that there was no meeting of the minds between the parties on mandatory arbitration. Second, the court found several provisions in agreement unconscionable. The district court found procedural unconscionability existed because the Distribution Agreement was a contract of adhesion in that the plaintiffs lacked autonomy to negotiate any of its terms. The district court also found several provisions of the Distribution Agreement substantively unconscionable. The court noted that the alleged labor code violations typically have a one-to-four-year limitations period. The defendants had reduced the limitation period to sixty days. The court found that the shortened limitations period was unduly harsh and supported substantive unconscionability. The district court also considered the substantive limitations on the remedies afforded to the plaintiffs. In the end, the district court concluded that because the Distribution Agreement contained several unconscionable provisions that would significantly obstruct the plaintiffs' ability to bring claims against the defendants, it could not be severed to save its application. For these reasons, the court held that the entire agreement was unenforceable.

Red Fit, LLC v. Red Effect International Franchise, LLC, No. 363686, 2024 WL 2790504 (Mich. Ct. App. May 30, 2024). Plaintiffs appealed the trial court's ruling that granted defendants' summary judgment motion and denied plaintiffs' motion to extend the deadline for filing witness lists. The court of appeals affirmed the trial court's decision granting defendants' summary disposition because the claims were properly disposed of due to the arbitration clause contained in each of the operative agreements. The court also affirmed the trial court's ruling denying plaintiffs' motion to extend the deadline for filing witness lists because the trial court's decision to deny plaintiff's motion did not fall outside the range of reasonable or principled outcomes.

Fuentes v. Jiffy Lube International, Inc., No. 18-5174, 2023 WL 5984284 (E.D. Pa. Sept. 14, 2023). The United States District Court for the Eastern District of Pennsylvania granted franchisor Jiffy Lube International, Inc.'s ("Jiffy Lube") motion to compel arbitration of a former employee's claims that no-poach provisions in its franchise agreements artificially depressed wages of Jiffy Lube franchisee employees. The court found that under California law, the former employee's online acknowledgment to an arbitration agreement during the standard employee on-boarding process was sufficient to put him on notice that the agreement to arbitration was a condition of his continued employment. The notice acknowledged by the former employee contained an option to formally opt-out of arbitration. However, if an employee failed to opt-out within thirty days, then continued employment constituted mutual acceptance of the arbitration agreement. Because the former employee failed to opt-out, the court granted Jiffy Lube's motion to compel arbitration.

Bissonnette v. LePage Bakeries Park St., LLC, 601 U.S. 246 (2024). The Supreme Court of the United States vacated and remanded the lower court's dismissal of a case in favor of arbitration which found that delivery driver franchisees were not exempt from the Federal Arbitration Act ("FAA").

Plaintiffs were a class of franchisees which had entered into distributor agreements with a baked goods company to purchase and then market, sell, and deliver bakery's products by truck to retailers in designated territories. The Connecticut franchisees brought a putative class action against the defendant alleging unpaid or withheld wages, unpaid overtime wages, and unjust enrichment pursuant to Fair Labor Standards Act and Connecticut wage laws. Defendant moved to dismiss or, in alternative, to compel arbitration under the FAA pursuant to the terms of the distributor agreements. Plaintiffs argued that they were exempt from arbitration because they fell within the FAA's exemption for transportation workers. The district court dismissed on the basis that the plaintiff's were not transportation workers since they had a much broader scope of responsibility under the distributor agreements and therefore were not principally truck drivers. The Second Circuit Court of Appeals affirmed, but on the basis that the distributors' commerce is in bakery, not transportation services. In a unanimous decision, the

Supreme Court held that a transportation worker need not work for a company in the transportation industry to fall within the FAA's exemption from coverage for any "class of workers engaged in foreign or interstate commerce." Because (1) there was no requirement for a transportation worker to work for a company in the transportation industry; and (2) the franchisees engaged in the transportation of the baked goods across borders via channels of interstate commerce playing a role in the free flow of goods, the court vacated and remanded the case.

BDD Group, LLC v. Crave Franchising, LLC, No. 24-CV-10035, 2024 WL 2854265 (E.D. Mich. June 5, 2024). Plaintiffs filed a motion to modify the court's order to provide that Michigan law would govern the subject arbitration proceeding and that the arbitration proceedings were to take place in Michigan. The court denied the motion because the arbitration agreement governed the choice of law and venue requirements.

Brown v. MUY Pizza-Tejas, LLC, No. 1:23-CV-1816-MLB, 2024 WL 3491659 (N.D. Ga. July 18, 2024). In a collective action brought by a pizza delivery driver under the Fair Labor Standards Act ("FLSA") against the owner of 352 Pizza Hut restaurants, the district court granted in part, and denied without prejudice in part, defendants' motion to dismiss and compel arbitration. The court granted the motion to dismiss and motion to compel arbitration for two employees who signed arbitration agreements electronically because their self-serving declarations were insufficient to create triable issues for the court on the issue of enforceability of the arbitration agreement. The district court denied without prejudice the motions for the remaining two employees because genuine issues of material fact existed regarding the validity of their signatures on their alleged arbitration agreements. The court set a hearing to determine whether limited discovery was needed to resolve that dispute for the court to decide the matter on the merits.

Sorroza v. Express Services, Inc., No. G062052, 2024 WL 3219183 (Cal. Ct. App. June 28, 2024). Sorroza signed a mutual arbitration agreement governed by the Federal Arbitration Act ("FAA") when he began working at Express, a franchisor of full-service staffing firms. Sorroza was placed at a container manufacturer where he operated a forklift in the shipping and receiving department and loaded and unloaded trucks that transported goods across state lines. Sorroza sued Express, who then moved to compel arbitration and dismiss Sorroza's claims. Sorroza opposed Express's motions, arguing that he was exempt from the FAA's coverage because he belonged to a class of workers engaged in foreign or interstate commerce. Sorroza filed a declaration in support of his position and Express filed objections to the declaration on hearsay grounds. The trial court overruled the hearsay objections and denied the motion to compel arbitration, finding that Sorrozo was exempt from the FAA coverage. Express appealed. The California Court of Appeals affirmed the lower court's rulings, holding that Sorroza's statements in his declaration were authorized admissions that fell within an exception to the hearsay rule. The appellate court also affirmed that Sorroza fell within the exemption for FAA coverage because Sorroza belonged to a class of workers who loaded and unloaded goods on and off trucks moving across state lines.

Ensambles Hyson, S.A. de C.V. v. Sanchez, No. 23-CV-1887 JLS (KSC), 2024 WL 2859576 (S.D. Cal. June 6, 2024). Ensambles Hyson, S.A., Rain Bird Corporation, and Rain Bird International, Inc. ("Petitioners") are interrelated companies, and a global manufacturer of irrigation products and services headquartered in California. Hyson maintains a facility in Mexico where Respondent Sanchez worked. Sanchez's employment offer letter included an arbitration agreement with a delegation clause. After sixteen years of employment, Hyson fired Sanchez. Sanchez initiated a wrongful termination action against Petitioners by filing a complaint with the Local Conciliation and Arbitration Board in Tijuana, Mexico (the

"Mexico Proceedings"). Two years later, Petitioners initiated an action in California seeking to compel Sanchez to raise his claims in arbitration and to require Sanchez to stop litigating the Mexico Proceedings through pursuit of an anti-suit injunction. The district court granted the petition to the extent Sanchez's employers sought to compel him to participate in arbitration. However, the district court denied the request for the anti-suit injunction because Petitioners failed to satisfy their burden.

The district court was asked to answer a question of first impression: whether an anti-suit injunction can be granted to enforce an arbitration agreement containing a delegation clause before questions of arbitrability are settled. In resolving the matter, the district court relied on a three-part test established by the Ninth Circuit Court of Appeals for evaluating the propriety of foreign anti-suit injunctions. Step one consists of two questions: (1) whether the parties and the issues are the same in both the domestic and foreign actions; and (2) whether the domestic action is dispositive of the action to be enjoined. The essential question is whether all the issues in the foreign action can be resolved in the local action. Step two requires courts to evaluate whether the foreign litigation would (1) frustrate a policy in the forum issuing the injunction; (2) be vexatious or oppressive; (3) threaten the issuing court's in rem or quasi in rem jurisdiction; or (4) result in prejudice or affect other equitable considerations. The Ninth Circuit's step three requires courts to consider whether the impact on comity would be tolerable. Relevant considerations include the scope of the requested inunction and whether the dispute implicates public international law or government litigants. The district court applied this Ninth Circuit analysis and concluded that the Petitioners failed to satisfy the threshold inquiry in step one. The court held that an anti-suit injunction cannot be granted to enforce an arbitration agreement until questions of arbitrability are settled.

The district court determined that delegation clauses in arbitration agreements impede step one analysis. Courts in cases with enforceable delegation clauses are limited to deciding whether the agreement exists, which undermines the court's ability to decide questions key to the threshold considerations laid out by the Ninth Circuit. In analyzing step one, the district court asked whether all issues raised in the Mexico Proceedings (1) were subject to the employment agreement; and (2) would those issues be resolved if the domestic action were to be decided in Petitioners' favor. The court found the answer to both questions to be "no" because arbitrability determinations are indispensable to the same-issues/dispositive inquiry's interrelated requirements. The district court determined that it could not dispose of all issues raised by the wrongful termination claim brought in the Mexico Proceedings. It was only asked to determine whether a written agreement to arbitrate existed and if that agreement contained a valid delegation clause. Because the agreement contained an enforceable delegation clause, it concluded that it could not rule on whether Sanchez's claims are subject to arbitration. Therefore, Petitioners' motion for the anti-suit injunction was denied because they failed to satisfy the threshold requirements for obtaining the injunction as the arbitrability of the claims raised in the Mexico Proceedings remained unsettled.

Nevertheless, because this was a question of first impression, the district court continued its analysis under the Ninth Circuit's three-party test. It evaluated the four factors in step two to determine whether they might justify an anti-suit injunction and determined that none of the factors supported entry of the injunction. In its analysis of the step three factors, the court determined that filing an anti-injunction suit would disrupt comity with the Mexican tribunal. This is because stopping the Mexico Proceedings at a stage where substantial resources had been invested and a resolution was nearly reached before confirming the issue of arbitrability, would have a distinctive and intolerable impact on comity.

After denying Petitioners' motion, the district court then analyzed whether to deny the motion with or without prejudice, and if without prejudice, what the next steps in the action should be. The court reasoned that a key element in the court's analysis—the arbitrability of Sanchez's claims—remained an open issue. Because the district court's reasoning hinged on an undefined variable, it denied the motion without prejudice.

Anthony v. Van Over, No. 3:22-cv-416, 2023 WL 6317685 (E.D. Tenn. Sept. 27, 2023). Fifty-four franchisees filed suit against their franchisor, its officers, and others allegedly involved in selling franchises on the grounds that the franchisees were fraudulently misled about a variety of statistics related to profitability and the time required to successfully manage and operate the franchises. Defendants moved to compel arbitration, which the court granted after affirmatively answering two questions: (1) does an arbitration agreement exist; and (2) is there "clear and unmistakable" evidence that the parties intended to delegate questions of arbitrability to the arbitrator?

All the franchise agreements had unambiguous arbitration agreements, and all expressly referenced that the arbitration would be guided by AAA rules. In granting the motion to compel arbitration and declining the invitation to consider whether certain claims fell outside the scope of what the parties had agreed to arbitrate–including an argument that non-signatories of the franchise agreements should not be compelled to arbitrate–the court relied on the Sixth Circuit's previous decision holding that, as matter of law, "incorporation of the AAA rules (or similarly worded arbitral rules) provides 'clear and unmistakable evidence' that the parties agreed to arbitrate 'arbitrability.'" *See* ***Blandon v. Domino's Pizza Franchising, LLC***, 962 F.3d 842, 846–48 (6th Cir. 2020).

Raab v. Nu Skin Enterprises, Inc., No. 38842-5-III, 536 P.3d 695 (Wash. Ct. App. 2023). Several franchisees sued in Washington alleging that Nu Skin and its top distributors misrepresented the financial potential of Nu Skin distributorships and the legitimacy of the Nu Skin business enterprises, and also provided preferential treatment to higher-level distributors. The complaint sought relief under Washington's Consumer Protection Act ("WCPA") and its Anti-pyramid Promotional Scheme Act ("WAPSA"), among other things. The parties' contracts required mandatory arbitration of all disputes in Salt Lake County, Utah, applying Utah law, so defendants moved to dismiss the Washington case and filed a petition with the federal district court in Utah seeking to compel arbitration in Utah. Plaintiffs opposed both motions for multiple reasons, including Washington's strong public policy in favor of protecting consumers. The Washington state court denied the motion to dismiss on the grounds that it was the proper venue given Washington's strong public policy interests in deciding cases brought under consumer protection statutes like WCPA and WAPSA. The Utah federal court ruled that the Washington state court's decision had preclusive effect, denying the motion to compel and dismissing the action. Nu Skin sought discretionary review from the Washington Court of Appeals.

The Washington Court of Appeals held that: (1) a motion to dismiss for "improper venue" was inapplicable to cases in which the defendant seeks to enforce a forum selection clause, citing a 2013 U.S. Supreme Court decision based on Fed. R. Civ. P. 12(b)(3), and decisions from Oklahoma and Vermont (which have similar procedural rules) following suit; (2) while the arbitration forum selection provisions of the contract were subject to the Federal Arbitration Act ("FAA"), the question of who decides arbitrability (the court or the arbitrator) is determined using state-law principles, and courts should not assume that the parties agreed to arbitrate arbitrability absent clear and unmistakable evidence they did so; (3) enforcement of the FAA is left largely to state courts because the FAA itself does not provide independent federal question jurisdiction, meaning that an arbitration clause that is enforceable in federal court is equally enforceable in state court, and pointing out an inconsistency in 9 U.S.C. § 4 that causes ambiguity on this issue; (4) the parties' dispute qualified as a "Dispute" under their contract; and (5) the validity and enforceability of forum selection clauses in state law actions are matters of state law and, in Washington, need not be enforced where enforcement would be unreasonable. The Court of Appeals remanded to the state court to determine whether the parties' contract was unconscionable under Washington law.

Pioneer Hotel Group, Inc. v. Choice Hotels International, Inc., No.: 1:23-cv-00173-REP, 2023 WL 7135059 (D. Idaho Oct. 30, 2023). The United States District Court for the District of Idaho denied defendant Choice Hotels' motion to dismiss plaintiff's complaint for improper venue. Plaintiff denied that the parties ever entered into a franchise agreement containing the arbitration provision that Choice Hotels sought to enforce. The court found there was a dispute between the parties as to whether a franchise agreement was signed by the plaintiffs so the court could not conclude as a matter of law that there was a contract entered into between the parties.

Basinski v. Keller Williams Realty, Inc., No. 1:23-CV-299-DAE, 2023 WL 8653172 (W.D. Tex. Nov. 7, 2023). Plaintiffs sued a franchisor, its founder and president, and several other individuals associated with the franchise (together, "Defendants"), alleging seven tortious interference claims involving five market centers. Defendants moved to compel arbitration pursuant to an arbitration clause contained in four separate Market Center License Agreements. The court partially granted Defendants' motion to compel arbitration for six of the Plaintiffs' claims, but it found that there was not a valid agreement to arbitrate between Plaintiffs and one of the market centers. Therefore, the court denied the Defendants' motion to compel arbitration, and permitted the claim to proceed.

Adler v. Gruma Corp., No. CV22-06598 (RK) (JBD), 2023 WL 7490006 (D.N.J. Nov. 13, 2023). The court granted defendant's motion to compel arbitration of claims brought by certain distributors of defendant's products, finding that New Jersey's interest in the matter was not materially greater than that of Texas, and therefore, upheld the distribution agreement's mandatory arbitration clause. The court noted that any arguments pertaining to unconscionability must be resolved in arbitration.

Jane Doe v. Massage Envy Franchising, LLC,, No. H050069, 2023 WL 8801517 (Cal. App. 6th Dist. Dec. 20, 2023). The California Court of Appeals considered whether the defendant franchisor could compel arbitration of the plaintiff's claim seeking damages for a sexual assault that allegedly occurred at a franchisee's massage clinic. Plaintiff Jane Doe ("Doe") alleged that she was sexually assaulted by a massage therapist at a Massage Envy franchise in San Jose, California. Doe sued both the franchisee who independently operated the establishment and the franchisor, Massage Envy Franchising LLC ("Massage Envy"). Thereafter, Massage Envy moved to compel arbitration, but the trial court denied the motion on the basis that a reasonable person in Doe's position would not have understood that they were entering a contract with Massage Envy. On appeal, the California Court of Appeals reversed the trial court's decision, holding that the arbitration agreement between Doe and Massage Envy was enforceable.

This dispute related to two separate clickwrap agreements between the parties. Sometime before the alleged assault, Doe created a profile on Massage Envy's online booking service which required her to check a box adjacent the text "I agree and assent to the Terms of Use Agreement." The Terms of Use Agreement was hyperlinked. However, Doe was not required to access the agreement before checking the box. The Terms of Use Agreement contained an arbitration provision that broadly encompassed any and all disputes that arose between the customer and Massage Envy. After completing all the necessary requirements, Doe checked the box and created her profile.

A few months later, on June 12, 2019, Doe arrived at the franchise location for a massage appointment. While checking in, Doe was handed an electronic tablet, and she was instructed to complete a digital Wellness Agreement. Near the end of the agreement, there was a checkbox that had text presented in the same way as it was during the profile creation screening with the same link to the Terms of Use Agreement. Doe never clicked on the hyperlink to the Terms of Use Agreement. Instead, she quickly completed the form and returned the tablet to a staff member.

The Court of Appeals reversed the trial court's denial of the motion to compel arbitration, holding that Doe had reasonable notice and expressly assented to the Terms of Use Agreement when she created her online profile. In support of its motion to compel, Massage Envy argued that Doe assented to the Terms of Use Agreement twice, first during the creation of her online profile and again when she checked-in for her appointment on June 12, 2019. Applying California law contract law, the court concluded that Doe agreed to arbitrate any disputes with Massage Envy because she assented to the Terms of Use Agreement when she created her online profile. However, the court rejected Massage Envy's argument that an enforceable contract was formed when Doe completed the Wellness Agreement.

The court distinguished the two agreements based on its previous decision in ***Doe v. Massage Envy Franchising, LLC***, 87 Cal. App. 5th 23, 26 (2022), which involved an in-person check-in. Specifically, the tablet check-in process at the franchised location was nothing like a typical clickwrap agreement because a person is not informed that they are signing up for a new service or setting up an account. Applying that reasoning, the court found that the Doe agreed to the arbitration clause when she created her online profile and granted Massage Envy's motion to compel arbitration. Finally, the court found that the delegation clause in the agreement was enforceable. Therefore, it determined that the arbitrator must address the issues raised by Doe regarding the unconscionability of the arbitration provision.

Jaiswal v. Dickey's Barbecue Restaurants, Inc., No. EDCV231921JGBSPX, 2024 WL 607370 (C.D. Cal. Jan. 18, 2024). The district court denied Defendant Dickey's Barbecue Restaurants motion to dismiss pursuant to an arbitration provision because the court found that the forum-selection clause in the arbitration provision and litigation carve-out were unconscionable.

Singh v. Batteries Plus, LLC, No. 2:24-cv-00223-KJM-DB, 2024 WL 213525 (E.D. Cal. May 13, 2024). Following an unsuccessful mediation, Plaintiff, Ashwant Singh ("Singh") a franchisee of Batteries Plus ("Franchisor"), filed a lawsuit in California state court against the Franchisor alleging multiple violations of state laws. Franchisor filed a demand for arbitration and then removed the state case to federal court based on diversity jurisdiction. Singh filed objections before the American Arbitration Association. Defendants moved to compel arbitration and Singh objected on the grounds that there was no valid agreement, the arbitration provision was unconscionable, and even if the arbitration provision was enforceable, it does not extend to the claims against the other individual sales development officers who were also defendants in the case. The court rejected these arguments and granted the motion to compel arbitration.

The defendants met their burden to establish a valid agreement to arbitrate existed, and the arbitration provision covered the dispute. The court was not swayed by Singh's argument that the table of contents to the Franchise Agreement was missing and the arbitration provision was allegedly 'buried' in text. The court also found no procedural unconscionability and only minor substantive unconscionability, but not with respect to the venue, and mere inconvenience or additional expense was not sufficient. The severability provision in the Franchise Agreement also allowed the substantive unconscionable provisions regarding damages to be severed from the arbitration provision. With only minimal procedural unconscionability and the severance of the substantively unconscionable provisions, the court found the arbitration agreement valid. Finally, the court found that the two co-defendants, the Vice President of Franchise Development and Real Estate Project Manager of Batteries Plus, were acting as agents and their alleged misconduct related to the Franchise Agreement, so they were entitled to the benefits of the arbitration provision. Because arbitration is a contractual right, only parties to an arbitration agreement generally have standing to exercise their right to compel arbitration, however, California courts have held non-signatories who "were acting as agents" have standing to compel arbitration.

A.W. v. Best Western International, Inc., No. 2:21-CV-4934, 2024 WL 1340264 (S.D. Ohio Mar. 29, 2024). In this TVPRA case, the court allowed a franchisor to file a third-party complaint against its franchisee for its potential involvement in the TVPRA allegations made against the franchisor. While the court struck Best Western's third-party contribution and indemnification claims, it denied plaintiff's motion to sever and stay the third-party suit because of the overlapping facts, parties, and evidence. This case is discussed in Chapter 6, Section X.

T.P. v. Best Western International, Inc., No. 2:21-CV-4933, 2024 WL 1347451 (S.D. Ohio Mar. 29, 2024). In this case, the district court allowed a franchisor to file a third-party complaint against its franchisee based on TVPRA allegations. Notwithstanding that result, the court struck Best Western's third-party contribution and indemnification claims. It further denied plaintiff's motion to sever and stay the third-party suit because of the overlapping facts, parties, and evidence. This case is discussed in Chapter 6, Section X.

Oakberry SD UTC, LLC v. Oakberry ACAI, Inc., No.: 23cv1883-BEN (MSB), 2024 WL 3463651 (S.D. Cal. July 18, 2024). The United States District Court for the Southern District of California granted defendant, Oakberry ACAI, Inc.'s motion to stay the case and compel arbitration in a breach of contract lawsuit. where plaintiff licensed defendant's trademark and other operational and intellectual property. Plaintiff alleged that the defendant sold them a disguised franchise in violation of the California Franchise Investment Law, Cal. Corp. Code sections 31000, et seq. The plaintiff also alleged breach of contract, intentional misrepresentation/fraudulent concealment and unjust enrichment. The court held that although plaintiff argued it was fraudulently induced to enter into the trademark licensing agreement by misrepresenting the true nature of the agreement to avoid compliance with California franchise laws, plaintiff did not argue that it was fraudulently induced to agree to the arbitration provision. As to whether the entire agreement was just a trademark licensing agreement or something different (like a misrepresented franchising agreement that would violate state law) was a subject for the arbitrator to decide.

B. BINDING NON-SIGNATORIES

Burnett v. National Association of Realtors, 75 F.4th 975 (8th Cir. 2023). The Eighth Circuit Court of Appeals denied franchisor, Keller Williams Realty Inc.'s ("Keller Williams"), motion to compel a plaintiff class of home sellers to arbitrate its federal antitrust claims against it. The class of home sellers filed a lawsuit against Keller Williams along with the National Association of Realtors and other real estate broker franchisors alleging that rules imposed by the defendants to require home sellers to compensate buyer side real estate brokers created anti-competitive restraints on trade. Keller Williams attempted to enforce an arbitration provision included in the listing agreements between the plaintiffs and plaintiffs' real estate brokers, which were not parties to the lawsuit. Using Missouri law, the court agreed with the district court's finding that Keller Williams could not enforce the arbitration provision in the listing agreement because it was not a party to the listing agreement or third-party beneficiary.

Bennett v. Anheuser-Busch Commercial Stratefy, LLC, No. 222CV01239MCEKJN, 2024 WL 1241916 (E.D. Cal. Mar. 22, 2024). The United States District Court for the Eastern District of California granted defendant's motion to compel arbitration because the employee suing brewer Anheuser-Busch agreed to be bound by defendant's dispute resolution program when he became employed. The court also determined that the delegation clause in the agreement required arbitration.

Yeh v. Superior Court of Contra Costa County, No. A166537, 95 Cal.App.5th 264 (Cal. App. 1st Dist. Sept. 6, 2023). In this decision, Mercedes-Benz USA, LLC ("MBUSA") could not enforce an arbitration provision against a purchaser in a Retail Installment Sales Contract ("RISC") entered into between a dealership and the purchaser, to which MBUSA was not a signatory. The purchaser's claims against MBUSA were premised on MBUSA's express and implied warranties for the purchased vehicle, rather than any obligations imposed on MBUSA by the RISC. Therefore, the court determined that the claims against MBUSA were not "intimately founded and intertwined" with any obligations under the RISC, such that MBUSA could compel arbitration as to the express and implied warranty claims.

Bacon v. BMW of North America, LLC, No. H050174, 2023 WL 8801304 (Cal. Ct. App. Dec. 20, 2023). Bacon purchased a BMW sedan and signed a contract with the dealership that included a mandatory arbitration provision that bound the purchaser, the dealership, and the dealership's assignees. Bacon sued the dealership and BMW of North America, the manufacturer, and asserted violations of the Song-Beverly Consumer Warranty Act, breach of contract, violations of California's Consumer Legal

Remedies Act, and other related claims. BMW, who was not a party to the contract, moved to compel arbitration, which the trial court granted. Bacon appealed arguing that the trial court erred in compelling arbitration because the manufacturer was not a party to the sales contract, BMW could not enforce the contract as a third-party beneficiary, and equitable estoppel did not apply to BMW's effort to force the arbitration. The California Court of Appeals agreed with Bacon, reversed the trial court's judgment, and awarded Bacon his costs on appeal.

Black Rock Coffee Bar, LLC v. BR Coffee, LLC, No. 3:20-cv-976-SI, 2024 WL 1436028 (D. Or. Apr. 3, 2024). The United States District Court for the District of Oregon vacated an arbitration award in favor of franchisor, Black Rock Coffee Bar, against the franchisee ("BR Coffee") and its owners and other parties (the "BR Parties"). The court found that before referring a dispute to an arbitrator, the court determines whether a valid arbitration agreement exists. The BR Parties submitted sufficient evidence that the arbitrator ignored binding precedent provided to him, thereby demonstrating that the arbitrator knew of the law and disregarded it. Thus, the arbitrator's order granting Black Rock's motion to amend and include the additional parties was a manifest disregard of the law and exceeded the arbitrator's powers. The court determined the BR Parties never received a fundamentally fair hearing and all errors were inextricably intertwined so the arbitration award must be vacated.

Singh v. Batteries Plus, LLC, No. 2:24-cv-00223-KJM-DB, 2024 WL 213525 (E.D. Cal. May 13, 2024). Plaintiff, Ashwant Singh ("Singh") a franchisee of Batteries Plus ("Franchisor"), objected to arbitration with the franchisor, on the ground that the arbitration provision in the franchise agreement did not extend to the claims against the other individual sales development officers who were also defendants in the case. The court rejected the argument and found that the two co-defendants, the Vice President of Franchise Development and Real Estate Project Manager of Batteries Plus, were acting as agents and their alleged misconduct related to the

Franchise Agreement, so they were entitled to the benefits of the arbitration provision. Because arbitration is a contractual right, only parties to an arbitration agreement generally have standing to exercise their right to compel arbitration, however, California courts have held non-signatories who "were acting as agents" have standing to compel arbitration. This case is discussed in Chapter 8, Section VI, Subsection A.

Arbogast v. Sky Zone, LLC, No. 2:23-cv-00427, 2024 WL 3378936 (S.D.W.V. July 11, 2024). The United States District Court for the Southern District of West Virginia denied Sky Zone, LLC's ("Sky Zone") motion to compel arbitration against a fifteen-year old minor injured on its trampoline obstacle course, holding that the mother lacked authority to enter into Sky Zone's participation agreement ("Participation Agreement") consenting to arbitration on her behalf and because she disaffirmed the release when she reached eighteen years of age. The court cited authority holding that West Virginia law provides that contracts by minors are generally not void, but voidable only, and may be ratified or disaffirmed after majority, and a contract is generally upheld when: (1) it was freely and fairly entered into between parties in equal bargaining positions; and (2) it does not interfere with a public interest. With these facts, the court held that neither element was satisfied. Allowing a parent to sign away rights of a minor child to recover for a potential injury incurred while participating in a commercial activity conflict with a public policy and the parties were not in an equal bargaining position. The Participation Agreement is a contract of adhesion offered on a "take it or leave it" basis. Further, the minor disaffirmed the Participation Agreement upon reaching the age of eighteen.

C. CLASS/COLLECTIVE ARBITRATION

Bryant v. Domino's Pizza, No. 22-11319, 2024 WL 1638616 (E.D. Mich. Apr. 16, 2024). The court denied plaintiff's motion for leave to amend its collective-action complaint because it would be futile. Each of the proposed plaintiffs were subject to an arbitration agreement they signed with Domino's and each arbitration agreement contained a delegation clause that assigned questions of arbitrability to an arbitrator. The court also denied plaintiff's request for more time to find a viable plaintiff that was not subject to an arbitration agreement because the case had been pending for nearly two years. And because there was no lead plaintiff, the court dismissed the case without prejudice.

D. AWARD CONFIRMATION

Choice Hotels International, Inc. v. Jai Sai Baba, LLC, No. GLS 23-146, (D. Md., Aug. 25, 2023) (district court in Pennsylvania stayed action and ordered arbitration; after franchisor prevailed in arbitration, district court in Maryland denied franchisor's motion to confirm award and granted franchisee's motion to transfer venue of confirmation action to original district court in Pennsylvania). This case is discussed in Chapter 8, Section III.

Your CBD Stores Franchising, LLC v. Buckwalter, No. 8:23-cv-1550-VMC-AAS, 2023 WL 6676671 (M.D. Fla. Oct. 12, 2023). CBD Stores Franchising, LLC ("CBD Franchising") filed a petition to confirm an arbitration award, and the franchisee, Brett W. Buckwalter ("Buckwalter") filed a competing motion to vacate the final arbitration award. The court found in favor of the franchisor and granted the petition to confirm the arbitration award.

Buckwalter defaulted under multiple franchise agreements with CBD Franchising. The franchise agreements contained arbitration clauses and personal guaranties. CBD submitted a Demand for Arbitration which was properly served on the franchisee by email and federal express. The franchisee responded to each email from the American Arbitration Association ("AAA") with messages that he did not want the AAA to represent him, that he closed the stores and was no longer in need of an arbitrator, and that he did not acknowledge the terms or payment for the arbitration. In response, AAA advised Buckwalter that the arbitration would proceed regardless of whether Buckwalter decided to participate. The arbitration did proceed, Buckwalter did not appear at the arbitration proceeding and the arbitrator awarded $363,276.09 to CBD Franchising. CBD Franchising then initiated the action to confirm the award and Buckwalter responded, pro se, that he was never given a notice of the final hearing and would have attended if given notice of the hearing by AAA. The court found that it had an obligation to confirm the award unless the facts met one of the limited standards under the Federal Arbitration Act to vacate. Because CBD Franchising met the threshold requirements to confirm the award, it must be confirmed. The court found that no reasons existed to vacate the award, that Buckwalter was provided at least constructive notice of the hearing, and the petition to confirm was granted.

Massage Green International Franchise Corp. v. Bunsey, Misc. No. 23-12707, 2023 WL 7127506 (E.D. Mich. Oct. 30, 2023). The court adopted a Report and Recommendation by the magistrate judge to confirm franchisor Massage Green International Franchise Corp.'s arbitration award, and rejected the franchisee's argument that they were not properly served so the award was *void ab initio*. The court found the franchisees were given adequate notice per the rules of the American Arbitration Association.

Massage Green International Franchise Corp. v. Bunsey, No. 24-1007, 2024 WL 3358158 (6th Cir. July 10, 2024). Franchisor Massage Green demanded arbitration after the Bunseys closed their franchised spa. After the Bunseys failed to respond to any notices or communications regarding the arbitration demand, the arbitrator awarded Massage Green damages for the breach, attorneys' fees and costs, arbitrator costs, and the AAA administrative fees. Massage Green then filed a petition to confirm the arbitration award, which the district court approved because the Bunseys' attempt to modify the award was time-barred by the FAA's three-month limitation. The Sixth Circuit Court of Appeals affirmed the district court's decision.

Carepatrol Franchise Systems, LLC v. TSI Investment Group Inc., No. B323525, 2024 WL 1710882 (Cal. Ct. App. Apr. 22, 2024). After a franchisor and franchisee arbitrated over the value of a franchise, the arbitrator awarded the franchisee nothing and awarded the franchisor approximately $320,000 in attorneys' fees and costs. Franchisor filed a petition to confirm the arbitration award and the trial court confirmed the award and entered judgment. The franchisee appealed and the appellate court affirmed the arbitration award confirmation because the arbitration was conclusive and binding, and franchisee failed to identify any basis for judicial review of the arbitration award, any statutory right or public policy inconsistent with the arbitration award, or any reversible procedural error.

Ice Rak, LLC v. Rita's Franchise Co., No. 8:23-CV-2659-WFJ-TGW, 2024 WL 1118810 (M.D. Fla. Mar. 14, 2024). Court granted franchisor's motion to compel arbitration against non-signatory limited liability company that conducted franchised business, formed by individuals who signed franchise and other agreements with franchisor.

Hyatt Hotels Corp. v. Unite Here Loc. 11, No. 22-56196, 2024 WL 107930 (9th Cir. Jan. 10, 2024). The appellate court reversed the district court's vacatur of an arbitral award compelling a party to secure a third-party's assumption of a card-check neutrality agreement that the third-party never signed. The appellate court reasoned that the district court should have given deference to the arbitrator's interpretation rather than turning to the substantive merits of the award.

Personal Best Karate, Inc. v. Mosca, No. 23-P-958, 2024 WL 3548864 (Mass. App. Ct. July 26, 2024). Franchisor Personal Best Karate filed a demand for arbitration against franchise owners in Massachusetts (the "Moscas") after they failed to respond to any notices or communications that Personal Best Karate was terminating the franchise agreement. The arbitrator found the Moscas in default of the agreement and awarded attorneys' fees and costs. When Personal Best Karate moved to confirm the arbitration award, Moscas opposed the motion arguing that the judge was required to consider whether the noncompete restriction in the franchise agreement was unconscionable. The Massachusetts Court of Appeals affirmed the trial court's decision because the Moscas failed to adhere to the thirty-day limit of challenging an arbitration award and because the Moscas forfeited their right to present substantive and procedural arguments on unconscionability before the arbitrator. The court also held that the Moscas' appeal was frivolous and allowed Personal Best Karate to pursue appellate fees and costs.

Subway International, B.V., v. Subway Russia Franchising Co., No. 21-cv-7362, 2024 WL 2720266 (S.D.N.Y. May 28, 2024). The United States District Court for the Southern District of New York granted franchisor Subway International, B.V.'s ("Subway") petition to confirm an arbitration award and denied Subway Russia Franchising Company, LLC's ("Subway Russia") cross-petition to vacate the award, finding that Subway Russia's default under the master franchise agreement authorized Subway's non-renewal of the agreement. Subway Russia did not provide sufficient evidence to establish that Subway's petition to confirm was untimely, that the arbitrator exceeded her authority, that the arbitrator demonstrated evident partiality, that the award was substantively wrong, that the refusal to allow certain discovery violated fairness, or that the AAA committed procedural error.

Subway Franchise Systems of Canada, ULC v. Subway Developments 2000, Inc., No. 24-cv-593 (AS), 2024 WL 3090480 (S.D.N.Y. June 21, 2024). Subway Developments 2000, Inc. ("Developer") filed an arbitration against Subway Franchise Systems of Canada, ULC ("Subway") alleging that Subway wrongfully terminated two development agreements between the parties. The development agreements required that Subway pay the developer fifty percent of the amount it would otherwise be entitled to receive during the arbitration until a final decision. A few months into the arbitration, Subway took the position that it was excused from making the interim payments and the arbitrator ordered Subway to continue making the payments. Subway then filed an order to vacate the decision. Subway argued that the arbitrator's order exceeded her authority and so must be vacated pursuant to the Federal Arbitration Act. The district court upheld the arbitrator's decision finding that Subway has not met its burden of showing that the arbitrator acted outside the scope of her authority.

E. WAIVER

Breadeaux's Pisa, LLC v. Beckman Bros. Ltd, 83 F. 4th 1113 (8th Cir. 2023). The Eighth Circuit Court of Appeals affirmed the lower court's ruling denying a franchisor's motion to stay pending arbitration after the franchisor elected to file an action in federal court to enforce post-term restrictive covenants against one of its franchisees. Breadeaux's Pisa, LLC ("Breadeaux's") initiated an action in federal court seeking equitable relief against a former franchisee for continuing to operate a pizza shop after expiration of the franchise agreement. The franchise agreement allowed the franchisor a choice to enforce its rights by filing a lawsuit or through mediation and then arbitration. After a series of adverse judgments, the franchisor refused to proceed to discovery and sought to avoid the adverse court rulings by filing a demand for arbitration and staying the court proceedings. By electing under the franchise agreement to resolve its disputes through filing a lawsuit and only deciding to attempt mediation after a series of negative decisions, the court concluded the franchisor waived its contractual arbitration rights. The Eighth Circuit Court of Appeals noted that Section 3 of the Federal Arbitration Act ("FAA") typically gives defendants, not plaintiffs the right to stay a litigation to enforce arbitration rights. However, a condition to the grant of a stay under Section 3 of the FAA is that the applicant not be in default in proceeding with the arbitration. The court held the waiver by Breadeaux constituted a default under Section 3 of the FAA and affirmed the lower court denial.

F. OTHER CLAIMS

Medical Search Consultants, LLC v. Pasture Gate Holdings, Inc., No. 1:23-cv-00118-MR-WCM, 2023 WL 8532400 (W.D.N.C. Dec. 8, 2023). Medical Research Consultants, LLC ("MRC") is a franchisor of a healthcare recruiting and placement concept. MRC entered into a franchise agreement with the defendant, Pasture Gate Holdings, Inc. ("Pasture") authorizing Pasture to open a franchise in the Atlanta region. MRC alleged that, after signing the franchise agreement, the franchisee made plans to open a competing recruiting firm and conspired with a competitor to compete directly with MRC and unlawfully misappropriate MRC's marks. MRC filed a lawsuit against the franchisee entity, owners and the new entity formed to allegedly compete against the MRC for breach of contract, misappropriation of trade secrets and trademarks in violation of various federal and state laws. The United States District Court for the Western District of North Carolina stayed the arbitration against all defendants. Although only two of the defendants were party to the arbitration provision in the franchise agreement, stay was appropriate because the factual issues regarding the claims were inextricably intertwined, and allowing the claims to proceed in litigation could result in inconsistent results.

VII. Statutes of Limitations

Wirtgen America, Inc. v Hayden-Murphy Equipment Co., No. 3:22-cv-00308, 2023 WL 591704 (M.D. Tenn. Sept. 11, 2023). A Minnesota dealer opposed a Tennessee-based supplier's motion for leave to amend its declaratory judgment action on grounds that it was barred by the 6-year statute of limitations for contract claims. The trial court granted leave to amend because the action was not one for breach of contract itself, but rather a claim for a declaration of rights under the distribution agreement which was not time-barred by the statute of limitations for the breach of contract claim. This case is discussed in Chapter 4, Section III.

HP Holding LLC v. Red Roof Inns, Inc., No. CV 23-20907 (RBK/MJS), 2024 WL 2720463 (D.N.J. May 28, 2024). The district court granted a hotel franchisor's motion to dismiss plaintiffs' tortious interference and breach of contract claims with prejudice because they were time barred under New Jersey's six-year statute of limitations and the three-year limitation period in the parties' franchise agreement. The court also granted defendants' motion to dismiss plaintiffs' claim under the New Jersey Franchise Practices Act ("NJFPA") without prejudice because the allegations fell short of the $35,000 threshold required to state a claim under the statute. The court granted plaintiffs' motion to amend its complaint provided it does not re-raise claims the court dismissed with prejudice.

VIII. Collateral Estoppel/Res Judicata

W.J. Deutsch & Sons LTD. v. Zamora, No. 1:21-cv-11003-LTS, 2023 WL 5609205 (S.D.N.Y. Aug. 30, 2023). The United States District Court for the Southern District of New York granted a Spanish wine manufacturer's ("Zamora") motion to dismiss its former distributor's ("Deutsch") efforts to vacate an international arbitration award in favor of Zamora. The court rejected Deutsch's argument that the arbitrator manifestly disregarded the law and rendered a decision so ambiguous that it failed to constitute a final and definite award. The court found that Deutsch's complaint failed to clear the "high hurdle" necessary for vacating arbitration awards.

Deutsch was a distributor of Zamora's wine in the United States for almost a decade before Zamora canceled their agreement in 2018 alleging that the distributor had failed to meet its contractual purchase objectives. The parties disputed how wine brands were quantified for purposes determining purchase requirements and the parties entered arbitration to resolve the dispute. During the arbitration, Zamora issued a second termination for failure to meet purchase requirements for another wine brand and stopped shipping to Deutsch altogether. The panel ruled in Deutsch's favor, but awarded no damages. It also ruled that Zamora breached the agreement by failing to transfer a trademark as promised and ordered Zamora to transfer the trademark. Deutsch then filed another arbitration proceeding requesting the panel (1) confirm Zamora's first termination notice was invalid; (2) determine the validity of the second termination notice; (3) require Zamora to buy out its interest in the trademark holding company, as the agreement required; and (4) award Deutsch damages.

The arbitration panel issued an opinion concluding that, although the 2018 termination notice was invalid, the breach was cured by the prior panel's order for specific performance, and the termination notice did not trigger any obligation to buy out the Deutsch's interest in the trademark holding company. However, certain factual issues remained unresolved, so the panel determined further proceedings would be necessary. Deutsch sought clarification from the panel and the panel denied the request. Deutsch filed this lawsuit in New York federal court, asking the court to vacate the second arbitration ruling, arguing that the panel acted in manifest disregard of the law. The court granted Zamora's motion to dismiss finding that the panel never decided to ignore any legal principle, and Deutsch was unable to identify the panel's unwillingness to apply relevant law.

Alfredo's Foreign Cars, Inc. v. Stellantis US LLC, No. 22-CV-10478 (KMK), 2024 WL 964967 (S.D.N.Y. Mar. 5, 2024). A family-owned dealership brought an action against Stellanis, f/k/a FCA ("FCA") alleging that its method of evaluating dealers violated the Robinson-Patman Act and the New York Franchise Dealer Act and further constituted a breach of the implied covenant of good faith and fair dealing inherent in the parties' agreement. The court granted in part and denied in part FCA's motion to dismiss. In denying the motion to dismiss, the court determined that federal common law did not preclude the court from hearing the case because some federal rights were at issue. The court granted the motion to dismiss for all other claims, reasoning that *res judicata* applied because plaintiff chose to pursue an initial agency proceeding that was related to the facts of the current claim prior to filing in state court.

IX. Class Actions

Gifford v. Dr. Pizza, Inc., No. 2:22-CV-00707-TS, 2023 WL 8376177 (D. Utah Dec. 4, 2023). In this case, the court granted a motion for conditional class certification and notice to potential plaintiffs relating to a Domino Pizza franchisee's alleged violations of the Fair Labor Standards Act. The franchisee was alleged to have failed to appropriately compensate delivery driver automobile expenses, thereby allowing wages to fall below the federal minimum wage.

Ayala v. Nissan N. Am., Inc., No. 23-11027, 2024 WL 489723 (11th Cir. Feb. 8, 2024). Class certification denied to two automobile technicians who sought to hold the manufacturer liable on an FLSA claim. This case is discussed in Chapter 7, Section II.

Christie Stinson v. Yum! Brands, Inc., Nos. 3:23-CV-00183-DJH, 3:23-CV-00201-DJH, 3:23-CV-00206-DJH, 3:23-CV-00214-DJH, 3:23-CV-00274-DJH, 3:23-CV-00290-DJH, 2023 WL 8724007 (W.D. Ky. Nov. 15, 2023). The United States District Court for the Western District of Kentucky granted six separate classes of plaintiffs' motions to consolidate class actions against Yum! Brands, Inc. and certain of its franchisees for damages resulting from a de fac breach where the plaintiff's social security numbers and private information was compromised by a cyberattack on defendants' computer systems. The court found that each of the complaints rested on common issues of law and fact, there was no prejudice to the defendants in consolidating the cases, and it would save judicial resources, time, and expense.

Air-Con, Inc. v. Daikin Applied Latin America, LLC, No. CV 18-1800 (RAM), 2024 WL 1016184 (D.P.R. Mar. 8, 2024). This case involved a claim under the Puerto Rico Dealer's Act and the trial court dismissed the dealer's claim on statute of limitations grounds. This case is discussed in Chapter 3, Section V.

Roman v. Jan-Pro Franchising International, Inc., No. 3:16-cv-05961-WHA, 2024 WL 2412387 (N.D. Cal. May 23, 2024). The United States District Court for the Northern District of California granted the plaintiffs' motion for final approval of settlement and attorneys' fees, costs, and expenses in a wage-and-hour misclassification class action finding that the settlement was fair, reasonable, and adequate. The original class action case against defendant, Jan-Pro Franchising International, Inc. ("Jan Pro") was filed in Massachusetts district court in 2008 and eventually dismissed. The California plaintiffs were severed from that case and transferred to California in 2016. The court granted summary judgment to Jan Pro based on then-case law governing classification of independent contractors. However, at the same time as plaintiffs' appeal, the California Supreme Court adopted the "ABC test" for determining employee classification cases under *Dynamex Operations West, Inc. v. Superior Court,* 4 Cal.5th 903 (2018).. The California Supreme Court determined the *Dynamex* decision applied retroactively and then granted plaintiffs' motion for class certification as to the failure to pay minimum wage for mandatory training, failure to reimburse for expenses incurred for uniforms and cleaning supplies, and unlawful deductions of management fees and marketing fees. In December 2023 the parties settled and counsel moved for final approval. The court analyzed the eight "Churchill Factors:" (1) the strength of plaintiffs' case; (2) the risk, expense, complexity, and likely duration of further litigation; (3) the risk of maintaining class action status throughout the trial; (4) the amount offered in settlement; (5) the extent of discovery completed and the stage of the proceedings; (6) the experience and views of counsel; (7) the presence of a governmental participant; and (8) the reaction of the class members of the proposed settlement. Applying these factors, the court found that they weighed in favor of settlement, and further, that the settlement was fair, reasonable, and adequate. The court also found that in calculating counsel fees, it would approve an amount of the total settlement fund equal to one third of the fees instead of the standard twenty-five percent benchmark. The court weighed the strong result achieved for the class in making the determination. However, it reduced the service award for the named plaintiffs due to countervailing concerns surrounding service awards.

Fuentes v. Jiffy Lube International, Inc., No. 2:18-CV-5174, 2024 WL 2723840 (E.D. Pa. May 28, 2024). The United States District Court for the Eastern District of Pennsylvania granted plaintiff's motion for class certification and final approval of a settlement between a class of former employees of Jiffy Lube franchises and franchisor, Jiffy Lube International, Inc. ("Jiffy Lube"). The former employees alleged that the no-poach clause in Jiffy Lube's form of franchise agreement (1) had the effect of benefitting Jiffy Lube franchise shop owners at the expense of employees and consumers; (2) allowed Jiffy Lube locations to retain employees at below-market wages, without attractive benefits, working conditions, or opportunities for advancement; and (3) constituted unfair competition and collusion in violation of antitrust law. The court approved the $2 million all cash settlement as well as attorneys' fees, reimbursement of expenses, and service award to the class representative.

Hoffman v. Deja Vu Pizza LLC, No. 1:22-CV-00006, 2024 WL 3582363 (D.N.D. June 6, 2024). Plaintiff, a pizza delivery driver for a Papa John's franchise in Wisconsin, brought a wage and hour collective action under the Fair Labor Standards Act ("FLSA"). Hoffman also asserted a claim for unjust enrichment. In this decision, the district court certified a class of similarly situated Papa John delivery drivers under Fed. R. Civ. P. 23. The court found that Hoffman established numerosity, commonality, typicality, and adequacy as required under Rule 23(a). Plaintiff also showed that common issues of law and fact predominated among class members and that a class action was superior to other available methods for efficiently adjudicating the controversy under Rule 23(b). The district court also held that plaintiff met her burden under the FLSA collection action analysis and was entitled to proceed to the certification step of the collective action process under the statute.

X. Discovery Issues

DMO Norwood LLC v. Kia America, Inc., No. 22-CV-10470-ADB, 2023 WL 5353744 (D. Mass. Aug. 21, 2023). Plaintiff, DMO Norwood LLC ("DMO") was an authorized Kia dealership that sued Kia America, Inc. ("Kia") for terminating the parties' dealership agreement. During their relationship, DMO participated in one of Kia's sales incentive programs. After conducting an on-site audit, Kia discovered twenty-two Kia vehicles on DMO's lot that had been reported as retail sales for incentive purposes. Further into Kia's investigation, it discovered fourteen additional vehicles that DMO improperly reported. In the lawsuit, DMO alleged that Kia terminated the agreement in retaliation for DMO's voluntary withdrawal from a sales incentive program. Kia filed a Counterclaim against DMO for breach of contract, alleging that DMO breached the dealer agreement by falsely reporting certain vehicles as sold and thereby profiting from unearned sales incentives. Kia moved to compel DMO to produce certain documents and respond to an interrogatory regarding its vehicle inventory and sales reporting.

Kia argued that each of its discovery requests were relevant to help test DMO's defense that any discrepancies between the reported sales and actual sales were the product of honest mistakes. The trial court agreed with Kia and shifted the burden to DMO to show that the requests were either irrelevant or improper. DMO alleged that Chapter 93B of Massachusetts Statutes limits the scope of Kia's requests to information about the vehicles identified through Kia's investigation. The court rejected DMO's argument because of Kia's Counterclaim. Even though Chapter 93B was applicable, the court found no language in the statute that limits a litigant's right to discovery. Therefore, the court granted Kia's motion to compel DMO to produce the documents. The court also rejected DMO's argument that the interrogatory request was too broad and that it imposed an undue burden. The court deemed that the original response directing Kia to specific documents was insufficient because Kia could not obtain an adequate answer without inferring DMO's possible defenses.

M&D Cycles, Inc. v. American Honda Motor Co., No. 22-cv-172-SM-AJ, 2023 WL 7182107 (D.N.H. Sept. 29, 2023). New Hampshire law requires motor vehicle manufacturers to pay a dealer the fair market value of undamaged signs and all special tools and equipment in usable and good condition within ninety days of terminating a dealer. In this case, Honda moved under Federal Rule of Evidence 702 and *Daubert* to exclude plaintiffs' damages expert testimony. The expert had forty-plus years as an owner of a Honda Motorsports dealership and had been through a private sale of his dealership, but he had no specific experience with pricing or selling for special tools, service manuals, signage, or other items not typically sold to consumers, and he had never been through a dealership termination. The court found his lack of experience significant in deciding to exclude his testimony, as well as his failure to examine the special tools, service manuals, and signage at issue (he relied on the terminated dealers' representations) and lack of any records confirming his market research or marketing methodology. The court reserved judgment on whether the expert could testify as a lay witness under Rule 701 or whether such testimony would just be duplicative of the testimony provided by the terminated dealer.

Puerto Rico Energy, LLC v. Puerto Rico, No. 20-1591 (ADC), Civil No. 20-1725(ADC), 2024 WL 866326 (D.P.R. Feb. 28, 2024). The United States District Court for the District of Puerto Rico denied the discovery requests of two gasoline wholesalers ("PRE") who filed a lawsuit against Puerto Rico alleging that its "Gasoline Law" ("Gasoline Law") was preempted by the federal the Petroleum

Marketing Practices Act ("PMPA"). Puerto Rico's Gasoline Law prohibits gasoline wholesalers from having any control over any non-gasoline service station business that is located on the premises of a gasoline service station. PRE sought declaratory and injunctive relief, plus damages, alleging that enforcement of the Gasoline Law constituted an unconstitutional taking of their property rights. The court consolidated the two actions. The court denied the PRE's request for further discovery finding that (1) the frequency and extent of the discovery requested throughout the litigation constituted abuse of the discovery process; and (2) based upon the doctrine of legislative privilege of state officials. This case is discussed in Chapter 3, Section II.

Woods v. JDHQ Hotels LLC, No. 4:23-CV-04026-RAL, 2024 WL 1886468 (D.S.D. Apr. 30, 2024). The district court denied defendant's motion to compel production of information and documents because plaintiff's collateral source information was not discoverable to prove a claim defendant failed to plead, and because Fed. R. Civ. P. 34 does not require a plaintiff to complete a HIPAA authorization.

Store Master Funding XXIX, LLC v. Triangle Capital Properties, LLC, No. 4:23-CV-01194, 2024 WL 2159967 (S.D. Tex. May 14, 2024). Defendants moved for a continuance to conduct additional discovery before responding to plaintiff's motion for summary judgment because plaintiff included information with its summary judgment motion that was not produced during discovery. The court granted defendants' motion to continue because defendants adequately identified the necessary additional discovery needed prior to responding to plaintiff's summary judgment motion and because defendants diligently pursued discovery.

In Re Application of Venequip, S.A. v. Caterpillar Inc., 83 F.4th 1048 (7th Cir. 2023). The petitioner, Venequip, S.A., a Venezuelan heavy-equipment supplier ("Venequip"), entered into dealer agreements Caterpillar Sàrl ("CAT Sàrl"), a Swiss subsidiary of Illinois-based Caterpillar, Inc. ("Caterpillar"). CAT Sàrl terminated its agreement with Venequip and Venequip commenced an action in Geneva in 2021, alleging breach of contract. Venequip then filed applications in U.S. federal district courts for discovery under 28 U.S.C. § 1782(a) from Caterpillar and related entities. The district court in the Northern District of Illinois denied the application and Venequip appealed. The Supreme Court in *Intel Corp. v. Advanced Micro Devices, Inc.*, provided guidance to courts when analyzing discovery applications, focusing on the need for discovery, intrusiveness, and comity considerations (the "Intel Factors"). The district judge considered Intel Factors and additional factors like the contractual choice of forum and law, and Caterpillar's agreement to providc discovery in Swiss court. On appeal, Venequip argued the judge misapplied the Intel Factors. The Seventh Circuit affirmed the district court's decision, finding the district judge properly weighed the Intel Factors.

EYM Pizza of Georgia LLC v. Pizza Hut LLC, No. 3:24-CV-0646-X, 2024 WL 1743363 (N.D. Tex. Mar. 27, 2024). In advance of a hearing on plaintiffs' motion for a preliminary injunction seeking to avoid termination of plaintiffs' franchise agreements involving 142 Pizza Hut restaurants, the parties moved for expedited and limited discovery in relation to claims over a forbearance agreement and related claims for tortious interference. Finding good cause to allow the injunction-related discovery to proceed, the district court granted in part and denied in part the motion. The outcome of the motion for preliminary injunction is discussed in Chapter 4, Section IV.

Toyota Motor Sales, U.S.A., Inc. v. Allen Interchange LLC, No. 22-CV-1681 (KMM/JFD), 2023 WL 7648895 (S.D. Cal. Nov. 15, 2023). Plaintiff Toyota Motor Sales, U.S.A. ("Toyota") filed suit against defendant for mislabeling auto parts in gray markets. In response to Toyota's discovery request, defendant filed a motion for a protective order, requesting that any discovery it provided be labeled "Attorneys' Eyes Only," not be shared with Toyota's in-house counsel. Toyota asserted that it would be "flying blind" throughout the course of litigation if the court were to enforce the order. The court disagreed with Toyota's argument and denied Toyota's requests to share the confidential documents with its in-house counsel. The court reasoned that because in-house counsel was in charge of competitive decision-making for the company, permitting them to access the confidential discovery would likely only aid Toyota in finding future claims. After making its decision, the court cautioned defendants to proceed cautiously moving forward. First, the court requested that the parties attempt to negotiate with each other if outside counsel felt a particular discovery response marked "AEO" was necessary to share with Toyota's in-house counsel before filing an additional amended protective order. Second, the court demanded that it be alerted if the defendant abused the "Attorney's Eyes Only" label.

Windy Cove, Inc. v. Circle K Stores, Inc., No. 21-cv-1416-MMA-DEB, 2023 WL 6284466 (S.D. Cal. Sept. 7, 2023). The court denied plaintiffs' motion to exclude Dr. John Umbeck and granted defendants' partial motion to exclude Mr. Donald Malaby. This case is discussed in Chapter 4, Section I, Subsection B.

Hlavinka Equip. Co. v. CLAAS of Am., Inc., No. 8:22CV379, 2024 WL 665087 (D. Neb. Feb. 16, 2024). Hlavinka Equipment Co. ("Hlavinka") brought a motion to compel against Defendant CLAAS of America, Inc., ("CLAAS") to respond to various discovery requests. CLAAS argued that the discovery requests were overbroad and irrelevant. The court disagreed. Therefore, the court granted Hlavinka's motion to compel, finding that each request was relevant to the contested issues.

XI. Default Judgment

AAMCO Transmissions, LLC v. Up to Parr, LLC, No. 22-3212-PJM, 2023 WL 5510081 (D. Md., Aug. 25, 2023). Default judgment granted to franchisor in trademark misappropriation case where court made "exceptional case" finding supporting award of attorneys' fees and costs. This case is discussed in Chapter 5, Section II.

Full Tilt Boogie, LLC v. KEP Fortune, LLC, No. 2:19-cv-09090-ODW, 2023 WL 6446188 (C.D. Cal. Oct. 3, 2023). The United States District Court for the Central District of California determined on summary judgment that owner-members of a franchisor were jointly and severally liable to a franchisee for violations of California Franchise Investment Law ("CFIL"). Two sets of counsel for franchisor withdrew due to discovery sanctions and owner-members decided not to retain new counsel, so franchisor's answer was withdrawn and the court entered default because the franchisor entity could not proceed pro se in a California court. The franchisee elected rescission as a remedy, so the owner-members of franchisor were excused from a hearing to prove up damages, and the court entered a million dollar judgment against the franchisor and owner-members who were jointly and severally liable due to prior summary judgment ruling. Both sides moved to alter or amend the judgment and the district court denied both motions. As to the franchisee, the district court determined that it had not satisfied the local rules requiring a "meet and confer" before and at least 28 days before hearing. As to the franchisor and owner-members, the district court determined that they had not been deprived of due process or improperly excluded from the hearing on damages because rescission was simply a remedy for CFIL violations for which they had already been found liable, not a separate and distinct claim.

Everything Yogurt Brands, LLC v. Bianco, No. 23-CV-01161 (LJL), 2024 WL 3497757 (S.D.N.Y. July 22, 2024). Plaintiffs, affiliated companies engaged in the franchising of various brands, including Villa Pizza, South Philly Cheesesteaks & Fries, and Cozzoli's Pizza, moved for default judgment against various franchisee defendants primarily located in Italy. The district court ordered plaintiffs to show cause why New York was the proper forum for the litigation and why the court had personal jurisdiction over the defendants to enter a default. The franchise agreements at issue only contained a choice of law provision and not a forum selection clause calling for litigation in the United States District Court for the Southern District of New York. Instead, the parties had agreed to arbitrate their disputes in New York City. After briefing, the district court denied the motion for default judgment because plaintiffs' submissions clearly showed an absence of personal jurisdiction. In so doing, the district court rejected plaintiffs' argument that the parties consented to being hauled into a federal court in New York because of the arbitration clause. In the court's view, the parties' consent to arbitration in New York could not be extended to impose jurisdiction in the district court. The court also held that it does not have general personal jurisdiction over the defendants because there was no allegation in the complaint that suggests any of the defendants had ever been to New York or were engaged in any continuous or systematic course of business there.

MaidPro Franchise, LLC v. City Maid Pro, Inc., No. 23 CIV. 9172 (VM), 2024 WL 3219888 (S.D.N.Y. June 27, 2024). MaidPro filed a trademark infringement action against City Maid, and following the defendant's failure to answer, MaidPro moved for default judgment. The district court held that MaidPro established the defendant's liability and further determined that plaintiff was entitled to a permanent injunction and $10,000 in statutory damages.

Mister Softee, Inc. v. Omar, No. CV 23-3845, 2023 WL 6619637 (D. N.J. Oct. 11, 2023). A Mr. Softee ice cream truck franchisee continuously operated outside of its territory, and after being terminated for doing so, both continued to operate using Mr. Softee trademarks and failed to abide by a two-year non-compete agreement. The district court in New Jersey granted Plaintiff's default judgment for a permanent injunction, expectation damages in the amount of future royalties, and attorneys' fees and costs, under claims for breach of contract and trademark infringement.

Fusa Franchisor SPV LLC v. SBG, Inc., No. 2:23-CV-02673-AB-E, 2024 WL 3298288 (C.D. Cal. May 1, 2024). Court granted default judgment against defendants because plaintiff adequately alleged defendants breached the franchise agreement and the personal guaranty and because the sum requested was reasonable and proportionate to the conduct.

Jeunesse Global Holdings, LLC v. Berry, No. 2:18-cv-513-CW, 2023 WL 8789513 (D. Utah December 19, 2023). The United States District Court for the District of Utah granted Jeunesse Global Holdings, LLC's ("Jeunesse") motion for default judgment in the amount of $316,304.00 against defendant former distributor, Mark Berry after Jeunesse terminated his distributorship for breaching the terms of the parties' distribution agreement by improperly diverting customers to a competitor's website and failing to respond to the complaint.

Sonesta RL Hotels Franchising, Inc. v. Patel, No. 1:23-CV-12548-JEK, 2024 WL 457046 (D. Mass. Feb. 6, 2024). The court granted in part and denied in part plaintiff, Sonesta RL Hotels' motion for default judgment for its claims against defendants Kunal Patel and Lotus Sky, LLC after defendants failed to file an answer or defend their case. The court awarded plaintiff $722,768.51 for contract damages and all of the litigation costs that plaintiff requested. However, the court reduced the attorney fees, finding that billing around seventy-five hours for filing a complaint, serving defendants, filing a motion for an entry of default, and filing a motion for default judgment was unreasonable. Therefore, the court reduced the requested amount of $27,958.00 to $20,800.00.

Wheelmaxx Inc. v. Maraaj Singh Mahal, No. 122CV01506KESSKO, 2024 WL 1343128 (E.D. Cal. Mar. 29, 2024). The district court granted in part and denied in part plaintiff's motion for default judgment on claims against defendants after defendants failed to take any action to defend their case. The court granted default judgment on plaintiff's breach of contract, trademark infringement, and unfair competition claims but did deny plaintiff's trade dress infringement claim because plaintiff failed to sufficiently allege a claim. The court also awarded plaintiff attorneys' fees and costs for damages proved by the plaintiff after the default judgment was entered by the court.

Honest Abe Roofing Franchise, Inc. v. DCH & Associates, LLC, No 2:22-cv-00387-JRS-MG, 2024 WL 3161264 (S.D. Ind. Apr. 4, 2024). Franchisor, Honest Abe Roofing Franchise, Inc. ("Honest Abe") filed suit against its former franchisees for breach of contract and trademark infringement. Defendants appeared for a single status conference, but thereafter failed to appear or defend, and Honest Abe moved for default judgment, seeking $185,941.39 in damages, $83,976.10 in attorney fees, and an injunction enforcing the post-termination obligations in the franchise agreement. The court granted the requested damages, finding that the allegations of the complaint sufficiently establish liability for the damages, which were contractual and the amount was sufficiently established by documentary evidence. The court reached the same conclusion with respect to the attorneys' fees. Finally, Honest Abe sought an injunction to enforce: (i) a two-year, fifty-mile noncompete; (ii) return of confidential information; (iii) cease and desist use of Honest Abe trademarks. The court analyzed whether Honest Abe could demonstrate: (1) that it had suffered an irreparable injury; (2) that remedies available at law, such as monetary damages, were inadequate to compensate for that injury; (3) that, considering the balance of hardships between the plaintiff and defendant, a remedy in equity was warranted; and (4) that the public interest would not be disserved by a permanent injunction. The court granted the cease-and-desist and return of confidential information finding it met the four prongs for injunctive relief. The court also found that trademark violations enjoy a presumption of irreparable injury and inadequate remedy at law, there was no great hardship to defendants to stop using information and trademarks to which they have no right. However, the court declined to grant the injunction on the non compete provision, as the franchise agreement provided for a two-year non compete from the time of termination which had almost expired and Honest Abe requested an additional two-year period. The court declined to extend the period or grant an injunction to enforce the two months remaining in the original noncompete. The court found Honest Abe had made no attempt to quantify its damages from Defendants' violation of the noncompete, and it had not sought actual damages aside from those established by contract.

Sit Means Sit Franchise Inc. v. SMSHTX, LLC, No. 2:23-cv-01464-CDS-DJA, 2024 WL 3202561 (D. Nev. June 26, 2024). The United States District Court for the District of Nevada granted franchisor, Sit Means Sit Franchise, Inc. ("SMS") default judgment against a former franchisee for Lanham Act and Trade Secrets claims. In the order, SMS obtained (1) a permanent injunction enjoining defendants from continuing to use SMS' trademarks, confidential information, and system to operate their unauthorized dog training businesses; and (2) damages in the amount of $74,520.07 as well as attorneys' fees.

XII. Enforcement and Collection

Interim Healthcare, Inc. v. Falcon Healthcare, Inc., No. 07-24-00043-CV, 2024 WL 1868948 (Tex. Ct. App. Apr. 24, 2024). After a bench trial awarded a franchisee monetary damages and non-monetary relief, the franchisor filed a notice of appeal and a motion seeking to require the franchisee to secure a supersedeas bond. The franchisee also filed a motion seeking a bond to secure the damages awarded against a potential loss by the franchisor on appeal. After the court denied franchisor's motion and granted franchisee's motion, franchisor appealed. The Texas Court of Appeals denied the franchisor's motion because the trial court did not abuse its discretion in requiring the franchisor to post the bond to secure the judgment obtained by the franchisee.

XIII. Withdrawal/Disqualification of Counsel

Sizzling Black Rock Steak House Franchising, Inc. v. Harold L. Kestenbaum, PC, No. 21-11621, 2024 WL 1699504 (E.D. Mich. Apr. 2, 2024). Sizzling Black Rock Steak House Franchising, Inc. ("Plaintiff") filed a lawsuit against its franchise attorneys, Harold Kestenbaum and his law firm ("Defendants") for legal malpractice and negligent misrepresentation. Plaintiff alleged that the defendants drafted area representative agreements that contained "evergreen" royalty provisions which would allow the area representatives to continue earning royalties after termination of the area representative agreements if they failed to develop the required number of restaurants but had otherwise fulfilled their contractual duties. Plaintiff argued that the inclusion of these provisions was against its express directions. Defendants moved for summary judgment, claiming, among other things, that the allegations were time-barred, and the negligent misrepresentation claim was duplicative of the legal malpractice claim. The court rejected Defendants' argument that the malpractice claims were time-barred, noting that the statute of limitations should start from the end of the ongoing professional relationship, not merely from the execution of the agreement under which the claim arose. The court did, however, dismiss the negligent misrepresentation claim as duplicative of the malpractice claim since both were based on the same facts and sought similar remedies.

Sizzling Black Rock Steak House Franchising, Inc. v. Harold L. Kestenbaum, PC, No. 21-cv-11621, 2024 WL 3442417 (E.D. Mich. July 17, 2024). The United States District Court for the Eastern District of Michigan adopted a magistrate judge's report and recommendation in a lawsuit filed by plaintiff franchisor, Sizzling Black Rock Steak House Franchising, Inc. ("Franchisor") against its franchise law firm for allegedly erroneously including an evergreen royalty provision in an area representative agreement. The court adopted the recommendation on defendant's motion for summary judgment on the negligence claim determining that material facts bearing on the merits of that claim exist but granting summary judgment on the negligent misrepresentation claim as it was duplicative of its legal malpractice claim and should be dismissed.

XIV. Confession of Judgment

Choice Hotels International, Inc. v. Thakorji, Inc., No. 22cv3092-PX, 2023 WL 8257947 (D. Md. Nov. 29, 2023). On April 24, 2023, the court entered an Order of Confessed Judgment against the defendants in favor of Choice Hotels International Inc. ("Choice Hotels") after Choice Hotels alleged that the defendants failed to make payments under terms of the franchise agreement between the parties. The defendants then filed a motion to vacate the judgment by confession and enforce arbitration, citing the arbitration clause in the franchise agreement. Choice Hotels argued that the incentive note under which the defendant failed to make payments did not contain the same arbitration language. The court found the defendants' argument sufficient to establish a material dispute, thereby meeting the local rule standard that there must be "substantial and sufficient grounds for actual controversy" to vacate a confession of judgment. The court granted, in part, the defendants' motion to vacate the confessed judgment, based on the presence of a credible claim of arbitrability.

XV. Third Party Beneficiaries

Reed Auto of Overland Park & Reed Automotive Group, Inc. v. Landers McClarty Olthate KS, LLC, No. 2:19-CV-02510-HLT, 2023 WL 5446552 (10th Cir. Aug. 24, 2023). In this case from the Tenth Circuit Court of Appeals, a Chrysler Dodge Ram car dealership appealed a decision by the trial court that it was not a third-beneficiary or successor to a settlement agreement between two neighboring Chrysler Dodge Ram franchisees.

Overland Park Jeep ("Overland") and the defendant, Landers McClarty Olathe KS, LLC ("Landers") operated Dodge Ram dealerships in adjacent territories in Kansas City. Overland's and

Landers' exclusive territory rights were governed by their respective franchise agreements with Fiat Chrysler Automotive and subject to a Kansas law requiring dealers have "good cause" to relocate and report the relocation, addition, or consolidation of any dealer to the Kansas Department of Revenue ("Kansas Department"). Landers desired to move into Overland's territory triggering a right for Overland to file a protest with the Kansas Department. Landers and Overland settled the dispute and, together with the franchisor, entered into a settlement agreement in 2007 under which Landers agreed not to protest any Overland move so long as Overland did not protest any future move by Landers.

Fast forwarding years later, Reed Auto of Overland Park, LLC ("Reed") purchased Overland's business pursuant to an asset purchase agreement. The settlement agreement was never disclosed and was not listed as an assumed or excluded contract under the asset purchase agreement. When Reed decided to relocate, Landers filed a protest with the Kansas Department. Reed fought the protest at considerable cost until Overland made Reed aware of the settlement agreement. Reed then filed suit against Landers for breaching the settlement agreement, arguing it was either a successor to Overland or a third-party beneficiary to the settlement agreement. The trial court granted Landers' motion for summary judgment on the third-party beneficiary claim and resolved the successor claim in favor of Landers. Reed appealed.

Applying Michigan law under the choice of law provision in the settlement agreement, the court determined that Reed was not a successor to Overland. Reed did not follow or replace Overland as a matter of law since it acquired only certain assets of the business, assume only limited liabilities, and entered into a new franchise agreement with the franchisor. The court also concluded that Reed was not a third-party beneficiary to the settlement agreement because Michigan applies a limiting test that requires a review of the agreement to see if the contracting parties knowingly took an obligation directly for the benefit of a third party. The court found that the promise by Landers not to protest was made solely to Overland and not to any other dealers. Further, since Reed was not a successor to Overland, the language prohibiting Landers from protesting a move by any of Overland's successors, assigns, heirs and legal representatives, did not apply to Reed. The court therefore affirmed the judgment of the district court. This included upholding a decision by the trial court not to grant Landers the attorneys' fees it tried to recover under the settlement agreement against Reed because the settlement agreement was not enforceable as between Overland and Reed.

XVI. Waiver of Jury Trial

Pizza Hut, LLC v. Pandya, 79 F.4th 535 (5th Cir. 2023). The Fifth Circuit Court of Appeals affirmed a judgment against a franchisee ("Pandya") in the amount of approximately $6.7 million in favor of franchisor, Pizza Hut ("Pizza Hut") after determining that the district court did not err in granting Pizza Hut's motion to strike Pandya's request for a jury trial.

Pandya was a multi-unit franchisee of Pizza Hut and entered into franchise agreements over the years to operate forty-three locations in Pennsylvania and one in Connecticut, each for twenty-year terms. After Pizza Hut terminated Pandya's franchise agreements for allegedly failing to pay fees and violating brand standards, the parties entered into a forbearance agreement to allow the restaurants to stay open while Pandya searched for a buyer. After the search was unsuccessful, the parties entered into a transfer agreement, pursuant to which the parties explicitly waived their respective rights to a jury trial in any litigation between or among them. Thereafter, a dispute arose between the parties, and Pizza Hut terminated the forbearance agreement and filed a lawsuit against Pandya alleging various breach of contract and intellectual property claims. Pandya counterclaimed, alleging that Pizza Hut breached the transfer agreement and asserted counterclaims for: (1) fraud/fraudulent inducement; (2) breach of fiduciary duty; (3)

tortious interference with prospective business relations; (4) tortious interference with existing contracts and business relations; and (5) business disparagement and defamation. Pandya also demanded a jury trial.

The court granted Pizza Hut's motion to strike Pandya's request for a jury trial based on the waiver in the transfer agreement and the case proceeded to a five-day bench trial, after which Pizza Hut was awarded $6,688,751.14 in damages and interest. Pandya appealed.

The court noted that if a jury waiver was entered into voluntarily and knowingly, then it is well settled by the Supreme Court that parties can expressly waive this right. The circuit courts were split on who has the burden to establish or negate that the waiver was done voluntarily and knowingly. However, the Fifth Circuit followed the Sixth Circuit in holding the party objecting to the enforcement of a waiver in a facially valid contract bears the burden of showing the waiver's unenforceability. Facially valid contractual waivers, like other valid contractual provisions, are assumed enforceable unless the party seeking to avoid the waiver proves otherwise.

The court held that Pandya failed to allege that the jury waiver specifically was procured by fraud. Pandya alleged in his counterclaims that Pizza Hut fraudulently induced him into signing the Transfer Agreement by representing that it would help him find a buyer although it never intended to do so. Pandya argued that Pizza Hut added the jury waiver at the last minute, after obtaining litigation counsel, to gain a litigation advantage, yet Pandya failed to allege any of this in his counterclaims. He only alleged that Pizza Hut fraudulently induced him into signing the transfer agreement. This allegation was insufficient to render the jury waiver provision void. Accordingly, the district court correctly held that Pandya's fraud claim did not invalidate the jury waiver.

Courts generally consider four factors to determine if a jury waiver was knowing and voluntary: (1) whether the parties had an opportunity to negotiate the terms of the agreement; (2) whether the waiver provision was conspicuous; (3) the bargaining power of the parties; and (4) the business acumen or professional experience of the party opposing the waiver. The court held that each factor supported upholding the transfer agreement's jury waiver.

First, the record supported the district court's determination that Pandya negotiated the transfer agreement's terms. Though Pizza Hut inserted the jury waiver at the end, Pandya questioned certain terms in that paragraph on the last turn before signing.

Second, the transfer agreement was short for a legal document at nine pages, and Pizza Hut did not place the waiver where it would be easily skippable. Instead, the jury waiver was in the final paragraph before the signatures. Since Pandya circled the paragraph containing the waiver, the court concluded was aware of it.

Third, the court rejected Pandya's argument that Pizza Hut had more bargaining power because Pandya admitted that he was the largest owner of Pizza Huts in Pennsylvania, and Pizza Hut thus had a strong interest in keeping his restaurants open. Pandya also successfully negotiated several favorable terms in the contract. So while there was "some inequality of bargaining power," Pandya did not have "the kind of 'extreme bargaining disadvantage' or 'gross disparity in bargaining position' that occurs only in certain exceptional situations.

Fourth, the court found that Pandya failed to demonstrate that he lacked sufficient business acumen since he stated in his complaint that he is a well-known and successful businessman with multiple companies. The court therefore affirmed the lower court decision.

XVII. Intervention

Oakland Family Restaurants, Inc. v. American Dairy Queen Corp., No. 2:21-CV-12530-TGB-APP, 2024 WL 473480 (E.D. Mich. January 10, 2024). The United States District Court for the

Eastern District of Michigan granted the motion filed by the Michigan Department of the Attorney General to intervene in a case where Dairy Queen challenged the constitutionality of certain provisions of the Michigan Franchise Investment Law, as applied to an agreement between defendant Dairy Queen and plaintiffs. The Attorney General filed the motion within sixty days of receiving notice that Dairy Queen would be challenging the law and 28 U.S.C. § 2403(b) gave the Attorney General the unconditional right to intervene in the case. This case is discussed in Chapter 8, Section III.

XVIII. Standing

Rigollet v. Le Macaron Development, LLC, 383 So. 3d 132 (Fla. Dist. Ct. App. 2024). The Florida District Court of Appeals reversed the lower court's dismissal of a franchisee's ("Rigollet") counterclaim against La Macaron Development, LLC ("LMD"), the affiliated financing arm of his franchisor, for: (1) fraud in the inducement; (2) violation of the Florida Deceptive and Unfair Trade Practices Act; (3) violation of the Florida Franchise Act; (4) breach of contract; and (5) breach of the implied covenant of good faith and fair dealing. Rigollet entered into a franchise agreement and personal guaranty with LMD granting him the right to open and operate Macaron pastry shops. In connection with the franchise agreement, Rigollet borrowed $200,000 from LMD pursuant to a promissory note to finance the opening of the franchise pastry shops. After the relationship soured, LMD brought fifteen counts against Rigollet including breaches of the franchise agreement, personal guaranty and promissory note. Rigollet counterclaimed. The lower court granted LMD's motion to dismiss for lack of standing arguing Rigollet did not incur any damages independent of the franchisee and any damages were losses, expenses, or damages of the franchisee. The court found the trial court erred in finding he was not a contracting party and Rigollet sufficiently alleged that he was a party to the contracts identified in the counterclaim, namely the promissory note and personal guaranty, and the court noted that that

LMD sued Rigollet for breach of the very same contracts. The court also found that it was unclear which party–Rigollet or his franchise entity–was the "person invested" in the franchise to maintain a claim under the Florida Franchise Act, and therefore, Rigollet's counterclaim alleged sufficient facts to support all five of his claims.

New Jersey Coalition of Automobile Retailers, Inc. v. Ford Motor Co., No. A-1051-22, 2024 WL 1461817 (N.J. Super. Ct. App. Div. Apr. 4, 2024). New Jersey Coalition of Automotive Retailers, Inc. ("NJCAR"), a trade association whose members consist of franchised new motor vehicle dealerships, sought declaratory and injunctive relief against the Ford Motor Company, but the trial court found that NJCAR lacked standing under the New Jersey Franchise Practices Act ("Act") so it did not address the merits. NJCAR appealed, arguing that it had associational standing to raise claims under the Act and that the trial court erred by analyzing statutory standing rather than associational standing. In New Jersey, associational standing has three prongs: (1) an association must demonstrate that its individual members would have standing to sue; (2) the interests it seeks to maintain are germane to the purpose of the organization; and (3) neither the claim asserted nor the relief requested requires individual participation by the association's members.

The court of appeals held that NJCAR had associational standing to bring the action because all three prongs were met. The court held that the first prong was met because there was a legal controversy that individual NJCAR members would have standing to bring the action under the Act. The second prong was met because NJCAR's purpose of advocating on behalf of its members and promoting public policies to ensure a competitive and fair marketplace are germane to the proper enforcement of the Act. Finally, the third prong was met because NJCAR sought only declaratory and injunctive relief, not damages based on a statute violation, and therefore, the litigation did not require the participation of individual members. The appeals court reversed the trial court's decision and remanded the case to address the merits of the summary judgment motions.

Plante Consulting LLC v. Ford Motor Co., No. 23-CV-2475(KAM)(TAM), 2024 WL 1556891 (E.D.N.Y. Apr. 10, 2024). The district court granted the defendant's motion to dismiss the franchisee's complaint for lack of standing because the franchisee failed to plead an actual or imminent threat to satisfy the concrete injury requirement for Article III standing.

XIX. Other Issues

Creative Management, Inc. v. 7514 Tonnelle Ave., LLC, No. A-3050-20, 2023 WL 8450777 (N.J. Super. A.D. Dec. 6, 2023). Creative Management, Inc. ("CMI") entered into a credit agreement whereby CMI agreed to sell and deliver fuel to defendants at their gas station. In a subsequent transaction, CMI sold defendants a point-of-sale ("POS") software system. Nearly three years later, defendants told CMI that they would no longer need their services. Thereafter, CMI filed suit against defendants seeking $31,125.40. Defendants filed a counterclaim for breach of contract alleging that SMI overcharged them and a violation of the New Jersey Consumer Fraud Act ("CFA").

At trial, the court dismissed the defendants' CFA claim, and the jury awarded CMI $18,244.05 for the gasoline it sold to the defendants. The jury also awarded the defendants $111,318.89 for its counterclaim. CMI moved for a judgment notwithstanding the verdict ("JNOV") as to the counterclaim, and alternatively, requested a new trial. The court denied both motions. On appeal, CMI argued that the trial court erred in denying its JNOV motion for the following reasons: (1) defendants failed to meet its burden of proof under the Uniform Commercial Code ("UCC") to prevail on its counterclaim; (2) the judge failed to include a relevant question on the jury's questionnaire sheet; and (3) the judge admitted inaccurate summaries from the defendant. In response, defendants filed a cross-appeal arguing that the judge erred in dismissing their CFA claim. The appellate court affirmed the trial court's decisions. The court noted that CMI's UCC argument failed because CMI never asserted that the defendants failed to conform to the UCC, nor did they ask for a specific jury instruction. Further, the court found that the summaries were appropriately admitted because CMI had an opportunity to object. Applying the UCC, the court found that CMI was not entitled to a JNOV. Lastly, the court rejected the defendants' argument because the defendants did not fall under the category of "consumers" as defined under the CFA.

Meier v. Meier, No. A-23-395, 2024 WL 3261408 (Neb. Ct. App. July 2, 2024). A wife appealed a divorce decree, arguing that the trial court erred in classifying her husband's twenty-five percent business interest in a restaurant franchise, and associated loans from his parents, as marital assets and marital debt. The Nebraska Court of Appeals held that the trial court abused its discretion by classifying the husband's twenty five percent business interest and associated personal loans as marital property because the husband owned his interest in the franchise prior to the marriage. The court determined that the premarital ownership made the interest in the franchise nonmarital property. It was persuaded in part and because the wife took no part in the franchised business. The court also held that the loans were borrowed not for the joint benefit of the parties, but to maintain the nonmarital twenty five percent interest in the franchise. For this reason, the loans constituted nonmarital assets and should have been excluded from the marital estate.

Baymont Franchise Systems, Inc. v. The Bernstein Co., No. 18CV620 (EP)(AME), 2023 WL 8436432 (D.N.J. Dec. 5, 2023). After the district court granted franchisor Baymont's summary judgment motion and entered judgment for Baymont, the franchisee defendants moved for reconsideration of the decision. The district court denied the motion for reconsideration, finding there was no basis for reconsideration because the defendants failed to provide any new or additional evidence supporting their claims against

Baymont, because the franchisor's breach did not entitle the defendant franchisees to stop paying and continue operating the franchised hotel, and because defendants' arguments rested on the possibility of proving an immaterial fact that the district court had previously rejected.

Troutt v. Watson, No. COA23-535, 2024 WL 446399 (N.C. Ct. App. Feb. 6, 2024). North Carolina Court of Appeals dismissed shareholder's interlocutory appeal on the trial court's order to dissolve two franchise LLCs because there was no evidence that the shareholder would be deprived of a substantial right by not obtaining immediate appellate review.

CHAPTER 9

International Developments

I. Introduction

This reporting period (2023-2024) features updates from Australia, Belgium, Canada, China, Japan, New Zealand, Poland, South Korea, Sri Lanka, Taiwan, and the United Kingdom.

II. Australia

By Eugenia Kolivos, Michael Joffe and Anika Di Pietro, Corrs Chambers Westgarth[1]

A. LEGISLATIVE UPDATE

1. Franchising Code of Conduct

On May 7, 2024, the Australian Government released its response to the Final Report of the Review of the Franchising Code of

[1] Eugenia Kolivos is the Head of Intellectual Property and Partner in TMT at Corrs Chambers Westgarth, Australia's leading independent law firm. Michael Joffe is a Senior Associate and Anika Di Pietro, Associate. Together the team advises extensively on franchising arrangements and related regulatory compliance in Australia, having assisted many organisations establish and maintain their franchising operations in Australia. The team also advises more broadly on IP transactions and licensing models, product launches, marketing,

Conduct (the "Review"), agreeing to implement 21 of the 23 formal recommendations made by the Review in full, and agreeing in principle to the remaining two recommendations.

By way of background, the Franchising Code of Conduct (the "Code") is a binding industry code made under the *Competition and Consumer Act 2010* (Cth) ("CCA") which regulates franchisee and franchisor conduct. The Review was publicly released on February 8, 2024 and assessed the Code's fitness for purpose, with specific regard to provisions relating to new vehicle dealership agreements and the operation of the Franchise Disclosure Register ("FDR"). The Review found that the Code is generally fit-for-purpose and should be remade prior to its expiry in April 2025, with some changes to improve its operation. It is these suggested changes that the Government has responded to.

The Government's response to the following twenty-three recommendations is as follows:

1. *Franchising sector statistics*- the Government agreed that more comprehensive and robust data on the franchising sector would support franchisors, franchisees, and policymakers to better understand the sector and assess the effectiveness of its regulation. Therefore, it will require the Australian Small Business and Family Enterprise Ombudsman ("ASBFEO"), to improve the comparability and publication of existing data sets held by itself, the Australian Competition and Consumer Commission ("ACCC"), and other state and federal government agencies.
2. *The Code should be revised*– the Government agreed that the Code should be remade regarding the recommended changes before it expires in April of 2025.

branding and consumer law regulation, data protection and privacy laws as well as technology acquisitions and deployments across all industries, with a particular focus on the life sciences, digital and healthcare sectors.

3. *Inserted statement of purpose–* the Government agreed to inserting a clear statement of purpose into the Code to provide clarity as to what it is intended to achieve for franchisees and franchisors.
4. *Service work by motor vehicle dealerships-* the Government agreed to ensure the next edition of the Code will clarify that service and repair work performed by motor vehicle dealerships is within its regulatory scope.
5. *Five-yearly reviews-* the Government agreed to ensure there will be statutory reviews of the Code every five years.
6. *Simplify pre-entry information given to prospective franchisees-* the Government expressed support for consolidating and streamlining information made available to franchisees in a way that reduces unnecessary compliance burdens whilst maintaining franchisee protections. It therefore plans to merge the 'key facts sheet' into the 'disclosure document' (which are currently provided separately).
7. *Simplify franchisor obligations–* the Government agreed to simplify franchisors' disclosure obligations in relation to existing franchisees.
8. *Reasonable opportunity to make a return on investment-* currently, only new vehicle dealership franchise agreements are required to provide a reasonable opportunity for franchisees to make a return on their investment. The Government agreed to extend this requirement to all franchise agreements in the new edition of the Code.
9. *Compensation for early termination–* currently, only new vehicle dealership agreements are required to include provisions for compensation for franchisees, in the event of early termination. The Government agreed to extend this requirement to all franchise agreements in the new edition of the Code.
10. *Enhance visibility and usage of the FDR-* the Government agreed to leverage existing mechanisms to promote the public visibility and use of the FDR (which contains high-level information about franchised businesses) in recognition of the widespread support expressed by stakeholders for the FDR to

remain a part of the Australian regulatory environment, despite its generally low utilization.

11. *Additional information on the FDR*- the Government agreed to implement requirements for additional information relating to dispute resolution and adverse actions brought by enforcement agencies to be included on the FDR.
12. *Education to encourage franchisors to consult franchisees regarding business model changes*– the Government agreed to require the ASBFEO to lead the development of best practice guidance in relation to improving the nature of and access to education materials for the sector.
13. *Simplify termination provisions for serious breach*– the Government will work with the franchise sector to simplify provisions relating to termination for serious breaches in a way which will not diminish protections for franchisees.
14. *Best practice guidance regarding franchisee-initiated* exit- the Government agreed to require the ASBFEO to lead the development of best practice guidance in relation to improving the nature of and access to education materials for the sector.
15. *Limit unreasonable restraints of trade*- the Government agreed to direct the Competition Taskforce to consider how restraints of trade and other un-competitive terms in franchise agreements may be affecting franchise workers. It will also request that the ACCC provide guidance as to when a restraint of trade provision may constitute an unfair contract term under the ACL.
16. *Create a comprehensive online government resource*– the Government agreed *in principle* that education and awareness are important elements of an effective regulatory framework.
17. *Improve standards of conduct through best practice guidance*– the Government agreed to require the ASBFEO to lead the development of best practice guidance. The Government agreed that small businesses need greater support to recognize and act against unfair contract terms and trading practices under the ACL.
18. *Additional powers to ASBFEO*- the Government agreed to amend relevant legislation to provide the ASBFEO with the

power to name franchisors which have failed to meaningfully participate in alternative dispute resolution ("ADR").

19. *Low-cost legal advice for franchisees*- the Government agreed to expand the ASBFEO's 'Tax Concierge Service' to support small businesses, including franchisees, to access low-cost legal advice on ADR prospects.
20. *Role of franchise interests in ACCC complaints process*- In July 2024, a designated complaints function within the ACCC was established. It has agreed to implement a process for interested parties that represent the interests of small businesses (such as franchisees) to apply to become a designated complainant under the prospective scheme.
21. *'No adverse costs' orders for franchisees bringing matters against a franchisor for breach of the Code or the ACL*- the Government agreed *in principle* to support improving access to justice for franchisees and low-cost means of resolving franchising disputes. The Government noted that 'no adverse costs' orders are not common in Australian federal legislation and that it would consult further on how this might be implemented within the context of the administration of justice.
22. *Increase scope of penalties and investigation powers*- the Government agreed to increase the scope of penalties under the Code to all substantive obligations it places on parties and to set those penalties at 600 penalty units. As of August 2024, the amount of a penalty unit is AU$313. This is subject to indexation pursuant to the formula in section 4AA of the *Crimes Act 1914* (Cth). It will also consider increasing the penalty for infringement notices issued under the CCA for a breach of the Code to 60 penalty units. Division 2A of Part IVB of the CCA provides for the issuance of infringement notices to persons for an alleged contravention of a civil penalty provision in an industry code, as an alternative to proceedings for an order for the payment of a pecuniary penalty: see section 51ACC.
23. *Licensing regime*- the Government agreed to establish a Taskforce in the Treasury to conduct a comprehensive cost-benefit analysis of introducing a licensing regime to regulate

most aspects of the franchisee-franchisor relationship. The Taskforce will consult widely and provide their advice to the Government.

It is anticipated that draft legislative amendments to the Code will be released later this year for public consultation and come into effect by April 2025.

2. Unfair Contract Terms in Franchise Agreements

The ACCC's long-stated objective of strengthening and introducing penalties for unfair contract terms ("UCT") was realized when reforms to the ACL came into effect on November 9, 2023. The changes apply in relation to standard form contracts with small businesses or consumers entered into or renewed, or any UCTs that are varied, on or after November 9, 2023. The ACCC was also afforded powers to seek significant financial penalties from businesses who breach these prohibitions.

The maximum financial penalty for businesses under the new penalty regime are the greater of:

1. AU $50,000,000;
2. three times the value of the "reasonably attributable" benefit obtained from the conduct, if the court can determine this; or
3. if a court cannot determine the benefit, 30 per cent of adjusted turnover during the breach period.

The UCT regime is likely to apply to many franchise agreements, to the extent they constitute standard form contracts entered into by small businesses that have fewer than 100 employees, or make less than AU $10 million in annual turnover. This is because prospective franchisees are likely to have limited or no opportunity to negotiate the terms of the relevant agreement. Accordingly, the ACCC considers that a significant proportion of franchisees and master franchisees operating in Australia are likely to be protected under the UCT regime.

B. CASE LAW UPDATE

AHG WA (2015) Pty Ltd v Mercedes-Benz Australia/Pacific Pty Ltd., No. VID 604 of 2021, FCA 1022 (Fed. Ct. of Australis, 2023). In this case, a claim was asserted against Mercedes-Benz Australia/Pacific Pty Ltd ("Mercedes-Benz AU") by 38 of its dealers after it did not renew their dealership agreements and implemented an agency model. The prior franchising model involved dealers buying wholesale stock from Mercedes-Benz AU, selling vehicles at prices with dealer-set profit margins, and developing their own goodwill with customers. The new agency model was a globally implemented strategy of its holding company and required dealers to act as agents of Mercedes-Benz AU, selling stock that the franchisor owned and receiving a fixed commission on sales. The Court dismissed the dealers' claims, finding that, in exercising its contractual power of non-renewal so that it could implement an agency model, Mercedes-Benz AU had not acted unconscionably, for an improper purpose nor in breach of its statutory duty to act in good faith under the Code (as the dealers had alleged). Although the dealers were financially disadvantaged by Mercedes-Benz AU favoring their own interests, this did not render the conduct unconscionable or in bad faith.

The Court held that a franchisor is unlikely to be acting unconscionably by exercising its power of non-renewal to change business models because franchisees accept the possibility of non-renewal when they enter franchise agreements. It confirmed that the obligation of franchisors and franchisees to act in good faith duty under the Code does not require a contract to continue indefinitely or prevent a party from acting in its own legitimate commercial interests – it simply requires that a party act honestly when exercising its power of non-renewal without cause. Similarly, the dealers' claims relating to the appropriation or loss of their goodwill were rejected by the Court, which confirmed that a franchisee's goodwill does not survive the expiry of the franchise agreement. Finally, the Court also affirmed that an Australian subsidiary does not necessarily exercise a contractual power for an improper purpose merely because it was influenced by its international holding company.

Health food and beverage retailer, Delicia Franchising Pty Ltd (ACN 623 553 631) ("Delicia"). Delicia admitted in an undertaking provided to the ACCC that it breached the Code, following an ACCC-led investigation in respect of the organization's failure to satisfy disclosure requirements. The investigation found that Delicia's annual marketing fund financial statements for the 2020, 2021 and 2022 financial years did not disclose sufficient detail of the fund's recipients and expenses. Under the Code, franchisors are required to provide franchisees with annual marketing fund statements if the franchise agreement requires franchises to contribute to a marketing fund. The undertaking is a reminder to franchisors to provide sufficiently detailed marketing fund statements and provide them to franchisees. Failure to do so may amount to a breach of the Code and invite significant penalties.

III. Belgium

By Kristof Zadora and Dylan Verhulst

A. LEGISLATIVE UPDATE

On February 9, 2024, the Belgian Parliament adopted a legislative proposal modifying article 28 of Book X of the Belgian Economic Code on the rules regarding the precontractual information obligation for commercial collaboration agreements, which includes franchise agreements. The rules on the precontractual information obligation for franchise agreements are codified in Title 2, Book X of the Belgian Economic Code. The modified article 28 of the Book X of the Belgian Economic shall enter take effect on September 1, 2024.

B. BELGIAN ECONOMIC CODE

1. Precontractual information documents

According to article 27 of Book X of the Belgian Economic Code, franchisors are obligated to provide franchisees with a draft of the franchise agreement as well as a separate information document. The legislative amendment as adopted on February 9, 2024, concerns information documents, usually referred to as "precontractual information documents."

A precontractual information document serves to provide franchisees with the necessary information to enter into the franchise relationship in an informed manner and consists of two parts: (1) the so-called "key contractual provisions" and (2) details pertaining to the assessment of the franchise agreement.
In the past, franchisors were required to provide information on the "obligations" and "consequences of non-compliance of the obligations" included in the franchise agreements, which often resulted in the inclusion of an exhaustive list of clauses in the precontractual information document. That did not serve franchisees' understanding of their obligations under the franchising agreement.
By clarifying what the "key contractual provisions" entail, the legislative amendment seeks to enhance the efficacy of precontractual information documents in highlighting critical aspects of the franchise relationship.

2. Key information obligations

The legislative amendment introduces a list of elements that are considered to encompass the key contractual provisions. Franchisors need to include the following elements in the precontractual information document (insofar as those elements are included in the franchise agreement):

1. Whether the agreement is concluded with or without specific regard to the person ("*intuitu personae*").
2. The duration of the agreement and the conditions for its renewal and termination as well as its financial consequences, especially in terms of charges and investments.
3. The direct remuneration to be paid by the franchisee to the franchisor and the method of calculating the indirect remuneration received by the franchisor and, where appropriate, the method of review during the course of the agreement and at the time of its renewal.
4. The start-up or recurring costs such as marketing, informatics, transportation, training borne by franchisee and the conditions for their modification.
5. The exclusivity reserved to the franchisor.
6. The non-compete clauses, their duration, the conditions and the consequences of not achieving them.
7. The obligations regarding maximum prices.
8. The obligations regarding minimum turnover and minimum purchase and the consequences of not achieving them.
9. The restrictions on the use of intellectual property rights.
10. The restrictions on access to and rights of use of client data during and after the agreement imposed on the franchisee.
11. The restrictions on online sales and online promotion.
12. The pre-emption rights or option to purchase for the benefit of the franchisor and the rules for valuing the business when such rights or options are exercised.
13. The clauses concerning the relationship and dependence between the agreement and the lease or any other agreement concerning the operating establishment.
14. The reasons for the express termination of the agreement as well as its financial consequences, regarding charges and investments.
15. The jurisdiction clause, choice of law, and procedural language.

In accordance with article 27 of Book X of the Belgian Economic Code, the precontractual information document needs to be provided to the franchisee at least one month before the conclusion of the franchise agreement.

3. Sanctions

Non-compliance with the enhanced precontractual information obligations may bring about substantial consequences for a franchise relationship. Article 30 of Book X of the Belgian Economic Code provides that in a case of non-compliance with the rules on the precontractual information in franchise relationships, the franchisee may invoke the nullity of the franchise agreement within two years after the conclusion of the agreement or certain clauses thereof, depending on the nature of the event of non-compliance.

That sanction is relative, as the franchisee can waive its right to invoke the nullity within one month after the conclusion of the franchise agreement. The waiver needs to state the grounds for waiver of the right explicitly.

4. Conclusion

The evolution of precontractual information obligations in Belgian franchise law reflects a concerted effort to promote transparency, fairness, and legal certainty in franchise arrangements. By clarifying the key contractual provisions, legislators aim to safeguard the interests of both franchisors and franchisees. As stakeholders navigate the complexities of franchise agreements, adherence to the revised regulatory framework is paramount to mitigate legal liabilities and foster mutually beneficial business relationships.

C. BELGIAN CIVIL CODE

1. Introduction

The recent adoption of Book 6 of the Belgian Civil Code has profound implications for franchise relationships in Belgium. The new Book 6 of the Belgian Civil Code was adopted by the Belgian Parliament on February 1, 2024, and replaces certain key provisions of the old Civil Code. It focuses specifically on extra-contractual liability. One of the most significant changes introduced by Book 6 is the reversal of the principle regarding confluence of contractual and extra-contractual liability, which in turn has significant implications for the legal regime of quasi-immunity of contractual agent. Those legal developments may prompt franchise stakeholders to reassess their contractual frameworks and risk management strategies.

2. Reversal of the principle on concurrence of contractual and extra-contractual liability

Before the introduction of the new Book six of the Belgian Civil Code, in principle it was not possible for a party to claim for liability against their contractual counterparty and their counterparty's agents on an extra-contractual basis (except in a limited number of occasions such as criminal offences), the so-called prohibition on concurrence of contractual and extra-contractual liability.

That principle has been reversed in the new article six. four, § one of the Belgian Civil Code, which allows for the aggrieved party to apply either contractual liability or extra-contractual liability in a contractual context, subject to contractual frameworks and statutory legal rules. The reversal of the principle is being justified by referring to the errors in logic of the previous principle and stressing the importance of the actual will of the contractual parties to set forth the applicable liability rules between them, rather than the general "implied" will of contractual parties to merely apply the contractual liability regime in a contractual context.

3. *Impact on contractual agents in a franchise context*

The prohibition on concurrence of contractual and extra-contractual liability also applied to the contractual agents of the parties to an agreement before the introduction of the new Book six of the Belgian Civil Code. As such, contractual agents were protected from extra-contractual liability in the same manner as the contractual parties themselves, i.e. the so-called quasi-immunity of contractual agents. Given the fact that a franchise relationship may involve a wide array of contractual agents going from independent contractors, employees, directors, sub-franchisees etc., the quasi-immunity of contractual agents has a lot of impact on the risks involved in a franchise relationship.

With the reversal of the principle on confluence between contractual and extra-contractual liability in a contractual context, the quasi-immunity of contractual agents is abolished under Belgian law. By providing aggrieved parties with recourse against contractual agents, the new Book 6 aims to ensure that franchisees and franchisors are held accountable for their actions while also safeguarding the rights of individuals who may suffer harm because of franchise operations. As such, the traditional boundaries of liability within a franchise context are put into question.

4. *Contractual risk management strategies*

It is self-evident that the adoption of the new Book 6 raises practical considerations for franchise stakeholders. Nevertheless, in accordance with the new article six, four, § two of the Belgian Civil Code contractual agents are granted the right to invoke the same defenses as their principal against aggrieved parties, ensuring a degree of parity. As such, contractual agents may rely on the contractual clauses included in the franchise agreement of their principal, including liability limitation clauses. Therefore, parties may seek to strategically include clauses in franchise agreements that address non-contractual liabilities of contractual agents, subject to legal constraints and considerations. Clarity and specificity in contractual provisions are crucial to delineate the respective rights and obligations of franchisors, franchisees, and contractual agents.

Taking the former into account, existing franchise agreements must be reviewed and, if necessary, amended to account for this paradigm shift set forth by the new legal framework. Franchise stakeholders should anticipate the potential for non-contractual liability claims against contractual agents and take proactive steps to mitigate risks.

5. Timing and conclusion

Looking ahead, the effective date of entry into force of Book 6 remains a critical point of consideration for franchise stakeholders. While January 1, 2025, is tentatively earmarked as the date of entry into force, franchise stakeholders should remain vigilant for any developments or clarifications regarding the implementation timeline.

In conclusion, the adoption of the new Book 6 of the Civil Code signals a paradigm shift in non-contractual liability within franchise relationships in Belgium. By embracing these changes and adopting proactive risk management strategies, franchisors and franchisees can navigate the evolving legal landscape with confidence and ensure the continued success and sustainability of their franchise operations.

IV. Canada

By Noah Leszcz[2]

A. INTRODUCTION

The past year has been an exciting one for franchise law in Canada. From continued growth in franchise jurisprudence to the introduction of a new franchise legislation, there are several noteworthy developments in Canadian franchise law. This section focuses on the most noteworthy of those developments.

B. LEGISLATIVE UPDATE

1. Saskatchewan's Newly Enacted Franchise Legislation

On May 8, 2024, Saskatchewan joined Ontario Alberta, Ontario, Prince Edward Island, New Brunswick, Manitoba, and British Columbia, becoming the seventh province in Canada with a franchise statute. While the new Saskatchewan franchise legislation (the "Act") has been enacted, the Act has yet to come into force, and will do so on an undetermined date that will be set by the Lieutenant Governor in Council. Though the Act largely mirrors the same requirements found in existing Canadian franchise legislation, including the obligation to provide pre-sale disclosure and to enforce contractual rights in accordance with the duty of good faith and fair dealing, there are some notable differences as compared to the other provincial statutes.

---

[2] Noah Leszcz is a partner in the Franchise Law and Business Groups at Cassels Brock and Blackwell LLP in Toronto, Canada. Noah practices business law, with a focus on franchising, licensing, distribution, emerging companies, and intellectual property. He works with a diverse group of franchise and distribution companies, assisting with legal and regulatory issues, contractual drafting, M&A transactions, intellectual property, and compliance with Canadian franchise disclosure legislation. Noah routinely assists international franchise clients seeking to expand their brands to Canada.

2. Differences to Other Regulated Provinces

1. *Definition of a "Franchise"*- The definition of a "franchise" is narrowed under the Act as compared to the existing Canadian franchise laws. Previously, a franchise in Canada existed where a franchisor has a right to exercise significant control or to provide significant assistance. In contrast, the Act requires that the Franchisor does in fact exercise significant control or provide significant assistance. (Bill 149, An Act respecting Franchises, 4th Sess, 29th Leg, Saskatchewan, 2023, s 2(1)). This difference will turn focus from the wording of the agreement to the conduct of the parties and will provide greater opportunities for businesses seeking to avoid application of the Act.
2. *Substantial Compliance*- The Act provides that a mere defect in form, technical irregularity, or error not affecting the substance of a disclosure document, will not give rise to a rescission right if a disclosure document is otherwise substantially in compliance with the Act. This also applies to statements of material change. Previously in Canada, only British Columbia's laws contained this substantial compliance concept.
3. *Prescribing Regulations*- The Act grants significant power and discretion to the Lieutenant Governor in Council to make regulations and provides that any additional information or documents to be included in disclosure documents for Saskatchewan may be prescribed by regulation. As of the date of publication, there are no draft regulations available for review.
4. *Changes to Québec Language Laws- Effective June 1, 2023,* Québec's Bill 96, An Act respecting French, the official and common language of Québec, brings significant changes to the use of French in commercial contracts, most notably requiring that all "contracts of adhesion" be translated into French prior to the execution of any such agreements.

3. *Contracts of Adhesion and Standard Clauses*

Under Bill 96 (*Provigo Distribution inc. c. Supermarché A.R.G. inc.*, J.E. 98-39, REJB 1997-03777 (C.A.); *Ashan v. Second Cup Ltd.*, J.E. 2003-736, REJB 2003-39565 (C.A.); *Régie d'assainissement des eaux du bassin de)* a contract of adhesion is where: (1) the drafting of the essential stipulations or clauses is done by one party and they are imposed on the other contracting party, and (2) the inability of that other contracting party to freely discuss or negotiate those essential stipulations. Parties are now required to present the counterparty with a French version of such contracts prior to contracting in the language of their choosing.

While much debate has ensued as to whether franchise agreements are typically contracts of adhesion, Québec courts have on many occasions found this to be the case. Accordingly, if franchisees are not provided a bona fide opportunity to negotiate the essential terms of a franchise agreement, there is a high likelihood that such agreements will be deemed contracts of adhesion and therefore require translation into French.

4. *Display of Non-French Trademarks*

The current Québec Charter has long required any inscription on a product, its container or wrapping, or a document supplied with the product such as instruction manuals, to be drafted in French. Previously, there was a significant exception regarding the requirement to translate to French for non-French trademarks. Businesses could display their trademark in a language other than French on their packages and labels without having to translate, as long as a French version of the trademark was not registered. This trademark exception was interpreted over the years as applying to both registered and non-registered trademarks (i.e., those marks with 'common law' protection).

Bill 96 has amended the Charter by removing all doubt as to whether the trademark exception applies to unregistered trademarks. Effective June 1, 2025, the exception will only apply to registered trademarks that do not have a registered corresponding French version. Further, the Charter of the French Language, CQLR c C-11, s 51.1 states that even if a trademark is registered, any generic or descriptive part of the trademark must be translated into French on the product or on a "medium permanently attached to a product."

5. *Trademarks and Advertising: Public signs, posters, and commercial advertising*

Previously, public signs, posters, and commercial advertising were required to be in French. Effective June 1, 2025, a non-French trademark must be registered to be entitled to an exception from the requirement to translate to French, provided no corresponding French version has been registered. If a French version is registered, then it must appear in the advertising. In any case, if a poster, sign, or advertisement is visible outside of a business premises, even if the non-French trademark is registered, French must be predominant on such signage.

6. *Use of French by Businesses Operating in Québec*

Currently, businesses with 50 or more employees operating in the province must "generalize the use of French at all levels of the enterprise". Bill 96 amends this threshold to 25 or more employees, with such amendment coming into force June 1, 2025. A business subject to "francization" will, among other things, need to provide its employees with working documents and tools, such as information technologies, in French.

7. *Impact on Business-to-Business Relationships*

Bill 96 further reinforced the existing right of consumers to insist on being served in French. Not only must businesses service their consumers in French, those which offer goods and services to a public other than consumers, such as other businesses or enterprises, must also inform and service that public in French. It appears that these amendments extend to business-to-business relationships.

Importantly, it appears that even if a franchisee explicitly or impliedly waives the right to be served in French or signs an updated agreement with the waiver and acceptance language, the franchisee will most likely remain able to request to be dealt with in French at any future time, at which point the franchisor may be required to satisfy this request.

8. Penalties and Risks of Non-Compliance

Failure to comply with requirements imposed by Bill 96 carries severe penalties. With respect to the translation requirements, a first offense can carry a fine of up to $30,000, and every day an agreement that is non-compliant constitutes a separate offense. As well, agreements can be rendered void by a court without the contracting party having to prove that the contravention of the Québec Charter caused any prejudices. Damages can also be awarded, and directors may incur personal liability.

1. *Amendments to the Competition Act-* Canada's federal *Competition Act* applies across all provinces and territories, irrespective of the lack of franchise-specific legislation in certain jurisdictions. As of June 23, 2023, the *Competition Act* was amended to prohibit "Wage-Fixing" and "No-Poaching" Agreements.

   This new section may expose parties to significant penalties (prison sentences of up to 14 years and/or fines with no statutory limit), as well as to potential civil liability (including by way of class actions for damages). However, the Final Guidelines, enacted by the Competition Bureau provide further guidance and expressly acknowledge franchise agreements as part of the list of business agreements and arrangements where the Bureau will "generally not" pursue a criminal investigation.

The Final Guidelines state that it "may revisit these Guidelines in the future in light of experience, changing circumstances, and legal developments."

2. *No-Poaching Agreements*- The Bureau confirms that the no-poaching prohibition is limited to instances where unaffiliated employers agree not to poach "each other's" employees. Therefore, agreements must be reciprocal or mutual in nature to violate the no-poaching prohibition, and "one-sided" or "one-way" agreements, where only one party agrees not to poach another's employees, will not be considered an offense. Further, the Bureau cautions that "separate agreements between two or more employers that result in reciprocating promises not to poach each other's employees" may trigger liability.
3. *Wage-Fixing Agreements*- The prohibition against wage-fixing deals with more than just wages, also making it an offense for unaffiliated employers to enter into agreements to fix, maintain, decrease or control the "terms and conditions of employment." Terms and conditions of employment include the responsibilities, benefits, and policies associated with a job. This includes job descriptions, allowances such as per diem and mileage reimbursements, non-monetary compensation, working hours, location and non-compete clauses, or other directives that may restrict an individual's future job opportunities.

C. CASE LAW UPDATE

The following is a high-level summary of the notable case law from the franchise jurisprudence in Canada from the previous year.

1. Alternative Dispute Resolution Issues

1010805 Alberta Ltd v Sundial Growers Inc, 1010805 Alberta Ltd v Sundial Growers Inc, 2024 ABKB 173. In this case, the court was asked whether it had jurisdiction to review arbitration issues. The applicant had signed a Franchise Agreement with Spirit Leaf which was later acquired by Sundial Growers (which had acquired all shares of Alcanna Inc). The applicant brought arbitration proceedings against Spirit Leaf and Sundial to determine whether Sundial breached or induced the breach of the Franchise Agreement by acquiring Alcanna. The Arbitrator found that Spirit Leaf breached the statutory duty of good faith and were ordered to pay nominal damages to the Claimant in the amount of $1,000. The court determined that it had sufficient jurisdiction because the parties had not explicitly referred any question of law to the arbitration. As per Section 44(3) of the Arbitration Act, parties are restricted from appealing awards to the court on questions of law explicitly referred to the tribunal for decision. The standard of review for questions of contractual interpretation was confirmed to be reasonableness, and that the Arbitrator did not err in her interpretation of the relevant contracts, nor in her costs award. The Arbitrator awarded only nominal damages ($1,000) as there was no conduct that gave rise to the level where punitive damages would be contemplated.

Aroma Franchise Company Inc. et al. v Aroma Espresso Bar Canada Inc. et al., Aroma Franchise Company Inc. et al. v. Aroma Espresso Bar Canada Inc. et al., 2023 ONSC 1827. In this case, the court confirmed that once an arbitrator issues an Award, any allegations of bias are to be brought before the Court. The Court confirmed that challenging awards based on reasonable apprehension of bias amounts to a claim of unequal treatment and a court application can be brought before arbitration is terminated, once the substantive issues have been rendered, on the grounds of bias.

Coffee Time Corporation v 1685247 Ontario Limited, 2023 ONSC 3353. In this case, the court examined a damages claim resulting from the termination of an overholding franchisee. The franchisor, Coffee Time, sought summary judgment from its former franchisee in respect of royalties, advertising fees, and rent purportedly owed under the franchisee's sublease. The Court found that the franchise agreement and the sublease had continued in an overholding capacity and addressed a variety of defenses such as limitation periods, interest, and potential damages arising from breaches to the lease. This case confirmed that parties should carefully review their contractual rights to ensure that they are claiming amounts to which they are legally entitled.

Taprobane Group Holdings Ltd v. Brownies Foods Ltd., No. S229423, 2023 BCBS 227 (Vancouver, 2023) BCSC 227. In this case, the court found that separate disclosure is required for separate franchise grants to *related* franchisees under British Columbia's franchise legislation. The legislation provides a disclosure document exemption from the obligation to provide disclosure where: (1) an additional franchise is granted to an existing franchisee, (2) the new franchise is substantially the same as the existing franchise that the franchisee is operating, and (3) there has been no material changes since the first grant was awarded. In this case, the franchisor entered into two separate franchise agreements with two distinct entities owned by the same parties and failed to provide adequate disclosure. The Court found that additional franchises being granted to a related franchise does not form part of this exception. Despite the principals of both entities being the same, the Court rejected the application of the exemption, granting the franchisee's rescission claim.

2. Issues Pertaining to Franchisor Obligations

In ***Spina v Shoppers Drug Mart Inc., Spina v. Shoppers Drug Mart Inc.,*** No. 10-414774, 2023 ONSC 1086 (Ontario Sup. Ct. 2023) ONSC 4595. In this case, the court found that if franchisors provide services not listed in a franchise agreement, and the franchisee accepts these services, the franchisee may be barred from disputing fees charged for that service. Additionally, the court confirmed franchisors can set discretionary fees higher than the cost of the services provided.

Hagley v A&W Food Services of Canada Inc., 2023 BCCRT 899. In this case, the Tribunal addressed that there is a distinction between franchisor and franchisees for the purpose of personal injury matters. As the franchisor does not own or control the franchised restaurant, it should not have been named as a defendant in a personal injury claim from a slip and fall incident outside of the franchised restaurant.

Jayasena Management Corp. et al. v Savannah Wells Holdings Inc. et al., 2023 ONSC 100 (Ontario Sup. Ct. 2023) BCCRT 899. In this case, the court held that the sale of an existing franchise was not eligible for a franchise disclosure exemption, thereby entitling the franchisees to rescind the franchise agreement. For the resale disclosure exemption to apply, the franchisor must merely play a passive role in the transfer. In this case, the fact that a franchisor required a purchaser to sign a new franchise agreement instead of assigning the existing agreement was sufficient to render the exemption inapplicable. Additionally, if a franchisor provides a potential resale franchisee with information about a particular franchise, that may be sufficient to demonstrate there was active involvement on the part of the franchisor.

Chapter 9

V. China

By Dominic Hui[3]

A. INTRODUCTION

These few years are very exciting for lawyers practicing in China as there have been a considerable number of new laws and amendments to existing laws implemented – they have been covered by various practitioners in different venues. For franchisors with operations or franchisees in China, we have selected a few pieces of new laws and new administrative documents which will affect the operations of franchise and distribution chains in China.

B. LEGISLATIVE UPDATE

1. Corporate Amendments to Company Law

Many franchisors maintain subsidiaries or joint ventures vehicles in China for various reasons: including serving as the sub-franchisors for China, supporting the franchisees, or for supply chain purposes. On July 1, 2024, amendments to the *PRC Company Law* which were passed on December 29, 2023 came into effect ("*New Company*

---

[3] Dominic Hui is a partner of Ribeiro Hui. His practice covers a wide range of commercial and business issues covering establishment of the proper business vehicle in Greater China, day to day business operations and to spin-off, divestiture and subsequent expatriation of profits. He has led practice groups and represented multi-nationals in mergers and acquisitions, group restructure, plant closures with layoffs and employment transfers, sales/distribution, franchising and licensing in medical, fashion and luxury goods, catering, software, publications and household and various consumer products businesses in the Greater China Region. The transactions invariably involved intellectual property rights and he is well accustomed in dealing with intellectual property issues, particularly on taxation and asset protection in relation to cross-border intellectual property transactions. He was the Co-Chair of the International Franchising Committee of the International Bar Association, between 2021-2023 and is currently a member of the ABA Forum on Franchising's International Division committee.

Law") and will have a profound impact on the operation of all limited liability companies ("LLC") in China, including foreign-invested enterprises .

The *New Company Law* covers substantial changes in areas such as capital contribution, corporate governance, and management responsibilities. Here, we will discuss some key changes and will provide some high-level guidance for compliance with the new requirements.

2. Capital Contribution Period

The old law does not provide a time limit on the capital contribution to be made by a shareholder. The *New Company Law* stipulates a shareholder must pay its subscribed capital in full within five years from the date of its incorporation. This requirement applies to unpaid capital for companies formed before the *New Company Law*, and to additional capital earned after an increase of capital. On July 1, 2024, the State Council also promulgated and enforced the *Provisions on the Implementation of Registered Capital Registration Management System of the Company Law of the PRC* to address some practical questions regarding the new rules for capital contribution.

The *Provisions on Registered Capital* grants a 3-year transition period (Article 2 of *Provisions on the Implementation of Registered Capital Registration Management System of the Company Law of the PRC)*. For companies established before the *New Company Law*, the provision takes effect with a remaining subscribed capital payment term ("Contribution Period") exceeding five years, the transition period will span from July 1, 2024, to June 30, 2027. For an LLC incorporated before July 1, 2024, but the remaining Contribution Period for its shareholders is less than five years from July 1, 2027, the LLC does not need to make any adjustments during the transition period. However, if the remaining Contribution Period exceeds five years, then the same must be adjusted to be within 5 years during the transition period.

For franchisors this change is important as on many occasions shareholders determined the registered capital at a higher amount as under the old law there was no time limitation for capital injection, while normally the shareholders will cease to inject further capital after the entity becomes profitable. For an LLC with a significant amount of outstanding capital contribution, if it is not possible to contribute all the registered capital in the five year time limit or the old capital level is considered as excessive, it may need to consider whether to reduce the amount of registered capital through proper capital reduction procedures as soon as possible. A highly relevant point is, from July 1, 2024, any capital reduction will be subject to publication, and any creditor can oppose such reduction *(Article 224 of the New Company Law)*. .

3. Legal Representative

Under the old law only the chairman of board, the sole executive director (in lieu of board of directors), or the general manager of the LLC could serve as the company's legal representative, regardless of whether this person is executing the company's business operations. The *New Company Law* gives an LLC greater flexibility when designating its legal representative by expanding the scope of the appointment of legal representative to any director who executes company affairs on the company's behalf or the general manager (Article 10 of *New Company Law*). However, the *New Company Law* does not elaborate upon or provide an ambit for the term "executives company affairs". It appears that this condition can be readily satisfied by a current legal representative to keep his position for example by attending board meetings with resolutions on major business matters and execution of contracts. Moreover, in the case of prosecution of officers for regulatory violations, the *New Company Law* denies the classic defense of absence of knowledge of the wrongful acts and requires the legal representative to have exercised diligence. Thus, for his own protection, the *New Company Law* indirectly requires the legal representative to be more hands on and responsible for the LLCs' business operations.

Further, for franchisors this change is important. It is common for franchisors to name their senior executives in the States to be the legal representative of an LLC in China. There may need to re-consider if such appointments should be varied if the senior executive will frequently travel to China. Further, a tailor-made handbook clearly defining the respective scopes of authority of different officers may help to manage the risks hereto.

4. Duties of Loyalty and Diligence of Management Team

The old law required the directors, supervisors, and senior management personnel to perform duties of loyalty and diligence, but there is no definition and/or description on the scope of the duties of loyalty and diligence, except a list of prohibited acts. The *New Company Law* defines the duties of loyalty and diligence with more detailed responsibilities of the directors, supervisors and senior management personnel as follows:

1. Regarding the duty of loyalty, senior officers should take measures to avoid conflicts of interest between their own interests and those of the LLC, and they should not use their authority to seek improper benefits; and

2. Regarding the duty of diligence, they should perform duties in the best interests of the LLC with the reasonable level of care normally expected of a management personnel (Article 180 of the *New Company Law*).

The controlling shareholders and actual controllers of a company who do not serve as directors of the company, but in an executive role also owe the duties of loyalty and diligence to the company. In addition, if the controlling shareholders and actual controllers instruct the directors and senior managers of the company to engage in acts harmful to the interests of the company or its shareholders, the controlling shareholders and actual controllers shall be jointly and severally liable for the damages and losses of the company with the directors and senior managers (Article 192 of the *New Company Law*). However, as the wording of the provisions are currently unclear, judicial precedents and further clarification is necessary to understand the impact of the legislation. Therefore, for franchisors, it is prudent to prepare the compliance policies and to draft the minutes carefully to manage the risks thereof.

5. Employee Representative

Under the old law, non-state-owned companies including the foreign-invested enterprises may (but it is not a must) have employee representatives on their board of directors. The *New Company Law* extends the employee representative rule to non-state-owned LLCs that have more than 300 employees. The employee representative must be elected by the company's employees through the employees' congress or meetings. Subject to the number of employees, there are the options of appointment of the employee representative to the board of directors or the board of supervisors under the *New Company Law*.

For an LLC with less than 300 employees, there is no need to appoint an employee representative to the board of directors:

1. Where the company already has a board of supervisors (3 or more members), there should be no less than 1/3 employee representatives on the board of supervisors as required under the old law. In this case, the old supervisory system will satisfy the new requirement on employee representative(s).

2. Where the company has a board of directors and one supervisor only, the company can have (but is not obliged) an employee representative among the directors. Alternatively, the company is allowed to keep the structure of a board of directors/executive director and one supervisor without an employee representative.

An LLC with more than 300 employees must have at least one employee representative either on the board of directors or on the board of supervisors (Article 68 of the *New Company Law*).:

1. Where the company already has a board of supervisors (3 or more members), there should be no less than 1/3 employee representatives on the board of supervisors as required under the old law. The same already complies with the new requirement on the employee representative(s), and there is no need to change the old supervisory system.

2. Where the company has a board of directors and one supervisor only, the company must have an employee representative among the directors.

Obviously, a head count should be upon the implementation of the *New Company Law* in July. The author is taking the view that having an employee representative at the board of supervisors should be the mainstream choice for LLCs with 300 employees.

C. CHINA JOINS THE APOSTILLE CONVENTION

On March 8, 2023, China officially submitted the instrument of accession to the Hague Convention of October 5, 1961, Abolishing the Requirement of Legalization for Foreign Public Documents ("*Apostille Convention*"). The *Apostille Convention* came into force in China on November 7, 2023. The accession of China to the *Apostille Convention* abolished the need for legalization of documents (by the Chinese Embassy/Consulate) for local use such as documents for the Ministry of Commerce ("MOFCOM") franchisor recordal applications.

As many franchisors may note, there was a small change in the documentation requirements of MOFCOM several years ago. There are more documents that MOFCOM occasionally require and many of them should be notarized and legalized before the *Apostille Convention*. The implementation of *Apostille Convention* is going to save significant time and costs.

D. ANTI-MONOPOLY LAW IN THE CONTEXT OF FRANCHISING

1. The Kerry Education case

On July 12, 2022, Beijing Municipal Administration for Market Regulation ("Beijing AMR") decided to impose an administrative penalty on Beijing Kerry Alliance Education Technology Co., Ltd ("Kerry Education") (Jing Shi Jian Long Fa [2022] No. 0622). Kerry Education owned the exclusive right to use and sub-license an American English education brand in China and had a franchise chain of English language training for children. Kerry Education fixed prices through policies, and the franchisees were required to observe the same. Beijing AMR held that Kerry Education's fixing of the franchisee's sales price constituted a vertical monopoly agreement to fix the resale price which had negative effects on competition. Beijing AMR finally imposed a fine of three percent of its 2020 sales pursuant to the *Anti-Monopoly Law of PRC* ("*AML*").

This may be the first case in which a franchise agreement has been recognized as a vertical monopoly agreement with administrative penalties in China.

The *AML* prohibits monopoly agreements in vertical relationships that: (1) fix prices for resale to third parties and (2) restrict the lowest price for resale to third parties. The resale relationship is not limited to sales of specific goods between suppliers and distributors. The services provided by a franchisor to a consumer under the franchise model may also be considered a "resale". Beijing AMR held that Kerry Education's conduct in fixing the price of the franchisee's courses constituted a monopoly agreement which:

1. Excluded and restricted competition among franchisees within the brand;
2. Restricted competition between franchisees and other brand operators in the same business; and
3. Harmed the interests of consumers.

Kerry Education argued that franchising and its pricing control should be exempted from Article 15(7) of the then-current anti-trust law effective in 2008, other circumstances prescribed by law and the State Council. However, Beijing AMR considered the following perspectives and concluded that the franchising, in this case, was not an exemption ground for its pricing control conduct:

1. There is no legal basis that the fixing resale price clauses are the necessary components of the franchising business.
2. Kerry Education failed to prove that the price restriction is necessary to preserve their unified business model and the consistency of their brand; and
3. Kerry Education failed to prove that the franchise agreements do not substantially restrict competition in the relevant market.

2. Safe Harbor Rule for Vertical Agreements

Several weeks before the Kerry Education case on June 24, 2022, China passed the amendment to the AML which was effective from August 1, 2022 ("*New AML*"). The *New AML* introduced safe harbor rules in respect of vertical monopolistic agreements. According to Article 18 of the *New AML*, a vertical monopoly agreement shall not be prohibited, if the operator can prove that its market share in the relevant market is lower than the threshold prescribed by the State Council's enforcement authorities and meets other conditions set by the State Council's enforcement authorities ("Safe Harbor Rule"). In addition, the relevant provisions on unlawful vertical monopoly agreements will not apply if there is evidence to prove that such an agreement does not have the effect of eliminating or restricting competition.

Following the introduction of the Safe Harbor Rule in the New AML, the draft *Regulation for Prohibiting Monopoly Agreements* ("*Draft Monopoly Agreement Regulation*") used to propose included a 15% market share threshold with detailed guidance on the burden of proof and application procedures (Article 15 of the draft *Regulation for Prohibiting Monopoly Agreements*). On April 15, 2023, the final version of *Regulation for Prohibiting Monopoly Agreements* ("*Monopoly Agreement Regulation*") largely follows the *New AML* and adopts most of the provisions in the draft version. However, the provisions as to the 15% market share threshold were not found in the final version (Article 17 of the *Regulation for Prohibiting Monopoly Agreements)* and the relevant provision is replaced with a general statement allowing the authority to decide the threshold of Safe Harbor Rule. Therefore, there is uncertainty in determining how the Safe Harbor Rule applies without a specified market share threshold, and it appears that the authority has the discretion to determine and adjust the threshold from time to time.

Regarding another defense for establishing or fixing the minimum resale price arrangement, in practice, there are genuine difficulties to prove that pricing-fixing and minimum resale price will not exclude or restrict the competition.

3. Observations

Although the Safe Harbor Rule provides a potential argument to the franchise business and is expected to alleviate the compliance burden for the franchisors without significant market share, fixing the minimum resale price arrangement shall continue to attract scrutiny from the anti-monopoly enforcement authorities. It appears that we need to wait for the next case to understand more about the stance of the authority and the courts on the Safe Harbor Rule.

Another takeaway from Kerry Education case is there is a genuine need to monitor the conduct of the sub-licensors or sub-franchisors. In the Kerry Education case, the brand suffered significant negative impact to its reputation.

Notice on improving the comprehensive regulatory system to promote the standardized and orderly development of commercial franchising (consultation draft)

On June 25, 2023, the MOFCOM, the Cyberspace Administration of China, the Ministry of Public Security, the State Administration of Market Supervision, and the China National Intellectual Property Administration, jointly issued the *Notice on Improving the Comprehensive Supervisory System to Promote the Standardized and Orderly Development of Commercial Franchising (consultation draft)* (the "*Draft Notice").* The *Draft Notice* provides guidance on the compliance of the commercial franchise.

The *Draft Notice* reiterates the definition of a franchise. A franchise must contain the following three elements (Point 1 of the *Draft Notice)*:

1. The franchisor, through an agreement, grants franchisees the right to use the franchisor's business-operational resources, including registered trademarks, logos, patents, and proprietary technologies;
2. The franchisees conduct business under a uniform business mode of operation; and
3. The franchisees pay franchise fees to the franchisor according to the agreement.

A uniform business mode means a collection of management models, business methods, image logos, product or service channels, etc., established and maintained by the franchisor and allowed to be replicated and used by the franchisee.

It further provides that the directly owned outlets for the purpose of record include: (1) the directly owned outlets of branches and subsidiaries (wholly owned or absolutely controlled) of the franchisor; (2) the directly owned outlets of the franchisor's parent company; and (3) individual businesses or sole proprietorships owned by the franchisor's controlling shareholders. For a hotel management franchisor, the hotels it directly operates and manages can be regarded as the directly owned outlets for the purpose of recordal. Online stores are the not directly owned outlets for the purpose of recordal.

Further to the above, the Draft Notice also proposes:

1. The parent companies, subsidiaries or other affiliates of the franchisors engaged in franchising activities are also required to make the recordal, if the franchisor has completed the recordal (Point 4 of the *Draft Notice*).
2. The sample franchise contract should include a "cooling-off period" clause as stipulated in Article 12 of the Franchise Regulations. It is recommended that the cooling-off period should not be less than 30 days, despite the current law does not impose a minimum period. The Draft Notice also indicates that the authority should intervene if a franchisor refuses to refund the payment made after the right of recission has been exercised.
3. If the statements and undertakings made by the franchisor in the commercial publicity have a significant impact on the conclusion of the franchise contract, the same should form part of the disclosure documents (Point 7 of the *Draft Notice*. The actual wording is “they should form part of the contractual documents”. However, the author believes the authority actually meant “they should form part of franchise disclosure documents”), and the parties shall be liable for breach of contract if they violate such representations.
4. The *Draft Notice* emphasizes the requirement of making the annual report. For franchisors who fail to complete the annual report within the specified period, the relevant departments shall order correction in accordance with the law, and in case of refusal to make corrections and seriousness of the situation, they shall be subject to administrative penalties and announcements in accordance with the Regulations and relevant laws and regulations (Point 8 of the *Draft Notice*).

5. The authorities will strengthen supervision of franchise activities in related industries such as foods and beverages, and retail by working with each other closely (Points 9 and 11 of the *Draft Notice*). In turn, this will increase the likelihood of seeing concerned actions from various departments, even in different locations.

The Draft Notice is not yet effective, but it is obvious that the authorities are paying more attention to the franchising sector.

VI. Japan

By Kentaro Tanaka and Taro Matsumoto[4]

A. CASE LAW UPDATE

Seven-Eleven Japan Case (*Supreme Court, 12 July 2023, Reiwa 5 (Gyo-Hi)*). In this case, the Supreme Court considered whether a franchisee is regarded as a "worker" under the Labor Union Act. The defendant, Seven-Eleven Japan Co., Ltd., operated a convenience store franchise model under which the plaintiff was a union organized by convenience store owners. First, the union filed a petition for relief with the Labor Relations Commission, claiming the franchisor's refusal to engage in collective bargaining constitutes an unfair labor practice, but the Central Labor Relations Commission denied the union's claim, expressing that each owner did not fall under the category of a "worker," and the petition for relief was dismissed. Following the denial, the union filed a lawsuit against

---

[4] Kentaro Tanaka is a partner at TMI, where he is central to TMI's franchise practice. He has particular expertise in franchising, M&A and other strategic transactions. He has represented franchisors in various industries and regularly advises clients on cross-border transactions involving franchising and M&A. He has written and contributed to numerous leading publications on franchising and M&A.

Taro Matsumoto is an associate of the Intellectual Property Group of TMI Associates. He is admitted to practise in Japan. His areas of expertise include franchising and intellectual property law (particularly with respect to the entertainment and sports fields). He represents domestic and foreign clients in franchising matters and entertainment and sports matters.

the franchisor, claiming that the convenience store owners are regarded as "workers" under the Labor Union Act.

Under the Labor Union Act, a "worker" is defined as "those persons who live on their wages, salaries or other equivalent income, regardless of the kind of occupation." If workers under the Labor Union Act were to organize a labor union that meets the requirements of Sections 2 and 5 of the Labor Union Act (a legal union), the union will be entitled to enjoy protections under the Labor Union Act, including criminal immunity, civil immunity, acquisition of juridical personality, and remedies for unfair labor practices. The Central Labor Relations Commission will then determine the applicability of the term "worker" from the perspective of whether it is appropriate to apply the protections under the Labor Union Act to ensure equality in negotiations with the other party, by taking into account the following factors:

1. *Basic factors:*
   a. Whether an individual incorporated into the organization is an integral or essential part of the other party's workforce for the conduct of the other party's business;
   b. Whether the other party unilaterally and routinely determines the individual's working conditions and the nature of the work based on the manner in which the contract is entered into; and
   c. Whether the individual's compensation is characterized as compensation for the provision of labor or something similar.

2. *Supplemental factors:*
   a. Whether or not the individual has a basic relationship to respond to individual business requests from the other party; and
   b. Whether or not the individual was under a certain time and place restriction and was performing labor under the direction and order of the other party.

3. *Negative factors:*
   a. Whether the individual has the status of an independent business entity.

The Court in the Seven-Eleven case held that the convenience store owners were not "workers" under the Labor Union Act because: (1) it is the owners, not the franchisor, who made the assignments of labor, and thus the owners could not be said to be integrated into the franchisor's organization as an indispensable or essential labor force for the conduct of the franchisor's business, and the monthly disbursements and other payments made by the franchisor to the owner were not compensation for labor or similar consideration; and (2) the owners do not assign permanent full-time employees to positions such as store managers, delegate to them the direction and supervision of employees or the preparation of work shifts, nor prepare or use their own curricula or manuals for the training of employees, and although owners tend to be involved in store operations for long periods of time, the owners, at their discretion, hire a large number of part-time employees on a permanent basis and assign them to store management duties, depending on the profitability of the store and other factors.

A lesson from this decision is that the Court found that convenience store owners were not generally considered to be an integral part of Seven-Eleven's business organization because several of the plaintiff union members (convenience store owners) delegated store management duties to store managers and devoted much of their own operating time to management decision-making duties. In other words, even if the convenience store owners themselves are engaged in store operations for long periods of time, the fact remains that they are providing labor for their "own business" at their own discretion and cannot be evaluated as essential or indispensable labor for the conduct of Seven-Eleven's business.

In the ***Kumon Case***, which came to a different conclusion than the Seven-Eleven case, the above review process was also an important factor. The Tokyo Labor Relations Commission found that the Kumon (a tutoring school franchise in Japan) franchisor's refusal to bargain collectively with a union whose members were classroom-leader franchisees constituted an unfair labor practice. In the Kumon case, the Commission found facts that were different from those of the Seven-Eleven case in the following respects:

1. Various subsidies from the franchisor reduced the burden of loss on franchisees;

2. There was very little discretion in classroom management, teaching methods, etc.; and
3. Franchisees were required to be directly involved in teaching students.

As to point (3) above, the Supreme Court's judgment emphasized that in the Seven-Eleven case, the franchisees were not required to perform the duties themselves (in many cases, part-time workers were employed), while in the Kumon case, the Tokyo Labor Relations Commission order pointed out that the franchisees were required to provide direct guidance to the students. This point would affect the other factors as well. Therefore, the fact that a franchisee is free to assign other persons to carry out its duties is considered significant grounds for denying that the franchisee qualifies as a worker under the Labor Union Act

VII. New Zealand

By Stewart Germann[5]

A. LEGISLATIVE UPDATE

New Zealand is one of the most deregulated countries in the world to conduct small to medium-sized business. There is no specific legislation controlling the operation of franchising in New Zealand and other countries like New Zealand include Singapore and the United Kingdom.

---

[5] Stewart Germann is a partner in the firm of Stewart Germann Law Office (SGLO) and has over 40 years' experience in franchising law. He acts for franchisors in New Zealand, Australia, USA and the UK. He has spoken at many franchising conferences world-wide. SGLO is New Zealand's longest established specialist franchising law firm and Stewart is included in the International Who's Who of Franchise Lawyers for 2023. Also, Stewart has been awarded his CFE designation and is the only New Zealand lawyer with that qualification.

B. CASE LAW DEVELOPMENTS

The following cases are examples of the High Court granting and enforcing injunctions where the factual situation warrants protection of the system, intellectual property and all aspects of the franchise.

Vision Personal Training Franchises Pty Ltd & Anor v. Williams & Ors [2023] NZHC 2848. This case was an application for an interim injunction in the form of "springboard injunction" designed to remove the advantage of a head start that a person has gained through illegitimate activity. The objective of a springboard injunction is to level the playing field between the parties by placing a defendant back in the position it would have been in but for the breach. The Vision PT business is a personal training franchise in Australia and New Zealand and the First Plaintiff operated the franchise. The Second Plaintiff was an intellectual property holding company and there are 48 Vision PT franchises in Australia. The First Defendant operated the three New Zealand Vision PT franchises in Ponsonby, Parnell and Takapuna and they are the only franchises in New Zealand. The Second Defendant operated a personal training studio called "The Right Fit" at Epsom in Auckland.

To obtain an interim injunction the plaintiffs had to show whether there was a serious question to be tried, the balance of convenience meaning assessing which course of action is likely to involve the least risk of injustice if it turns out the course taken is wrong, and the overall justice of the case. The plaintiffs were successful in obtaining interim injunctions restraining the defendants from disclosing the operations manual and financial information to third parties.

Prominent Investments Ltd v Quest Apartment Hotels (NZ) Ltd [2023] NZHC 2968. The plaintiff Prominent as franchisee and the defendant Quest as franchisor are parties to a franchise agreement which gave Prominent the right to operate a Quest franchise from premises in Ponsonby, Auckland, for a term of five years. The franchise agreement also entitled Prominent to have three further terms of five years each provided it complied with certain terms and conditions as set out in the franchise agreement. On 22 April 2021, Justice Duffy granted the plaintiff an interim injunction but on 27 June 2022 Quest applied for orders that the interim injunction be rescinded. Quest said that there had been a material change of circumstances such that there was no longer a serious question to be tried in the application of Prominent and that the balance of convenience did not favour interim relief continuing. So having considered the facts, Justice Robinson dismissed Quest's applications to rescind the injunction and strike out parts of Prominent's claim. It should be noted that the plaintiff is a client of Stewart Germann Law Office and we are recorded as solicitors for the plaintiff.

Whites96 Ltd & Anor v. The Wheel Magician Ltd [2023] NZHC 3046. This case was an appeal against an interim injunction prohibiting the former franchisee of a mobile wheel repairs system business from competing with the franchisor. The franchise agreement was between Whites96 Limited and the directors of The Wheel Magician Limited being Alan and Lisa Thomas. Wheel Magician used the facilities in a mobile van to carry out repairs to the car wheels of customers at the premises of customers. The wheel repair systems were set out in a Manual available to franchisees. The franchise agreement contained a restraint of trade provision which applied both during the term and upon the expiration or earlier termination of the agreement for any reason. For various reasons The Wheel Magician Limited terminated the franchise agreement and Whites96 Limited alleged breach of the restraint of trade clause in post-termination obligations in four ways being:

1. Continuing to operate a mobile wheel repair business in the area prohibited by the restraint of trade clause;
2. Soliciting and providing services to Wheel Magician's customers;

3. Appropriating, using or duplicating Wheel Magician's systems and continuing to employ Jakob White (a former employee of Wheel Magician.).

The appeal was allowed, and the Judge concluded for the purposes of the interim injunction that the restraint of trade provision was reasonable and as such it was enforceable. The High Court confirmed that the interim injunction would continue to apply on the same terms as were imposed in the District Court.

Team Group Realty Ltd trading as Harcourts Paremata v Cardno & Ors [2024] NZHC 553. Team Group Realty operated the Harcourts Real Estate franchise in the Paremata and Porirua areas of Wellington and the five respondents were engaged by Harcourts as real estate agents and its sales manager. In December 2023 all five respondents resigned within a matter of days of each other and five weeks later a rival real estate agency called Bayleys opened a new office in the area and all five respondents began advertising and marketing as newly engaged agents for Bayleys. On 9 February 2024 Harcourts wrote to the respondents seeking undertakings that they would comply with non-competition, confidentiality and non-solicitation obligations as contained within the various agreements. When those undertakings were not forthcoming, Harcourts filed an application for an interim injunction.

The Court ordered that the first through fourth respondents be restrained from undertaking any business or employment which directly or indirectly competed with that of the applicant within the Tawa to Pukerua Bay area. Further, the interim order required the first through fourth respondents to comply with their obligations relating to the applicant's confidential information and property and to return and/or destroy any confidential information belonging to the applicant, and to return any other property belonging to the applicant.

One New Zealand Group (formerly trading as Vodafone New Zealand Ltd) v. Redfone Ltd & Anor [2024] NZHC 633. One New

Zealand Group (formerly Vodafone New Zealand Limited) applied for the defendant's summary judgment in relation to a claim by Redfone Limited, Grant Knox and Linden Knox. Vodafone had decided not to renew the franchise agreement and on 8 May 2017 Vodafone terminated the Redfone Agreement.

This case involved the applicant, One New Zealand Group (formerly trading as Vodafone New Zealand Limited). The Court ordered that the summary judgment should be granted to Vodafone as neither of the plaintiffs' causes of action could succeed. Some of the facts were disputed but, in the end, the High Court Associate Judge determined that the defendant summary judgment should be granted to Vodafone as neither of the plaintiffs' causes of action could succeed. The Associate Judge confirmed that Vodafone validly terminated the Redfone agreement, and that Vodafone did not act unreasonably or in bad faith. Vodafone's application against the plaintiffs was granted and confirmed.

VIII. Poland

By Sławomir Uss and Krzysztof Misarko[6]

---

[6] Sławomir Uss has worked at SK&S since 1998 and has been a Partner of the law firm since 2012. He specializes in M&A transactions, corporate law, commercial law and civil law. He advises on M&A transactions, restructuring projects, and the merger, division, transformation of companies, joint ventures as well as corporate ownership conflicts. He has a vast experience in advising international teams of lawyers providing advisory services to companies investing in Poland. Sławomir focuses on advising FMCG companies (including the biggest Polish FMCG wholesaler, at the same time having one of the biggest FMCG franchise retail networks) and real estate (in particular, retail). He has been active in Polish aspects of numerous cross-border transactions. Additionally, he has extensive experience providing comprehensive advice in the aviation sector and has advised Wizz Air in all its Polish activities since the incorporation of the airline in 2003.

Krzysztof Misarko joined SK&S in 2012 and represents clients in civil law and commercial disputes, unfair competition, energy sector litigation, corporate disputes, arbitration, post M&A disputes, insolvency and restructuring

A. LEGISLATIVE UPDATE

1. *Franchise Bill*

Franchise contracts, although highly popular and frequently used in Poland, are not separately regulated and codified, but are executed based on the general rule of freedom of contracts. There are views (especially coming from, not surprisingly, the associations of franchisees) that this allows franchisors to impose unfair conditions for franchisees, who need additional protection.

For these reasons, the previous government (There were general elections in Poland in the Fall 2023, and as a result the former government ceased to have a majority at the Parliament after being in power for the last 8 years. There is a new coalition government since December 2024) prepared a first-ever bill to regulate the franchise contract in the Polish Civil Code. The draft was quite revolutionary and proposed implementing obligatory (implied) terms both to new and existing franchise contracts, which could not be changed by the parties simply by way of agreement. These new terms sometimes imposed quite far-reaching obligations on franchisors, while also providing franchisees with new rights and additional protections.

Below are some examples of proposed obligatory terms aimed at protecting franchisees:

---

proceedings, personal rights and torts, and property law disputes. He also represents clients in precedent and high-profile cases against decisions by the public authorities, including disputes against the President of the Competition and Consumer Office. Besides litigation, Krzysztof advises clients in relation to day-to-day business needs, especially in the FCMG and TMT sectors. In particular, Krzysztof assists clients in corporate matters, including representation during shareholders' meetings, and in drafting and preparing various types of contracts, including a standard template of sale and distribution contracts for one of Poland's biggest wholesalers and franchise agreement templates for one of the franchise networks.

1. Fourteen days before the franchise agreement could be signed, a franchisor would be obliged to provide a potential franchisee with a brochure containing information on the franchisor and franchisee's future financial and legal situation, including (i) the estimated value of the franchisee's expenditures needed to start a business under a franchise contract; (ii) the estimated value of the franchise's future turnover following the execution of the franchise agreement; (iii) a general description of the franchisor's business including the number of executed franchise contracts; (iv) a list of contracts that the franchisee would be obliged to sign with third parties to perform the franchise contract.
2. The franchisee would be entitled to terminate the franchise agreement and claim damages, if the franchisor did not provide him with the above-described brochure before the execution of the franchise agreement, or the information contained therein was false or misleading.
3. The franchisor would have to observe this procedure also when presenting an offer to the franchisee to amend the existing franchise contract. Yet again, the franchisee would be entitled to terminate the contract and claim damages, if the new brochure was not provided or information was false or misleading.
4. The franchisee would be entitled to ask the court to decrease the franchisor's remuneration, if franchisee's own income became significantly lower due to circumstances not attributable to the franchisee itself.
5. A contract executed for an indefinite period could be terminated by the franchisor upon a 6-month notice, while the franchisee would be able to terminate the contract only upon a 3-month notice.
6. Both parties would be able to terminate the contract with an immediate effect only in cases of qualified breaches, described in law.

7. Franchisor's potential claims for liquidated damages would cease to exist if the franchisor failed to send a demand for payment to the franchisee within one year following the breach of contract.
8. A potential non-compete clause imposed on the franchisee could only cover the obligation not to create a competitive franchise system within a year of the franchise contract being discharged.

2. Mixed reception

The bill was widely commented upon, but the reception was mixed. While some saw it as a step in the right direction, others indicated that it might give too much power to the franchisees, make franchise contracts inflexible by implementing obligatory, unchangeable terms of such contracts, and thus limiting future growth of franchise networks.

One of the most controversial issues was the information brochure. Such statutory regulation was inspired by other jurisdictions, where the law already requires the franchisor to disclose information to franchisees at the pre-contractual phase (for example, Franchise Disclosure Document in the U.S., which is to be provided to the franchisee 14 days before the contract is executed or any payment is made to the franchisor). The main reason for imposing such an obligation on the franchisor was to give the franchisee additional information and ensure that the undertaking of any obligation by the franchisee was a result of informed consent. While the aim of the regulation was praised, the amount of information to be disclosed under the proposed bill was controversial. Specifically, there were concerns that franchisors would not be able to precisely inform the franchisees about their future income or their expenditures, as this may vary depending on the given franchisee, their economic situation, experience and current market conditions – while the other party (franchisee) might even be entitled to terminate the contract and claim damages if such information was false or misleading.

Thus, there were voices to reduce the disclosure obligation at least in this part.

3. Current status

After the general elections in October 2023, the new government pulled the bill out from the Polish Parliament. However, the Minister of Justice declared that the new government would continue work on the bill in camera. The current status of the bill is unknown.

Following the apparent freeze of work on the bill (or at least lack of information about their progress), in April 2024 the Franchisees and Concessionaires Association published a study called "Franchise to change" and demanded that the new Parliament implement not only a comprehensive statutory regulation of franchise agreements itself, but also regulate the relationship between franchise networks and other market participants, while also making necessary changes in labor law, competition rules, tax law and other important areas of regulation of social and economic life.

Although nothing is certain at this point, we assume that we may expect some kind of franchise legislation in the coming months in Poland, which will be aimed at giving additional protection for franchisees, while imposing additional obligations and controls on franchisors. The crucial issue will be of course the balance between these two issues and its impact on the existing and new franchise networks. One can only assume that changes of such magnitude to the existing contracts will be a fertile ground for future disputes and that challenging times lie ahead both for franchisors and franchisees.

IX. South Korea

By Sun Chang, Heeyoung Lim, Se Won Min

A. LEGISLATIVE UPDATE

1. The KFTCS's Guidelines on Assessing Unfair Business Practices in the Franchise Industry

On February 8, 2024, the Korea Fair Trade Commission ("KFTC") announced 2024 Major Operational Plans and as one of such Plans, the KFTC also issued a new set of Guidelines for Assessing Unfair Business Practices in the Franchise Industry (the "Guidelines") regarding the Fair Transactions in the Franchise Business Act ("Franchise Act").

Having been in effect since March 25, 2024, the Guidelines give a clear roadmap and detailed explanation to overseas franchisors that directly enter into franchise agreements with Korean franchisees about how the Franchise Act will apply and provide an overview of unfair trade practices in the franchise industry through specific examples of each type of unfair trade practice in violation of the Franchise Act.

Specifically, illegality of unfair trade practice is primarily assessed based on whether the acts are likely to restrict fair trade by restricting the franchisee's freedom of choice or being disadvantageous to the franchisee. For example, the Guidelines stipulate 11 types of unfair trade practices and examples of legal violations thereof as follows:

1. *Refusal to deal*- Refusal to aid with business, unreasonable refusal to renew a franchise agreement, and unreasonable termination of a franchise agreement.
2. *Restrictive transactions*- Restraint of price, restraint of counterparty, restriction on the sale of goods or services by a franchisee, enforcement of compliance with the sales territory and other restraints on business activities of franchisees

3. *Abuse of bargaining position-* Forced purchase, coercing provision of benefit, establishing or amending contracts with unfair terms and conditions, interference with business activities, forced sales targets, and imposing disadvantages.
4. *Imposing unreasonable compensation for damages-* Setting and imposing excessive penalties, transferring obligation to compensate for damages to consumers, imposing unreasonable business penalties, and other acts of imposing unreasonable compensation for damages.
5. *Other unfair trade practices-* Solicitation of competitor
6. *Unfairly forcing franchisees to improve store environment-* Unfairly forcing the franchisee to improve store environment or violating the obligation to bear costs for store environment improvement.
7. *Unfair restriction of business hours*
8. *Unfair infringement of the franchisee's protected business area-* Violating the obligation to specify and stipulate the protected business area of a franchise, unfairly changing the protected business area, and unfairly infringing the protected business area
9. *Taking retaliatory measures*
10. *Holding advertising or promotional activities without franchisees' prior consent*
11. *Interfering with franchisee association's activities-* Imposing disadvantages for forming, joining, or participating in a franchisee association, and signing a franchise agreement on the condition of joining or not joining a franchisee association.

2. Recently Amended Franchise Act

Along with the Guidelines, effective July 3, 2024, the amended Franchise Act introduces a new requirement for franchise agreements to specify the type of mandatory items and their supply price calculation methods. This requirement must be incorporated in existing franchise agreements within six months from the effective date. In this regard, the Guidelines specifically set out which may fall under mandatory items.

For example, general industrial products such as disinfectants, dishwashing detergents, equipment cleaners, sanitary products, cleaning products, soup containers, side dish containers, and mask care that are not directly related to the taste or quality of food which is a primary product of the franchise business are not mandatory items. They are not specially customized by the franchisor for the uniformity of the franchise business and are easily available on the market.

Next, with respect to franchisors' obligation to obtain franchisees' prior informed consent to advertising and promotional events, the Guidelines stipulate specific methods for obtaining prior informed consent and individual agreements for advertising and promotional events. The guidelines also provide examples of conduct that may constitute a violation of such obligation especially in relation to mobile gift vouchers, which have been the subject of much recent concern. Under the Guidelines, the following activities would be prohibited:

1. Issuing mobile gift vouchers in a promotional event without entering into an agreement with the franchisee in advance or obtaining the franchisee's consent
2. Issuing mobile gift vouchers in promotional offers to all franchisees even though less than seventy percent of all franchisees have agreed to the issuance of mobile gift vouchers
3. Entering into an agreement with a franchisee to handle mobile gift vouchers in a promotional event and failing to include the franchisee's cost-sharing ratio (e.g., the percentage of the mobile gift voucher fee, the percentage of

the difference between the face value of the mobile gift voucher and the actual amount of goods sold, etc.)

4. Moreover, abuse of superior bargaining position in relation to mobile gift vouchers would be regulated.
5. Forcing franchisees to accept mobile gift vouchers without their consent and forcing them to unilaterally bear related costs such as commissions.
6. In the event the price of a product increases after mobile gift vouchers exchanged for the product have been issued, resulting in a difference between the face value of the gift vouchers and the actual sales price of the product, making the franchisees solely bear this difference without reasonable grounds.
7. Causing damages to franchisees by not settling the payment for the sales made by using mobile gift vouchers within the previously agreed-upon period without reasonable grounds, such as delays in payment by the gift voucher issuing company.

3. Implications

The KFTC announced that it will inspect and correct unfair practices by franchisors that pose a risk of unjust enrichment, and to share relevant information with the industry to encourage voluntary improvements in trading practices. Given the newly announced Guidelines, the KFTC is highly likely to use them as a basis for investigating and sanctioning franchisors.

Meanwhile, the KFTC announced that it will expand the document submission order system introduced in the Monopoly Regulation and Fair Trade Act and the Subcontracting Act to the Franchise Act, the Large Retail Business Act, and the Agency Act. The document submission order system is a system in which a court can order parties to submit documents necessary to prove damages and calculate damages. Considering that the KFTC intends to take strict measures and extend the document submission order system for franchisors and franchisees, it is advisable for franchisors to carry out compliance reviews before offering franchise businesses.

B. CASE LAW UPDATE

Korea Fair Trade Commission, 2018GaMaeng2254, May 18, 2023. The defendant, BKR, operates franchise business in Korea under the master franchise agreement with BK Asiapac Pte., Ltd., who owns the rights to develop and operate a global franchise brand, "Burger King" within Asia Pacific region. Since 2015, the defendant has stated in its franchise disclosure document that advertising contributions collected from franchisees will be allocated for promoting the brand. However, contrary to this disclosure, the defendant used a portion of the advertising fund for "new product development and consumer surveys." On May 31, 2023, the KFTC found that the defendant's disclosure regarding the use of advertising funds collected from the franchisees' was inconsistent with the Franchise Act, specifically Article 9 Section (1)1, which prohibits providing false or exaggerated information. The KFTC issued correction order to the defendant. The case underscores the importance for franchisors to transparently and accurately disclose the purpose of collecting funds from its franchisees in franchise disclosure documents.

Korea Fair Trade Commission, 2021GaJo1286, February 20, 2024. The defendant, emart24, operates as a franchisor in the convenience store sector. Amid COVID-19, two franchisees experienced operational loss and requested adjustments to their business hours. However, the defendant failed to respond to these requests, effectively denying the adjustments. Additionally, the defendant collected assignment franchise fees for assigning existing franchise agreements, even when only the franchise's name changed without further modification. Moreover, the franchisor neglected to inform its franchisees following advertising and/or promotion activities, for which the franchisees were required to cover all or a portion of the expenses.

On February 20, 2024, the KFTC determined that the defendant's refusal to allow the franchisee to adjust their business hours due to operational losses violated the Franchise Act. Specifically, Article 12-3 of the Act prohibits franchisors from unfairly restricting franchisee's business hours. The KFTC deemed the defendant's refusal unjustifiable, when franchisees experienced sluggish sales during late-night hours, leading to operational loss.

In defense, the defendant argued that the franchisees received financial incentives for operating their stores for 24 hours and did not incur losses when factoring in these incentives. Regardless, KFTC found that the defendant's failure to approve adjustment constituted violation of the Franchise Act. Notably, the franchise agreement did not specify any financial incentives for maintaining 24-hour operations, and the Franchise Act does not endorse such incentives in revenue calculations.

Additionally, KFTC determined that collecting assignment franchise fees from unchanged franchisee ownership, except for a name change, violated the Franchise Act. Article 12 of the Franchise Act prohibits unfair trade practices, including exploiting the franchisor's superior bargaining position to disadvantage franchisees. The Enforcement Decree of the same Act further prohibits coercing franchisee into bearing costs or providing economic benefits to the franchisor.

In its ruling favoring the franchisee, KFTC recognized the defendant's superior bargaining position, as franchisees relied on them for procuring goods and operated under their control. KFTC also recognized that franchisees had to make significant investments into their units, risking financial losses if transactions with the defendant were terminated. KFTC deemed the collection of franchise fees in this situation coercive, noting that the name changes incurred minimal costs and efforts from the defendant. Furthermore, since the franchise agreement at hand did not permit an assignment unless the assignee pays the assignment franchise fee, KFTC considered such payments inherently coercive.

Finally, KFTC issued a warning to the defendant for neglecting to inform its franchisees after conducting advertising and/or promotional activities for which the franchisees were obligated to bear some or all the costs.

Under Article 12-6 of the Franchise Act, franchisors must notify franchisees within three (3) months following the end of the fiscal year if they have undertaken advertising or promotional activities that require franchisees to cover some or all the expenses.

KFTC reasoned that although franchisees were aware of their contribution to advertising and promotional costs as stated in the franchise disclosure document and agreement, Article 12-6 of the Franchise Act aims to ensure both franchisors and franchisees are informed about such expenditures. The statute encompasses all instances where franchisee funds are utilized, irrespective of the extent.

The case illustrates KFTC's stance on addressing a franchisor's abuse of its superior bargaining position within a franchise transaction and its efforts to restrict unfair trade practices. It also sheds light on the rationale behind the Article 12-6 of the Franchise Act.

X. Sri Lanka

By Thivanka Hettiarachchi and Kasuni Ranaweera[7]

---

[7] Thivanka Hettiarachchi is a Partner at Sudath Perera Associates. She holds a Bachelor of Laws (LL.B) degree awarded by the University of Colombo and is currently pursuing the degree of Master of Laws in Commercial Law. She serves as an Attorney-at-Law in the Supreme Court of Sri Lanka. Her areas of practice

Chapter 9

A. LEGISLATIVE UPDATE

1. Overview

Sri Lanka lacks a codified law governing the arena of franchising. Therefore, the judicial evolution in franchising grasps the central attention in determining its legal parameters. In this backdrop, the enjoining order dated March 22, 2024, granted by the Commercial High Court of Sri Lanka against Rusi Pestonjee, the local franchisee of McDonald's Corporation has paved the path for reshaping and reaffirming the prevailing laws and norms on franchising. It is thus analyzed the present status of the said litigation ***McDonald's Corporation v Rusi Pestonjee CHC* 07/2024 IP**, and its legal implications. It shall, however, be noted that the matter is subjudice and can accrue further developments.

2. Factual Context

The Plaintiff, McDonald's Corporation, is a company duly incorporated under and in terms of the laws of the United States of America. The Plaintiff entered into a Development Agreement with the Defendant in 1997, which subsequently facilitated the basis for entering into certain franchise agreements with the Defendant. The Defendant has acted as the local franchisee of the McDonald's System thereunder, which is a comprehensive restaurant system for the retailing of a limited menu of uniform and quality food products. Therefore, the foundation of the McDonald's System and the essence of this Agreement are said to be the adherence by the franchisee to

---

are Commercial and Corporate Litigation, Intellectual Property Litigation and Dispute Resolution.

Kasuni Ranaweera is an Associate at Sudath Perera Associates. She holds a Bachelor of Laws (LL.B) degree awarded by the University of Colombo and a Diploma in Commercial Arbitration (Honors) offered by the Institute for the Development of Commercial Law and Practice (ICLP). She serves as an Attorney-at-Law in the Supreme Court of Sri Lanka. She is attached to the Litigation and Dispute Resolution Department of the firm.

the standards and policies of McDonald's which provide for the uniform operation of all McDonald's restaurants within the McDonald's System.

Therefore, the Plaintiff took up the position that the use of McDonald's trademarks and service marks was subject to the Franchisee's full compliance with the foregoing standards and policies, which provided the basis for the Plaintiff's valuable goodwill and wide family acceptance of the McDonald's System. The Defendant has carried out McDonald's restaurants nearly in 12 outlets, out of which only five have valid franchise agreements in force. The franchise agreements with respect to three outlets are said to have expired. Also, four outlets are alleged to have been operated without a valid franchise agreement. Nevertheless, the Defendant has agreed to act in compliance with its contractual undertakings even though they are time lapsed.

However, the Plaintiff argued that the purported conduct of the Defendants has rendered the existing agreements between the parties obsolete. It is alleged that the Defendant has, *inter alia*, failed to meet the prescribed standards of quality, service, and cleanliness in McDonald's Restaurants. Also, the Defendant has allegedly produced reports affirming food security, which, however, were authenticated by a non-prescribed company. It has been unearthed through the onsite inspections that the franchisee has nevertheless taken no such measures to ensure food security, as shown in the said reports. Therefore, it was the Plaintiff's contention that the non-maintenance of the McDonald's restaurants in Sri Lanka up to the standard prescribed by the franchisor has caused the cessation of their contractual relationship and accordingly, the franchisor has terminated the respective franchising agreements forthwith.

3. Legal relief sought by the Franchisor

In this context, the Plaintiff filed the present action claiming ownership over McDonald's trademarks, service marks and the

Claimant's iconic reputation. The major allegation against the franchisee was that its conduct contrary to the franchise agreements has infringed the intellectual property rights of the franchisor under the Intellectual Property Act, No. 36 of 2003 ("IP Act"). The Plaintiff therefore sought the jurisdiction of the Commercial High Court holden in Colombo under and in terms of the IP Act.

Accordingly, the Plaintiff *inter alia* sought enjoining orders preventing the Defendant *inter alia* from:

1. Advertising to the public that the Defendant is a franchisee of the Plaintiff;
2. Using the name McDonald's and/or any name in any way or manner similar to the name McDonald's;
3. Using any name that would convey to the public that the said Restaurant is in any or manner connected to the Plaintiff;
4. Adopting and/or using the McDonald's system, inclusive of serving and/or selling McDonald's food and/or menu items;
5. Using any of the trademarks and/or names and/or devices belonging to McDonald's as set out therein.

It was pleaded that irrevocable and irremediable damage would be caused to the iconic goodwill and reputation of the franchisor in the event the court refused to grant enjoining orders as prayed for. In consideration of the foregoing, the Commercial High Court issued enjoining orders against the franchisee as prayed for, which have not been vacated thus far.

4. Legal Implication

The enjoining order obtained by the Plaintiff is instructive in the context of intellectual property rights attributable to franchising and its legal extents. On one hand, assignment of designated product specifications and use of the respective trademarks therewith by the franchisee is essential to establish uniformity of the franchisor's system. On the other hand, use of the franchisor's trademarks and other ancillary IP rights by the franchisee whilst failing to uplift its substantial goodwill, would cause prejudice to the rights of the franchisor. Therefore, a fair balance shall be struck between these conflicting interests of the parties to ensure an effective franchise relationship.

It is thus evident that a franchisee is not vested with exclusive power to make use of the IP rights assigned thereto, and the rights accrued by a franchisee shall be ascertained considering standards and obligations that the franchisee ought to have fulfilled. Therefore, non-compliance with the standards and obligations so undertaken gives rise to dissolution of the relationship between the franchisor and the franchisee.

This is a breakthrough in Sri Lankan franchising law, alerting the legislators and parties to the franchising agreement to re-evaluate the existing standards and laws to make Sri Lanka a safe haven for franchising.

XI. Taiwan

By Jane Wang, Charles Chen and Shelley Hsu[8]

A. INTRODUCTION

Franchising in Taiwan has experienced substantial growth, particularly in the food service and retail sectors, with both international giants such as Starbucks and local favorites bubble

[8] Jane Wang is a partner at Formosa Transnational Attorneys at Law. Her practices include IP litigation, data protection, licensing, antitrust, franchise, labor/employment, and emerging technologies. Charles Chen is an associate partner at Formosa Transnational Attorneys at Law. His practice focuses on intellectual property, corporate commercial matters, franchising, licensing, labor/employment and competition/antitrust. Shelley Hsu is a commercial lawyer with expertise in various related legal fields, including intellectual property law, company law, franchise law, and technology laws and regulations.

milk tea shops like FIFTYLAN, Ching-Shin Fu-Chuan and Kebuke expanding their presence. Despite challenges such as the Covid pandemic, franchising has proven resilient, with an increase in both the number of franchise brands and stores. Key associations like the Taiwanese Chain Stores and Franchise Association (TCFA) and the Association of Chain and Franchise Promotion, Taiwan (ACFPT) play pivotal roles in fostering the growth of franchising by providing essential support services and acting as platforms for industry promotion.

From a legal perspective, Taiwan's approach to franchise regulation is relatively liberal. Unlike some jurisdictions with comprehensive dedicated statutes that consolidate all relevant provisions, Taiwan's franchise regulations are dispersed across various laws and regulations. These include the Fair Trade Act, Multi-Level Marketing Supervision Act, Copyright Act, Trademark Act, Patent Act, Labor Standards Act, Civil Code, and relevant tax regulations. Additionally, administrative orders, decisions by the Fair Trade Commission, and court rulings play significant roles in shaping Taiwan's franchise law landscape. Therefore, in this discussion, we will begin by outlining the regulatory framework of franchise law in Taiwan and subsequently analyze its recent developments.

Brief Overview of the Regulation Framework of Franchise Law in Taiwan

1. Market Entry

Regarding the principle of freedom of contract and the aim of attracting foreign investment, Taiwan typically imposes no restrictions on foreign franchisors entering the Taiwanese market. However, if a foreign investor acquires shares in a Taiwanese company or establishes an entity in Taiwan, advance foreign investment approval is necessary. Nonetheless, foreign franchisors wishing to operate in Taiwan are not obligated to establish joint ventures or transfer management authority to Taiwanese citizens.

2. *Intellectual Property Rights*

Intellectual property rights are paramount in franchising, with mechanisms in place for brand search, registration, and enforcement, particularly in trademark protection.

Brand search- To gather information on franchise businesses in Taiwan, individuals can conduct a trademark search on the Taiwan Intellectual Property Office (TIPO) online database. The Trademark Search system allows users to search for registered trademarks using keywords. This provides details on trademark applicants, specific words used, and the status of pending or registered trademarks.

Brand protection- Taiwan's trademark registration operates on a first-to-file basis. Applicants can register trademarks through TIPO, gaining exclusive rights for 10 years. Intangible elements like sounds or smells can also be registered.

The Trademark Act prioritizes protecting well-known trademarks and prevents trademark squatting. Brand owners can pursue invalidation or opposition procedures against squatters at TIPO. The statute of limitations for these remedies is 5 years from trademark publication.

Enforcement- Taiwan is actively reinforcing the protection of intellectual property (IP) rights, with dedicated institutions such as the Intellectual Property and Commercial Court and the Intellectual Property Rights Police (IPRP). These institutions are focused on enforcing IP rights, particularly for trademarks and patents. In 2023, the IPRP handled a significant number of cases, making seizures in 2,972 instances of intellectual property right infringement. If a registered trademark is infringed upon, the trademark owner has the right to demand the cessation of infringement, seek compensation for damages, and request the destruction of infringing articles and materials under the Trademark Act. Offenders may face imprisonment for up to 3 years, a fine not exceeding NT$200,000, or both penalties. Additionally, owners of well-known or famous unregistered trademarks can pursue civil relief under the Fair-Trade Act in Taiwan.

3. Tax

Tax considerations for franchisors and franchisees involve profit-seeking enterprise income tax, value-added business tax, and individual income tax, among others. While there is no specific tax structure optimized for franchise businesses, the type of business entity and business structure will have important tax implications.

4. General Laws and Dispute Resolution Mechanisms

General laws, such as those related to good faith in contracts, agency distributor models, employment, consumer protection, competition, anti-corruption, and dispute resolution, impact franchising in Taiwan. Franchise agreements are also required to comply with regulations on pre-contractual disclosure, mandatory clauses, and guarantees. Dispute resolution mechanisms include litigation and alternative methods like mediation and arbitration. While Taiwan is not a signatory to the New York Convention on Arbitral Awards, arbitration is a robust and effective option for resolving both domestic and international disputes. Furthermore, issues like joint liability for employee actions in franchise businesses remain subject to interpretation and persuasive legal precedent, highlighting the evolving nature of franchise law in Taiwan.

B. LEGISLATIVE UPDATE

Since 2022, the cases heard by the Supreme Court in Taiwan have focused on general contractual issues that could impact franchise businesses. These issues encompass contract interpretation, differentiation of franchise contracts, unfair competition, and infringement of trademark rights. It is worth noting that issues concerning the disclosure of information continue to hold significant importance in this domain.

C. CASE LAW UPDATE

1. Contract interpretation

Supreme Court 2023 Tai Shang Zi, No. 1966 Civil Court Decision. In a case concerning a franchise contract relationship, the Supreme Court addressed a clause in the contract stating that "this contract is valid from June 20, 2019, to June 20, 2022, totaling 3 years" (clause 2). According to clause 4, the appellant was required to pay the appellee 1.68 million New Taiwan Dollars (approximately USD 57,000) as a franchise fee to operate the appellee's Sanliang Tea trademarked Zhonghe Yuanshan store and was prohibited from requesting a refund of the franchise fee, in whole or in part, for any reason thereafter. However, Clause 16 also stipulated that, "The actual operating time, including the trial selling date, of Party B (the appellant) joining Party A (the appellee) must be more than 6 months. If the operation is terminated in less than 6 months, Party B must compensate Party A with a penalty for breach of contract of 100 thousand New Taiwan Dollars."

The Supreme Court concluded that the interpretation of Clause 16 permits the inference that the appellant could unilaterally terminate the business after operating it for more than 6 months without being obliged to continue operations for the full three years. Article 247-1 of the Civil Code states that 'If a contract has been constituted according to the provisions which were prepared by one of the parties for contracts of the same kind, the agreements which include the following agreements and are obviously unfair under that circumstance are void.

1. To release or to reduce the responsibility of the party who prepared the entries of the contract.
2. To increase the responsibility of the other party.
3. To make the other party waive his right or to restrict the exercise of his right.
4. Other matters gravely disadvantageous to the other party.

As it has done many times in the past, the Supreme Court reaffirmed that contract interpretation must consider not only the entirety of the contract, but also usages of trade and the principle of good faith. Moreover, Taiwanese cases on franchising suggest that the courts are minded protecting the franchisee because they typically have less economic power than the franchisor. This tendency may be particularly obvious in the common scenario where the franchise contract has been drafted by the franchisor. Nevertheless, because contract law is highly contingent upon the specific circumstances of each case, whether a franchisee holds a preferential position in the interpretation of franchise contracts is a question that will have to be answered by future jurisprudence.

2. Unfair Competition

Supreme Court 2021 Tai Shang Zi No. 3161 Civil Court Decision. In a case involving unfair competition arising from similar products, the Supreme Court provided clarification on the terms 'symbol,' and 'secondary meaning' as defined in the Fair Trade Act. It explained that 'symbol' refers to a characteristic with distinctiveness or secondary significance. Under the Taiwan Fair Trade Act, the term ‘symbol’ refers to the appearance, container, and other aspects that enable consumers to recognize the source of a product. It is like the concept of trade dress. This characteristic distinguishes the source of a product and hence aids relevant businesses or consumers in distinguishing between different goods. 'Distinctiveness' denotes a characteristic that is particularly prominent, allowing relevant businesses or consumers to recognize that the product was produced by a business manufacturer upon seeing it. 'Secondary significance' refers to a characteristic initially lacking distinctiveness, but through long-term use, consumers become conscious and associate it with the product's origin, creating an additional meaning that distinguishes the source of the goods.

The appellee stated that the pleated design had been used on the exterior of the suitcases for years without changing. Therefore, it should be considered the symbol of a well-known product. Nevertheless, the Supreme Court determined that since up to 50% of general consumers were unaware of the appellee's brand and 46.08% thought that the defendant's products were not from plaintiff's licensed or franchised companies. Hence, the Court did not think that the pleated design had been established clearly enough in the minds of consumers. As a result, relying solely on this design to identify the source of the suitcases marketed by the appellee may not be appropriate, especially considering that the suitcases prominently feature the NaSaDen or Centurion brand logos on the front. These logos should be sufficient to enable consumers to identify the source of the products at the time of purchase. Additionally, the prices and sales channels of the two types of products differ significantly. Consequently, the appellee's claim of infringement warrants further examination. The case was remanded to the Intellectual Property and Commercial Court and later settled by the Parties.

It should be noted that the Taiwanese courts have gradually established an objective and comprehensive framework for determining confusion involving widely-known products. The term 'to cause confusion,' as provided in subsection 1 of Article 22 of the Fair Trade Act, refers to a situation where there is a real risk that an average customer, with ordinary attention and memory, might confuse the two products. The courts determine whether such a risk really exists by considering a variety of factors including the ubiquity of the product's symbol, the degree of distinctiveness, the similarity between the symbols, the products, and the business operations, consumer overlap, pricing differences, and the existence of a competitive relationship. (*See* Supreme Court 2020 Tai Shang Zi No. 2369 Civil Court Decision, Intellectual Property and Commercial Court 2022 Min Gong Su Zi No.8 Civil Court Decision.)

D. DUTY OF DISCLOSURE

As per the Fair-Trade Commission Directions, franchisors are required to furnish their franchisee(s) with crucial franchise information in writing at least 10 days before commencing the franchise operation relationship, or within a reasonable timeframe determined in specific cases, or as agreed upon by both parties. This information includes:

1. Startup costs
2. Operating expenses
3. The licensed intellectual property, periods of validity, the scope of licensing and restrictions on use of relevant trademarks, patents and copyrights
4. Methods and nature of operational assistance, training and guidance
5. Plans for setting up other franchisees in the same franchise system in a franchisee's existing area of operation
6. Restrictions applied to the franchise relationship during the period of the agreement
7. Conditions and process for alteration, termination and cancellation of a franchise agreement

While the guidance in the Fair-Trade Commission Directions is evolving towards greater flexibility, these seven requirements remain crucial as may be seen in recent Fair Trade Commission decisions.

For instance, in 2024, SEVEN TEA Company Limited, a renowned Taiwanese beverage chain, failed to provide complete and comprehensive information regarding four crucial aspects of the franchise agreement with the 'Seven Tea' brand before entering into the franchise operation relationship. These aspects include pre-operational purchase of goods and raw material expenses, purchase of goods and raw materials during the franchise operation period, POS machine software-related expenses, purchase of goods, raw materials brand and specifications from the franchisor or their designated persons during the franchise period, and specifications of capital equipment to be purchased from the franchisor or their designated persons during the franchise period.

This omission of vital information was deemed by the Fair Trade Commission to significantly affect the fairness of the transaction and hence violate Article 25 of the Fair Trade Act. As a result, SEVEN TEA was fined NT$200,000.

E. CURRENT DEVELOPMENTS, CHALLENGES AND PROSPECTS

Covid-19 emerged in Taiwan in 2021, leading to a widespread outbreak that persisted until 2022, when the Omicron variant became the predominant strain in the country. The easing of lockdown measures due to Covid-19 has been a gradual process. The impact of Covid-19 ended in mid-2023.

In the post-pandemic era, Taiwan's franchise law development has remained relatively stable, mirroring the growth of various industries. In 2022, Taiwan's gross domestic product (GDP) amounted to around USD 760.91 billion and is projected to reach just over USD 1 trillion by 2029. Taiwan's service sector has emerged as a crucial component of its economy, with franchising becoming a primary mode of modern commercial operations. Taiwanese franchises have ventured overseas, especially in China and Southeast Asia, supported by initiatives like the government's New Southbound Policy. However, some smaller enterprises face challenges in expanding abroad due to resource constraints, highlighting the need for support. To stay competitive, franchise businesses must adapt to globalization and technological advancements.

Overall, given Taiwan's strategic location in the western Pacific Ocean, its pivotal role in the industry supply chain, and its well-established regulatory framework and investment environment, foreign enterprises are likely to invest, and related businesses will continue to thrive. This will lead to new opportunities and raise significant issues in the field of franchise law.

XII. United Kingdom

By Nicola Broadhurst and Alasdair McDowell[9]

A. INTRODUCTION

Whilst there has been no franchise specific legislation in the United Kingdom this year, there have been three franchise specific cases in England. Since England has a common law system these cases are important to the development of franchise law in the jurisdiction and this contribution therefore summarizes those cases.

---

[9] Nicola Broadhurst is a commercial partner and the Head of Franchise and ESG at the UK law firm Stevens & Bolton LLP. She advises a broad range of both franchise and commercial clients and has in depth experience on all aspects of franchise transactions including preparing the franchise documentation and adapting international franchise agreement for use in the UK. She has a particular focus on international expansion and ethical franchise practices and is the chair of the British franchise Association's Legal Committee. She is also the director of the American Bar Association's Franchise Forum's international division and a council member of the IBA's European Regional Forum, chairing its ESG working party. She is consistently top ranked by leading legal directories for her expertise in franchising.

Alasdair McDowell is an associate solicitor in the Commercial and IT team at Stevens & Bolton LLP and is also part of the firm's Franchise Practice and its Hospitality and Leisure Group. Alasdair has both transactional and litigation experience and advises a wide range of franchise and commercial clients on their franchise arrangements and expansion plans, including preparing development agreements and franchise documentation and advising on strategic approaches to potential disputes.

B. CASE LAW UPDATE

London Business House Limited and another v Pitman Training Limited and another [2023] EWHC 1077 (Comm). In this case, the High Court found that there was an element of exclusivity in a franchise agreement despite the absence of an express exclusivity provision. London Business House Limited ("LBH") entered into a franchise agreement with the franchisor, Pitman Training Limited ("Pitman") for a franchised territory in Nottingham. LBH was not a successful franchisee and the franchise agreement ended early during the initial term. LBH claimed that this was because Pitman was supplying materials to another training entity within LBH's franchised territory, whilst Pitman alleged that LBH's business failed because of LBH's shortcomings as a franchisee.

Another Pitman entity called Derby Business College Limited ("Derby") was in fact providing training services in a territory that overlapped with LBH's franchised territory. The agreement between Pitman and Derby was for Derby to provide government funded training with unbranded training materials provided by Pitman, whilst LBH provided Pitman branded training courses on a private paying basis using Pitman branded training materials. In practice, however, Derby did passively sell privately funded training courses. LBH raised Derby's existence and the fact that it was offering courses on a private paying basis in LBH's territory in an email to Pitman sent during the franchise agreement. LBH had by that point already fallen into arrears on its franchise payments and the email to Pitman alleged that that Derby's activities were having an impact on LBH's sales. The issue of Derby was not resolved to LBH's satisfaction and LBH's solicitors subsequently wrote to Pitman to explain that Derby's activities had meant that LBH's business was not viable and that it had no alternative but to cease trading. In response, Pitman's solicitors wrote to LBH terminating the franchise agreement. LBH subsequently brought claims against LBH for breach of contract and misrepresentation.

The Judge found that, despite there being no express exclusivity provision in the franchise agreement, taken as a whole it did have an element of exclusivity. However, that exclusivity was limited to the Pitman brand, rather than to trading as a whole. Accordingly, Pitman was entitled to provide materials to Derby to use on a white labelled basis without being in breach of the franchise agreement. However, since Pitman had also provided Pitman branded training certificates to Derby (rather than white labelled certificates) this amounted to a breach of the exclusivity granted to LBH for the use of the trademarks and was a breach of contract.

As to the misrepresentation claim, the Judge found that the exclusivity position was not misrepresented to the Claimant and, that it had certainly not been misrepresented fraudulently. To the extent that there was any claim for negligent or innocent misrepresentation this was excluded by the franchise agreement which contained an entire agreement clause excluding any pre-contractual statements or representations not included in the agreement.

Whilst the provision by Pitman of headed certificates to its contractor Derby bearing the Pitman branding did constitute a breach of contract, this was not material enough to be a repudiatory breach and LBH's claim was therefore limited in scope to damages for breach of contract. Further, rather than have the effect of terminating the contract, LBH's solicitors' letter was itself a repudiatory breach (as it indicated an intention no longer to comply with the terms of the franchise agreement) allowing Pitman to terminate. LBH was therefore not entitled to claim for the wider losses of losses of future business, and their claim for losses for breach of contract failed on the grounds that it caused no losses to LBH.

The judgment in ***London Business House*** is an illuminating illustration of the centrality of exclusivity to franchise agreements under English Law as well as the limits of exclusivity and the risks of overlooking it. It remains to be seen whether the courts in future cases adopt the ***London***

Business House approach of finding exclusivity in similarly drafted franchise agreements. The claimant in London Business House succeeded on one very narrow ground of breach of contract but failed to recover damages on causation grounds. In different circumstances, the finding of breach could have had significant financial consequences for Pitman.

1. Two High Court judgments in 2023 concerned issues that arose at the point of renewal

Winkworth Franchising Limited v. Nicholas Goble, No. LM-2022-000174, 2023 EWHC 2883 (Comm. 2023). In this case, the High Court found that a franchisor was entitled to terminate the suite of franchise agreements it held with its franchisee due to the franchisee's breach. Winkworth Franchising Limited ("Winkworth") the franchisor, entered into five franchise agreements with Mr. Goble through which he traded under the Winkworth estate agency brand from locations in Southwest London. Each franchise agreement had a twenty-year term and could be extended for two additional periods of ten years. Towards the end of the term of the franchise agreements, Winkworth requested audited accounts from Mr. Goble pursuant to clause 14.12 of the franchise agreements. The franchise agreements allowed Winkworth to refuse to renew and terminate the franchise agreements if Mr. Goble failed to do so.

Mr. Goble initially refused to provide audited accounts by the deadline on the grounds that they had not yet been prepared. Winkworth therefore agreed that Mr. Goble could provide unaudited accounts instead. However, Mr Goble did not provide the accounts by either the initial or the extended deadline set by Winkworth. Accordingly, rather than agree to Mr. Goble's request to extend the franchise agreements, Winkworth instead served counternotices on Mr. Goble refusing to extend the franchise agreements and informing him that the franchise agreements had come to an end.

In the subsequent legal proceedings, Mr. Goble alleged that Winkworth was trying to find a breach to either take control of his franchised businesses or impose new franchise agreements with more favourable terms. Mr. Goble also argued that the parties could not have intended to enter into an agreement which had the effect that even a minor breach of the requirement to provide accounting information, could allow Winkworth to terminate the franchise agreements.

Instead, Winkworth should be obliged to demonstrate that the breach in question was material. Finally, Mr. Goble argued that Winkworth had not clearly stated that their requests were made pursuant to clause 14.12 (which they should have done given what Winkworth said were the serious consequences of failing to comply) and in any event Winkworth were estopped from relying on Mr. Goble's breach because they had agreed to accept unaudited accounts in the place of audited accounts.
The Court rejected Mr. Goble's arguments, noting that Winkworth was entitled to rely on an agreed contractual term and terminate the franchise agreements on that basis. There was no need to add a requirement of materiality because "[i]t is not for the court to re-write the bargain…entered into in the franchise agreement" in the absence of estoppel. The available evidence reflected that Mr. Goble had been told that the request was made pursuant to clause 14 of the franchise agreement. Whilst the judge did find that agreeing to accept unaudited accounts amounted to an estoppel preventing Winkworth from relying on Mr. Goble's failure to provide audited accounts, it did not affect the issue of breach because Mr. Goble had also failed to provide the unaudited accounts that Winkworth agreed to accept instead by the requisite deadline. Accordingly, Mr. Goble was in breach of the franchise agreements, entitling Winkworth to refuse renewal and to terminate.

The Judgment in ***Winkworth Franchising*** was given in the context of a summary judgment application, rather than after a full trial at which witnesses were cross examined. The outcome was therefore based on the construction of the franchise agreements and the facts as appeared from documentary evidence. It is therefore necessary to exercise caution in respect of the scope of the principles that can be drawn from this judgment. With that caveat in mind, however, the judgment reflects that the English courts will be reluctant to interfere with the agreement made by the parties, and that franchisees need to take care to comply strictly with their obligations at renewal if they wish to renew.

The Burke Partnership (a firm) v. The Body Shop International Limited No. BL-2022-000847, 2023 EWHC 2897 (English High Court, 2023) EWHC 2897 (Ch). The Body Shop is a well-known British skincare, perfume and cosmetics company, which was founded in the 1970's. It was one of the earliest organizations to use the franchise model in the UK and The Burke Partnership was one of its legacy franchises, having held franchises for territories in Norwich and Cambridge since the early 1980's. Both franchise agreements were materially identical and were for a five-year term. They contained a clause allowing The Burke Partnership to extend the term for a further five years (on the same terms) provided they gave written notice at least three months prior to expiration and subject to them having complied with the terms of the franchise agreements.

The franchise agreements were renewed every five years on the same terms until, in 2021, The Body Shop purported to refuse a request for an extension and to terminate the Norwich franchise agreement for the following key reasons:

the franchise agreement was "no longer fit for purpose" in its current form as it did not reflect the Body Shop's operations and the term of the franchise agreement was in effect perpetual and was therefore terminable on reasonable notice in accordance with English contract law.

The Body Shop subsequently sent a letter to the Burke Partnership purporting to terminate its Cambridge franchise agreements in similar terms. In the litigation that followed, The Body Shop argued that, on its proper construction, the franchise agreements entitled The Burke Partnership to only one extension of the five-year term on the basis that it would be unusual for commercial parties to expect the agreements they entered into to be indefinite and any such right therefore ought to have been expressly set out in the franchise agreements. Given that The Body Shop's interpretation conflicted with The Burke Partnership's contention that the franchise agreements could be renewed on identical terms every five years, The Body Shop's formulation should be preferred in accordance with English contract law. Any ambiguity in the wording ought to be construed in The Body Shop's favour.

However, the Judge rejected The Body Shop's argument holding that The Burke Partnership were entitled to renew the franchise agreement every five years for an additional five-year term and on the same terms (including the term granting the right to renew) on giving appropriate notice. His reasoning included that:

Firstly, these franchise agreements were not perpetually renewable because they contained a compulsory renewal mechanism and required compliance with the terms for renewal. If the franchisee was in breach of the agreement, it would not have met the condition to renew and this was sufficient to avoid the agreement being a perpetual agreement; Secondly, neither party had considered how their commercial relationship might develop at the point of contracting. Whilst parties to modern franchise agreements might not expect franchise agreements to be repeatedly extended, the position was different in the nascent franchising landscape of England in the early 1980's. The Courts would only consider the intention of the parties at the time the contract was formed. Additionally, the fact that the franchise agreements were no longer suitable commercially was not relevant and did not allow The Body Shop to avoid complying with their terms.

The Judge added he would have made the same finding had he found the agreement to have been perpetual. Whilst modern parties might not enter into a franchise agreement containing provisions of that nature, the court should not *"construe the Agreements with hindsight"*: the terms of the agreement reflected the commercial position that existed at the time.

As there was already a contractual means for terminating the agreements, the Judge refused to imply a term into the agreement allowing the agreements to be terminated on reasonable notice, adding that the franchise agreements did not lack commercial or practical coherence in the absence of the proposed implied term.

The English courts have historically held parties to their bargain and refused to allow one party to resile from an agreement on the grounds that it no longer suits them commercially. The court's judgment in ***Burke Partnership*** affirms that, as well being a useful reminder that the parties' commercial concerns should be considered at the time of the contract formation, not the present day. It also demonstrates English Courts' reluctance to imply terms into a commercial agreement unless absolutely necessary.

Page(s)

Cases

INDEX